PRAISE FOR

MADAME FOURCADE'S SECRET WAR

"A hell of a yarn . . . Why the heck have we never heard of [Marie-Madeleine] Fourcade? The only woman to lead a major French resistance network. A woman who in later life was elected to the European Parliament. And who, upon her death in 1989 at the age of seventy-nine, became the first woman to be granted a funeral at Les Invalides, the complex in central Paris where Napoleon Bonaparte and other French military heroes are buried. Olson posits a few possible reasons for Fourcade's relegation to the footnotes of history. The inescapable one, though, circles back to where we began: her gender. . . . Brava to Lynne Olson for a biography that should challenge any outdated assumptions about who deserves to be called a hero."
—*The Washington Post*

"Fast-paced and impressively researched . . . Olson writes with verve and a historian's authority. . . . With this gripping tale Lynne Olson pays [Fourcade] what history has so far denied her. France, slow to confront the stain of Vichy, would do well to finally honor a fighter most of us would want in our foxhole."
—*The New York Times Book Review*

"Lynne Olson is a gifted author and her books about the Allies in World War II are carefully researched and compulsively readable. . . . Thankfully, a new generation of writers is expanding our knowledge of individuals whose roles in World War II deserve more attention." —*The Christian Science Monitor*

"A brilliant, cinematic biography of resistance leader Marie-Madeleine Fourcade . . . Olson's weaving of Fourcade's diary artfully and liberally into her own writing and her heart-stopping descriptions of Paris, escapes, and internecine warring create a narrative that's as dramatic as a novel or a film. Olson honors Fourcade's fight for freedom and her 'refusal to be silenced' with a gripping narrative that will thrill WWII history buffs."

—*Publishers Weekly* (starred review)

"Olson, who in *Last Hope Island* and *Citizens of London* mined lesser-known world-war history to great effect, has penned the incredibly absorbing and long-overdue chronicle of the exploits and accomplishments of French Resistance hero Mme Marie-Madeleine Fourcarde. . . . This masterfully told true story reads like fiction and will appeal to readers who devour WWII thrillers à la Kristen Hannah's *The Nightingale*." —*Booklist* (starred review)

"As well researched and engrossing as her previous books, showcasing her adroit ability to weave personal narratives, political intrigue, and wartime developments to tell a riveting story, Olson's latest is highly recommended to readers interested in World War II, the history of espionage, women's history, and European history."

—*Library Journal* (starred review)

"A comprehensive, often exciting narrative . . . [Olson's] solid descriptive passages help re-create the tension and anxiety Fourcade and her friends felt as they risked everything to save France. . . . The author brings into the spotlight a woman whose courage and endurance helped shape history yet whose full story had not yet been told. 'For several decades following the war,' writes the author, 'histories of the French resistance, which were written almost exclusively by men, largely ignored the contributions of women.' Olson rectifies that omission. . . . An engaging, informative addition to World War II history." —*Kirkus Reviews*

"In *Madame Fourcade's Secret War,* Lynne Olson tells one of the great stories of the French Resistance, a story of one woman's courage amid great danger, a story of heroism, defiance, and, ultimately, victory." —ALAN FURST, author of *A Hero in France*

"Lynne Olson has added yet another brilliant chapter to her vital historical project: documenting the extraordinary efforts of individuals, such as spymaster Marie-Madeleine Fourcade, who helped liberate twentieth-century Europe from Nazi occupation. Much like Madame Fourcade herself, Olson goes to great lengths to unearth truth and preserve dignity for those who lived and died during Hitler's reign of terror—and for that, both the author and her daring subject deserve high praise."

—MADELEINE K. ALBRIGHT, former Secretary of State

"In *Madame Fourcade's Secret War,* Lynne Olson is at the top of her game, giving us the renowned beauty and elite French socialite Marie-Madeleine Fourcade, who surprised everyone—including herself, perhaps—by becoming one of the most consequential players in the high-stakes spy game in Nazi-occupied France. Fourcade's nerve, resolve, and extraordinary inner resources shine and inspire here. . . . A fascinating portrait of uncommon audacity."

—PAULA MCLAIN, *New York Times* bestselling
author of *Love and Ruin* and *The Paris Wife*

"If Lynne Olson had set out to write a novel, she could not have come up with a more fascinating character than Marie-Madeleine Fourcade, the glamorous young woman who led the largest French spy network in World War II. This is a case where fact is far more riveting than fiction. Olson chronicles Fourcade's extraordinary story with her customary eye for every revealing detail and every breathtakingly dangerous twist."

—ANDREW NAGORSKI, author of *Hitlerland,*
The Nazi Hunters, and *The Year Germany Lost the War*

"Lynne Olson has long been among my favorite historians, and in *Madame Fourcade's Secret War* she's written the most gripping account of Second World War spycraft I've ever read. The story of Marie-Madeline Fourcade—head of Alliance, the largest intelligence network in the French Resistance—is staggering in its scope and detail, and utterly enthralling from scene to nail-biting scene. This is serious history told with all the verve of fiction, and a vital corrective to the largely male Resistance narrative. . . . An absolute must-read not just for history buffs but for anyone who cares about human courage."

—BEATRIZ WILLIAMS, *New York Times* bestselling
author of *The Summer Wives*

"In the real-life character of Madame Fourcade, Lynne Olson has found a heroine who seems to come tailor-made for the movie screen: She is beautiful, rich, effortlessly elegant, and an absolutely indomitable spy for the ages. Olson's clear, unadorned writing style and her meticulous marshaling of facts will keep you on the edge of your seat as Fourcade endures psychological and physical hardship in service of her singular goal—to keep France free of fascism. For all of us who have wondered what we would do in a time of crisis, Olson holds up Madame Fourcade and her relentless fight for the French Resistance as a model of how to fight back when faced with unthinkable evil. . . . Fascinating and timely."

—ELIZABETH LETTS, *New York Times* bestselling
author of *The Perfect Horse*

"Madame Fourcade's war should never have been a secret, and it takes a historical sleuth like Lynne Olson to bring it, at last, into glorious light. I read this extraordinary book with wonder and admiration, seeing a movie on every page that was both true to life and somehow bigger than life. The canvas is vast, the characters vibrant, the history we thought we knew suddenly as fresh as tomorrow."

—JAY COCKS, screenwriter of *The Age of Innocence,*
Gangs of New York, and *Silence*

BY LYNNE OLSON

*Madame Fourcade's Secret War: The Daring Young Woman
Who Led France's Largest Spy Network Against Hitler*

*Last Hope Island: Britain, Occupied Europe, and the
Brotherhood That Helped Turn the Tide of War*

*Those Angry Days: Roosevelt, Lindbergh, and America's
Fight over World War II, 1939–1941*

*Citizens of London: The Americans Who Stood with
Britain in Its Darkest, Finest Hour*

*Troublesome Young Men: The Rebels Who Brought Churchill
to Power and Helped Save England*

*A Question of Honor: The Kosciuszko Squadron; Forgotten
Heroes of World War II* (WITH STANLEY CLOUD)

*Freedom's Daughters: The Unsung Heroines of the
Civil Rights Movement from 1830 to 1970*

*The Murrow Boys: Pioneers on the Front Lines of
Broadcast Journalism* (WITH STANLEY CLOUD)

MADAME FOURCADE'S SECRET WAR

CARTE D'IDENTITÉ
Nom *Imbert*
Prénoms *Marie Suzanne*
Profession *Secrétaire*
Née le *28 Aout 1906*

MADAME FOURCADE'S SECRET WAR

The DARING YOUNG WOMAN
WHO LED FRANCE'S LARGEST SPY
NETWORK AGAINST HITLER

LYNNE OLSON

RANDOM HOUSE

NEW YORK

2020 Random House Trade Paperback Edition

Copyright © 2019 by Lynne Olson

All rights reserved.

Published in the United States by Random House, an imprint and division of Penguin Random House LLC, New York.

RANDOM HOUSE and the HOUSE colophon are registered trademarks of Penguin Random House LLC.

Originally published in hardcover in the United States by Random House, an imprint and division of Penguin Random House LLC, in 2019.

PHOTO CREDITS: page 14: Assemblée-Nationale; pages 16, 71, 191, 241: Chemins de Mémoire; pages 34, 242, 328 : Compagnons de la Libèration; page 37: Les Français Libres; page 54: National Portrait Gallery (UK); pages 126, 216, 282: Alamy; page 138: Musée de la Reddition pages 131, 179, 370, 372: Patrick Rodriguez-Redington; page 184: Fondation de la France Libre; page 201: Yad Vashem; page 235: Rev. Jerome Bertram; pages 246, 268: Creative Commons; pages 279, 375: Dorie Denbigh-Laurent; page 301: Collection Résistance et Mémoire; page 317: Des Isnards family; pages 325, 332: Granger.

LIBRARY OF CONGRESS CATALOGING-IN-PUBLICATION DATA
NAMES: Olson, Lynne, author.
TITLE: Madame Fourcade's secret war: the daring young woman who led France's largest spy network against Hitler / Lynne Olson.
DESCRIPTION: New York: Random House, [2019] |
Includes bibliographical references and index.
IDENTIFIERS: LCCN 2018049180 | ISBN 9780812985030 (paperback) |
ISBN 9780812994773 (ebook)
SUBJECTS: LCSH: Fourcade, Marie-Madeleine, 1909–1989. | World War, 1930–1945—Secret service—France—Biography. | Spies—France—Biography. | Women spies—France—Biography. | Spies—Great Britain—Biography. | Women spies—Great Britain—Biography. | Espionage, British—France—History—20th century. | World War, 1939–1945—Secret service—Great Britain—Biography. | World War, 1939–1945—Underground movements—France. | World War, 1939–1945—Women—France.
CLASSIFICATION: LCC D810.S8 O4765 2019 | LCC DDC 940.54/8644092
[B]—dc23
LC record available at https//lccn.loc.gov/2018049180

Printed in the United States of America on acid-free paper

randomhousebooks.com

9 8 7 6 5 4 3

Title-page and part-title-page images from Everett Historical/Shutterstock.com
Maps by M. Roy Cartography
Book design by Barbara M. Bachman

For Stan and Carly

They appeared from out of the shadows, and suddenly you felt that you had always known them. The connection formed by a threat to one's country is the strongest connection of all. People adopt one another, march together. Only capture or death can tear them apart.

—*Marie-Madeleine Fourcade*

Fact had outpaced fiction in producing the copybook "beautiful spy." This was Marie-Madeleine.

—*Commander Kenneth Cohen,*
MI6 official in charge of French intelligence
operations during World War II

CONTENTS

SELECTED CAST OF CHARACTERS

ALLIANCE NETWORK

with Coustenoble, was one of Fourcade's closest deputies in the early days of the network.

JEAN BOUTRON—A survivor of the British attack on the French naval fleet at Mers-el-Kébir in July 1940 and another key figure in Alliance's initial operations, who took an undercover job as Vichy's deputy naval attaché in Madrid.

CHARLES BERNIS—Regarded as the leading theoretician of French military intelligence, he coordinated and supervised the flow of information sent by Alliance to the British. He later was the network's chief in the south of France.

GABRIEL RIVIÈRE—Burly and ebullient, he headed Alliance's operation in Marseille and ran a fruit and vegetable shop as cover for his clandestine activities.

ÉMILE AUDOLY—A Marseille grain merchant who was in charge of collecting intelligence about cargoes and ship movements in the Mediterranean.

JACQUES BRIDOU—A former Olympic bobsled racer and Fourcade's brother, he served as Alliance's first emissary to MI6 in London.

HENRI MOUREN—Chief of the Saint-Nazaire shipyard in Brittany, he provided the network with a detailed map of the important German submarine base there.

ANTOINE HUGON—A garage owner and chief of Alliance's operations in Brittany, who delivered Mouren's map of Saint-Nazaire to Fourcade.

LUCIEN VALLET—A young former army officer who served as the network's chief radio operator in the first year of its existence.

GAVARNI (FIRST NAME UNKNOWN)—A hot-tempered former air force officer who worked briefly as Fourcade's chief of staff.

JEAN SAINTENY—One of Alliance's most skilled and daring agents, he ran its sector in Normandy, which played a major role in the success of D-Day.

SECOND WAVE (RECRUITED 1942–1943)

MONIQUE BONTINCK—Fourcade's young personal courier and assistant, whose demure appearance was at odds with her bold fearlessness.

FERDINAND RODRIGUEZ—A British radio operator sent to Alliance by MI6, he, along with Bontinck and Faye, was among Fourcade's closest colleagues and confidants in 1942–43.

ERNEST SIEGRIST—A former Paris policeman who was in charge of Alliance's security and was also a master forger of identity cards and other documents.

COL. ÉDOUARD KAUFFMANN—A former air force colleague of Léon Faye's, he was head of Alliance's sector in the Dordogne.

MAURICE DE MACMAHON, THE DUKE OF MAGENTA—A colorful flying ace and scion of one of France's most illustrious noble families, who was put in charge of Alliance operations in the country's occupied zone.

LUCIEN POULARD—An air force pilot recruited by Faye, he served as Faye's adjutant and then as chief of Alliance's sector in Brittany.

PIERRE DALLAS—Another air force recruit of Faye's, he headed Alliance's Avia unit, which handled the logistics of parachute drops and aircraft ferry service from Britain.

MARGUERITE BROUILLET—A social worker who sheltered Fourcade and other Alliance agents from Vichy and German police and later became a close friend of Fourcade's and a key Alliance operative herself.

PHILIPPE KOENIGSWERTHER—A former spy for the BCRA, the Free French intelligence agency, who became head of Alliance operations in Bordeaux.

GEORGES LAMARQUE—A brilliant young mathematician, he ran an Alliance subnetwork called the Druids that covered all of France and played a major role in keeping the faltering network alive in the last two years of the war.

JEANNIE ROUSSEAU—One of Lamarque's Druids, she was responsible for one of the greatest Allied intelligence coups of the war through her collection of information about Germany's V-1 and V-2 terror weapons.

ROBERT LYNEN—The most celebrated child actor in France in the 1930s, he was recruited by Fourcade as a courier in Alliance's Marseille headquarters.

JEAN VINZANT—A coal and wood merchant, he oversaw Alliance's operations in the Corrèze, which included clandestine landings of RAF aircraft to pick up and drop off network agents at an airfield near the town of Ussel.

ANDRÉ COINDEAU—An engineer from Nantes who was in charge of Alliance's intelligence gathering at the port of Saint-Nazaire later in the war.

JEAN PHILIPPE—A police superintendent in Toulouse who joined Alliance in 1942 while still working for the Vichy government. After the war, he was honored by Yad Vashem for his refusal to round up Jews.

ANNE DE MEREUIL—A reporter for the French fashion magazine *Marie-Claire* and an old friend of Fourcade's who hid Fourcade and two members of her staff in her apartment in Lyon.

MARGUERITE BERNE-CHURCHILL—A doctor in Lyon who also offered Fourcade a hiding place there and who later joined the network's headquarters staff in Paris.

THIRD WAVE (RECRUITED 1943–1944)

ROBERT DOUIN—A sculptor and artist whose hand-drawn map of German gun emplacements and fortifications on the Normandy beaches played a role in the Allied success of D-Day.

JACQUES STOSSKOPF—A naval engineer at the Lorient submarine base who was regarded by his countrymen as a Nazi collaborator but who was in fact providing valuable intelligence about the German U-boats to Alliance and the British.

HELEN DES ISNARDS—A former air force pilot and the scion of a prominent aristocratic family, he headed Alliance's operations in southeast France.

PIERRE NOAL—A young doctor who served as Fourcade's deputy when she crossed enemy lines in late 1944 to provide intelligence to the Allies on German troop movements in eastern France.

AUTHOR'S NOTE

MARIE-MADELEINE FOURCADE, THE MAIN CHARACTER IN this book, was a woman of complexities, one of which was how she chose to refer to herself. Throughout World War II, her surname was Méric, the name of her first husband, from whom she had long been estranged. She took the name Fourcade—the surname of her second husband—after the war and used it when she wrote her memoirs; it is the name by which she is known in France today. To avoid the confusion of going back and forth between the two names, I've used Fourcade throughout.

PROLOGUE

I T WAS THE MIDDLE OF THE NIGHT.

The air in the barracks detention cell was hot and sultry—typical July weather for the southern French town of Aix-en-Provence. Not surprisingly, the woman lying on the cot was bathed in sweat. But the reason wasn't just the stifling heat. It was also fear. A few hours earlier, she had been captured by the Gestapo while combing through intelligence reports from her resistance network.

The Germans who had taken her captive knew she was an Allied spy, but they had no idea of her true identity. According to her papers—forged, of course—she was a French housewife named Germaine Pezet. Dour and dowdy, she wore spectacles, was drably dressed, and had lusterless jet-black hair. It was the latest of her many disguises, this one concocted in part by a dentist in London who had made the dental prosthetic that had helped transform her appearance. No outward trace remained of the chic blond Parisienne she'd been before the war—a woman born to privilege and known for her beauty and glamor.

For Marie-Madeleine Fourcade, those prewar years seemed like ancient history. Immediately after the German occupation of France, she'd joined the resistance—part of a "minute elite," as Kenneth Cohen, a top British intelligence official and close friend of hers, called the comparative handful of French men and women who rose up in 1940 to defy the Nazis.

In 1941, at the age of thirty-one, she became *la patronne*—the boss—of what would emerge as the largest and most important Allied intelligence network in occupied France. Throughout the war, it supplied the British and American high commands with vital German military secrets, including information about troop movements; submarine sailing schedules; fortifications and coastal gun emplacements; and the Reich's new terror weapons, the V-1 flying bomb and the V-2 rocket.

Over the course of the conflict, Fourcade, the only woman to head a major resistance network in France, commanded some three thousand agents, who infiltrated every major port and sizable town in the country. They came from all segments of society—military officers, government clerks, architects, shopkeepers, fishermen, housewives, doctors, artists, plumbers, students, bus drivers, priests, members of the aristocracy, and France's most celebrated child actor. Thanks to Marie-Madeleine's determined efforts, almost twenty percent were women—the highest number of any resistance organization in France.

Her group's formal name was Alliance, but the Gestapo called it Noah's Ark because its agents used the names of animals and birds as their aliases. Marie-Madeleine had come up with the idea and assigned each agent his or her *nom de guerre*. Many of the men bore the names of proud and powerful denizens of the animal and avian kingdoms: Wolf, Lion, Tiger, Elephant, Fox, Bull, Eagle, to name a few. For her own code name, she decided on Hedgehog.

On the surface, it seemed an odd choice. A beguiling, bright-eyed little animal with prickles all over its body, the hedgehog was—and is—a beloved figure in classic children's books. In *Alice in Wonderland,* hedgehogs are used as croquet balls by the Queen of Hearts. In Beatrix Potter's stories about Peter Rabbit, one of her most endearing characters is a hedgehog named Mrs. Tiggy-Winkle, who was based on Potter's own pet hedgehog.

But the hedgehog's unthreatening appearance is deceiving. When challenged by an enemy, it rolls up in a tight ball, which causes all the spines on its body to point outward. At that point, as a friend of Marie-Madeleine's once noted, it becomes "a tough little animal that even a lion would hesitate to bite."

Until July 1944, Marie-Madeleine Fourcade, like the hedgehog, had managed to elude her foes. Many others in her network had not been as fortunate. For the previous year and a half, the Gestapo had engaged in a full-scale offensive to wipe Alliance out. Hundreds of her agents had been swept up in wave after wave of arrests and killings; whole sectors had been annihilated. In the summer of 1944, Fourcade had no idea how many of her people were still alive. Dozens, including some of her closest associates, had already been tortured and executed.

After each crackdown, the Gestapo was sure they had destroyed the group. But they had not reckoned with its leader's resourcefulness and fierce persistence. Every time a regional circuit was decimated, she managed to cobble together a new one.

In Aix-en-Provence, however, it appeared that her luck had finally run out. After her arrest, she'd been told that a high-ranking Gestapo official was coming from Marseille the following morning to question her. She knew that when he arrived, her real identity would almost certainly be discovered. She feared she would be unable to withstand the brutal interrogation and torture to which she would be subjected before her execution. Briefly, she considered swallowing the tablet of cyanide she'd been given in London in anticipation of such a moment.

But she knew that the end of her life would likely mean the end of Alliance as well. After all the contributions her network had made to the Allied war effort, including to the success of the D-Day landings just a month before, Fourcade couldn't abide the idea of its destruction. She had to find a way to escape.

THROUGHOUT MY WRITING CAREER, I have specialized in works of history that tell sweeping, panoramic stories, chiefly set during World

War II and featuring a multitude of characters. As much as I've enjoyed writing these books, I've often felt a sense of frustration at having to dismiss in a few sentences or paragraphs individuals who, in my opinion, deserved far more attention than I was able to give them.

That was especially true of my last book, *Last Hope Island: Britain, Occupied Europe, and the Brotherhood That Helped Turn the Tide of War*. I was drawn to a number of compelling figures in it, but none more than Marie-Madeleine Fourcade. How could one not be fascinated by the story of this cultured young woman from a well-connected family who had dreams of becoming a concert pianist but ended up as arguably the greatest wartime spymaster in Europe?

M.R.D. Foot, the British historian widely considered the leading authority on European resistance movements in World War II, has observed that "resisters shared one characteristic besides bravery: contrariness. They were disputatious, argumentative, non-conformist, did not enjoy being ordered about." Fourcade is the embodiment of that observation.

All her life, she rebelled against the norms of France's deeply conservative, patriarchal society, in which women were largely confined to their domestic duties as wives and mothers and still did not have the right to vote. "She was very independent," noted her younger daughter, Pénélope Fourcade-Fraissinet. "She had a mind of her own from the beginning."

When the war broke out, Fourcade had long been estranged from her husband, a French army officer serving in North Africa. She had two young children whom she dearly loved but did not see for months, even years, during the conflict.

When she took over as a *chef de résistance,* she initially had doubts about whether male resistance members would accept her leadership. Although some were hesitant at first, most were won over by her courage, resilience, formidable organizational skills, and determination to stay in the field with her agents. The converts included a bevy of traditionalist former military officers who, as one observer later wrote, were "not inclined to feminism." "She had enormous charisma," recalled Charles-Helen des Isnards, whose father had been one of Fourcade's top lieutenants. "She was one of those people who dominate a room just by being in it."

In the years immediately following the war, Fourcade was showered with tributes for her remarkable wartime achievements, but today she and Alliance are relatively unknown outside of France. Although there have been floods of books and films about the French resistance, little has appeared about her and her network—or, for that matter, about any other intelligence organization. The lion's share of attention has gone to groups and individuals specializing in sabotage and other forms of open rebellion against the Nazis. A second strand of resistance activity—escape lines—has also received considerable notice. Yet as exciting and dramatic as their stories were, neither played a crucial role in winning the war. Saboteurs and other resistance fighters in France were certainly important after D-Day, but they did little to obstruct the Germans before then. Escape networks did heroic work in smuggling shot-down Allied airmen and others out of occupied Europe and back to freedom, but their actual contribution to victory was small.

By contrast, the third strand of activity—espionage—was vitally important to the Allied cause from the first day of the war to the last. In order to plan both defensive and offensive operations against the Germans, Allied military commanders were dependent on spies in France and the rest of occupied Europe to inform them where the enemy was and what he was doing. In France, dozens of intelligence networks sprang up to meet that need. Some, like Alliance, worked closely with MI6, Britain's chief foreign intelligence agency. Others were associated with Charles de Gaulle and his Free French movement in London. Yet despite their oversized impact on the war's outcome, intelligence networks have gotten short shrift from historians, novelists, and filmmakers, largely because of the secrecy of their operations.

In the late 1960s, Marie-Madeleine Fourcade pulled back the veil cloaking her wartime activities in her gripping memoir, *Noah's Ark,* which was rightly described by MI6's Kenneth Cohen as "a Homeric saga" of her and Alliance's daily life under German occupation. But like Fourcade herself, the memoir is little known today.

Another explanation for Fourcade's relative obscurity is her gender: As a female *chef,* she does not fit into the traditional historical narrative of the French resistance—namely, that its leaders were men. "To this day historians of the Resistance persist in the belief that no women led Resistance networks, blatantly ignoring the work of Marie-Madeleine Fourcade," the British historian J. E. Smyth noted in 2014.

One of the reasons for this book, then, is to tell her story and give her the credit she is due. But I also wrote it to shine a spotlight on the thousands of agents she led—ordinary men and women who refused to accept the destruction of human values and the dishonor and degradation of their country.

Many years after the war, an American journalist asked Jeannie Rousseau, one of Marie-Madeleine's operatives, why she had risked her life to join Alliance. "I don't understand the question," replied Rousseau, who was responsible for one of the greatest Allied intelligence coups of the war. "It was a moral obligation to do what you are capable of doing. It was a must. How could you not do it?"

1936–1942

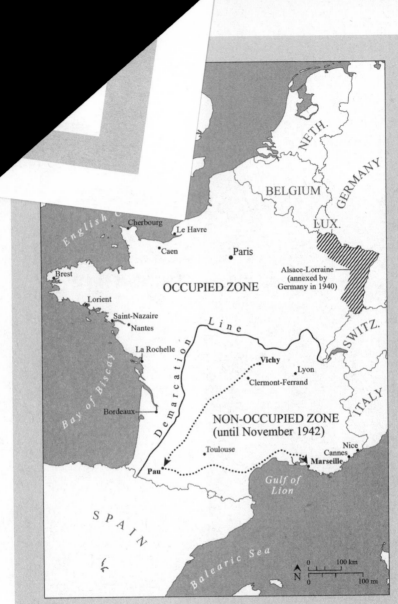

FOUNDED IN VICHY IN SEPTEMBER 1940 BY GEORGES
LOUSTAUNAU-LACAU AND MARIE-MADELEINE FOURCADE,
THE CRUSADE INTELLIGENCE NETWORK (LATER CALLED
ALLIANCE) MOVES ITS HEADQUARTERS FROM VICHY TO
PAU IN EARLY 1941 AND TO MARSEILLE LATER THAT YEAR.

CHAPTER 1

LEAPING INTO
THE UNKNOWN

ER SISTER'S DRAWING ROOM WAS ALREADY CROWDED WHEN Marie-Madeleine Fourcade arrived. In one corner, Georges, her brother-in-law, was deep in discussion with a cluster of male guests. Spotting her sister in another corner, Marie-Madeleine crossed the room to join her.

Yvonne introduced her to several women, who, after acknowledging the newcomer, returned to their conversation about children, their latest travels, and their incessant problems with servants. At one point, between sips of tea, a small, birdlike woman named Yvonne de Gaulle held forth on the soothing virtues of the countryside and how important it was to have a house in the country where a busy man like her husband could find a quiet refuge.

Her attention wandering, Marie-Madeleine glanced around the room. She recognized several of the men—a number of them military officers like Georges, along with a scattering of diplomats, journalists, and business leaders. Ever since she'd returned to Paris, her sister and brother-in-law had included her in their circle of influential friends, many of whom frequented the lively late-afternoon salon that the couple had established at their apartment on rue Vaneau, not far from the French capital's government ministries and embassies.

She caught the eye of Georges, who beckoned to her. As she joined the group around him, she was aware of the appreciative glances directed her way. Cool and elegant, with porcelain skin and high cheekbones, the twenty-six-year-old blonde was used to being the object of male scrutiny.

After introducing her to a couple of guests she had not yet met, Georges mentioned her passion for cars and fast driving and boasted about her success in a recent long-distance car rally. For a minute or two, she and the others debated the merits of various cars, including the speedy model she owned—a Citroën Traction Avant. But the conversation soon returned to the subject that had preoccupied the men from the moment they had arrived that afternoon: Nazi Germany's shocking occupation of the demilitarized Rhineland just a few weeks before.

On March 7, 1936, German troops had marched into the Rhineland, a strip of western Germany straddling the Rhine River and bordering France, Luxembourg, Belgium, and the Netherlands. After Germany's defeat in World War I, the area had been declared a buffer zone, and a ban had been imposed on any installation there of German forces or fortifications. Adolf Hitler's defiance of the ban was his most flagrant violation to date of the 1919 Versailles Treaty and his most dramatic challenge thus far to the Western allies Britain and France.

If either country had responded with force, Hitler's troops, as he later acknowledged, would have retreated immediately. But neither the British nor French lifted a finger to stop the incursion—a failure that appalled those at Georges and Yvonne's salon on that lovely April afternoon.

Several of the guests were army intelligence officers, who, for the last three years, had been providing information to the French government detailing Hitler's mounting preparations for war. Indeed, in the past few months they had passed on advance intelligence of the Rhineland incursion itself. To all these warnings, government officials and the top military command had paid little heed.

The top brass were equally indifferent to increasingly urgent calls by some of their underlings for the modernization and reform of the

French military. As one observer later put it, "The minds of the French generals had ground to a halt and were already thickly coated with rust." In their preparations for a future war, members of the high command remained committed to the kind of defensive warfare that had eventually brought the Allies, at an extremely high cost, a victory in World War I. They paid little or no attention to the swift technological advances in the development of such offensive weapons as planes and tanks. They also went out of their way to block the advancement of younger, more vigorous officers who preached the need for a revolution in military tactics and strategy.

Two of the most prominent members of that younger group—Lieutenant Colonel Charles de Gaulle and Major Georges Loustaunau-Lacau—took center stage in the discussion on rue Vaneau, engaging in a debate that quickly escalated into a full-blown argument. It soon became obvious to Marie-Madeleine that the two officers viewed each other as rivals, which, considering how much they had in common, was perhaps not surprising.

They both were products of Saint-Cyr, France's foremost military academy, and the elite École Supérieure de Guerre, the country's graduate war college. Both had fought in World War I, been wounded, and received multiple citations for bravery. After the war, they had served at different times on the staff of Marshal Philippe Pétain, the hero of the Battle of Verdun, who had held several key postwar posts—commander in chief of the army, inspector general, and minister of war. The forty-five-year-old de Gaulle and the forty-two-year-old Loustaunau-Lacau were brilliant, ambitious, and egocentric, with a rebellious streak that had gotten them in considerable trouble at various times with Pétain and other military superiors. Each loved the spotlight, and neither wanted to share it with the other.

After Germany occupied the Rhineland, de Gaulle had submitted an article predicting its disastrous consequences to the influential journal *Défense Nationale,* which refused to publish it. Now, leaning against the apartment's fireplace mantel, he criticized the high command's tactical and strategic ineptness, blasting its reliance on prepared fortifications like the Maginot Line and arguing for the creation of a fast-moving mechanized army working closely with and supported by aircraft. Loustaunau-Lacau interrupted, dismissing de Gaulle's idea of a strike force as unworkable. As they argued, they seemed to agree on only one point: If the French military were not immediately reshaped, the army would collapse, and the country would be crushed by Germany in a war that was drawing ever closer.

Fascinated by the verbal fireworks between them, Fourcade had no idea of the profound impact that both men would soon have on her life.

AS IT HAPPENED, FOURCADE had much in common with these two iconoclastic officers, including a strong will and a taste for risk and rebellion—traits not often seen in young Frenchwomen from well-to-do families like hers. But then again, few genteel Frenchwomen had the kind of unconventional pedigree and upbringing that she did.

Boldness and daring seemed to run in Marie-Madeleine's family, with one of her distant ancestors, the Marquis de Bacqueville, topping the list of risk takers. Like many Frenchmen in the eighteenth century, the marquis had been fascinated by the idea of flying. Unlike his compatriots, he decided to test the possibility himself. On March 19, 1742, he appeared, with large white wings attached to his arms and legs, on the roof of his house in Paris, overlooking the Seine. The fifty-four-year-old nobleman had told friends and acquaintances of his planned experiment, and a large crowd, including the writer Jean-Jacques Rousseau, had gathered in the streets below.

Wings outstretched, the marquis hurled himself off the roof—and promptly plunged several feet. But then a light wind came up, keeping him aloft and pushing him slowly across the river, to the gasps and cheers of the spectators. It appeared that he might actually make it to the opposite shore when the wind died as abruptly as it had risen, and he fell on top of a houseboat in the Seine, breaking his leg. For months, the marquis was the butt of jokes among le tout Paris. And yet, as his descendants were quick to point out, he actually did fly, if only for a few moments.

In her own way, Marie-Madeleine's free-spirited mother, Mathilde Bridou, displayed a similar zest for leaping into the unknown. Soon after she married Lucien Bridou in the early 1900s, he was assigned to Shanghai as an executive for Messageries Maritimes, a French shipping line responsible for most of the passenger and trade traffic to and from France and its large colonial empire.

When Mathilde made it clear she planned to accompany Lucien to Shanghai, her family was aghast. How could she expose herself, not to mention any children she and Lucien might have, to the dangers of living in China—the appalling climate, the myriad diseases, the earthquakes, the constant danger of riots and revolution? Mathilde brushed off all such warnings, although when her second daughter, Marie-Madeleine, was born in 1909, she had agreed to return home to Marseille for the birth.

Like their parents, Marie-Madeleine and her siblings, Yvonne and Jacques, were captivated by the teeming city in which they grew up. Known as the Paris of the Orient, Shanghai was one of the world's leading seaports, as well as the largest, richest, and most modern metropolis in Asia. It was by far the most prominent of China's five so-called treaty ports, which the Chinese, under duress from Britain, France, and other Western countries, had opened to foreign trade in the nineteenth century.

In the first three decades of the twentieth century, Shanghai was considered the essence of exoticism, mystery, and excitement. As an open city, it required neither a visa nor passport to enter, providing a haven for an extraordinarily eclectic array of immigrants, among them White Russians fleeing from the Bolsheviks; Chinese warlords and revolutionaries; American and European gangsters and spies; drug smugglers; and international arms dealers.

To many, Shanghai epitomized "the stylish, the new, the audacious in everything from dress to politics." As one observer put it, "You could be a cosmopolitan Parisian or Londoner, but you simply were not chic enough unless you had been to Shanghai."

Much of Shanghai's foreign population, including Marie-Madeleine's family, lived in spacious, airy, European-style houses on tree-lined avenues in the city's French quarter. But it was Shanghai's vibrant waterfront and its bustling downtown streets that most attracted the young Marie-Madeleine, who, with her sister and brother, were given free rein by their equally adventurous parents to explore the city. She had a slight limp—the result of a congenital hip displacement that she had inherited from her mother—but it never seemed to slow her down.

On the Bund, Shanghai's major avenue, cars and trams shouldered their way through throngs of bicyclists, rickshaw coolies, and peasants carrying ducks and other foodstuffs on bamboo poles, everyone seemingly indifferent to the blare of car horns and the whistle blowing and shouted commands of Shanghai's policemen, most of them turbaned Sikhs from the raj. The noise was cacophonous, with at least a dozen different languages assaulting one's ear.

On the Whangpoo River, the boom of ships' horns added to the din. As crowded as the Bund, the river was alive with wooden sampans, barges, and junks, their sails spread wide, dodging between the moorings of passenger ships and freighters from all over the world, as well as British and French warships, their decks bristling with guns.

"My mother loved the scenery of China and was always drawing our attention to everything around us," Fourcade recalled. "She would take us all out, including my father, on the Chinese canals, on a houseboat that was provided to our family. We'd float under the marvelous bridges and look at the villages and countryside."

On occasion, the Bridou children, accompanied by their Chinese amah, ventured beyond downtown Shanghai into the old Chinese city, its dark, narrow, cobblestone streets packed with beggars, fortune-tellers, letter writers, and street vendors, from whom they would buy sweets—one of Marie-Madeleine's favorite childhood memories.

As cosmopolitan as Shanghai was, the British dominated the city economically and politically and set the tone for the foreign community. At the French *lycée* she attended, Marie-Madeleine became friends with several British girls. "They wanted to speak French, and I wanted to speak English, and we all ended up bilingual," she later remarked. During those years, she fell in love with all things British, including afternoon tea.

IN 1917, MARIE-MADELEINE'S IDYLLIC life in Shanghai abruptly ended when her father contracted a tropical disease and died soon afterward. Mathilde Bridou moved the family to Paris, where Marie-Madeleine was enrolled in a convent school catering to the daughters of aristocratic and otherwise well-connected families. She then studied at a leading Paris conservatory, with the hope of becoming a concert pianist.

At the age of seventeen, however, she abandoned her dreams of a music career when she met, fell in love with, and swiftly married a handsome, dark-haired Army captain named Édouard-Jean Méric, a graduate of Saint-Cyr and the son of a general. She was attracted to him personally but also to the fact that his next posting would be in Morocco, an exotic milieu that promised a return to the excitement and adventure that she had relished during her childhood.

In the late 1920s, France boasted the second-largest colonial empire in the world, with a population of 100 million people and territory of 4.5 million square miles spread over Africa, Asia, and the Middle East. As one of the most valuable jewels in the French colonial crown, Morocco was a training ground for France's military and civil service elite, and as such it was a plum assignment for an up-and-coming intelligence officer like Édouard-Jean Méric.

His assignment was to monitor various restive Arab tribes in the country and to act swiftly to quash any signs of potential uprisings against the French. In the early months of their marriage, Marie-Madeleine, who learned Arabic, would often accompany him on horseback to his meetings with tribal chiefs. She particularly enjoyed the sumptuous fourteen-course feasts—"tagines of every kind, roast lamb, couscous, and so much else"—that the chiefs staged for their French visitors. She also was a frequent volunteer at a makeshift French clinic for local residents, where her duties included helping to deliver babies.

Although Méric was impressed by her keen interest in his work, he was less pleased by the delight Marie-Madeleine took in the lively social life in Rabat, Morocco's capital. Eight years older than she, he had no time for what he viewed as the frivolity of such activities as cocktail parties, dinners, and picnics in the desert, at which other young officers paid considerable attention to his beautiful young wife.

A year after their wedding, Marie-Madeleine gave birth to a son, named Christian. Two years later, her daughter, Béatrice, was born. Although she adored her children, she was growing increasingly unhappy with her husband and his conservative views, especially those about how she should behave. He wanted her to be what he called a proper wife, focused only on him and their family—a view that clashed with her freewheeling, independent ways. In 1933, the couple separated.

From then on, Marie-Madeleine had virtually nothing to do with Méric; in her memoirs, written more than thirty years later, there is no mention of him. As her French biographer, Michèle Cointet, put it, she would never again "allow a husband to decide her wishes, govern her acts, or judge for her what she will do with her life."

After their separation, Marie-Madeleine moved with her children to Paris, to be near Yvonne, Georges, and their family on rue Vaneau. Soon after she arrived, she became part of a small circle of young women in the upper reaches of Paris society, many of whom were married but who, like her, were unwilling to confine themselves to domestic duties. Her closest friend was Hélène ("Nelly") de Vogüé, a twenty-eight-year-old blonde noted as much for her intellect as for her beauty. The daughter of a wealthy industrialist in eastern France, Nelly had studied at the École des Beaux-Arts in Paris and was both an accomplished painter and a gifted writer. In 1927, she had married Comte Jean de Vogüé, a scion of one of France's most illustrious aristocratic families. But the great love of her life was the writer Antoine de Saint-Exupéry, whom she met two years after her marriage and whom she served as both mistress and muse. She would be named his literary executor after Saint-Exupéry's death late in World War II.

Like Nelly and her other friends, Marie-Madeleine was anxious to do more with her life than abide by French society's restrictive ideas about how women should behave. In the late 1920s and early 1930s, she and other affluent young Frenchwomen were caught up in the car rally craze that swept the country. Owning a car was still a rarity in France, and women who could afford one were now handed the freedom to come and go as they pleased, without having to depend on anyone else.

Marie-Madeleine also took flying lessons and acquired a pilot's license. And in 1935, she did something equally daring for a woman of her social class—she got a job. She worked at Radio-Cité, the country's first commercial radio station, initially in its advertising department and then as a producer of entertainment programs, partnering with the writer Colette on a half-hour series for women. Extraordinarily successful from the beginning, Radio-Cité was responsible for, among other things, launching the broadcast careers of singers like Édith Piaf and Maurice Chevalier and offering France's first radio news programs.

For a young woman who possessed both money and ambition, the early and mid-1930s were an exciting time to be in Paris, with its vibrant social, artistic, and literary life. To its many admirers—expatriates and natives alike—it was the cultural capital of the world. Writers, painters, musicians, dancers, sculptors, and intellectuals of every stripe from all over the world continued to flock there, just as they had for decades.

At the same time, however, the French capital—and the country as a whole—was enmeshed in mounting political, economic, and social turmoil. France had long been known for what one historian called its "people's ineradicable love of political squabbles," but by the 1930s, its traditional divisiveness had metastasized into intolerance, bitterness, and outright strife.

In the nineteenth and early twentieth centuries, French governments had been noted for their short tenures, but since the end of World War I, such instability had grown considerably worse. During that period, more than forty governments had come and gone—an average of one every six months. None lasted long enough to come to grips with the country's severe economic and social problems. With France in a state of permanent political crisis, cabinet ministers focused their efforts on staying in office, which usually meant spending little time on substantive issues. The already deep cynicism of the French people toward government officials was further exacerbated by a string of financial scandals in the 1930s involving bribes paid to ministers and parliamentary deputies by businessmen and bankers seeking favorable government treatment.

All this was happening during a decade of intense crisis throughout the world, marked by the global ravages of the Great Depression and the rapid rise of Hitler and other totalitarian leaders. Like much of the rest of Europe, France was hit hard by the Depression, with tens of thousands of businesses collapsing and the unemployment rate skyrocketing to more than twenty percent. Racked by infighting and claims of corruption, the various governments in power during the 1930s failed to cope with these challenges, leaving a vacuum that was filled by direct action by extremist groups from both the left and the right.

The French Communist Party, which dominated much of the country's labor movement, was responsible for fomenting a massive wave of wildcat strikes across the country that caused significant disruption to factory production. On the right, a host of nationalist groups, some of them fascist, sprang up like mushrooms after a rain, with several seeking the violent overthrow of France's parliamentary system.

As the country teetered on the brink of anarchy, the last thing its people and government wanted was to confront the looming threat of another war with Germany. The last one had devastated France, and its citizens had never fully recovered. More than 1.4 million Frenchmen had been killed in World War I, the highest proportion of deaths per capita of any of the great power combatants. Another 4.2 million men were wounded. The northern part of the country, which had been occupied by the Germans, was left in ruins, and the French were still struggling to restore the region's decimated industries.

Most French citizens, for all their corrosive divisions, were united in the belief that France must never fight another such war again. Such pacifism came as a profound shock to Marie-Madeleine, who, having spent most of her life as an expatriate, had an idealized view of her homeland, with its traditions of patriotism, service, and honor. She had grown up hearing about the glories of France's victory in the 1914–18 war, without being exposed to the grief and despair it had caused.

Deeply affected by the discussion at Georges and Yvonne's apartment, Marie-Madeleine thought about getting involved herself in the debate over France's failure to confront German aggression. But what could she possibly do? The day after the gathering, Georges Loustaunau-Lacau gave her the answer.

LATE THE FOLLOWING MORNING, she received a phone call from the major. He had enjoyed meeting her, he said, and would like to see her again. He added that he had something confidential to tell her. Could they meet soon, preferably someplace discreet?

For a moment, she hesitated. What did he have in mind? A romantic assignation, perhaps? He was, she acknowledged, an attractive older man, but she was still a married woman. Yet she could not help being intrigued by him. Although relatively short, especially when compared with Charles de Gaulle, he had broad shoulders, piercing eyes, palpable energy, and a powerful, charismatic presence that, in her opinion, his tall, icy debating partner did not share.

She told him yes, then suggested he come to her apartment. After hanging up, she had immediate second thoughts. Lighting a cigarette, she went to her closet and took out her outfit for the day—a plain gray suit, white blouse, and flat shoes—meant as a signal that she was not in the mood for seduction.

But, as it happened, neither was he. As soon as he arrived, Loustaunau-Lacau apologized for being so forward on the phone. But, he added, time was of the essence: "You seemed interested in what I said yesterday at your brother-in-law's. I want to tell you more and to ask you to help me in a task that I cannot do alone."

GEORGES
LOUSTAUNAU-
LACAU

Specifically, he said, he wanted her to join him in a new venture he had begun: the creation of a confidential journal for Frenchmen of influence that would argue the case for the need of immediate reform of the French military. The situation, he added, was even worse than she could imagine. It was essential to open the eyes of the country's leaders as quickly as possible to the intentions of the German general staff.

Their work would start immediately. "One of my Belgian friends has procured secret dossiers that expose the intentions of the German high command," he said. "I need to get them quickly. Such documents must not travel by mail. You have a car. You must go to Brussels and collect them. I will pay all expenses."

Caught up in this real-life spy drama, Marie-Madeleine agreed—a decision that would radically change her life. From that moment, she wrote later, she and Loustaunau-Lacau began building an intelligence network against Nazi Germany.

CHAPTER 2

THE CHAOS OF DEFEAT

O VER THE NEXT TWO YEARS, MAJOR LOUSTAUNAU-LACAU, AIDED by Fourcade, recruited a stable of informants in France, Switzerland, Belgium, and Germany who passed on reports about the buildup of the German armed forces. Although neither of the two was aware of it, Winston Churchill, then an antiappeasement backbencher in the British House of Commons, had created a similar private network, seeking out authoritative sources in Germany and elsewhere who could provide evidence of the growing Nazi military menace.

A natural conspirator, Loustaunau-Lacau adopted the code name Navarre, after Henri de Navarre, a hot-blooded prince and master intriguer who became King Henry IV of France in the late sixteenth century. Like many of his friends and acquaintances, Fourcade addressed him and referred to him as Navarre for the rest of his life.

Serving as Navarre's intermediary, she drove her Citroën to the various countries to meet with informants and pick up their material. Navarre's main source was Berthold Jacob, an intrepid German-Jewish journalist who had left Germany shortly before the 1933 Nazi takeover and operated an independent press service in the French city of Strasbourg, near the German border. Jacob's investigative articles revealing Germany's preparations for war had so infuriated the Nazis

MARIE-
MADELEINE
FOURCADE

that he was lured to Switzerland in 1935, kidnapped by the Gestapo, and taken to a prison in Berlin. Thanks to strenuous protests by the Swiss government over the violation of their country's sovereignty, Jacob was released after six months and returned to France, where he continued his work for the press service—and Navarre—until the outbreak of war.

But as Navarre saw it, Nazi Germany was not the only threat to peace and the security of France. He was also deeply concerned about the activities of the Soviet Union and the French Communist Party. In his view, the French Communists, backed by the Soviet government, "were the reckless agents of a Germany that was waiting for her hour of revenge against France."

That belief had some evidence to support it. Since the 1920s, the Soviets had secretly provided Germany with facilities deep within their country for the making and testing of tanks, aircraft, and poison gas and for the training of Luftwaffe pilots and Wehrmacht troops—all activities that had been prohibited by the Versailles Treaty.

In addition, the Soviets, in partnership with French Communists, had operated an extensive spy network in France, which gathered considerable intelligence about the country's defense industries and military. According to Navarre, the French army was a particular target of Communist subversion, which included an intensive propaganda campaign by the French Communist Party aimed at demoralizing French troops and sowing defeatism within their ranks.

Convinced that a growing Communist influence in the army was imperiling French security, Navarre took matters into his own hands. In the mid-1930s, he created a secret organization of army officers, called the Corvignolles, to combat what he saw as Communist attempts to encourage army indiscipline and to destroy morale. The Corvignolles' mission was to conduct surveillance of those in the army who were suspected of being Communists and to pass on information about their activities to top military officials.

Although Navarre was hardly alone in his anticommunist views—many if not most of his military colleagues shared them—his group's vigilantism could not have come at a more politically inopportune time. In 1936, the Popular Front—a coalition of left-wing parties supported by the Communists—took control of the government. The following year, Navarre, not surprisingly, was cashiered from his post in the German section of the Deuxième Bureau, the French army's intelligence agency. "A man of the utmost daring and rebelliousness," he "positively relished being in hot water—wonderful to serve under, impossible to command," the British historian M.R.D. Foot later noted.

Seemingly undaunted by his dismissal, Navarre transferred his energies to setting up a small publishing empire, comprised of several political, military, and cultural journals that were aimed, for the most part, at influential business, government, and military circles. Many of the publications' articles detailed the growing military might of Germany, the dangers of communism, and the shocking unpreparedness of the French army and air force. In this new venture, as in Navarre's earlier enterprises, Fourcade served as his deputy.

In March 1938, two years after she'd begun working with Navarre, Nazi Germany annexed Austria, to which the British and French governments again turned a blind eye. Six months later, at the Munich Conference, the two Western allies surrendered a huge chunk of Czechoslovakia—the Sudetenland—to the German leader, along with its vital fortifications and major centers of industry. Providing a sharp corrective to the euphoric mood of those who believed that the Munich agreement had brought "peace in our time," Navarre wrote in one of his journals: "It is neither by speeches nor by these missions that the insane excesses of Hitler's Germany will be defeated." In the same journal, he published, in considerable detail, the entire order of battle of Hitler's land, sea, and air forces, compiled from reports sent to him by Berthold Jacob.

Yet it wasn't until September 1939, following Hitler's invasion of Poland and the Allies' declaration of war against Germany, that the French military brass implicitly acknowledged the truth of Navarre's Cassandra-like prophecies. He was recalled to active duty and sent as a military intelligence officer to the Ninth Army, whose command post was in the east of France, near the Ardennes forest in southern Belgium.

Throughout 1939 and into 1940, Navarre and other French intelligence officers passed on reports to top government and military leaders of German plans for an invasion of France through the Ardennes. Both leadership groups rejected the intelligence, preferring to believe that any future German offensive would come through the flatlands of central Belgium, just as it had at the beginning of World War I. Navarre was enraged. From his Ninth Army post, he publicly lambasted what he saw as the incompetence of the French high command, which he said amounted to treason. For French military leaders, this latest insubordination was the final straw. In March 1940, he was arrested and charged with demoralizing French troops, which, under a wartime emergency decree, was punishable by death.

His case came before a magistrate on May 10, 1940, the same day that Hitler launched his blitzkrieg of Western Europe, during which German units went into battle precisely as he had predicted. For Navarre, the timing could not have been better. The magistrate acknowledged that the major had been correct in charging his military superiors with extreme negligence. He was let off with a stern reprimand—and then was sent to fight the Germans as commander of a battalion near the Maginot Line, France's supposedly impenetrable chain of fortifications.

On May 14, another of Navarre's predictions came true. The main German force, consisting of more than 1.5 million men and 1,800 tanks, thundered through the Ardennes, outflanking the Maginot Line. Smashing into the least protected sector of the French frontier, it routed the ill-equipped French forces assigned to guard it and crossed the Meuse River into France. In just three days, the German offensive had split the Allied forces in two.

In Paris, a wave of panic enveloped the government and military. As Navarre and de Gaulle had forecast four years before on rue Vaneau, the vaunted French army was collapsing like the proverbial house of cards.

THREE WEEKS LATER, MARIE-MADELEINE Fourcade fled Paris, joining a mass exodus. With the Germans closing in on the capital, the French government had decamped six days before, sneaking out in the middle of the night without making any arrangements for the evacuation or defense of the city.

In keeping with its panicked residents' funereal mood, Paris was shrouded in a thick, choking fog of smoke and soot from nearby oil and gas tanks that had been set alight by retreating troops. Soot covered the trees and streets, and some people noticed an eerie lack of birdsong as they left. Most of the birds, it turned out, had been killed by the black pall of smoke.

Overall, more than six million French citizens, resembling "an anthill that had been knocked over," flooded south—the largest single movement of people in Europe since the Dark Ages. The scene was pure chaos, filled with "all the ugliness of panic, defeat, and demoralization" of a disintegrating society, remarked the American diplomat George Kennan, who witnessed the flight. Thousands of children became separated from their families, and for months afterward, anguished parents placed ads in newspapers trying to find their missing offspring. According to one refugee, "We had lost all points of reference. All our habits and all the rules of life were floating."

Several weeks earlier, Marie-Madeleine had had the foresight to send her own children—ten-year-old Christian and eight-year-old Béatrice—to Noirmoutier, an island off France's Atlantic coast, in the care of her mother. She had had advance warning from Navarre, who, before he left for the front, told her that the situation was hopeless and that when the time came for her to leave Paris, she should head for his country home in Oloron-Sainte-Marie, a village in southwestern France near the French-Spanish border. She followed his advice, setting off by car with her maid, her dog, and a married couple who were friends of hers.

For a day and a half, her Citroën inched slowly southward in an endless line of cars, wagons, trucks, taxis, delivery vans, and even pushcarts and hay wagons. Other refugees—pushing wheelbarrows and prams piled high with children and possessions—trudged along both sides of the road. An American journalist, caught up in the middle of the exodus, said it was like "a stream of lava flowing past, the unstoppable river which came from the unimaginable eruption somewhere in the north."

Finally, Marie-Madeleine and her party reached Berry, a rural region in the Loire Valley, where she hoped to stay with a close friend, Aurore Sand—the granddaughter of the famed novelist George Sand. Sand's house, however, was already filled with friends and relatives fleeing the Germans, so she handed over to Marie-Madeleine the keys to the historic Château de Nohant, her grandmother's home.

At the château, which was more like a large country house than a castle, Sand had written many of her books and hosted some of the most important writers, painters, and composers of her time, including Balzac, Flaubert, Turgenev, Delacroix, and Liszt. Arguably her most noted guest was her lover, Frédéric Chopin, who lived off and on at Nohant for more than eight years.

After a meager supper that evening, Marie-Madeleine wandered through the château, finally sitting down at a piano in the salon. It was here, she knew, that Chopin had composed some of his masterpieces, including the Polonaise in A-flat Major, the Sonata Funèbre, two nocturnes, and four mazurkas.

That night, however, she identified most with another of Chopin's works—his Étude op. 10, no. 12, otherwise known as the Revolutionary Étude. An exile from his native Poland, Chopin had written the etude to commemorate his countrymen's celebrated—and failed—uprising against their Russian occupiers in 1831. Marie-Madeleine caressed the piano's keys and then began to play, pouring her grief and rage over the impending fall of France into Chopin's passionate, thundering piece. Afterward, she went to sleep in his bed.

She clung to her anger over the next several days as she and her companions continued their journey, traveling by night to avoid the Stuka dive bombers that strafed the refugee-crowded roads and sleeping by day in ditches, woods, and other places that were hidden from view. In one of the many small towns and villages through which they passed, she and her party were given shattering news: Marshal Pétain, who had just replaced Paul Reynaud as France's prime minister, had ordered French troops to lay down their arms and had petitioned Nazi Germany for an armistice.

In a broadcast to his countrymen, the eighty-four-year-old Pétain attributed France's defeat to "too few arms, too few allies," and the country's own moral failures, which included a lack of discipline and an unfortunate "spirit of pleasure." At the same time, he expressed his compassion and concern for the millions of refugees still choking France's roads and appealed to them and their compatriots to "rally to the government over which I preside during this difficult ordeal."

As shocked as she was by Pétain's capitulation, Fourcade was even more stunned by the joyful reaction of the people around her to the news. They laughed, kissed each other, and drank to Pétain's health. Such happy scenes, which the novelist Arthur Koestler later described as "the apocalypse [disguised] as a family picnic," were repeated throughout the country. As Fourcade saw it, the French, in their understandable relief that the war had ended for them, failed to recognize that in the process, they and their country had lost their souls.

On June 25, Pétain announced the terms of the armistice. German troops would occupy the northern three-fifths of the country, including Paris, the industrial north, and the Atlantic coast, with its valuable string of seaports. The remaining two-fifths, to be controlled by

Pétain's government and to be known as the free zone, would be made up of France's southern provinces. The French also would retain control of French North Africa and the country's other colonial possessions, as well as its fleet. The spa town of Vichy, in the center of France, was designated the new French capital.

Stopping for a few days in Saint-Jean-de-Luz, a lovely little seaside village on the Atlantic, Marie-Madeleine was invited to dinner by acquaintances there. They showed no interest in the stories she told them of what she had seen during her flight from Paris— abandoned toddlers crying for their parents, demoralized soldiers throwing down their arms and joining the exodus, refugees huddling in fear as German dive bombers appeared overhead. When she was finished, her acquaintances merely shrugged. It was time, they told her, to forget about such misfortunes and focus on the future and France's return to normality.

Appalled by such complacency, Marie-Madeleine refused to heed their advice, launching into a long diatribe against what she saw as Pétain's cowardice. Her hosts had had enough. "How dare you say this!" one of them snapped. "How dare you insult the name of the marshal!" Marie-Madeleine sat in silence for the rest of the meal. Never had she felt so alone.

In early July, she finally made it to Navarre's country home in Oloron-Sainte-Marie. His family, however, had no idea where he was or what had happened to him. For more than a month, Marie-Madeleine stayed with them while awaiting news of his fate. Finally, word came that he was alive, although badly hurt in a battle near the Maginot Line. Late in August, he hobbled home, forty pounds lighter and in terrible pain from unhealed bullet wounds in his neck and back. Despite his grave injuries, he had escaped from the German hospital to which he had been taken and had made his way several hundred miles across occupied France, slipping into the free zone and back to Oloron-Sainte-Marie.

As he recuperated, Marie-Madeleine did her best to tamp down her impatience over her prolonged stay in this peaceful rural haven. Finally, she could contain herself no longer. She pointedly noted to

Navarre that Charles de Gaulle, his longtime colleague and rival, was now in London. The most junior brigadier general in the French army, de Gaulle had been appointed undersecretary of war just eight days before his dramatic escape to the British capital on June 17. He was the only French official willing to abandon his homeland to continue the fight against Hitler. From London, de Gaulle had made a BBC broadcast to France, urging his countrymen to join him in a movement to resist both the Vichy government and the Nazis. "Whatever happens," he declared, "the flame of French resistance should not and will not be extinguished."

Marie-Madeleine argued that they should follow de Gaulle to London and become part of his Free French operation. Her mentor rejected the idea outright. In England, he said, they would be refugees, just like de Gaulle, dependent on the British for everything. At that point, almost no one in the British government, with the prominent exception of Winston Churchill, took de Gaulle and his minuscule band of followers seriously.

Instead, Navarre said, he and Marie-Madeleine should remain in France and resist from within. The place to start, he said, was the country's epicenter of defeatism—Vichy itself. He had many contacts there, he pointed out, thanks to his prewar political activities.

Marie-Madeleine's heart sank. It was a phony capital, she told Navarre. What could they possibly accomplish there? He replied that in order to collect intelligence, they must go to its source—France's current seat of government. Only there could they learn more about the country's political and military situation.

Less than a week later, they were on their way to Vichy.

CHAPTER 3

FIGHTING BACK

L OOKING MORE LIKE AN OPERETTA STAGE SET THAN THE CAPITAL of a major European country, Vichy was as far removed from the chaos and fear afflicting much of the rest of France as one could possibly imagine. But that was exactly what the Pétain government wanted—a quiet, out-of-the-way place, with no smoke-belching factories, restive workers, or would-be resisters.

For more than two centuries, Vichy, famed for its reportedly health-restoring spring water, had attracted the well-to-do from all over Europe, who came there each year to take the cure. Along with its baths, Vichy boasted a casino, restaurants, tearooms, daily band concerts, and several Belle Époque hotels. When they arrived in early July, Pétain and his staff had taken over the Hotel du Parc, with its wrought-iron balconies and rooms awash in blue and pink toile de Jouy fabric depicting charming, restful pastoral scenes. While most ministries had been assigned offices in other hotels, the ministry of the interior, responsible for policing the free zone, was incongruously housed in the town's sprawling Grand Casino, which boasted a Moorish cupola encased in gold tiles.

"Never was Vichy . . . as busy and as gay as in the summer of defeat in 1940," noted the CBS correspondent David Schoenbrun.

Wives and mistresses of government officials, in their best summer dresses, took daily strolls along the town's tree-lined main avenue, opposite the beautiful Parc des Sources. There were endless queues in front of Vichy's most fashionable restaurants, with the competition for tables particularly fierce at the dining room of the Hotel du Parc, where Pétain and leading members of the government held court.

The cheerful holiday atmosphere, however, was just a facade. Behind it, the government had embarked on a mission to kill parliamentary democracy in France and install an authoritarian regime modeled on that of Nazi Germany. On July 8, in the casino's theater, the French parliament yielded to pressure and voted to turn over all its powers to Pétain and, by extension, to Pierre Laval, Pétain's deputy and the power behind the throne. Henceforth, the legislature would assemble only at Pétain's request. He in turn would govern at the sufferance of the Germans—and would continue to do so only as long as he did what they ordered.

After several conversations with Pétain and others in Vichy, William Bullitt, the U.S. ambassador to France, wrote to President Franklin Roosevelt that "the physical and moral defeat [of the French leaders] has been so absolute that they have accepted completely for France the fate of becoming a province of Nazi Germany. Moreover, in order that they may have as many companions in misery as possible, they hope that England will be rapidly and completely defeated by Germany."

From its beginning, the Vichy government instituted policies of persecution and repression of French citizens, particularly Jews. In early July 1940, less than a month after France's capitulation, Vichy began enforcing anti-Semitic measures in its territory without receiving orders from Berlin to do so.

Yet despite the growing oppression, Pétain and his government could do no wrong in the eyes of many if not most of the French, regardless of which part of the country they lived in. They saw Pétain as their savior, whose wisdom and firm direction would help heal the trauma of their country's collapse. Shortly after the capitulation, Jean Guéhenno, an anti-German writer and literary critic in Paris, noted with disgust that the French radio "says 'the Marshal' in the same way it would say 'my love.' " According to the French historian Henri Michel, "the Marshal's authority was accepted by all with more than resignation. He offered consolation and hope."

When Pétain had announced the armistice terms to the French people, he told them that a "new spirit of sacrifice" was needed. In order to recover from the anguish of defeat, he declared, France must undergo a complete transformation of its society, adhering to the conservative spirit of his government's new motto—*Travail, famille, patrie*—rather than to France's national motto since the French Revolution—*Liberté, égalité, fraternité*. Obedience to authority and devotion to work, he made clear, must replace the idea of freedom and equality. There must be a return to tradition, to working the land, and to so-called family values, which in his and Vichy's eyes meant accepting men as the unquestioned authority figures of the family and viewing women solely through the prism of motherhood and caregiving.

Even before Pétain, France had treated women as second-class citizens, refusing them the right to vote, to own or control property without permission from male relatives, or to have a bank account in their own name. As was true in America and elsewhere, many in France were profoundly shocked by the emergence of large numbers of young women in the 1920s and 1930s who had made clear their contempt for conventional feminine behavior through their independent ways, which included bobbed hair, short skirts, dancing, drinking, smoking, getting jobs, and having premarital sex.

In patriarchal France, the behavior of the "new woman" was considered brazen and threatening, and the Vichy government struck back hard. Among other new restrictions, it decreed the death penalty for performing an abortion, made it much more difficult to get a divorce, barred married women from working in the public sector, and ordered all female students in high school to take classes in housekeeping.

Marie-Madeleine Fourcade, of course, embodied everything the new regime detested. She was separated from her husband, had a mind of her own and ambitions that stretched far beyond housekeeping, and had given up care of her children in order to take part in a nascent resistance campaign against the Germans. "She never operated according to society's rules; she followed her own rules," said a longtime acquaintance. "Basically, she acted like a man."

Fourcade in turn was disgusted by Pétain's government and everything it stood for, and she hated its seat of power from the start. To her, Vichy was nothing but a nest of gossip, infighting, and intrigue, filled, as she put it, with the "aristocracy of defeat"—politicians, businessmen, civil servants, military officers, and others—all seeking jobs or other personal or political gain from the new government.

Conspiracies were being hatched everywhere. The conspiratorial Navarre managed to convince Pétain that he had given up his rebellious ways and now fully supported his former boss's policies. "The Marshal received me as if I was his son," Navarre told an acquaintance. "He does not look touched by the cyclone. To see him, one would believe that the disaster that has befallen France was only a badly cooked meal."

During their meeting, he persuaded Pétain to make him an official of the Légion Française des Combattants, a new national organization of military veterans created and funded by the government. Fourcade greeted the news with unconcealed exasperation. How would such a group fit into their plans for resistance? she asked. What exactly were they doing in Vichy, anyway? And what was her role supposed to be? Perhaps, she said, it would be better if she went to London after all.

Navarre tried to calm her down. "You know very well that I need you," he said. He added that they were going to do what they had done in the late 1930s: create a network to provide intelligence about the German armed forces, only this time those based in France. The British, he noted, were in desperate need of such information to help them survive the German onslaught that they were about to face.

But, he said, he personally must be above suspicion. His League position would allow him to circulate throughout the free zone, making contacts, collecting information, and covertly drumming up political support for a future transformation of the League into an instrument of resistance. In the meantime, he said, pointing his cigarette at Fourcade, she would do the actual work of recruiting agents and setting up the initial intelligence operation.

She was stunned by his directive. How could she possibly do that? She was a woman, after all, barely thirty years old. Did he really believe military men like himself would accept her as a leader? He swept her objections aside, pointing out that as his deputy in the interwar years, she had amassed considerable experience in the handling of agents and other aspects of the labyrinthine world of collecting intelligence. And as for being a woman, he said, that in itself was an excellent reason for her to do it because no one would suspect her.

When she failed to respond, Navarre shrugged and said that if she wasn't strong enough to take the job, he would do it himself. After hesitating for a moment, Fourcade decided she had no choice but to give in.

AT HIS MEETING WITH PÉTAIN, Navarre had persuaded the marshal to authorize and pay for the establishment of a reception and rehabilitation center for the many thousands of former servicemen who were still roaming the country after their sudden demobilization. Under the armistice, Vichy was allowed an army of just one hundred thousand men, which meant that the vast majority of France's wartime forces were no longer needed.

The idea of the center, Navarre told Pétain, was to provide meals, medical care, rest, recreation, and job advice, which hopefully would ease these young men's transition back to civilian life and keep them under control. What he didn't reveal was that the real purpose of the center would be to identify and enlist a select few as spies for his and Fourcade's new operation, to be known as Crusade. It would be, he told Marie-Madeleine, "the first stronghold of the interior resistance."

With Pétain's blessing and Vichy funds, Navarre and Fourcade leased one of the few hotels not appropriated for government offices and hired a small staff to run it, with Fourcade as its manager. Radio Vichy, meanwhile, announced the center's opening, inviting all former servicemen to come and take advantage of its programs.

From its first day, it was packed with former officers and enlisted men, lured by the promise of comfortable rooms, good food, a clinic, and recreational facilities. The place was so crowded that few of its guests noticed the intense conversations that Fourcade struck up with various individuals on the ground floor. Nor did they pay attention when some of those men disappeared up the stairs to the second floor, where the real work of recruitment went on.

This venture of Fourcade's and Navarre's was a rare phenomenon in France so early in the war. As the historian Julian Jackson observed, "The hackneyed phrase 'he or she joined the Resistance' is entirely inappropriate to 1940–41. Before it could be joined, resistance had to be invented. . . . Resistance was a territory without maps."

In the fall of 1940, most French citizens were still in a state of shock, not sure how to react, much less fight back. As one Frenchman remarked, "The French have no experience of clandestine life; they do not even know how to be silent or how to hide." At that point, too, the German occupiers seemed all-powerful. For most of the French, the paramount aim was simple survival.

Further complicating the issue was the fact that France's own government was actively cooperating with the Nazis. For many in the country, disobeying the dictates of Pétain and his men would have caused a greater crisis of conscience than obeying them. That was particularly true for most current and former members of the armed services, for whom unquestioning obedience to their superiors was an inviolable rule and who, in any case, revered Pétain perhaps even more than did the general public. In addition, the armistice explicitly prohibited members of the French military from engaging in any form of anti-German activity.

Yet it's also important to note that Navarre and Fourcade were not alone in plotting resistance within the confines of Vichy. Indeed, many of the earliest resisters in France were followers of Pétain, and a substantial number of them could be found in the Vichy government. Such facts fly in the face of conventional wisdom, which advances the theory that everyone in Vichy marched in lockstep with Pétain and agreed with his policy of collaboration with the Germans. In reality, Vichy was far from being a monolithic regime. It was made up of competing factions, drawn from a wide range of backgrounds and with different objectives.

One of those factions, albeit small, was populated by former and current military officers who revered Pétain as a great hero but who also were violently opposed to cooperating with the Germans. Prominent among them were Navarre and other members of the military intelligence community, who had been responsible for warning successive French governments in the 1930s about the growing threat of Hitler.

Ever since the late 1800s, France's intelligence services had viewed Germany as the country's most dangerous enemy and had directed most of their spying efforts against the Germans. In doing so, they had cooperated closely with their British counterparts, particularly MI6, Britain's foreign intelligence gathering agency. For more than fifteen years before the war, MI6 had maintained a significant presence in Paris, with British and French agents sharing information on Hitler's regime, including the activities of the Abwehr, the German military intelligence and counterintelligence department, and the Sicherheitsdienst (SD), which collected intelligence for Heinrich Himmler's SS.

The most notable anti-German rebel was General Gabriel Cochet, a senior officer in the French air force and a former head of the Deuxième Bureau. Two hours after Pétain announced the country's capitulation to Germany, Cochet called his staff together and told them that the marshal was wrong and that collaboration with Hitler would be a catastrophe. "We must learn to hide what we are doing, to camouflage our movements and our arms," he added. "We must at all costs continue the struggle against the enemy." Three months later, Cochet issued a public proclamation calling on the French people to "watch, resist, and unite"—and followed it with a succession of new tracts advocating resistance that began to attract small, uncoordinated groups of followers. Cochet could get away with such activities because for the first few months after the armistice, the Vichy government did little to stop such expressions of rebellion.

As it turned out, the Deuxième Bureau itself was a hotbed of anti-German activity. Its current head, Colonel Louis Baril, had sent a message of support and solidarity to MI6 shortly after the armistice. Baril's deputy, Colonel Louis Rivet, insisted to his staff that "the fight must go on, whatever happens," adding, "No other attitude is acceptable. Suspending hostilities for us is worse than an unforgivable mistake; it would be tantamount to infamy."

Under Rivet's aegis, military intelligence officials set up an undercover organization to track down German spies who had infiltrated the free zone in violation of the armistice. Called the Société des Travaux Ruraux (Society of Rural Works), this counterespionage outfit disguised itself as a private company whose job was to maintain and build rural sewage and drainage systems. Its real mission was to identify, arrest, and prosecute German agents.

According to the terms of the armistice, the only German officials allowed in the free zone were members of the so-called Armistice Commission, an organization whose mission was to monitor French compliance with the armistice. In fact, the commission was riddled with agents from the Abwehr and Gestapo. Dozens of other operatives from German intelligence and counterintelligence services also flooded the free zone, using various false identities. Among their tasks was to gather information on anti-Nazi activists who had found refuge in Vichy France.

Of all the covert anti-German activities carried out by Vichy military officers, however, none was as crucial as a secret codebreaking operation at a secluded château in the countryside of Provence. Its head was Captain Gustave Bertrand, the director of the Deuxième Bureau's radio and cryptography department.

In the early 1930s, Bertrand had acquired from a German informant top-secret documents related to the Reich's fiendishly complex Enigma code. When his government showed no interest in his coup, Bertrand passed the material to Polish cryptographers, who had long given top priority to breaking the military codes of Germany, Poland's hereditary enemy. As a result of Bertrand's largesse, the Poles in 1934 became the first to crack the Enigma code.

After Germany invaded Poland in September 1939, several of its top codebreakers fled to France, where they worked with Bertrand and his subordinates at the French military's radio intelligence and cryptography center, housed in an elegant château about twenty-five miles northeast of Paris. Bertrand's department cooperated closely with the British government's codebreaking operation at Bletchley Park, which, just before the war began, had received from the Poles a copy of the Enigma machine, along with detailed information on how to use it.

When the Germans marched into Paris, Bertrand evacuated his French and Polish codebreakers—not to a safe location outside France but, in an audacious and breathtakingly risky move, to the Provençal château in the free zone. The cryptographers rarely left the château, whose ground-floor windows were barred and kept shut, making working conditions distinctly unpleasant in the hot, sultry summer of 1940. As a further precaution, three cars were ready, day and night, to whisk the team and its equipment away in case of a sudden German or Vichy police raid.

For all their difficulties, the codebreakers in France never lost contact with Bletchley Park. Both operations continued their work of cracking the various Enigma military codes, with the Provence-based group providing the British with decrypts about the movements, locations, and equipment of the Reich's air, ground, and naval forces in France and other occupied countries.

WITH THE EXCEPTION OF Bertrand's operation, few of the early Vichy resisters had a clear idea in the first weeks of the armistice about how to translate their resolve into action. Like the others, Fourcade and Navarre were feeling their way. How would their new network function? Who would pay for it? How would they get the information collected by their agents to the British? And for Fourcade, the haunting question remained: How would these operatives react to a woman as their leader? Would they obey her?

Among her first recruits were a young air force pilot named Maurice Coustenoble and two of his colleagues, who had fetched up at the center after weeks of wandering around the country. Friends since flying school, they had fought in the battle for France and were furious when the armistice was announced.

Fourcade was initially doubtful about Coustenoble because of his unprepossessing appearance: slicked-back hair, waxed mustache, large dark eyes, and slender, slight frame. What could he have been in civilian life, she wondered. A professional ballroom dancer, perhaps, or some little clerk? But she was soon won over by his passion and directness.

Coustenoble told her that when his plane crash-landed near Bordeaux, he set fire to it and swore he'd find another way to fight. With his two friends, he had traveled throughout France trying to persuade other pilots, as well as anyone else they happened to meet, to join their effort. When they met Fourcade and discovered the real purpose of the center, they pulled from their pockets countless scraps of paper with names and addresses of would-be resisters scribbled on them.

Like most of the young men Fourcade enlisted, the three new recruits wanted to challenge the Germans right away. She told them that was impossible. The only way they could fight back now, she said, was by gathering intelligence. She offered to put them to work immediately. Their first task would be to recruit couriers for the network—people who had jobs like driving trucks or working on the railroad, which allowed them to travel unhindered throughout the country.

If they thought the job was too much for them, she said, they should say so. They looked at her pityingly, and she guessed what they were thinking: "It's odd that *she* should want to tell us what to do." For a moment, she feared they would back out. But after a brief pause, Coustenoble announced that they were ready.

As the weeks passed, this initial trickle of recruits for Crusade became a small stream. Most of the newcomers were former members of the French army and air force; almost none had served in the navy. Like their counterparts in the other two services, naval personnel believed strongly in unquestioning obedience to their superiors, almost all of whom strongly supported France's capitulation to the Nazis. But they also had a very personal reason for abhorring the thought of working with Britain against Germany. On July 3, 1940, the British navy, under Winston Churchill's orders, had destroyed much of the French fleet, then based in North Africa, to keep it out of German hands. In a matter of minutes, British shells had blown up the battleship *Bretagne* and destroyed or badly damaged several other ships. During the bombardment, more than twelve hundred sailors were killed.

The French people were outraged by what they saw as a deliberate massacre by the British—but none more so than the victims' naval comrades. After the British attack, Navarre grumbled, the odds of recruiting former navy personnel for Crusade had dropped to zero.

For a couple of months, it appeared he was right. Then Henri Schaerrer appeared on the scene. Swiss by birth, the twenty-four-

HENRI SCHAERRER

year-old Schaerrer had been a mechanical engineer in France's merchant marine before enlisting in the navy in April 1939. Assigned to the *Bretagne* at the beginning of the war, he was stationed on a destroyer at the time of the Dunkirk evacuation in June 1940 and barely escaped death when the ship was torpedoed and sunk.

From the moment they met, Fourcade recognized Schaerrer as a force of nature. Fun-loving and boyishly handsome, he exhibited a passion, energy, determination, and taste for adventure equaled by few of the other recruits she had signed up. To her and Navarre, Schaerrer promised to rally naval and merchant marine crewmen to the cause. He proposed to start in Marseille, the free zone's only major port, more than two hundred miles southeast of Vichy.

Along with Maurice Coustenoble, Schaerrer would prove to be one of the most valuable first links in the Crusade chain. Keeping his pledge to the network's leaders, he soon would add another crucial link—a naval officer who had almost died aboard the doomed *Bretagne*.

CHAPTER 4

SPYING IN MARSEILLE

I N THE LATE AFTERNOON OF JULY 3, 1940, LIEUTENANT JEAN BOUTRON, a thirty-five-year-old gunnery officer aboard the *Bretagne,* stood at his battle station—one of thousands of men doing the same on more than a dozen French warships moored at the North African port of Mers-el-Kébir.

Ten miles away, an armada of British ships—a battle cruiser, two battleships, an aircraft carrier, and several destroyers—lay in wait outside the port's entrance. Just three weeks before, the two countries' navies had been allies. Now the British threatened to open fire on the French fleet unless its commander surrendered or scuttled his ships. The deadline for his decision was 5:30 P.M.

Throughout the day, messages flew back and forth between the two fleets. The French commander, Admiral Marco-Bruno Gensoul, repeatedly rejected the British demands, declaring that he and his men would resist to the end. Confident that their former ally would not attack them, many of the French seamen read magazines or chatted idly with each other at their battle stations as the minutes ticked by and the deadline came and went.

At 6:00 P.M., British guns opened fire. The *Bretagne* was hit almost instantly; flames and smoke poured from its stern as sailors scrambled to control the blaze. A minute later, the ship's torpedo magazine exploded with an ear-splitting roar, enveloping the harbor in acrid clouds of smoke.

The *Bretagne* trembled, then listed sharply. Jean Boutron watched in shock as his shipmates began leaping into the water, struggling to stay afloat and trying to dodge the flames dancing on the oil-covered surface of the waves. Frantic cries of "Help!" and "Save me!" filled the air.

Then, as the ship slid beneath the water, Boutron himself was swept overboard. Unable to see anything in the oily blackness, he fought for a moment, then gave up the struggle. "An immense and complete indifference took hold of me," he recalled. "A quick thought of my mother and my son—that was all."

Several minutes later, he was pulled unconscious from the water, so covered in oil that a friend was able to identify him only by his wristwatch. Of the forty-five officers aboard the *Bretagne,* just Boutron and six others survived. Overall, 1,079 members of the ship's crew lost their lives, accounting for eighty-five percent of the deaths at Mers-el-Kébir.

JEAN BOUTRON

As they recuperated, the *Bretagne*'s survivors raged at the British for committing what they viewed as mass murder. Boutron was equally infuriated—but not at the British. For him, France's main enemies were Germany and the Vichy government. An outspoken critic of France's capitulation to Germany, he had erupted in anger in late June when Admiral François Darlan, the head of the French navy, ordered the fleet, the fourth-largest in the world, to accept the armistice, even though most of it was still intact and safely anchored in North Africa. "But we are not beaten!" Boutron shouted at the *Bretagne*'s captain when given the news. "Is the *Bretagne* beaten? The *Provence,* is she beaten? And the *Dunkerque* and *Strasbourg*—brand flaming new and full of guns and shells—are they beaten? And the rest of the navy? In any case, I am not beaten! And I'm not going to go along with this!"

The admiral agreed that the armistice was a catastrophe but said it was their duty to accept it. Boutron scornfully replied, "And now on behalf of this sacred discipline, we are chained to a defeat for which we are not responsible."

In the days before July 3, the dark-haired, quick-tempered lieutenant continued to skate dangerously close to insubordination, advising some of his shipmates at one point that the fleet should be scuttled. When they protested, noting that such a move would violate the terms of the armistice, he exclaimed, "This bloody armistice—we haven't finished paying for it! It's only just beginning."

After Mers-el-Kébir, most French sailors, including Boutron, were demobilized. Returning to his native Marseille, he agonized over his future. He was desperate to resist France's occupiers but had no idea where to go or what to do. And then one chilly afternoon, he ran into Henri Schaerrer on a Marseille street.

Several years before, Boutron, as an officer in the prewar merchant marine, had trained Schaerrer, then an officer cadet; the two had developed a close relationship as mentor and protégé. Delighted to see each other again, they had a few drinks at a Marseille bar and caught up on their lives. Although he had great affection for Schaerrer, Boutron was unsure about how far he could trust him. Yet as the conversation continued, he began to open up, acknowledging his anger over the armistice and admitting he was looking for a way to continue the fight, perhaps by joining the Free French in London. Schaerrer said he might do the same, although he hadn't quite decided. He wrote down Boutron's address and said he would be in touch.

A few days later, he appeared at Boutron's door. As it happened, he said, he had become involved in a new resistance group "with the same principles and goals as yours." He had talked to the group's leaders, who wanted to meet Boutron as soon as possible. The next day, the two men took the train to Vichy, where Schaerrer introduced Boutron to Navarre and Fourcade.

After hours of discussion, Boutron agreed to join Crusade. Sensing that he might have doubts about a woman as the network's second in command, Navarre made it clear that Marie-Madeleine Fourcade had his full confidence and that Boutron must accept her authority. She was, the chief added, "the pivot around which everything turns. She is the most valuable of us all." He described her in glowing terms, saying she had "the memory of an elephant, the cleverness of a fox, the guile of a serpent, the perseverance of a mole, and the fierceness of a panther."

During that first meeting, Boutron was assigned to work with Schaerrer as Crusade's advance guard in Marseille, which was to become the network's first major outpost. There they would begin to enlist agents from among the throngs of merchant seamen who sailed in and out of the port and who could report on, among other things, the identity of ships and cargoes and where they were headed.

IN EARLY DECEMBER 1940, Fourcade traveled by train to meet Boutron and Schaerrer's first two recruits, who were to take charge of the day-to-day operations in Marseille. She was happy to exchange the surreal, hothouse atmosphere of Vichy, if only briefly, for the gritty reality of the city where she had been born and which she considered her hometown.

After arriving at the Gare de Marseille–Saint Charles, she paused for a moment at the top of the steep stone staircase leading down from the station and gazed at the hilly city, with its narrow streets and alleys, spread out below her. Noisy and bustling, it pulsated with life. She took a deep breath and savored the salty tang of the sea air.

A center of trade and immigration since its founding by the Greeks around 600 B.C., Marseille was considered one of the most cosmopolitan cities in the world, surpassing, in the view of some, even Fourcade's beloved Shanghai. If one stood for eighty minutes on a corner of the city's best-known boulevard, the Canebière, he or she, according to local lore, would end up encountering people from more nations than Phileas Fogg did in Jules Verne's novel *Around the World in Eighty Days*.

Marseille's already huge immigrant population swelled even more after the German occupation of northern France. As the free zone's biggest city and only functioning port, it served as a beacon of hope for thousands of refugees—French from the occupied zone, British and other Allied soldiers left behind after the fall of France, Poles, Czechs, Belgians, Italians, and anti-Nazi Germans and Austrians, many of whom were Jews. All had flocked to Marseille for the same reason—to flee occupied Europe and the Nazis. By late 1940, the chances for escape had dwindled considerably, but the exiles, with no place else to go, continued to crowd the city's hotels, cafés, and waterfront bars, anxiously exchanging rumors of ship sailings and police raids.

Not coincidentally, Marseille also served as a hotbed of early French resistance to the Nazis. Because of its status as a key international port, it was obviously a magnet for fledgling intelligence-collecting groups like Crusade. But it also became the home of embryonic escape networks, which began to smuggle stranded Allied airmen and soldiers, as well as European refugees, from Marseille to neutral Spain and Portugal and from there to freedom.

For members of the resistance, part of Marseille's attraction lay in the fact that it was an easy place in which to hide. The sprawling metropolis was made up of more than one hundred districts, many of which were more like separate villages than conventional city neighborhoods. Located near the port, Marseille's Old Town, with its dark, twisting alleys and underground passageways leading to the cellars of houses, was a particularly difficult place in which to track down fugitives from the law, whether they were members of the resistance or Marseille's flourishing criminal underworld.

The city's centuries-old tradition of stubborn independence from the rest of France also helped the resistance cause. "Marseille residents by their nature consider themselves as different," an observer wrote in 1794. "The city's geographical situation, its mountains, its rivers, which separate it from the rest of France, its peculiar language, everything encourages this opinion. . . . Marseille is their country; France is nothing."

That sense of independence could be seen in the attitude of the people of Marseille to the new Vichy government and its German masters. When they were hired, policemen in Vichy France had to take the following oath: "I swear to fight against democracy, against Gaullist insurrection and against Jewish leprosy." In Marseille, however, the police department was widely considered to be pro-British and "discreetly anti-Nazi." When revelers in one Marseille bar raised their glasses to "de Gaulle and England," a couple of gendarmes passing by turned a blind eye. In the margins of a surveillance report about a Marseille resident who openly expressed support for a British victory, an anonymous police officer scribbled, "Who wouldn't wish for it?"

BEFORE FOURCADE'S ARRIVAL IN Marseille, Henri Schaerrer had assured her that the two new operatives had been well briefed about Crusade. But when she entered the café chosen for the meeting and walked toward the table where Schaerrer sat with the men, she heard one of them shout, "Good God! It's a woman!" Glancing at a sheepish-looking Schaerrer, she realized that his briefing had not included the fact that their new boss was female.

The shouter was Gabriel Rivière, a burly, mustachioed official of

Marseille's merchant marine association who, according to Schaerrer, knew more about maritime traffic in the Mediterranean than anyone else in the port. Once he recovered from his shock, the jovial Rivière made no further mention of her gender and immediately got down to business. He hated the Germans and would gladly join the network, he told Fourcade. To serve as a cover for his activities, he suggested that Crusade buy a wholesale fruit and vegetable business that was currently for sale, which would give him a cover for roaming at will around the port in search of possible recruits. A partner of his would actually run the business, Rivière's wife would work in its retail shop, and its warehouse would serve as a hiding place for Crusade's agents and couriers.

Taken aback by Rivière's sweeping proposal, Fourcade turned to Schaerrer's other new hire, Émile Audoly, a slight, reserved, and somewhat ethereal man, at least in comparison with the earthy Rivière. Audoly worked for a company of grain dealers, which gave him access to Marseille's docks, railway station, and warehouses. He could check the manifests of merchant marine and railway cargoes and could on occasion inspect the cargoes themselves.

In addition, both Rivière and Audoly were acquainted with merchant marine radio operators who were anti-German and were likely recruits for Crusade. If the network could provide them with radio transmitters, they could quickly pass on the intelligence they collected to the network's headquarters in Vichy.

Within a few days, Crusade's Marseille sector was up and running. Fourcade authorized the spending of 50,000 francs for the fruit and vegetable business for Rivière, whose main job would be to supervise the recruitment of agents. Audoly would be in charge of the actual collection of intelligence, focusing on the movements of ships and their cargoes. And Jean Boutron would oversee the sector's work as a whole.

FOR FOURCADE, ARRANGING THE MARSEILLE operation was the easiest part of this trip. She was far more concerned about her other assignment: to recruit an experienced intelligence officer to coordinate and supervise the information that she hoped would soon begin flooding in from the fast-growing number of Crusade agents.

For the job, Navarre had recommended a friend of his: Colonel Charles Bernis, a canny sixty-six-year-old veteran of the army's Deuxième Bureau. Regarded as the leading theoretician of French military intelligence, Bernis had written what was considered the definitive text on intelligence methods and procedures. In 1936, he had retired to the tiny principality of Monaco, whose government immediately hired him as the head of its military, police, and fire departments.

When she arrived in Monte Carlo, Fourcade was filled with trepidation. She met the short, stocky, gray-haired Bernis for lunch at the Café de Paris, the legendary Belle Époque restaurant on the city's main square. His unsmiling demeanor and the formality of his greeting when she introduced herself only increased her nervousness.

Bernis asked her if Navarre really thought the French could fight back. Absolutely, she replied. Navarre believed that the British would hold out and the Americans would eventually enter the war. Until then, the most important help the French could provide was to pass on intelligence to the British.

Bernis gave Fourcade what she interpreted as a mocking look and asked her if she knew what intelligence was. She knew that it was hard work, she said, and that she very much needed his knowledge and experience. Bernis glanced around, then motioned to her to accompany him. He rose from their outdoor table and led her down to a terrace overlooking the sea, where he gave her a detailed primer on intelligence gathering.

When she asked him how to judge the relative importance of information, Bernis said it wasn't an agent's job to decide what was important. Nor should an agent speculate or make judgments. When the British asked for information, the network's response must be as precise as possible. Nothing should be left to the imagination. An agent must report only on what he saw or heard, and let the recipients of the intelligence draw their own conclusions.

When she had finally finished with her questions, Bernis had some of his own. Wasn't she there to recruit him? Where was he to go? She readily provided the answers: He would work from the town of Pau in southwestern France, chosen because it was close to the Spanish-French border and also to the demarcation line dividing the free and unoccupied zones, making it easier for agents and couriers to slip back and forth between them. He would start in January 1941.

Then came a much thornier question: To whom would he report? After hesitating a moment, Fourcade said, "To me." Bernis stared at her without replying. Shortly afterward, the two silently began to walk down a flight of stone steps, heading for the train station.

As she kept pace with him, Fourcade asked if he was opposed to working for a woman. Again, silence. After what seemed to her an eternity, Bernis said that if he took the job, he would need an assistant. She replied that she already had someone in mind. A woman, he said with an ironic smile. Yes, she replied.

Just as they reached the station, Bernis gave her his answer, albeit obliquely. With a slight smile, he handed her a folder of papers just before she boarded her train. They turned out to be detailed reports of German army and naval concentrations on the southern coasts of France and Italy. Once inside her compartment, Marie-Madeleine was quietly exultant. As she later observed, she had passed the test.

WHEN SHE RETURNED TO VICHY, however, her ebullience over the success of her mission gave way to concern. Two months earlier, Marshal Pétain had met with Hitler in the small French town of Montoire and soon afterward announced that he and his government had embarked on a policy of official collaboration with Germany. According to the historian Robert O. Paxton, "Collaboration was not a German demand . . . [it] was a French proposal."

The Montoire meeting shook the faith of some nascent resisters in Vichy who had supported Pétain and believed he had been playing a double game since France's capitulation. In their view, although the marshal had been prevented by the armistice terms from acting openly against Germany, he secretly opposed the invaders and would eventually join the Allies.

One of those disillusioned by Montoire was a young Deuxième Bureau officer named Henri Frenay, who later wrote that in the immediate aftermath of France's capitulation to Germany, "there was no inherent contradiction between joining the struggle against Nazism and retaining one's faith in Pétain." But after Montoire, he noted, "all the hopes which the marshal had once aroused in me had now all but vanished." Soon after Montoire, Frenay left the Vichy government to organize a resistance movement called Combat, which would become one of the largest and most influential underground organizations in all of France.

In hindsight, it's clear that Pétain never intended to resist the Germans. At least in the beginning, however, he was susceptible to pressure from the anti-German faction in the government. In December 1940, that group persuaded him to arrest Pierre Laval, whom he had never liked, and oust him from his post as Pétain's deputy. The German high command in Paris, which strongly supported Laval, was furious and put pressure on Pétain to release and reinstate him. Although Laval was set free, the marshal dragged his feet on returning him to his post.

As a result of Montoire and this Vichy power struggle, the Germans had stepped up their pressure on Pétain, as well as their illicit presence in the free zone. The collaboration agreement, Navarre told Fourcade, had allowed the Nazis to infiltrate everywhere.

In the midst of the turmoil, Navarre lost his position as an official of the Légion Française des Combattants, the government-sponsored veterans' organization. Fourcade had repeatedly urged her mentor to cut his ties to Pétain and was relieved to hear the news of his dismissal. Yet she knew it also meant that Crusade would lose the funding that the Vichy government had been unknowingly providing.

The month before, Navarre had dispatched an emissary to London to put out feelers to both Charles de Gaulle and Britain's Secret Intelligence Service (MI6) about collaboration with Crusade. The intermediary was Marie-Madeleine's twenty-nine-year-old brother, Jacques

Bridou, who had been part of the network since its creation. A member of the 1936 French Olympic bobsled team, Bridou, who had trained as a lawyer, was as addicted to risk and adventure as his sister. He had worked as a journalist during the Spanish Civil War and had fought in the battle for France. Fluent in English, he had married a young Englishwoman just months earlier.

Navarre had given Bridou two letters to take with him to the British capital: one to de Gaulle and the other to MI6. Both included a detailed report about the creation and development of Crusade. In his letter to de Gaulle, Navarre assured his former colleague and rival of his wholehearted support and cooperation in continuing the struggle against Germany. He would be happy to work with de Gaulle's newly established intelligence service in London, he wrote, as long as his network could function on an equal basis with that of the Free French and could share with the British the intelligence his agents collected.

Travel from France's free zone to Britain was extremely difficult throughout the war but particularly so in late 1940, when escape lines and other resistance organizations had not yet firmly established their underground routes between France and neutral Spain. Bridou's plan was to travel to Morocco, where he hoped to find a way to reach the British redoubt of Gibraltar and from there get to London. He had no idea how long that would take or when he could return. A month after he left, Navarre and Marie-Madeleine still had not heard from him.

Meanwhile, Crusade's reception center for former servicemen was drawing unwelcome attention from Vichy officials. Deciding that it was no longer a safe cover, especially since Navarre had lost his Vichy position, he and Fourcade made plans to shut it down and move their operations to an office in another, less conspicuous hotel.

Yet for all the uncertainty and anxiety, there was much to celebrate at the end of 1940. In a matter of weeks, the embryonic network had grown from a handful of people to more than fifty agents. Most of them came together for a joyous Christmas Day lunch at the reception center—its last event before its doors closed forever.

CHAPTER 5

THE BIRTH OF ALLIANCE

BY THE MIDDLE OF MARCH 1941, CRUSADE HAD SNOWBALLED in size, spreading from Vichy and Marseille to other parts of the free zone and even penetrating North Africa and some areas of German-occupied France. In Vichy France, agents were at work in the south-eastern cities of Lyon and Dijon and in the Dordogne, a hilly, forested region in the southwest known for its medieval villages, verdant countryside, and prehistoric caves. The Dordogne was particularly important for Crusade because of its proximity to Bordeaux and its inland port, which had been transformed into a major base for German submarines, warships, mine-laying vessels, and torpedo transports.

Couriers for the network had begun to crisscross the country, collecting the agents' information and taking it to the picturesque resort town of Pau, where Colonel Bernis had established his operation in a small hotel called the Pension Welcome. Among the newly recruited couriers were the pilot and radio operator of a small plane used by the Vichy government to distribute its official mail throughout France, including the occupied zone. While doing their work for Pétain and his men, the crew also picked up and delivered Crusade reports to Pau.

Yet despite Crusade's rapid growth, Fourcade was haunted by worry about its future. After working sixteen-hour days, she lay awake at night trying to figure out how to keep the network alive. Four months had passed since her brother had left for London; she knew he had reached Morocco but had heard nothing since then. Since no formal ties had yet been established between Crusade and de Gaulle or MI6, the intelligence it had already gathered was going to waste. To make matters worse, she and Navarre had run out of money and were living on loans. Without new sources of funds, they soon would have to shut down the network.

Finally, on March 14, 1941, Fourcade received the phone call she had been waiting for. Her brother had returned to France, parachuted in by an RAF plane near Clermont-Ferrand, an industrial town some forty-five miles southwest of Vichy. She and Navarre immediately drove there to pick him up.

Jacques Bridou's parachute drop—his first ever—had not gone well: He had badly injured an ankle when he hit the ground, and he still seemed in shock from the experience. But he insisted on returning with them to Vichy, and on the way he related the story of his lengthy, difficult hegira to London.

The trouble had begun, he said, when he arrived in Gibraltar from Morocco and informed the admiral commanding the British base there that he had been sent by a new French underground network to make contact with de Gaulle and British intelligence in London. The admiral immediately concluded that Bridou was a German spy and put him on a troop ship to England, where he was met and arrested by Scotland Yard officers. They then took him to London for seemingly endless days of interrogation.

He insisted to his questioners that he was married to an Englishwoman and that his wife's father, a London businessman, could verify his identity. But his father-in-law, who had never met him and had had no message from Sylvia, his daughter, about Bridou's trip, vehemently denied that this stranger was in fact Sylvia's husband. Only when they were brought together was Bridou able to convince his wife's father that he was telling the truth.

Finally freed from British confinement, Fourcade's brother suffered another rebuff when he presented Navarre's letter to Charles de Gaulle at the general's Free French headquarters in west London. De Gaulle already knew about the existence of Crusade. In a report about Navarre's organization, one of his aides wrote, "We have to take into account this movement, as its importance is considerable in France." He added that if the Free French provided funds to Crusade, "it will in some ways become automatically attached to us, and we will gain uncontestable advantages." De Gaulle did not agree. After reading Navarre's letter, he icily turned down his rival's offer of joint cooperation. "Whoever is not with me," he declared, "is against me."

As Bridou described de Gaulle's negative reaction, Navarre appeared remarkably unperturbed. He seemed equally unsurprised when the younger man finally delivered some good news: MI6 had leapt at the idea of working with Crusade and had invited Navarre to travel to neutral Lisbon the following month for several days of consultation with a top official from their French operation.

Thrilled as she was by MI6's response, Fourcade suspected that this was what Navarre had had in mind from the beginning. Knowing de Gaulle as well as he did, how could he possibly think that his long-time rival would agree to an equal partnership? When she mentioned her suspicions to him, he smiled and blandly denied them.

IT WAS TIME NOW to take another step to ensure Crusade's survival. For weeks, Navarre had been under constant surveillance in Vichy. Indeed, he had been warned by a friend that Admiral Darlan, the former head of Vichy's navy who had replaced Pierre Laval as Pétain's deputy, was on the verge of ordering his arrest. Darlan had already taken into custody General Gabriel Cochet, who had been calling for resistance against the Germans since the armistice.

In late March 1941, Navarre decided to shut down the network's headquarters there and move it to Pau, some 350 miles to the southwest, consolidating it with Colonel Bernis's operation. Fourcade, who had never felt safe in Vichy, greeted the news with relief.

Founded in the eleventh century, Pau was the birthplace of Henri de Navarre, the future King Henry IV, whose castle overlooked the town. The city's fresh, dry air and stunningly beautiful setting in the foothills of the Pyrenees had drawn vacationers from British and European high society since the early nineteenth century.

Lined with palm trees, hotels, cafés, nineteenth-century mansions, and a casino, Pau's main boulevard ran along the top of a steep cliff, with spectacular views of the snowcapped mountains thirty miles to the south and subtropical gardens that cascaded down the cliff's slope to a lush green valley below. The area was particularly well known for its fox hunting and Europe's first eighteen-hole golf course—pastimes introduced by well-heeled British travelers. For Navarre and Fourcade, however, its main attractions were its nearness to the Spanish border and its quiet, remote location. It also helped that Navarre, who had grown up in the nearby village of Oloron-Sainte-Marie, was well known in Pau and regarded by many of its residents as a favorite son.

Among his admirers were the two elderly sisters who owned the Pension Welcome, Colonel Bernis's new base of operations. When the women politely inquired about the enormous intelligence maps of France that papered Bernis's room, he told them that he was a geographer who specialized in the study of the country's coasts and mountainous frontiers. And when Crusade agents and couriers began to come and go from the hotel, the sisters were informed that they were French soldiers who had escaped from German prisoner-of-war camps and whose presence in Pau must be kept secret. The women readily accepted Marie-Madeleine's presence at the hotel, believing she had come to help Navarre cope with the escaped POWs.

With more than a week to go until Navarre's appointment with MI6 in Lisbon, Marie-Madeleine decided to take a break from the network and visit her children, whom she had not seen since the previous fall, when they had paid her a brief visit in Vichy. Eight-year-old Béatrice was now living with Marie-Madeleine's mother at the family's summer villa on the Côte d'Azur near Cannes, while ten-year-old Christian was enrolled at a Catholic boarding school in the town of Sarlat.

When she picked Christian up at the school shortly before the Easter holidays, she decided it was time to tell him about her clandestine activities, hoping he would understand why he had seen so little of her over the previous few months. She clearly felt remorse over what she called her "apparent desertion," a sense of guilt deepened by his complaint that she never answered his letters. She told him she couldn't write because it might result in her getting caught. When Christian asked if her work was dangerous, she said she was doing what all Frenchmen should do in time of war. She assured him she tried very hard to stay out of danger.

Portraying her work as a secret game in which the players had to be exceptionally quiet and cunning, she took Christian with her as she did a bit of intelligence work on the way to the Côte d'Azur. She scouted a possible parachute dropping zone for future supply shipments from Britain, surreptitiously inspected a German airfield, and interviewed potential agents.

When she was done, they headed to her family's retreat. Three miles north of Cannes, she turned off the road and drove up a narrow, steep dirt path that led to the family compound where she had spent so many lazy summer days in earlier years. The white stucco walls of the main house, adorned with grapevines and wisteria, shimmered in the bright early-spring sunshine. Directly behind the villa was a small grove of pine trees. On one side, the land fell away in terraces to the road below; on the other side were two large eucalyptus trees and a lawn ending in a row of mimosa trees flaunting their bright yellow blossoms. A strawberry patch and orchards of peaches, cherries, and figs were located in the rear of the pine grove. Before the war, the fruit, along with cut flowers from the house's gardens, had been flown regularly to London and Paris markets.

Instead of stopping at the villa, Marie-Madeleine continued up the path until she reached a small Provençal farmhouse at the top of the hill. Her mother had rented out the villa for the war's duration, and she, her housekeeper, and Béatrice had moved into the farmhouse. Intrepid and adventurous as ever, Mathilde Bridou was fully aware of her daughter's and son's resistance work. Not only did she approve of it, she was not averse to becoming involved herself.

The bedrock of her family throughout the war, Mathilde had "a remarkably quick sense of humor that never entirely left her, no matter how appalling the situation, and her dancing brown eyes radiated warmth and love," her daughter-in-law, Sylvia Bridou, later recalled. "She was what the French call *spirituelle,* witty, sprightly, intelligent. All those qualities sustained her and those around her, throughout the troubled times ahead."

When Marie-Madeleine and Christian arrived at the farmhouse, Mathilde ran out to greet them, followed by Béatrice, Jacques, and Sylvia. After the embraces and kisses of welcome, Jacques led his sister to a pigsty behind the house, where he had dug a hiding place for the dozens of files containing the early records of Crusade that she had brought from Pau in the trunk of her car. It was the safest place she and Jacques could think of to hide them; nobody, they were sure, would ever dream of looking there.

For the next several days, Marie-Madeleine played with her son and daughter, helped her mother in the garden, took long walks, and gazed out at the spectacular views—the village of Mougins atop a nearby hill and the Mediterranean sparkling in the distance. But for all the pleasure she took in the family reunion and for all her joy at being with Christian and Béatrice again, she could not shake her concern about the future of Crusade. Would the encounter between Navarre and MI6 save the network? She could not bear to think about the alternative.

Then one morning, Henri Schaerrer suddenly appeared at the farmhouse, bringing the news for which she'd been waiting. Navarre had won MI6's support in Lisbon, he exclaimed. She must return immediately to Pau. Marie-Madeleine didn't hesitate. She packed her things, kissed her children and mother goodbye, asked her brother to drive her Citroën back to Pau, and left with Schaerrer to catch a train from Cannes.

The train was jammed, like most trains in France during the war, and Marie-Madeleine was forced to sit on her suitcase in a corridor for much of the overnight journey, surrounded by travelers asleep on the floor. But the wretched conditions failed to curb her elation. For Crusade, the real war was now beginning.

On the train, she told Schaerrer that she was going to set up a new chain of command. She decided to make Maurice Coustenoble her adjutant and to appoint Schaerrer to head the network's operations in the occupied zone. A whirlwind recruiter, Schaerrer "seemed to be everywhere and to know everyone," noted one colleague. "He was always ready to take on any job and get it done." Marie-Madeleine's only worry was that in his zeal to succeed, he had a penchant for risk taking that bordered on the reckless.

When she arrived back in Pau, however, her concerns about Schaerrer and other matters were eclipsed by the euphoria of the moment. At the Pension Welcome, the air was thick with smoke from the British cigarettes that Navarre had brought back from his mission and distributed to members of the network staff. As their jubilant celebration continued, Navarre pulled Marie-Madeleine aside to tell her about his adventure in Lisbon.

ON THE MORNING OF APRIL 14, Navarre had shown up at the designated meeting place—the tomb of the Portuguese explorer Vasco da Gama in the nave of the Church of Santa Maria de Belem. After a few minutes, a tall, spare Englishman joined him. He introduced himself to Navarre as "Keith Crane." In fact, he was Commander Kenneth Cohen, the head of MI6 operations in Vichy France.

The forty-one-year-old Cohen was an anomaly among MI6 officials, who tended to be wellborn former military officers with substantial private incomes, many of them charter members of the clubby, upper-class "old boy network" that had dominated British society for generations. A former naval officer and torpedo expert who had served in World War I, Cohen was Jewish—a rarity in MI6. He was fluent in French and Russian and was known for his sensitiv-

KENNETH
COHEN

ity, tact, keen mind, and deep understanding of international issues—
traits that were also unusual among his colleagues in the intelligence
service, most of whom were determinedly anti-intellectual.

Cohen's job was to recruit intelligence sources from within
France's free zone, and he regarded his meeting with Navarre as a
potential answer to MI6's prayers. In that first meeting, and in those
that followed over the next three days, Cohen repeatedly emphasized
the dire position in which Britain now found itself. After ten months
of standing alone against Hitler, the country faced imminent defeat.
Although the RAF had fended off the Luftwaffe in the Battle of Britain in the fall of 1940, German bombs continued to ravage London
and other British cities. German submarines, meanwhile, were stran-
gling the country's supply lines by laying waste to British merchant
shipping in the Atlantic.

Most of the German bombers and U-boats were being dispatched
from bases in France, the occupied country closest to Britain and
hence Hitler's springboard to victory. France would also serve as the
launching point for any invasion of Britain. In order for the British to

fight back, it was crucial that they learn everything possible about German operations there. Underscoring the point, Winston Churchill wrote to a subordinate days after the fall of France: "It is, of course, urgent and indispensable that every effort should be made to obtain secretly the best possible information about the German forces." Of particular importance was intelligence about the movements and dispositions of troops, ships, submarines, barges, and aircraft.

Yet at a time when Britain's very survival depended upon the timely detection of enemy intentions, MI6, whose operations in Europe had been virtually wiped out in the 1940 German blitzkrieg, did not have a single agent in place who could communicate back to London the information the government so desperately needed.

Globally renowned, MI6 had enjoyed a sterling reputation as an all-seeing, all-knowing spy organization for decades. Winston Churchill considered the British intelligence service "the finest in the world." So, interestingly, did Hitler and other Nazi higher-ups, including SS head Heinrich Himmler and Himmler's murderous deputy, Reinhard Heydrich. The truth, however, was far different. Starved of government funds after World War I, MI6 was underfinanced, understaffed, and woefully short of both talent and technology.

The agency's standing was complicated even further in the summer of 1940 when the government created another secret service, called the Special Operations Executive (SOE), whose job was to encourage sabotage and subversion by the citizens of occupied Europe. From the beginning, top MI6 officials saw SOE as a dangerous bureaucratic rival and did their best to destroy it.

As the Nazis tightened their control over Europe, the British military brass complained bitterly about MI6's failure to penetrate the fog that enshrouded German activities there. In the immediate aftermath of the blitzkrieg, "there was no contact between Britain and any of the occupied countries," one senior intelligence official remarked. "Nothing was known of the conditions inside those countries except for occasional reports from the few who still managed from time to time to escape."

Under tremendous pressure to get its agents into occupied territory, MI6 was saved by the providential arrival in London of the governments in exile of six occupied European countries, along with
Charles de Gaulle's Free French. In exchange for providing financial,
communications, and transportation support to the governments' secret services, MI6 gained control of most of their operations. These
foreign services in turn provided virtually all the wartime intelligence the British received about German activities in occupied Europe.

From the start, France was MI6's main focus, as well as its most
politically fraught challenge. Indeed, the agency had set up two separate French sections to try to keep to a minimum the complications
stemming from the extraordinary friction and rivalries that bedeviled
that geographically and politically divided country.

One section worked with the Bureau Central de Renseignements
(BCRA), de Gaulle's fledgling intelligence service, which was headed
by André Dewavrin, a young army officer and former professor at
Saint-Cyr. The first BCRA operative to be sent to France was Gilbert
Renault, a French film producer and ardent Gaullist, who, although
a complete novice at intelligence, put together a far-flung spy network, called the Confrérie de Notre Dame, that eventually covered
much of occupied France and Belgium. By early 1941, at least half a
dozen additional Gaullist intelligence groups, with cover names like
Johnny and Fitzroy, were reporting back to BCRA and MI6.

Meanwhile, the second French section, under Kenneth Cohen,
focused on members of the military intelligence services now head-
quartered in Vichy, who had worked so closely with MI6 before the
war. In spite of being part of Pétain's government, they remained
opposed to the German occupation and continued to pass on information to the British. Yet while Cohen regarded those Vichy connections as extremely valuable, he was particularly keen on working
with Navarre's organization. Although most of its agents were amateurs, it had in its ranks several seasoned military intelligence veterans, including Navarre himself. Additionally, it was not hampered by
the strictures and political dangers facing those who were still in the

government. Most important, it had dozens of agents already in place, not only throughout the free zone but in much of occupied France as well. In Cohen's view, it had the potential to become MI6's largest and most important spy network in the country.

During Cohen's meetings with Navarre, he emphasized that in order for Britain to stave off defeat, it must above all keep its maritime supply lines open. At any given time, some three thousand merchant ships were crossing the oceans linking Britain to its trading partners and colonies, carrying cargoes essential for its survival. Without fuel oil and natural resources like copper, lead, rubber, iron ore, nickel, zinc, and aluminum, Britain's industries would be brought to a standstill and its military forces would no longer be able to function. Likewise, Britain relied on imports for seventy percent of its food supply; if those shipments were cut off, its citizens would starve.

In early 1941, one of Churchill's private secretaries had passed on to the prime minister the latest in a series of dire reports of merchant ship sinkings. When the secretary remarked how "very distressing" the news was, Churchill glared at him. "Distressing?" he exclaimed. "It is terrifying! If it goes on, it will be the end of us." Top German officials agreed. Foreign Minister Joachim von Ribbentrop told the Japanese ambassador in Berlin that "even now England was experiencing serious trouble in keeping up her food supply. . . . The important thing [now] is to sink enough ships to reduce England's imports to below the absolute minimum necessary for existence."

For Admiral Karl Dönitz, commander of Germany's submarine fleet, France's defeat had been a gift from the gods. It gave him control of a string of ports on the northern and western French coasts, whose transformation into submarine bases, he believed, would spell the end of Britain as a free nation. Until the summer of 1940, Dönitz's "gray wolves" had been forced to sail hundreds of miles from their bases on the North Sea and Baltic to reach the Atlantic killing grounds. Now they could begin their marauding of British shipping from the gateway of the Atlantic itself, allowing them to prey on merchant ships for up to ten days longer than before.

Less than a week after the armistice agreement was signed, the first submarines began to arrive at Lorient, a quiet fishing village in Brittany, which Dönitz made his headquarters, and at its sister ports in Saint-Nazaire, Brest, and Bordeaux. Thousands of French workers were brought in to convert the ports' shipyards into U-boat repair yards, while German and French engineers designed and built huge submarine pens with concrete roofs thick enough to withstand Allied bombing raids.

Dönitz's wolf packs were now free to run amok. In the last six months of 1940, German submarines sank more than five hundred merchant ships in the Atlantic, totaling about 2.5 million tons. It's no wonder that Dönitz and his submariners called this period *die gluckliche Zeit* (the happy time).

Each succeeding month, the losses grew vastly greater. In April 1941, the amount of matériel sunk—nearly 700,000 tons—was more than twice the tonnage lost two months earlier. On a single night in April, as Kenneth Cohen and Navarre were meeting in Lisbon, a U-boat wolf pack sank ten of twenty-two ships in a British convoy. The overall figures were so devastating that Churchill ordered Whitehall to discontinue the publication of weekly sinkings.

As a result of the deepening shortage of food imports, rationing in Britain had become draconian. Britons were limited to one ounce of cheese and a minimal amount of meat per week and eight ounces of jam and margarine per month. Some foods, including tomatoes, onions, eggs, and oranges, had disappeared almost completely from store shelves.

Cohen made it clear to Navarre that the number one priority for his spy network would be to infiltrate the submarine bases on the French coasts and glean everything possible about the U-boats' movements, including their sailing schedules and routes. In return for that and other intelligence requested by the British, MI6 would fully fund and supply his organization. To commemorate this new British-French intelligence partnership, Cohen and Navarre rechristened the network. It would now be called Alliance.

When he returned to Pau, Navarre brought with him a treasure trove of material from MI6, including a large amount of money—

5 million francs—and a wireless transmitter, which Cohen assured him was the first of many more to come. According to the plan worked out by the two men, Alliance couriers would deliver intelligence reports to Pau, where they would be encoded and sent by the transmitter to MI6 in London.

Each member of Alliance was to be given a code name. Navarre was N1. After assuring an anxious Fourcade that he had not disclosed her gender or name to Cohen, Navarre said that she, as Alliance's chief of staff, would be known to the British only as POZ 55. Similarly, the code names of other network members consisted of three letters and two numbers, such as COU 25 for Maurice Coustenoble.

Finally, at the end of his briefing, Navarre handed Fourcade a stack of flimsy sheets of paper, each covered with dozens of single-spaced typewritten lines. The quid pro quo for MI6's largesse, they were questionnaires covering a vast array of subjects, among them the arrivals and departures of German submarines and ships; movements of enemy troops and supply trains; and the location of German airfields, antiaircraft defenses, weapons arsenals, and factories producing war matériel. Although a bit daunted by the scope of the information sought by MI6, Fourcade was at the same time delighted by its specificity. Finally, the British were letting the network know the exact information they needed.

With Alliance now linked officially with MI6, its work shifted into high gear—and grew considerably more perilous. At Navarre's suggestion, Fourcade prepared to travel to Paris to expand the network's reach there and in other cities in the German-occupied zone. She also was tasked with finding agents to report on the shipyards and submarine bases in Brittany.

Fourcade, as she was well aware, was still a neophyte as a spymaster, continuing to learn how to organize the network and run its day-to-day operations. In the Gestapo-infested French capital, this on-the-job training would involve risks far more lethal than any she had faced thus far.

CHAPTER 6

DANGER IN PARIS

IN THE TOWN OF ORTHEZ, THE SKY WAS BLUE AND THE AIR WARM, and spring flowers were finally blooming after a winter that had been punishingly hard. But at the town's railway station, the crowd waiting in line to board a train to Paris paid little attention to the beautiful weather.

Instead, on that late April day, their focus was on two German soldiers at the head of the line, who were studying the identification papers of each passenger. Orthez, thirty miles north of Pau, lay on the boundary dividing the Nazi-occupied north of the country from the free zone. To cross that demarcation line, French citizens needed an *ausweis,* a German-issued identity card that was difficult to obtain and was carefully examined each time its bearer traveled across the border.

From inside the Orthez station, Henri Schaerrer and Maurice Coustenoble watched as Marie-Madeleine Fourcade approached the table. She and her papers had obviously been targeted for special scrutiny; after a few minutes, she was abruptly removed from the line and led away by two female Nazi auxiliaries, known as "gray mice" because of the color of their uniforms.

Trading worried glances, Schaerrer and Coustenoble headed for the station's buffet. Fifteen minutes later, Fourcade joined them. Shaking with anger, she announced that the "witches," as she called the auxiliaries, had thoroughly searched her luggage and then had made her strip. Following her outburst, she fell silent, providing no answer to her lieutenants' unspoken question: What had she done with the questionnaires she was carrying to Paris?

It wasn't until they boarded the train and took their seats in an otherwise empty compartment that Marie-Madeleine slipped her fingers inside the double lining of her hat and took out several sheets of paper. Schaerrer groaned, and Coustenoble covered his face with his hands. Ignoring their dismay at her boldness, she handed Schaerrer one of the questionnaires. He would soon assume his new duties as chief of operations in the occupied zone, but before doing that, he'd been assigned to ferret out information about the U-boats based at the port near Bordeaux, including any intelligence he could gather about new sonar devices that reportedly had been installed aboard them.

When Marie-Madeleine asked him how he planned to go about his sleuthing, he replied with a grin that he'd get a U-boat crew member drunk, take his uniform, and board the sub. Marie-Madeleine was shocked by his audacity, seemingly forgetting her own penchant for risk taking. She said she hoped he was joking. Schaerrer didn't respond. A few minutes later, they arrived at the Bordeaux station, and he melted into the crowd leaving the train.

LIKE ORTHEZ, PARIS WAS experiencing a beautiful spring. The breeze was warm and soft, the chestnut trees were unfurling their pale green leaves, and the air was redolent with the scent of lilacs. But the city displayed none of the bustle and gaiety that were its usual hallmarks on such a glorious day. Gone were the incessant blare of car horns, the laughter and buzz of conversations among Parisians strolling along the boulevards or sipping their coffee at sidewalk cafés. The city was eerily, soullessly quiet—a silence only occasionally broken by the screech and roar of large black Citroën and Mercedes sedans carrying high-level Nazi functionaries along the Champs Élysées and other major thoroughfares. The Germans had banned all but a few thousand French-owned vehicles from the capital, forcing its residents to rely on bicycles, the metro, or vélotaxis (small wagons pulled by bicyclists) to get around.

Everywhere Fourcade went in Paris, she saw more humiliating reminders of its residents' subjugation by the Germans. Enormous black-and-red swastikas flew atop the Eiffel Tower and the Arc de Triomphe; over the Ritz, the Crillon, and the city's other grand hotels; and above public buildings like the French Senate and Chamber of Deputies. Wehrmacht troops goose-stepped along the Champs Élysées each afternoon, and German cannons were pointed menacingly down the four main boulevards radiating out from the Place de l'Étoile. Restaurants that once displayed "English spoken here" signs now made clear that *"Hier spricht man Deutsch."*

Paris and the rest of occupied France were under the command of the German military, which had been quick to requisition the capital's best hotels for their headquarters. The army's high command had taken over the Majestic, off the avenue Kléber, while the Luftwaffe occupied the Ritz, on the Place Vendôme, and the German navy chose the Hôtel de la Marine, on the Place de la Concorde. Outside each hotel, rifle-toting sentries stood guard, forbidding the French to enter without a pass. Banners draped over the entrances read DEUTSCHLAND SIEGE AN ALLEN FRONTEN (Germany is victorious on all fronts).

The Abwehr, the army's intelligence and counterintelligence branch, meanwhile, established its headquarters at the Hotel Lutetia, on the Left Bank's boulevard Raspail. Among its departments were the Geheime Feldpolizei, the German military police, whose main function was to arrest Allied agents and others suspected of anti-German activities.

When Fourcade arrived in the French capital on that late-April day, she already knew that the Germans had been trying to track her down. During a quick trip to Paris a few weeks earlier, she had stopped by the office on rue Corty that she and Navarre had occupied before the 1940 blitzkrieg. The building's concierge turned white when she saw her. Within days of the Nazi occupation of Paris, she told Fourcade, German police had searched the place and demanded to know where she and Navarre were and if the concierge knew a "Mr. Jacob," a reference to Berthold Jacob, the German journalist who had provided Navarre and Fourcade with the German army's order of battle in 1938.

The concierge asked Fourcade what she was going to do. Taking the keys to the office, she replied that she would stay there. She asked Pierre Dayné—a policeman on the Paris vice squad, whom she'd known for years—to report to the police that she had not returned to rue Corty. He then helped her move her furniture and other possessions from her old apartment on rue Vaneau into the office, which she planned to use as a *pied-à-terre* as well as a meeting place for agents. Before returning to Pau, she installed her maid, Marguerite, there to keep an eye on it.

But when she showed up during her second trip, she realized how naive she had been to think she had outwitted the enemy. Two Germans had paid a visit to the former office the day before, Marguerite said. She told them she was expecting a visit from Fourcade, and the pair ordered her to let them know when she arrived.

Marie-Madeleine thought for a moment, then said that when the Germans came back, to tell them her mistress had returned to Paris only briefly to attend the funeral of an uncle who had left her some money. After Marguerite agreed, Marie-Madeleine wandered through the apartment. Here, she wrote, were all the belongings she valued most—her piano, books, music, and the mementos she had saved from her early years in the Far East. As important as these items were to her, she realized she must let them go. She had no intention of ever entering that office again.

A friend of hers, an Armenian industrialist, gave her a key to his stately townhouse on avenue Foch, where she hid out in a sixth-floor maid's room. Avenue Foch was a thoroughfare with which Marie-Madeleine was very familiar: In the years before the war, she'd been a guest at dinner parties and other gatherings in several of the grand nineteenth-century mansions that lined it.

The engineer who designed the avenue in the 1850s had made it especially wide so that wealthy Parisians could easily drive their coaches from the Arc de Triomphe at one end to the Bois de Boulogne, a vast, verdant park that once served as a hunting ground for French kings, at the other. The wealthiest and most exclusive street in Paris, it seemed an oasis of peace, with its towering chestnut trees, manicured lawns and flower beds, and elegant wrought-iron railings fronting its houses.

But in this case, appearances were brutally deceptive. Under the Germans, avenue Foch had become the most dangerous spot in Paris. Most of the mansions' owners, who included members of the Rothschild family and other wealthy Jews, had fled or been displaced by the most feared German occupiers in the city—members of the various branches of Heinrich Himmler's SS.

The Sicherheitsdienst (SD), the SS's counterintelligence unit, established its headquarters at 84 avenue Foch and requisitioned several other mansions on the street. Created to investigate cases of espionage, sabotage, and treason against the Third Reich, the SD was responsible for the interrogation and imprisonment of members of the French resistance. It was the twin of another infamous Himmler-controlled entity—the Geheime Staatspolizei, or Gestapo, the SS's secret state police, whose members, known for their black leather trench coats and ruthless methods, were charged with ferreting out and arresting those it deemed enemies of the state. The Gestapo headquarters was on rue des Saussaies, not far from the Champs Élysées.

The French public, as well as the individuals who were targets of Nazi persecution, paid little attention to the faint distinction between the SD and Gestapo—or, for that matter, between the two SS agencies and the Abwehr, which was also involved in tracking down French spies and resisters and which became subordinate to the SS in 1942. The French used the term "Gestapo" to cover all of them. Regardless of the branch to which they belonged, the members of these services were united in using terror, torture, and murder in their relentless drive to crush anyone who dared defy the Reich.

AFTER INSTALLING HERSELF IN the maid's room on avenue Foch, Fourcade contacted Alliance operatives already at work in the city, setting up hiding places for them in case of emergency, and organizing "letterboxes"—locations like a bar or apartment where intelligence reports could be left or picked up. She also cast her net wide for additional agents, radio operators, and couriers.

Her initial catches were impressive: a childhood friend, now in the oil business, who provided information about the location of oil storage dumps near the city and the vast amounts the German army was siphoning from them, and another prewar friend, who produced reports about German orders from French companies for war matériel such as plane engines and propellers. She also recruited a distributor for a film company in Paris, who, while traveling throughout northern France to book films in local theaters, gathered information about German airfields, infantry bases, and depots for weapons and ammunition.

But Fourcade's greatest triumph during this scouting trip was discovering a middleman for the collection of intelligence at the Saint-Nazaire submarine base in Brittany. The intermediary was a garage owner named Antoine Hugon, who, surprisingly, had been awarded an Iron Cross by the German government for saving the life of a drowning German soldier during World War I. Although fervently anti-German, Hugon conspicuously displayed the Iron Cross on his lapel from the earliest days of the occupation. According to one observer, "it turned out to be the most useful shield an [Allied] agent could have." Named leader of Alliance operations in Brittany, Hugon in turn recruited Henri Mouren, the head of the shipyard at Saint-Nazaire, who agreed to provide information about German U-boats there and the facilities servicing them.

With these new Alliance agents, as with veterans like Schaerrer and Coustenoble, Fourcade developed an extraordinary sense of community. But with that closeness came fear. Not for herself—in the seven months she had been involved with the network, she had often been worried but never afraid. So far, Alliance and its agents had suffered no severe consequences for their work in the unoccupied zone. The Vichy government, while increasingly irritated by anti-German activity, had yet to strike back hard. Even in Paris, with the German threat ever present, Marie-Madeleine was not overly concerned about her own safety.

Rather, her fear was for the men and women whom she had enlisted in the cause. These people were not trained intelligence agents. They were what MI6's Kenneth Cohen called "enthusiastic volunteers," who had no real preparation for going up against the extremely skilled and dangerous operatives of the German counterintelligence services, whose only mission in France was to annihilate them and others like them.

For a brief but crushing moment, Fourcade was overwhelmed by a sense of futility. She and her agents were challenging the mightiest military power in the world. What could they possibly accomplish? Did she have the right to involve these amateurs in a venture that could lead to their deaths?

At the same time, she thought, what other option did she—and they—have? If France was to be saved, they must continue the fight, no matter how grave the danger or how unbalanced the odds.

AS SHE MOVED ABOUT Paris that spring, Marie-Madeleine was struck by how radically different her world had become in less than a year. She was completely cut off from the life she had enjoyed in Paris before the war—dinners at exclusive restaurants, shopping for designer clothes, dancing at nightclubs. Now, like those of most of her compatriots, her life was one of austerity and making do—of ration cards and scarce food, shabby clothing and wooden-soled shoes.

Yet some Parisians in her former social circle had seen little or no change in their privileged lives, except that they were now socializing primarily with their occupiers. At the end of 1940, the chairman of Paris's metro system staged his annual costume ball at his château near Paris. "The buffet was groaning," one partygoer remembered.

"Champagne flowed. German officers were in their best gala costumes. Here was Tout-Paris in the spheres of literature, the arts, politics, and theater." High-ranking German officials returned the favor, entertaining some of France's wealthiest and most noted citizens in their commandeered houses and apartments, where white-gloved servants served black-market steaks and the finest French wines.

If one had money and was in the Germans' good graces, it was still possible to find butter, coffee, and luxuries like pâté and caviar. Jewelry was still being sold by Cartier and Van Cleef & Arpels and haute couture clothing by designers such as Balenciaga, Dior, Nina Ricci, Paul Poirier, and Jacques Fath. Most of the designers continued to stage fashion shows during the occupation, but the audience needed special passes to get in. Some were given to the wives of German officials, but most were handed out to Frenchwomen.

Throughout the war, the occupiers dominated every cultural and social institution in Paris, among them the opera, art galleries, auction houses, cabarets, and music halls. German officers flocked to the city's grandest restaurants—Maxim's, La Tour d'Argent, Lapérouse, Fouquet's, Le Grand Véfour—which welcomed them as warmly as they had their prewar French clientele.

The Germans' ubiquitous presence in many of her old haunts infuriated Marie-Madeleine. It was important, she thought, to live her life on occasion as if they did not occupy her country's capital. She enlisted her best friend, Nelly de Vogüé, to join her in a plan to do just that. Nelly, who still lived in Paris, was eager to follow the examples of Marie-Madeleine and the two most important men in her life in defying the Germans. Her husband, a naval officer who'd taken part in the fighting at Dunkirk in 1940, had remained in France after the armistice and joined a resistance group in Paris. Her lover, Antoine de Saint-Exupéry, had flown reconnaissance missions for the air force until France collapsed and then had traveled to the United States to try to persuade its government to enter the conflict.

As part of her plan, Marie-Madeleine borrowed one of Nelly's couture outfits and had her hair cut and styled. Like many of her female compatriots, she believed that looking fashionable was one way of thumbing her nose at the Germans. "Fashion was, for the French . . . anything but trivial," noted the historian Anne Sebba. "Many French women . . . remained as fashion-concious as possible during the war in order to retain their pride, boost morale, and remain true to themselves, because fashion expressed their identity."

Marie-Madeleine and Nelly then went for lunch at Maxim's, which had been taken over by the famed Berlin restaurateur Otto Horcher and was regarded as having the most loyal German clientele in Paris. Its frequent customers included Luftwaffe chief Hermann Goering, who always ate there during his art-raiding trips to the French capital.

Until then, the only Germans whom Marie-Madeleine had encountered were low-ranking soldiers on the city's streets. Now, as Maxim's old headwaiter, Albert, guided the two women to their table, she saw bemedaled Wehrmacht and Luftwaffe officers dining on the best food and wine that Maxim's had to offer. As she passed them, she thought of her shabbily dressed agents, who often had little to eat, risking their lives to get rid of the men in that elegant room.

Not surprisingly, the appearance of the two beautiful, fashionably dressed blondes did not go unnoticed among Maxim's clientele. Marie-Madeleine took a secret delight in the appreciative stares directed at her and Nelly. What would these Germans say if they knew she was leading a network that was plotting their destruction?

CHAPTER 7

TAKING COMMAND

WHILE SHE WAS STILL IN PARIS, FOURCADE RECEIVED AN URGENT message from Navarre asking her to return immediately to the south. He did not explain why. Even though she had not finished all her work in the capital, she did as he asked, albeit reluctantly. Once again, she was searched by the "gray mice" as she crossed the demarcation line into the free zone.

At their meeting in Marseille, Navarre delivered some staggering news. He was leaving the next day for Algeria, he said, to help organize a coup against Vichy by dissident French army and air force officers in North Africa. If successful, they and the rest of the French armed forces there—140,000 men in all—would join with the British to fight the Germans. While he was gone, she would be in complete charge of Alliance.

Marie-Madeleine considered the idea of a coup to be stunningly wrongheaded. Yet she wasn't surprised that he supported it. Like many of the young former servicemen he and she had recruited, Navarre had made it clear he'd much rather fight the Germans than collect information about them. Indeed, he had told Kenneth Cohen in Lisbon that his eventual aim was to take up arms when the time was ripe.

But at the moment, Fourcade argued, that time was still in the far distant future. During her stay in the occupied zone, she had witnessed firsthand how dominant the Germans were; they had enough troops in France and elsewhere to crush any revolt. Even the mere thought of a revolt was premature, she declared, to which he shot back that nothing was premature in war.

While Fourcade was well aware of Navarre's taste for conspiracy and political intrigue, she knew that he was not the mastermind behind this audacious plot. Its architect was a buccaneering forty-one-year-old air force pilot named Léon Faye, who currently headed Alliance operations in North Africa.

WHEN FOURCADE FIRST MET FAYE in January 1941, she'd been immediately taken with him. Standing ramrod-straight in his dark blue uniform, the tall, lean major was physically attractive, she noted in her memoirs, with thick dark hair, an aquiline nose, and penetrating gray-green eyes. He possessed an unmistakable air of authority and more than a hint of roguish charm. But what struck her most were his passion, daring, and steadfast determination to strike back at France's occupiers.

An anomaly in France's military officer corps, Faye came from a much more modest background than did most of his cohorts. One of seven children of a police gendarme in the Dordogne, he had left high school at the age of seventeen to fight in the 1914–18 war. He'd distinguished himself in several major battles, including the bloodbath at Verdun. After the war, at the age of twenty, he was awarded the Croix de Guerre.

Bored by peacetime army life in France, Faye won a transfer to North Africa, where he discovered a new passion: flying. He transferred to the air force and became a pilot, eventually earning a promotion to head a squadron. In recognition of his obvious leadership skills, he was invited to apply for entrance to the elite, highly competitive war college, the École Supérieure de Guerre. Faye was at a significant disadvantage in terms of qualifications, not only because,

LÉON FAYE

unlike most of the other applicants, he had not attended the military academy at Saint-Cyr, but even more damning, he was a high school dropout. Still, he was fiercely determined to succeed, and after an intensive, months-long study regimen, he passed the examinations with distinction.

Shortly after he graduated from the military postgraduate school, World War II broke out. During the fighting in France, Faye commanded an air force reconnaissance group and was cited several times for bravery in his superiors' dispatches. Horrified by the armistice, he wangled another transfer to North Africa, where he became deputy chief of the air force and launched a campaign to persuade his aviator colleagues to continue the fight. At that point, the French air force in North Africa still had more than eight hundred planes but was woefully short of fuel, aircraft parts, and ground crew.

In January 1941, Faye traveled on an unofficial mission to Vichy to petition Pétain's government for more resources for his squadrons. His request was rejected outright, and he poured out his anger and disappointment to a former commander of his, General Pierre Baston, who happened to be a member of Navarre's and Fourcade's fledgling spy network. Baston stopped Faye from having a confrontation with Pétain and introduced him instead to Navarre and Marie-Madeleine. During their meeting, Faye talked about a potential uprising in a manner that, in Marie-Madeleine's words, "left me gasping." Since the government refused to support his plans to renew armed combat against the Germans, he would work to recruit other officers to take part in a putsch against Vichy to prevent the enemy occupation of North Africa.

To Fourcade's dismay, Navarre was entranced by the idea, asking how far the plot had advanced. Faye said that he was relatively confident of the support of the air force in Tunisia and Algeria and was now working on the navy, but that it would be more difficult with the army.

Neither Fourcade nor Jean Boutron, who also was present at the meeting, shared Navarre's enthusiasm. Boutron knew from firsthand experience that many if not most navy and army officers in North Africa—particularly in Algeria, where the Mers-el-Kébir sinkings had occurred—were violently pro-Vichy and anti-British. "Algeria had felt Mers el-Kébir as if she had been assaulted," he later wrote. "She was thoroughly anglophobic and anti-Gaullist."

Following their spirited discussion, Faye acknowledged that considerably more spade work needed to be done before the conspiracy could be launched. He returned to North Africa with two missions: to recruit spies for Alliance and to continue laying the groundwork for the mutiny.

Five months later, while Fourcade was in Paris, Navarre received a coded message from Faye that the time for the uprising was drawing near. He had been joined by a well-connected coconspirator, a young army captain named André Beaufre, who was on the staff of the governor general of Algeria and who had attracted support from a number of like-minded colleagues. Faye urged Navarre to travel to Algiers to take part in the final preparations. Knowing that Marie-Madeleine would surely oppose the idea, Navarre completed plans for his departure while she was gone and presented them to her as a fait accompli on her return.

He told her that army intelligence officials in Marseille, who were also working surreptitiously against the Germans, had supplied him with false identity papers and other travel documents. He would pose as a Monsieur Lambdin, a wine merchant who was traveling to Algiers to negotiate the purchase of the latest vintage of Algerian wine. "The next time you hear from me, I'll have taken over Algiers," he said.

Predictably, Marie-Madeleine was livid. He had interrupted her work in Paris for this? A rash scheme that in her view had virtually no chance of succeeding? Less than two months after making a pact with MI6 to supply critically important information to Britain, he was abandoning it, her, and the dozens of other people who were risking everything, including their lives, to work for Alliance. Indeed, his actions might well make their mission more dangerous. For the first time in their long association, she felt as if a wall—invisible and unbridgeable—divided them.

The following day, Navarre sailed for Algiers. The morning after his arrival, he met clandestinely with Faye, Captain Beaufre, and three other officers to discuss their progress toward activating the coup. Faye asked the Alliance chief to get in touch with his contacts in the officer corps of the French army in Morocco, which Navarre promised to do. But he also brought up the name of another possible coconspirator—an old friend of his from his Saint-Cyr days who was now deputy chief of staff of the 19th Army Corps in Algiers. Navarre had mentioned the plot to his friend, who had expressed great interest in it.

At Navarre's request, the others asked his friend to lunch, where further discussions were held. When the meal ended, the officer shook hands with everyone and told Navarre he would join the conspiracy.

Later that afternoon, the plotters met again. The table around which they sat was covered with maps and reports outlining possible means of attack. Suddenly the door to the room burst open, and a throng of Vichy policemen rushed in. One of them, a superintendent, brandished search and arrest warrants. The maps and reports were swept up, and Navarre, Faye, and the others were hustled into cars and taken to the main police station in Algiers.

AFTER NAVARRE'S DEPARTURE FOR ALGERIA, Fourcade had remained in Marseille, feeling more secure there than in Pau, thanks to the blind eye that many members of the local police force turned to burgeoning resistance activities in the city. Summoning her radio operator, Lucien Vallet, from Pau, she continued her work while waiting to hear from her absent leader.

A few days later, Gabriel Rivière, the head of Alliance's Marseille operations, burst into her office and shouted that Navarre and his fellow conspirators had been arrested in Algiers and that she had to leave at once. For a moment or two, Fourcade couldn't move or speak. When the shock wore off, she ordered Rivière to inform local agents immediately of the arrests. She then traveled to Pau to tell Bernis and the others.

As Fourcade knew, the question of whether the network was doomed by the jailing of its founder would be uppermost in the minds of its operatives. Bernis, for one, thought the answer was yes. When she told him about the arrest, he began to pack up his intelligence maps in preparation for returning to Monte Carlo. He had agreed to work with her, he made clear, only because Navarre had been in overall charge of Alliance. Now that his old friend had been captured, he said, his work was over.

Fourcade knew she could not afford to lose Bernis's support. Assuring him that the network would continue, she said she would inform the British that he was going to Monaco to take charge of the entire Mediterranean region. He thought for a moment, then agreed. He was giving her a chance, she knew, to prove she could hold Alliance together.

Another senior officer in the network—General Baston, who had introduced Faye to her and Navarre—was also dubious about its future. When Fourcade told Baston she planned to continue, he frowned and asked if she was going to carry on alone. Although his facial expression and tone of his voice indicated he didn't think she was up to the challenge, he agreed, somewhat reluctantly, to continue Alliance's work in Vichy.

As it happened, Fourcade had misgivings herself about whether she would be accepted as Alliance's leader. She also feared the impact of Navarre's arrest on the network's security. But those concerns soon faded. She was sure that Navarre would never reveal the group's existence to Vichy officials in Algiers, and they had no other way of knowing about it. As for her ability to command the network, hadn't Navarre emphasized to her and others that she was his designated successor? "She is the most valuable of us all . . . the pivot around which everything turns," he had told Jean Boutron. Once, when she told him that everything would end if he were captured, his response was: "No, you will simply carry on."

And while Bernis and Baston might still have their doubts about her, most of the younger operatives did not. To them, Navarre was a distant figure, while they had been operating under Fourcade's command since the network's beginning. As chief of staff, she had recruited many of them; found hiding places for them; taught them how to do their jobs, including coding and deciphering messages; received their information; provided money and other essential supplies; and presided over the meals they shared whenever they came to Pau. "She had a natural authority about her," recalled her daughter, Pénélope Fourcade-Fraissinet. "When she spoke, she made clear that that was the way it was going to be, that her directions must be followed." To the agents of Alliance, she was *la patronne,* the boss.

Her confidence restored, at least in part, she decided to move the Alliance headquarters to Marseille and returned there by train to begin the transfer. She had not yet figured out how and when she was going to tell MI6 about Navarre's arrest. Her main worry now was how British intelligence would respond to the news.

On the train, she wore a broad-brimmed hat to avoid being recognized and kept her head buried in a book, the philosopher René Descartes's classic treatise *Discourse on the Method*. As the stations rolled past, a man seated opposite her began nudging her foot with his. The third time it happened, she looked up with annoyance. He was wearing one of the most extraordinary outfits she had ever seen: checked trousers, a black jacket with a purple rosette, a wide cravat, and a Stetson hat, similar to the ones worn by American cowboys. She glanced at his face. It was Navarre.

He stared ahead with a blank expression. Her stomach churning, she looked down again, pretending to read Descartes. After a few minutes, he went out into the corridor to smoke, and she followed him. He whispered to her that he'd escaped from jail with the help of a high-level official in the Algiers office of the Surveillance du Territoire (ST), a branch of the French national police responsible for counterintelligence.

When they reached Marseille, he told her the full story of his arrest and flight from Algiers. He and the other conspirators had been betrayed by his friend from Saint-Cyr, who, after his lunch with them, had immediately informed Vichy authorities about the plot. Navarre, Faye, and the rest had been rounded up by French military police loyal to Vichy. However, as in Marseille, others in the police and state security agencies in Algiers secretly supported the British, including the ST commissioner there, who returned Navarre's false passport to him and let him go.

When Fourcade mentioned her plan to move Alliance's main operation to Marseille, he disagreed, saying they should return to Pau. Vichy, he said, wouldn't dare arrest him there; he had too many influential friends. Fourcade doubted that was true. Admiral Darlan, who had replaced Pierre Laval as leader of the Vichy government, had been enraged when he learned of the plot in Algiers, which marked the first time since the armistice that members of the armed forces dared to rise up against Vichy.

Convinced that Darlan would do his best to track down Navarre and make an example of him and the other conspirators, Fourcade urged him to flee to London. But he insisted he must carry on the fight in France. Finally, she agreed to return with him to Pau but said that he had to hide from public view. At her request, Henri Schaerrer, back from his assignment in Bordeaux, found Navarre an apartment overlooking Pau's main boulevard. The only other place he frequented was Alliance headquarters. He traveled there by bicycle, leaving his apartment at dawn and returning at dusk or later, when few people were around to observe him.

Two months earlier, the network had moved most of its operations to Villa Etchebaster, a large one-story house surrounded by a walled garden, on the outskirts of Pau. It was considerably more secluded and secure than Alliance's previous base, the Pension Welcome. Navarre's close call in Algeria prompted Fourcade to tighten security even more, transforming the villa into a kind of fortress, with hiding places for the network's radio transmitter, codebooks, and reports. She and others on the staff rarely ventured outside and designated Josette, their housekeeper, to do all their shopping.

Even though Navarre was back, Fourcade remained in charge. With almost two hundred agents now on Alliance's rolls and MI6 deluging the network with floods of questionnaires, she barely had time to draw a breath. To help speed up the transmission of intelligence to London, the British had dispatched three more transmitters. One was sent to Marseille, a second to Colonel Bernis's operation in Monaco, and a third held in reserve.

All of them were transported into France by Jean Boutron, who now served in an undercover role as Vichy's assistant naval attaché in Madrid. Although a godsend for Alliance and the British, Boutron's surprising new posting was his worst nightmare come true. In early 1941, while working for the network in Marseille, he had informed French naval officers there, as part of his cover, that he was preparing a study on the need for reorganization of the country's merchant marine. He did in fact complete the study, and the navy higher-ups were so impressed with it that they asked him to go to Madrid to give them ideas for reorganizing Vichy naval intelligence in Spain.

Boutron, who passionately hated Vichy and Pétain, was horrified by the offer. Navarre, however, was thrilled. "For months, I've been trying to think how to create a link to Spain to send messages and people back and forth from here to London," he said. "And now you've been handed this job on a golden platter. You've got to take it." With great reluctance, Boutron gave in.

Once in Madrid, he found the atmosphere in the embassy even more disagreeable than he had imagined. Before entering the French government in 1940, Pétain had been ambassador in Madrid, and the embassy staff talked of him as if he were a god. "Everyone worships Pétain here," Boutron grumbled in his diary. "Some can't speak for more than five minutes without mentioning something wonderful that the Marshal said or did." His new colleagues, he added, "pronounce the name of England with a pout and that of General de Gaulle with total contempt. . . . I am an iconoclast in a milieu of idolators."

As uncomfortable as Boutron was in this den of Vichy true believers, Navarre was right in his judgment of the extraordinary advantage his position gave to both Alliance and MI6. After making contact with an MI6 agent in Madrid, Boutron persuaded Vichy embassy officials to give him yet another assignment: to carry its diplomatic mailbags, which were sealed and thus exempt from customs inspection, back and forth between Spain and France. Marie-Madeleine had lent him her Citroën for his journeys between the two countries.

In his new role as courier, Boutron was able to transport questionnaires and other secret messages, along with equipment such as radio transmitters, from British intelligence to Alliance headquarters and carry the network's voluminous responses back to Madrid. In addition, Marie-Madeleine and the others at Pau were given a chance, albeit briefly, to examine some of the embassy's communications to the Vichy government and vice versa.

Yet for all of Alliance's successes that summer, Marie-Madeleine was plagued by a lingering sense of unease. She was still concerned about Henri Schaerrer, who, after reporting on the German submarine base near Bordeaux, was about to assume his new post as chief of Alliance's operations in the occupied zone. Just before he was to leave, MI6 sent an urgent message requesting information about the sailing of specific U-boats from the Bordeaux base. Marie-Madeleine was loath to send Schaerrer again, but he insisted on going, although not with his usual ebullience. She considered calling on another agent to do the job but in the end let Schaerrer go. When she urged him, as she always did, to take the greatest possible care, he muttered that no one was irreplaceable. With that, she later wrote, "the intrepid, the irreplaceable Schaerrer disappeared into the night."

A week later, Maurice Coustenoble, looking unusually worried and exhausted, returned from a mission to the southeast with the warning that Vichy was closing in on Navarre. His coconspirators in Algiers, Léon Faye and André Beaufre, had been transferred to a jail in Clermont-Ferrand to await trial for their part in the abortive mutiny, and Vichy officials were determined to see that Navarre joined them in the dock.

Coustenoble blurted out to Marie-Madeleine that Navarre must leave Pau immediately. She stood up, and the two of them went to find him. When she told him what Coustenoble had said, he replied he knew he had to leave but couldn't do so until the following day, when he planned to meet his wife and daughter at the cathedral in Pau to say goodbye. When Marie-Madeleine said the police surely had Navarre's family under surveillance, he shrugged, sat down at the desk where he had been working, and picked up his pen. She knew there was nothing she could say that would change his mind.

As the day crept by, she struggled to carry on with her usual routine—arranging new missions, encoding messages for Lucien Vallet to send to London, and deciphering MI6 transmissions that had just come in, including an announcement that its first parachute drop to Alliance would be made in two days.

When Navarre rose to leave late in the evening, Marie-Madeleine and Coustenoble said they were going with him. On their bicycles, the three pedaled silently down into the sleeping town, along the boulevard overlooking the valley. They slipped into Navarre's apartment, and Coustenoble insisted on a thorough search for anything incriminating. Finding stacks of compromising papers and reports in every corner of the apartment, he took them out and burned them.

As dawn approached, Navarre offered each of them a glass of Armagnac. Sipping from hers, Marie-Madeleine stared out an open window at the peaks of the Pyrenees some thirty miles away, glowing like beacons in the early morning light. Navarre told the two to go back and get a few hours' sleep. After he saw his family, he'd be with them at noon.

Neither did as he suggested. Coustenoble stood guard outside the apartment while Marie-Madeleine wandered around Pau until late morning, doing some shopping and spending a couple of hours at the hairdresser's. Because she and her Alliance colleagues had closeted themselves away during their time in Pau, few people in the town had any idea who she was. But instead of savoring her few hours of freedom, she felt sick from anxiety and lack of sleep. Late in the morning, she cycled back to Villa Etchebaster. When Josette came to open the garden gate, Marie-Madeleine saw from her agonized expression that the worst had happened.

In the drawing room, her staff stood silently, their faces a tableau of shock and despair. Coustenoble took her arm and hurried her upstairs to tell her what had occurred. Navarre's family had been followed from their home in Oloron-Sainte-Marie by more than a dozen Vichy policemen, who had been told their quarry was a German spy. They had stationed themselves in the back of the cathedral, and when Navarre came in, they rushed him. When he tried to run, he was fired at but not hit. He was now in the Pau jail, waiting to be transferred to the prison at Clermont-Ferrand.

Overcome by exhaustion, fury, and anguish, Marie-Madeleine broke down in tears. Coustenoble put his arms around her. "Enough, little one," he murmured. "A soldier doesn't cry." She needed to eat, he said, and he urged her to come to lunch. She shook her head.

He insisted she had to come: If she didn't, her staff would feel leaderless. She told him that she had to think for a while and that she would join them later. After a few minutes, she got up and went downstairs to the dining room. Taking a seat next to Lucien Vallet, she surreptitiously slipped the food on her plate onto his. Then she asked him the time of his next transmission to London. Three P.M., he replied.

About ten minutes before Vallet's transmission time, she handed him an encoded message. It read: N1 ARRESTED THIS MORNING STOP NETWORK INTACT STOP EVERYTHING CONTINUING STOP BEST POSTPONE PARACHUTING NEXT MOON STOP CONFIDENCE UNSHAKABLE STOP REGARDS STOP POZ 55.

MI6's reply, filled with expressions of regret and sympathy, came a few hours later. It ended with a terse question: "Who is taking over?"

Marie-Madeleine's answer was brief and emphatic. I AM AS PLANNED STOP SURROUNDED BY LOYAL LIEUTENANTS STOP POZ 55.

CHAPTER 8

A NETWORK IN PERIL

A S SHE STRUGGLED WITH THE TRAUMA OF NAVARRE'S ARREST, Fourcade found solace in the knowledge that the British had no idea that POZ 55 was a woman. Navarre had never told them the name or gender of his deputy. And she, concerned that they would reject her out of hand, had no intention of enlightening them.

Besides, she had other, more pressing matters to worry about, including how to prevent the Vichy police dragnet from closing around her and the rest of the network. With Navarre in jail, Boutron in Madrid, Bernis in Monte Carlo, and Schaerrer in Bordeaux, she was left with few confidants who could advise her in her battle to keep Alliance afloat.

But her sense of isolation didn't prevent her from acting. She immediately severed all connection with Pension Welcome, where Navarre had been a frequent and highly visible visitor. She informed its owners about his arrest, telling them that if the police came looking for her, they should say that she had gone to the Côte d'Azur.

After two sleepless days and nights, she finally collapsed into bed at the Villa Etchebaster, only to be awakened in the early morning by a new headquarters staffer named Gavarni—a tall, lean former air force officer with a quick temper and commanding presence—who told her that the police were ransacking the Pension Welcome and that she must leave immediately. He took her to the home of a friend for a few days, then installed her in a hotel in the center of Pau, whose anti-Vichy owner agreed to serve her meals in her room and not to fill out the forms required by the police for guests. In the interests of security, she never left the hotel during the day and only rarely at night.

The rest of the headquarters staff continued their work at the Villa Etchebaster, which, after careful consideration, was judged to be relatively safe, at least for the moment. The network's operations intensified, and huge stacks of intelligence reports, delivered to the hotel by Fourcade's radio operator, Lucien Vallet, piled up on the desk in her room. She spent her days reading them and encoding the most urgent, which were transmitted to MI6 by radio. The rest were dispatched to London via Madrid in Boutron's Vichy mailbags.

She held clandestine meetings with a steady stream of agents at the hotel to discuss the details of the intelligence that MI6, in its queries, asked them to track down. The majority of the questions, not surprisingly, had to do with the location and movements of German ships and U-boats to and from the French coasts. Alliance now had agents in place in twelve coastal ports, stretching from Normandy to the Côte d'Azur. Thus far, the best intelligence had come from agents in Saint-Nazaire, on the Brittany coast. One of the largest ports in Europe, Saint-Nazaire housed not only a large U-boat fleet but also some of the German navy's biggest ships, such as the battleships *Bismarck* and *Tirpitz*.

Antoine Hugon, the garage owner whom Fourcade had chosen as the network's leader in Brittany, was the conduit for the information from Saint-Nazaire, much of it coming from two spies Hugon himself had recruited—Henri Mouren, chief of the Saint-Nazaire shipyard, and Mouren's deputy, Jules Sgier.

One morning in the late summer of 1941, Hugon arrived unexpectedly at the Villa Etchebaster. To the astonishment of the Alliance staff, he began taking off his clothes—first his jacket, with the Iron Cross on the lapel, then his tie and shirt. Wrapped around Hugon's ample torso was an enormous cloth map, which he unwound and presented to his astonished audience for inspection. The map depicted the layout of the Saint-Nazaire submarine base and shipyard, including the recently built U-boat pens—all reproduced by Henri Mouren to scale, down to the last inch.

A major coup for Alliance, the map only increased MI6's insatiable appetite for information. In early August, the intelligence agency informed Marie-Madeleine that it was about to parachute in more support, including a new type of wireless transmitter and a British radio operator who would train her agents in the transmitter's use and also instruct them in an improved method of coding. When finished with those duties, he would travel to Normandy, where he had been assigned to create a new Alliance sector. The first Englishman to work in the field with the network, he would be known to Marie-Madeleine and her operatives only by his code name, Blanchet.

The parachute drop proceeded without a hitch, and she was thrilled with the bounty that MI6 sent. The new transmitter was smaller and easier to operate than its big, bulky predecessor; a new type of paper to be used for messages was silky and tissue-thin, making it easier to hide; and there were "lots of other little gadgets to help us in our work." The only potential problem was the radio operator himself.

To meet him, she abandoned the safety of her hotel room for a rare foray to the Villa Etchebaster. When she entered the drawing room, she stopped and stared. Standing before her was a living parody—a figure who looked as if he had just stepped out of a low-budget Hollywood movie made by a director who knew nothing about the French. The man sported a goatee and pince-nez and wore a short jacket and waistcoat, striped trousers, stiff shirt with cutaway collar, and a cravat. On his head was a bowler hat. Marie-Madeleine's agents burst into gales of laughter.

Trying to smooth over the awkwardness of the moment, she delivered a few words of welcome in English, only to be interrupted by Blanchet, who said in fluent French, albeit with a Cockney accent, that he had spent more of his life in France than England. It wasn't

until after the war that she found out his real identity: Arthur Bradley Davies, a thirty-nine-year-old former farm manager who had
lived in Normandy for some twenty years. After the Germans invaded France, he had fled to England and was recruited there by MI6.

Marie-Madeleine ordered Blanchet, whom she called Bla, to shave
off his beard and to tone down his flamboyant appearance. But his
outrageous outfit wasn't the only way in which he called attention to
himself. From the beginning, he acted oddly, giving his coding lessons in a loud voice in public places, asking too many questions about
the network's operations, and showing too much interest in everyone
who came to the Villa Etchebaster. Lucien Vallet advised her to get
rid of him.

But how could she turn down an agent from MI6, which, by all
accounts, was the most skilled intelligence service in the world? Although she didn't get rid of Bla, she remained uneasy about him until
he finally left for Paris, on his way to Normandy. Preceding him to
Paris was Vallet, the warm, witty young former army officer who had
worked with her as the network's chief radio operator for almost a
year and whom she regarded with great fondness. Fourcade had assigned him to take charge of the network's expanding radio operation
in the capital, but his departure was a loss she felt keenly.

Her regret over Vallet's leaving was followed by a far more shattering blow. For weeks, she had been deeply worried about Henri
Schaerrer, who had left for Bordeaux more than a month earlier.
Since then, she had heard nothing from or about him. Then, shortly
after Bla's and Vallet's departures, word came that the Gestapo had
captured Schaerrer, his pockets stuffed with documents from the submarine base, on the outskirts of Bordeaux. The first Alliance agent to
be arrested by the Germans, Schaerrer had been taken to Fresnes
prison outside Paris, the Germans' central holding facility for captured British agents and members of the French resistance.

The report of Schaerrer's arrest was accompanied by additional
bad news. The Vichy government, under increasing pressure from
the Nazis, had ordered its security agencies and police to take the
toughest possible action against all resistance movements and net-

works in the free zone. The repression began soon after the surprise German invasion of Russia in June 1941. In response to the German attack, Moscow had ordered the French Communist Party to launch an armed struggle against munitions factories and German troops in France, in hopes of weakening the Reich's Russian campaign. The Communists' first strike came on August 21 with the fatal shooting of a young German naval cadet in a Paris subway station. The Vichy government, in an attempt to appease Nazi authorities, ordered the execution of six French Communists who had had nothing to do with the ambush. Rather than halting the Communist attacks, the reprisal was followed by more assassinations: On October 20, a high-level German official was killed in Nantes, followed by another in Bordeaux. In retribution, ninety-seven additional French hostages were shot.

The French people, already restive over growing food and fuel shortages, were infuriated by the wanton killing of their compatriots, and resistance efforts against the Germans grew noticeably stronger, especially in the free zone. Vichy's repression also increased, thanks to Admiral Darlan's eagerness to conciliate the Third Reich. Believing that France's destiny was to serve as the leading vassal state in a Germanized Europe, Darlan did all he could to make that happen, including overseeing the sale of more than seventeen hundred trucks and thousands of tons of fuel to the Germans for use in their fight against the British in North Africa.

Hoping to extend military collaboration even further, the admiral also signed a tentative agreement allowing German armed forces to use French airfields in Syria, submarine facilities at Dakar, and ports in Tunisia for resupplying German troops. There were, however, still some Vichy officials who believed that the government should maintain at least a semblance of independence. In their view, Darlan's agreement was a step too far, and he was successfully pressured to cancel it.

But he suffered no such constraints when he allowed German security forces, including the Abwehr, SD, and Gestapo, to infiltrate the free zone, an action that violated terms of the armistice. An

American diplomat in Vichy reported to Washington that he encountered Gestapo agents everywhere—"at bars, restaurants, and the opera." Their presence was so ubiquitous, he said, that "you expect to find them in your bed—and perhaps you would not be wrong."

Darlan was furious when he discovered that the French army's counterintelligence branch did not share his laissez-faire approach to the presence of German spies throughout the free zone. In Marseille, for example, French counterintelligence agents had broken up an Abwehr espionage network operating on the Mediterranean coast. Eight radio transmitters were seized and twenty-six agents captured. By the end of 1941, more than three hundred Nazi operatives, many of them French nationals, had been arrested in the free zone and handed over to French military courts. Of these, sixteen had been executed.

During a cabinet meeting in the summer of 1941, Darlan attacked the army's counterintelligence efforts and ordered them stopped. "It's open war against us," the Deuxième Bureau's Colonel Louis Rivet later told a colleague. "We are now considered the bête noire of the regime."

Obeying Darlan's directives, Vichy's interior ministry took control of the country's urban police forces, and special police brigades were created to hunt down resisters. "At the grass roots, the police were torn between the directives they were being given and their deeply patriotic feelings," an army counterintelligence officer wrote. "Many officials remained favorable to us and were ready to continue the fight against the enemy within, but we had to admit that we were completely short-circuited."

Fourcade, for her part, had always been wary of putting any faith in Vichy. The crackdown ordered by Darlan simply confirmed her belief that no one in the government could be trusted. "Vichy is betting on a German victory," she told Jean Boutron late that summer. "There may be in this regime men who will help us. But there are not many of them, and we will find it difficult to discover them. It is better to consider all of them as dangerous and sometimes ruthless opponents. . . . So much the better if we have happy surprises."

Yet even as reports of repression rolled in during the fall of 1941, Alliance continued to extend its reach throughout the country. Six of its MI6-supplied radio transmitters—in Pau, Marseille, Nice, Lyon, Normandy, and Paris—were now sending intelligence back to London. At the same time, the network's operations in Paris and the rest of the occupied zone were rapidly growing. MI6 told Fourcade that it soon would send six additional transmitters to her, along with several million more francs to finance the network's continued expansion. In mid-October, she dispatched Gavarni, Coustenoble, and two other lieutenants to tour the network's sectors and urge their chiefs to redouble their efforts.

Although much of the intelligence she received from the sectors, particularly reports from the coastal areas, had been superb, some material, sent by operatives who clearly had a shaky command of the basics of intelligence gathering, caused her intense frustration. When she was sent reports, for example, about "a lot of Germans" observed traveling on trains, planes, or ships that were not identified, she shot back scathing responses demanding precise details of the enemy units and transports.

But that frustration was nothing compared to her anguish over the news she received one autumn day from Henri Mouren, the chief of the Saint-Nazaire shipyard. Bursting into her hotel room, he told her that postal inspectors had discovered incriminating documents in a Paris post office box, placed there by a postal worker who also served as an Alliance courier. French police shadowed the worker, who, over the next few days, met with more than a dozen other Alliance operatives. All were arrested.

"Who were they?" Fourcade whispered. She flinched when she heard the response. Antoine Hugon, who had brought her the Saint-Nazaire map, was among them. So were Lucien Vallet and Jules Sgier, Mouren's deputy at the shipyard and his closest friend.

In the midst of dealing with this latest calamity, Fourcade was tasked with overseeing the preparations for MI6's scheduled parachute drop, which yielded the biggest cache of money and materials yet. Containers holding 3 million francs and six transmitters floated down beneath their parachutes to a field in the Dordogne. Other parachutes carried new codes and questionnaires; an array of new devices for agents' use, among them soapboxes and tooth powder tins with false bottoms; and treats for the Alliance staff, including coffee, sugar, and tea. Another 3 million francs were transported by Jean Boutron from Madrid, and 4 million more would be kept in reserve for the network at a Barcelona bank. The overall total—a heart-stopping 10 million francs—was unmistakable proof of Alliance's importance to MI6 and the British war effort.

A million francs from the parachute drop were immediately dispatched to various patrols throughout the country to cover their expenses. Marie-Madeleine entrusted the remaining 2 million to Gavarni, whom she had just made her chief of staff. While presiding over the distribution of MI6's largesse, she also was hard at work reorganizing the Paris patrols. Four new agents were about to leave for the capital. They would be accompanied by Mathilde Bridou, Marie-Madeleine's mother, who wanted to visit friends in Paris and resisted her daughter's arguments that going there now was too dangerous.

On the day they all were to depart, Marie-Madeleine felt the same sense of unease she had had before Navarre's arrest. Coustenoble agreed. Together, they burned masses of intelligence reports stacked in her room, and Coustenoble spirited away the six new transmitters for safekeeping at his house in Toulouse.

Later that night, as Marie-Madeleine sat at her desk coding reports, two Alliance agents rushed into her room. Struggling to catch his breath, one of them shouted that Vichy police had raided the Etchebaster and rounded up everyone there. Now they were on the hunt for Marie-Madeleine. She must leave immediately.

With the exception of the two operatives, everyone at the Pau headquarters had been captured—Coustenoble, Gavarni, the rest of the staff at the Villa Etchebaster, the agents who had been dispatched to Paris, and several others who had come to Pau for consultations. Her mother, too, had been swept up in the net. The headquarters radio transmitter was destroyed before the police could seize it, but policemen found the new radios from London at Coustenoble's house. There was one bit of good news: The remaining 5 million francs from the British had not yet been discovered.

Fourcade hurriedly gathered up her reports and packed a suitcase. After the owner of the hotel smuggled her out and into a waiting car, he put on his pajamas and moved into the room she had just vacated, prepared to claim to the police that the room was his and the woman they were seeking had never been there. As the car containing Fourcade drove away from the hotel, it passed a police car speeding toward it. Her agents took her to the home of a married couple they knew in the town of Tarbes, about thirty miles from Pau.

Distraught over these attacks on multiple fronts, she thought about whom she could approach for help. She had lost all the agents who had acted as her eyes and ears, had no transmitter to communicate with London or anywhere else, and ruled out traveling to Marseille or any of Alliance's other sectors for fear of contaminating them. Concluding that her only hope was Jean Boutron, who had left Pau for Vichy several days before, she dispatched one of her rescuers to find him. Providentially, Boutron had not yet left on his return trip to Madrid, and when he heard what had happened, he rushed immediately to Tarbes, where Marie-Madeleine greeted him with a fervent embrace.

They discussed possible hiding places for her, all of which Boutron rejected. The only possible way to save her from prison and the network from destruction was to smuggle her across the border to Spain, he said. Like it or not, she must go with him to Madrid, reveal her true identity to the British, and seek their aid.

CHAPTER 9

THE MAILBAG

T O SMUGGLE MARIE-MADELEINE ACROSS THE FRENCH-SPANISH border was no easy task. Since she did not have official papers, real or forged, to cross into Spain, she had to be concealed somewhere in Boutron's car. As he saw it, the only possible hiding place was in one of the official Vichy mailbags that he carried back and forth between the two countries.

The logistics of travel also presented a problem. During most of the year, Boutron could drive the car—Marie-Madeleine's old Citroën—over a mountain pass in the central Pyrenees, which had served for centuries as a popular route for travelers between France and Spain. But it was now early December, and the pass was already heavily blanketed by snow. The only way for a vehicle to make a winter crossing over the mountains was to stow it atop a railway flat-car and take it by train to the Spanish border.

Marie-Madeleine wasn't Boutron's only stowaway. He would also smuggle to Madrid a young Frenchman who worked for an MI6 intelligence network based in Spain. The man would hide in the car's trunk while Marie-Madeleine would take refuge in a mailbag.

For hours, Boutron tried to figure out how to squeeze his *patronne*, who stood five feet six inches tall, into a jute sack that measured two feet by four feet. After experimenting with a number of contorted positions, the two of them found that if Marie-Madeleine removed all her clothes except her underwear and crouched with her head and torso curled over her knees, the sack could be closed, if only barely. The position was extraordinarily uncomfortable: Her chin dug into her chest, and her displaced hip began hurting after just a few minutes of being in the bag.

But Boutron assured her that she would be in it for only about two hours—just enough time for the car to be loaded onto the train, which would then travel from a French rail station through a five-mile tunnel to the Spanish border. He cut a couple of small holes in the bag, next to her nose and mouth, so that she could breathe, and gave her a pair of scissors in case she needed to make a quick exit.

The morning following their reunion in Tarbes, Boutron, Marie-Madeleine, and the other agent traveled to the French mountain village of Urdos, where the train station was located. Boutron drove slowly, to avoid getting there too early but also to escape the attention of police who might be on Marie-Madeleine's trail. In a wooded area outside the village, the male operative climbed into the trunk and Marie-Madeleine slipped into the sack, which Boutron closed and affixed with an official Vichy seal. He put it in the backseat of the car, along with two other mailbags. As he got back into the car, he asked Marie-Madeleine if she was all right. "From the bag," he recalled, "came a murmur which I resolutely took for an affirmation."

At the station, Boutron drove the car up a ramp to a siding, where the flatcar was waiting, along with the stationmaster, who delivered a jolt of bad news. The train for which Boutron had a reservation was arriving an hour earlier than expected, and there wouldn't be enough time to perform the complicated maneuver of hoisting the Citroën onto the flatcar. He would have to wait eight hours for the next train to the border.

Boutron was horrified. Marie-Madeleine, he thought, couldn't possibly survive in the bag that long. He told the stationmaster he had changed his mind and would try to cross the pass in his car. When the man responded that he was out of his mind, Boutron said he was used to driving in ice and snow and that he would take his chances. But he was turned back almost immediately by a French customs official, who said that traversing the pass was not only forbidden but impossible: The snow covering it was several feet deep.

Growing increasingly desperate, Boutron returned to the station, where railwaymen began the lengthy process of attaching ropes to the Citroën. More than two hours later, it had been raised onto the flatcar and moored. Watching the men work, Boutron tried to appear calm, but the effort was exhausting: Although the air was freezing, his face and hands were slick with sweat. When the train finally arrived and the flatcar was attached, Marie-Madeleine had been in the sack almost eight hours.

Boutron had planned to stay in the Citroën for the short journey, but the stationmaster ordered him off the flatcar and into a compartment. When he protested, he was told that it was far too dangerous: The tunnel had sharp curves, and the ropes mooring the auto could snap, hurling it against the tunnel wall. It had happened more than once before, the stationmaster added.

Painfully aware that Marie-Madeleine had heard everything the man said, Boutron made his way to his compartment near the front of the train. When it finally entered the tunnel, he clandestinely retraced his steps to the flatcar, struggling hard to keep his balance as the train rocketed around the seemingly endless curves. Finally reaching the Citroën, he climbed into it and announced with more good humor than he felt: "I'm back. If the car falls off, at least we'll be together." When Marie-Madeleine responded in a muffled voice, he let out a sigh of relief. He couldn't understand what she said, but at least she was still alive.

After what seemed an eternity, the train finally emerged from the tunnel and headed toward the bright lights of the Spanish customs post. "We're almost there!" Boutron exclaimed. "Just stick it out for a few more minutes. *Courage!*" At the moment, however, Marie-Madeleine had no *courage* to spare. Having been doubled up in the mailbag for more than nine hours, she was almost frozen and in excruciating pain.

She heard Boutron approach the flatcar with several workmen, who roughly unloaded the Citroën. From inside the sack, she could see the beams of flashlights sweeping over the mailbags. Boutron tried to speed up the process. "These are diplomatic bags with top secret information," he said to the Spanish customs officials. "Please hurry . . . I must get to Madrid as soon as possible . . . Important diplomatic mission . . . The Marshal . . ."

Finally, his cargo was cleared. With hearty shouts of *"Adiós"* and *"Vaya usted con Dios,"* Boutron drove the car down a ramp and into neutral Spain. After a few miles, he pulled off into a wooded area by the side of a mountain stream and released the male agent from the trunk. The two of them then took the mail sack containing Marie-Madeleine out of the car and opened it. Still curled up in a fetal position, she had no feeling in her limbs and was unable to move any of them. As the two men gently pulled her from the bag, she fainted. When she regained consciousness, she saw Boutron's stricken face. For a brief moment, he had thought she was dead.

He helped her sit up and gave her a cigarette. He also handed her a bottle of Napoleon cognac that he had bought on the black market in France as a gift for his MI6 contact in Madrid. The cigarette and a few sips of cognac revived her a bit, but she was still unable to walk. When she had recovered enough to travel, he carried her to the car, and once they reached Madrid early the following morning, he carried her up the steps of his rented house.

After telling his housekeeper that Marie-Madeleine was his cousin and that she would be staying with him for a couple of weeks, Boutron contacted Georges Charaudeau, a wealthy French businessman who lived part-time in Spain and was the intended recipient of the cognac. Charaudeau had formed a small anti-German intelligence organization of his own, in league with MI6, that operated in both Spain and France. Although he had no official connection with Alliance, he cooperated closely with Boutron in the Spanish capital.

Boutron asked Charaudeau to send a message to MI6's Kenneth Cohen, informing him of the arrival of POZ 55 and ASO 45 (Boutron's code name) in Madrid and the decimation of the network staff in

Pau. Later in the day, Cohen responded, instructing POZ to travel to London via Lisbon. Marie-Madeleine adamantly refused, declaring that she must be back in France by the New Year at the latest. In a second message to Cohen, she informed him of her decision, then added a bombshell piece of news: POZ 55 was a woman. After a few hours of silence, Cohen answered. He would send his deputy to Madrid, with full power to act on his behalf. The meeting would take place within a week.

While they waited for the MI6 representative, Boutron reported back to his undercover job at the Vichy embassy, while Marie-Madeleine, consumed with worry over the arrests in Pau, particularly that of her mother, recuperated from her ordeal. After a few days, she had regained enough strength to wander a bit around Madrid, but her outing only increased her depression.

As she strolled through the center of the city, she vividly remembered the frequent trips she had taken with her mother to Madrid in the 1920s and early 1930s and their keen enjoyment of the lively, bustling Spanish capital. Now Mathilde Bridou was in a Vichy jail cell, while Madrid, having suffered serious damage during the Spanish Civil War in the late 1930s, was a sad, tattered version of its former self. Many buildings were dilapidated and pockmarked with bullet holes, and the iron railings fronting their balconies were red with rust. Several had been reduced to rubble by the incessant bombing of Luftwaffe planes during the conflict, and weeds now flourished in the mountains of debris left behind.

Like Madrid's other squares, the Puerta del Sol, the vast expanse in the heart of the city where Marie-Madeleine and her mother had spent many happy prewar hours socializing with friends in its cafés and restaurants, was largely deserted—its fountain dry, its trees barren. As in Paris, a shroud of silence enveloped the city.

Also as in Paris, black-and-red German swastikas fluttered in the breeze almost everywhere Marie-Madeleine went. During the civil war, Nazi Germany had aided General Francisco Franco and his fascist army, and even though Spain was officially neutral now, Franco's government still favored the Reich.

Although Madrid, like the capitals of other neutral countries, had been inundated by intelligence agents from all over the globe, Gestapo and Abwehr spies predominated. The chiefs of both agencies—Heinrich Himmler and Admiral Wilhelm Canaris—were occasional visitors to the Spanish capital and, along with their subordinates, were feted at lavish parties by members of Madrid's high society, most of whom were pro-Franco and pro-Axis.

During her stay there, Marie-Madeleine was taken under the wing of Georges Charaudeau and his wife, a clothing designer whose fashion house catered to Madrid socialites and the wives of Franco's officials—and acted as a front for Charaudeau's pro-Allied intelligence activities. The Charaudeaus showered her with clothes unavailable in France—a black silk dress, sweaters, skirts, lingerie, and shoes with cork soles, to replace her ugly wooden-soled French shoes. She also received an abundance of British cigarettes, whisky, coffee, and tea.

Although she reveled in this bounty, Marie-Madeleine found the experience surreal. Here she was, in the midst of luxury, while cut off from everything and everybody she loved most in the world. She was haunted by thoughts of her mother and her agents in jail and by the plight of her two children, who now had no mother or grandmother to care for them. She would discover only later that they were being looked after by other members of her extended family.

THE MAN FROM MI6 turned out to be a tall, fair-haired, youthful-looking man in a British army uniform who introduced himself as Major Richards. His real name was Eddie Keyser, but Marie-Madeleine Fourcade knew him only as Richards until after the war.

Even though Keyser had been informed before he left London that the chief of Alliance was a woman, his dumbfounded expression when he met her betrayed his disbelief that this lovely blonde in her chic silk dress could possibly be head of a major intelligence network. After staring at her for several seconds, he glanced at Jean Boutron, who was standing beside her, as if to say, "This is a joke, isn't it? You are the real POZ 55." Boutron, however, made it clear that Fourcade was indeed *la patronne.*

When Cohen's deputy mentioned the deception, she stiffly replied that she had concealed her identity because she was afraid MI6 would abandon her network and agents if it learned that Alliance's leader was a woman. She felt she had to prove herself before letting Cohen and the others know who she was.

With a wave of his hand, Keyser brushed her worries aside and asked if she still wanted to work with his agency. Hearing the anxiety in his voice, Fourcade recovered her confidence. Her help—and that of her agents—was needed, regardless of her sex.

Before discussing the future, she gave Keyser the details of what had happened in Pau—the arrests of her agents and mother, the seizure of the transmitters that MI6 had just parachuted in, the fact that the millions of francs sent by London had not yet been discovered by the police. As she talked, she was perplexed by his seeming lack of surprise about the events she was describing. In fact, he seemed to know far more about what had occurred than she did. He passed along some new information, which made the network's situation appear all the bleaker.

Her agents in Pau, Keyser said, had been betrayed by the head of the Alliance patrol in the Dordogne, who had been having an affair with the daughter of a policeman there. Pulled in for questioning by the young woman's outraged father, the agent, who had been recruited months earlier by Maurice Coustenoble, informed the police about the British parachute drop in a nearby field and told them where they could find members of the reception committee. He also revealed the location of the network's headquarters in Pau and the identities of its staff.

Fourcade found herself barely able to speak. She asked Keyser if he had anything else to reveal. Keyser nodded. "Paris," he said, telling her that the Alliance agents captured in the French capital just days before the Pau raid had been turned over to the Germans and were now in Fresnes prison.

Her heart raced: Lucien Vallet, Antoine Hugon, and the rest of the operatives in Paris—now in the clutches of the Gestapo! In a strangled voice, she asked where he had gotten the information. From an agent of hers named Gavarni, he said. She replied that was impossible: Gavarni was in prison in Pau.

Actually, Keyser said, he had never been in prison. MI6 had received a recent cable from him explaining what had happened. After Gavarni's arrest, according to his message, he had met in Vichy with Commander Henri Rollin, the head of Surveillance du Territoire, the government's political counterintelligence agency. Fourcade's chief of staff had insisted to Rollin that the Alliance network had been broken up and was no longer a threat to Vichy. Telling Rollin that Fourcade had fled to England, Gavarni offered him a deal: In exchange for the release of himself and his Alliance colleagues, he would hand over the 2 million francs from London that she had given him for safekeeping. Rollin agreed to the proposition and allowed Gavarni to travel to Marseille and send a message to Fourcade via MI6, outlining the situation and asking her to approve the deal. According to Keyser, Gavarni reported that giving the money to Vichy would prove that the network had indeed collapsed.

Fourcade found it incomprehensible that the Englishman could keep so calm in the midst of this calamity. Above all, she was horrified by the idea that Gavarni would hand over such vast sums of money to Vichy—money that the network badly needed. She had promoted him to chief of staff because she had been impressed by his energy, quickness of mind, and leadership qualities. She especially valued his decisiveness after the Vichy raid on the Pension Welcome, when he had whisked her away to safety. As she sat there in Madrid, she found it almost impossible to believe that he could have done what Keyser said he had.

Jean Boutron was even more upset, calling Gavarni a "bastard," a "skunk," and a "traitor." Fourcade told him to calm down, noting that if Gavarni had indeed been a traitor, she, Boutron, and other Alliance agents would have been arrested long before.

Unconvinced, Boutron appealed to her to turn down Gavarni's proposal. But all she could think of was her mother and operatives in a Pau jail. Urged on by Keyser, she reluctantly agreed to give up the 2 million francs in exchange for the release of all the prisoners. After writing a message to Gabriel Rivière giving her approval, she handed it to Keyser, who coded it and sent it to London for transmittal to Marseille.

She would wait until her return to France to deal with Gavarni herself.

AS SHE TRIED TO come to grips with the latest bad news, Fourcade had a question of her own. Why, she asked Keyser, did MI6 send her an agent like the radio operator Blanchet, whose odd appearance and suspicious behavior had immediately raised red flags in everyone's mind? Was it meant to be some sort of test?

Keyser scowled and said no, then scolded her for such suspicions. But Fourcade persisted, describing in detail Bla's inquisitiveness and blatant carelessness. She wondered if Bla had somehow been involved in the arrests of her agents in Paris.

The MI6 officer dismissed her concerns. Blanchet may have been a little too talkative and agitated, he acknowledged, but there was nothing to fear from him. He was, in fact, considered one of the agency's best radio operators and thus far had been doing an excellent job in Normandy.

Fourcade asked Keyser if he was sure Bla was transmitting from Normandy. She said she'd heard from an Alliance agent in Paris that Bla had reported technical problems with his transmitter and had come to the capital to use one of the machines there. In fact, according to her agent, Bla had been in Paris for some time.

Keyser seemed slightly shaken by Fourcade's account and said he would report her fears to London. MI6's response, sent the following day, endorsed his support of Bla but, to alleviate Fourcade's worries, said that it would gradually ease him out of Alliance and send him to another network.

Fourcade was far from satisfied by MI6's ambiguous reaction, but there was nothing more she could do about it. She shared Jean

Boutron's jaundiced opinion that the British, with their high opinion of themselves and their nation, found it almost impossible to believe that one of their countrymen might be a traitor. Indeed, Stewart Menzies, the current head of MI6, had once been quoted as saying that "only people with foreign names commit treason." Fourcade could only hope that her network could survive that myopic attitude—and its potentially deadly consequences.

WHATEVER THE CAUSES OF the network's recent losses, their enormity, after the triumphs of the organization's first fourteen months, had badly shaken her. With a few exceptions, Alliance's first wave of agents had been wiped out. In her mind, Fourcade ticked off the sectors that still survived: Marseille, Vichy, Brittany, Nice, and Grenoble. There were a few other resources scattered throughout the country: several agents who had gone undetected in Paris, as well as a sprinkling of couriers and reserve radio operators. Overall, however, the network was in tatters and needed to be rebuilt from the ground up.

She took solace in the fact that MI6 remained fully committed to Alliance—and, from all appearances, to her as its leader. Such an attitude was remarkable, considering that the agency, like most of the British government, was an almost exclusively male preserve, with little tolerance for the idea of women in any sort of position of responsibility or authority. Claude Dansey—MI6's misanthropic, irascible deputy director who was the power behind the throne there—once had grumbled that "letting women run anything was against his principles." But neither he nor his colleagues could argue with the invaluable information collected by Alliance under Fourcade's command. Again and again, Keyser underscored how dependent his agency was on a continuing flow of information from her organization. "Your network *must* last," he declared.

For more than a week, he met daily with Fourcade to brief her in detail about the specific kinds of intelligence that the British now needed regarding the German military presence in France. As always, their most immediate priority was the sea, with the emphasis on information about port installations and the movement of ships and submarines.

Their meetings turned out to be eye-opening for both of them. Fourcade sketched verbal portraits of Alliance's remaining agents and described the difficulties they faced in collecting information. In turn, he briefed her on the vagaries of MI6 and British officialdom in general. He also outlined a plan to vastly expand MI6's methods of communication with Alliance, including the introduction of a new air operation between England and France, using small planes to pick up and take out Alliance agents, mail, and other important material.

With his typical audacity, Jean Boutron came up with his own contribution for improving the exchange of information. To help speed up the flow of messages back and forth between MI6, Alliance headquarters, and his own base in Madrid, he installed a radio transmitter in the attic of the Vichy embassy there, telling the embassy's radio operator that he had been authorized by Marshal Pétain himself to open up a secret wireless link with London. Using the transmitter, Boutron established a secure, direct link to Marseille, where Fourcade planned to install her base, as well as to London.

In the ten days they spent together in Madrid, Keyser and Fourcade developed a surprisingly close relationship. At their last meeting, they warmly shook hands, realizing, as Fourcade later wrote in her memoirs, that they had formed a real friendship. For them, the word "Alliance" had taken on a new, more personal meaning.

IN LATE DECEMBER 1941, Marie-Madeleine and Boutron prepared to return to France and get back to the work of spying on the Germans. But at the moment, she was preoccupied by a more immediate concern: Had her mother and agents in Pau been freed in response to the deal between Gavarni and Vichy authorities to which she had agreed?

Although still difficult, her return journey in the mail sack proved to be far less agonizing than the earlier trip. The train—and flatbed car—were already waiting when she and Boutron arrived at the Spanish custom post, which meant she had to endure only three hours of extreme discomfort instead of nine. Back in France, it took her only a few minutes to recover.

Her spirits rose even more when, on their way back to Marseille, she and Boutron rendezvoused with an Alliance courier, who informed her that Mathilde Bridou had been freed from jail several weeks before, thanks to the intervention of Georges Georges-Picot, Marie-Madeleine's brother-in-law and a colonel in the small post-armistice French army, who pulled strings in Vichy to obtain her mother's release.

Arriving in Marseille on the morning of New Year's Eve, Marie-Madeleine felt a momentary sense of happiness and peace after the chaos and trauma of the previous month. Here, everything was safe and familiar, including the vegetable and fruit warehouse and shop that she had bought the year before as a cover for Alliance activities. It had turned out to be a remarkably profitable business venture as well.

From Madrid, she had brought back a cornucopia of goods—cigarettes, coffee, tea, chocolate, and whisky—for her agents. She also handed over some money to buy food, on the black market if necessary, for a memorable New Year's Eve feast. For one night at least, they would block out the omnipresent fear and danger and simply take pleasure in each other's company.

That night, she glanced around the table in Gabriel Rivière's apartment, just above the warehouse and shop. There was Rivière himself, the burly chief of the Marseille sector, whose idea it had been to buy the produce business. Sitting next to him was his wife, Madeleine, who had become a close friend of Marie-Madeleine's. Also at the table was Émile Audoly, the grain merchant who provided invaluable intelligence about ship movements in the Mediterranean. And of course the ever-ebullient Jean Boutron, who, as Marie-Madeleine recalled, was "the king of the feast."

These beloved colleagues represented the advance guard of Alliance—men who had been at the core of the network since its beginning. But there were others at the table, too—several new agents who had recently joined the fraternity. As they ate and drank together, laughing and offering toasts to each other, "joy," in Marie-Madeleine's words, "took hold of us all."

At the end of the evening, however, reality intruded. Although her mother was now free, her agents arrested in Pau were still in jail. Now Rivière told her that Gavarni wanted to meet her soon to discuss his plan to free them. Gavarni believed, Rivière said, that the network was finished and that it should sever its ties to Britain.

The celebration was over, and the New Year had begun. It was time to return to the daunting task of saving Alliance.

CHAPTER 10

THE RETURN OF
LÉON FAYE

TWO DAYS LATER, FOURCADE SUMMONED GAVARNI TO THE VEGE-
table warehouse. She had resolved not to pass judgment on him until
she heard him explain his actions in Vichy. As she waited for him to
arrive, she thought back to his brief stint as her chief of staff and the
confidence she had placed in him. But she also recalled that immediately after Navarre's arrest, Gavarni had expressed doubts about
whether she as a woman would be fully accepted as Alliance's leader.
He supported her, he said, but others didn't. She asked him if they
objected to taking orders from a woman. He replied that they were
unsure about both her gender and her youth. Now she wondered if
he had been voicing his own skepticism.

Having no idea what to expect from him, Fourcade went to the
warehouse accompanied by Alfred Jassaud, Rivière's young deputy,
who stood guard outside its office door. When Gavarni appeared, Jassaud let him in. Despite her burgeoning doubts, Fourcade could not
forget how he had saved her from arrest, and she warmly embraced
him. It was clear, however, that the warmth was not reciprocated.
Instead of the deference and sympathy that he had shown her before,
his voice had a distinctly hard edge. She sensed he had come to try to
impose his authority on her.

He freely acknowledged that during his meeting with Henri Rollin, he had turned over the 2 million francs and had promised the Vichy official that the network's imprisoned agents would cut their ties with the British. When they were freed, he said, they would begin working for Vichy.

Unable to speak for a moment, Fourcade finally found her voice. She strenuously objected to the idea of betraying the British. Gavarni took out a cigarette, put it in his mouth, then threw it away. He was sick of the British, he yelled. Grabbing her by the shoulders, he declared that if he and she joined forces and worked for Vichy, they could become rich in the process by convincing MI6 to provide them with vast amounts of money.

Trying hard to smother a laugh, an incredulous Fourcade pushed him away, deliberately knocking over a small table to attract the attention of Jassaud. When he rushed in, she told him that Gavarni musn't miss his train back to Vichy and that he should be taken to the station immediately. Gavarni protested that she hadn't yet given him an answer. She said she needed time to consider the implications of his proposition. In the meantime he should tell Rollin that she had agreed to the dissolution of the network and that when Vichy had released all the agents still in jail, they could arrange another meeting. He nodded.

As he headed toward the door, Fourcade asked him why he had handed over the entire 2 million francs to Rollin, pointing out that he probably could have gotten the same result by surrendering just a few thousand. Gavarni didn't answer. Jassaud escorted him out the door and to the station.

Fourcade had no intention of abiding by her pledge to Gavarni. By seemingly agreeing to end the network, she and it had gained a reprieve. But she knew that the respite could not last long and that at some point she herself would be challenged by Vichy. For now, however, her most immediate problem was to find a new chief of staff.

IT TOOK HER ABOUT A WEEK. When she showed up at the vegetable warehouse one morning, Léon Faye was on the doorstep. The last time she had seen him was a year earlier, when, having been recruited by Navarre, he had left for North Africa to head the network's operations there and to embark on his ill-fated plan to organize an anti-Vichy coup.

After he, Navarre, and the coup's other ringleaders had been arrested in May 1941, Faye had languished in jail until the plotters were put on trial in September. Found guilty, he was sentenced to an additional two months and was released in late November. Navarre, meanwhile, received a much more severe sentence in retaliation for his escape from North Africa—two years in prison.

Just before the disaster in Pau, Marie-Madeleine had received a letter from Faye informing her of his release. He went on to say that his role in the failed coup had sparked the interest of a large number of his anti-German colleagues in the air force, who were eager to join him in fighting back against their country's occupiers. He, however, was not sure how to translate that interest into action. Caught up in the chaos of the arrests in Pau, Marie-Madeleine had destroyed his letter to prevent Vichy officials from finding it and then put it out of her mind. Once she reached Madrid, however, she was sorry she had done so, belatedly realizing that Faye and his friends could provide the reinforcements that Alliance so desperately needed.

And now, like magic, he was here. Although he had enticed Navarre to join the mutiny, thus setting in motion the cascade of problems now plaguing Alliance, Marie-Madeleine's heart skipped a beat when she saw him. His dark, unruly hair contained strands of gray, but other than that, his ordeal in jail seemed to have left little mark on him. He flashed a broad grin and embraced her.

Trying to hide her delight, she said, "At last! Is this the soonest you could get here?" He answered in the same playful vein: "I know—it's very bad of me." He spun a fanciful story of having just returned from a grand tour of Italy, North Africa, and the châteaux of France. Then, turning serious, he told her that he had promised Navarre after their trial he would return to see her once his sentence was completed. He wanted to take her to safety in Algiers, where friends of his would hide her.

When she asked what would happen to the network if she accepted his invitation, he said he'd been informed that Alliance no longer existed. In response, she invited him to join her for the day.

Her first visitors that morning were Ernest Siegrist and Georges Guillot, two Paris policemen who had been part of another anti-Nazi intelligence network, based in the French capital, that had been smashed by the Gestapo. Wanting to continue the fight, they had been put in touch with Alliance, which had asked MI6 to check them out. Marie-Madeleine told them that London had confirmed their story and that she would take them on as security men in Marseille. One of them would forge identity papers while the other would guard the headquarters and its agents.

The morning's next visitor was Denise Centore, a short, stocky professional historian whom Marie-Madeleine had just hired as her assistant. Centore complained about problems with the latest batch of invisible ink that had been dispatched from MI6 and brought in by Jean Boutron in his diplomatic bags. She showed Fourcade a recent message from an agent—a piece of light brown wrapping paper covered with dark brown writing that described German antiaircraft sites in Boulogne. The heat, Centore said, brought out the writing. After she explained to Faye how Alliance used innocent-looking parcels from the occupied zone to smuggle in information written in invisible ink, Marie-Madeleine instructed her to warn London about the problem.

Next to arrive was a courier bringing in copies of the radio messages sent that day from Marseille to London by Émile Audoly. One of them reported how an Alliance agent at the port had managed to open packing cases that ostensibly were the property of the German armistice commission. Inside were rifles and other war matériel destined for General Erwin Rommel's Afrika Korps, which was fighting the British in Libya. The message to MI6 included the sailing date of the ships carrying the supplies. Thanks to the intelligence, Marie-Madeleine later wrote, British bombers intercepted and destroyed the convoy.

One after another, the parade of visitors continued. Finally, early in the afternoon, Faye asked for a temporary halt. Fourcade had made her point: The network was alive and well, he acknowledged. Now he and she needed to get something to eat—and to talk. He suggested one of the black-market bars on the Canebière, but, fearful of being recognized, she said no. He finally took her to his room at a nearby hotel, where he laid before her a feast of bread and foie gras—gifts from a former air force colleague who had turned to farming in the Dordogne after the 1940 armistice.

As they enjoyed the foie gras and a bottle of Monbazillac, a fine dessert wine that also came from Faye's friend, she told him about the network's activities since Navarre's arrest. She described the raid in Pau, her meeting with Keyser in Madrid, and the program they had mapped out, including the new aircraft pickup operations and the urgent need for intelligence to help the British in the Battle of the Atlantic and in its struggle to close the Germans' Mediterranean Sea routes.

When Faye asked what her greatest concern was, she replied that she was in desperate need of new people who could rebuild the existing sectors and create new ones. He was silent for a moment, and then, as she hoped, he suggested himself and his former air force colleagues—about a dozen at first but, he assured her, soon to be followed by many more.

Marie-Madeleine was thrilled with the idea of his rejoining the network, along with a throng of new recruits, but she had to be extremely careful about how she handled the situation. She needed to make it clear to this assertive, charismatic officer that although she would love to have him, she would continue to lead Alliance, while he would act as her deputy. In making her pitch, she focused more on the responsibilities they would share than on his subordinate position, noting that if she were captured, he would ensure the survival of the network by continuing as its leader.

Then, indirectly, she mentioned her greatest concern about his plan: Would these friends of his, some of them senior officers whose world was totally male-oriented, be willing to take orders from a woman? Faye resolved her dilemma with a laugh and the remark: "I'm prepared to."

By the time she and Faye returned to the warehouse, it was dark, snowing, and bitterly cold. But warmed by her sense of triumph, Marie-Madeleine was unperturbed by the dreadful weather. Her euphoria lasted until she saw the stricken expression on Gabriel Rivière's face. He stood up, held her by the shoulders, and said she needed to be brave. Then he told her that Henri Schaerrer had been executed by the Germans.

According to Rivière, Schaerrer had been executed on November 13, 1941, four months after his arrest by the Gestapo near the submarine base outside Bordeaux. Rivière, who had been recruited as Alliance's Marseille chief by Schaerrer, said with a ferocity that Marie-Madeleine had seldom heard from him that Schaerrer would be avenged. She shook her head. Schaerrer would not want that, she said. She added, "We must carry on."

At the moment, however, she was incapable of doing anything. From the day she learned of Schaerrer's arrest, she had feared this would be the outcome. But she was unprepared for the devastation she felt when faced with the reality. It wasn't just that Schaerrer was the first Alliance agent to die. It was the loss of the man himself—this exuberant, fun-loving, incautious whirlwind of energy who had been there from the beginning and had done so much to breathe life into the network. Her grief was matched by a sense of guilt for putting him in harm's way.

Although she wanted to be alone, Rivière insisted she share that evening's meal with the rest of the Alliance staff, along with their tearful sharing of memories of their fallen friend. Later that night, she caught a tram to her apartment on the outskirts of Marseille. As she climbed the steep stone steps leading to her building, she prayed to the Virgin Mary for help in dealing with Schaerrer's death. She had no idea how terrible it would be, she murmured. She begged to be given the strength to continue.

In the darkness of her apartment, she opened the shutters and gazed out the window at the churning sea below her. Maybe she should cross it and go to Algiers, as Faye had first suggested. Maybe she should shut the network down and save its members from Schaerrer's fate. Her sleep that night was filled with nightmares.

She was awakened the following morning by a pounding at the door; when she opened it, she saw that the sun was already high in the sky. Standing before her was Marc Mesnard, the agent who handled Alliance's financial and other administrative matters. The staff was worried about her, he said, and had sent him to find her. She asked if he had heard about Schaerrer. Of course, he replied: It was awful, but she needed to focus on those who were still living. He urged her to get dressed and return with him to headquarters. She did so. She would mourn Schaerrer for the rest of her life, but Mesnard was right: She must think of the others and carry on.

AN HOUR OR SO LATER, Fourcade stood in front of her staff and told them that she had just appointed Léon Faye as her chief of staff. Looking out at her agents, she did her best to conceal her nervousness. Although most knew who Faye was, they had never worked with him directly. She also knew that her announcement put an end to the hope held by some of them that Navarre would somehow find his way back to the network. With her appointment of Faye, she was making it clear that she, and she alone, controlled Alliance. In an effort to reassure them, she added that it was Navarre himself who had asked Faye to come to their rescue.

Hearing that, the crowd, which had been silent until then, burst into scattered applause and then surrounded Faye to congratulate him. After sending out messages to Alliance's other sectors announcing Faye's appointment, Fourcade joined him on a journey around the free zone to begin the job of melding the survivors of the crippled network with its new members.

Their first stop was Pau, where Fourcade introduced Faye to Maurice Coustenoble and the other members of her team who had been captured there the previous November. They had just been freed from jail in Vichy, with the proviso that they were now to be intelligence agents for the Vichy government.

She ordered them to go into hiding and added that after they had recovered from their ordeal she would assign them to new sectors. She wanted Coustenoble to join her in Marseille in his old role as her adjutant, but he seemed wary about the idea and distant toward her. When he said he hoped she was still in charge, she realized that he was upset about Faye and his new position, and feared he was taking over. She assured Coustenoble that was not the case, making it clear she had missed him and wanted him back by her side. With that, his coolness vanished, and he began to call her "little one" again.

After Pau, Fourcade and Faye traveled to Toulouse, where he introduced her to some of the men he had recruited, among them Colonel Édouard Kauffmann, who had provided the foie gras and Monbazillac she had so enjoyed in Marseille the week before. A graduate of Saint-Cyr, Kauffmann had distinguished himself in the fighting at Verdun in World War I, then switched to the air force after the war, serving in Morocco and Indochina. In the 1940 battle for France, he had commanded air force units assigned to an army motorized division. Demobilized after the armistice, he had taken up residence at his country property in the Dordogne, where he cultivated artichokes and, according to Faye, "was thoroughly bored."

When Fourcade and Faye offered him the job of rebuilding Alliance's Dordogne sector, which had been destroyed in the November Vichy raid, Kauffmann accepted with alacrity. He told them he'd have things running well in no time. And, he added, he had no problems with a woman as leader of the network.

Another pilot recruited by Faye was Maurice de MacMahon, the Duke of Magenta, a colorful young flying ace who had been a member of the air force acrobatics team before the war and whose pedigree was arguably the most illustrious of any Alliance agent. His great-great-great-grandfather, John MacMahon, was an Irish doctor who immigrated to France, married a French noblewoman, and was given a title by Louis XV in 1750. John's son became aide-de-camp to the Marquis de Lafayette in America's Revolutionary War, and his grandson, Patrice MacMahon (Maurice's grandfather), was a Crimean War hero, a marshal in the French army, and the first president of France's Third Republic.

Fourcade had met Maurice de MacMahon in Morocco when she lived there in the late 1920s with her husband. She found him elegant, dashing, and audacious. She was equally enchanted by his wife, Marguerite, who also joined the network and who was described by Marie-Madeleine as "tall, willowy, and radiant: she was born a princess and looked like one in everything she said or did."

After the armistice, MacMahon had become a key official of the French Red Cross and, in that role, was given an *ausweis,* the German identity document that allowed him to cross at will from the free zone to the occupied zone. In the summer of 1942, Fourcade would put him in charge of the network's activities in the occupied zone.

Having added Kauffmann, MacMahon, and a dozen other airmen to the Alliance fold, Faye went out looking for more. From the day he became Marie-Madeleine's deputy, he was constantly on the move. Sleeping no more than a few hours a night, he crisscrossed France, recruiting and training new agents and creating new sectors. Thanks to his obvious leadership skills, coupled with his notoriety as the main orchestrator of the failed coup, he was regarded as a hero by many of the young operatives he brought in. But he always made it clear to them and others that Fourcade was *la patronne.* Officially, that was true: She was the head, he the deputy. Unofficially, however, they ran Alliance together, although when they disagreed, he accepted her word as final. Both personally and professionally, no one was closer to her during the war years.

As Alliance regrouped and expanded, its operations spread out across Marseille. While its local sector, run by Gabriel Rivière, continued to operate from the vegetable warehouse and shop, its national headquarters was located in a sprawling apartment on the city's Corniche, a picturesque roadway that overlooked the sea. A nearby villa was used to house visiting agents. Fourcade also bought a bar at the foot of the steps of the Saint Charles railway station, to serve, like the vegetable warehouse, as a cover. Managed by an agent named Émile

Hédin, the bar not only provided drinks for the public but also was a place where operatives and couriers on the move could leave messages and receive instructions. Ernest Siegrist and Georges Guillot, the two recently hired policemen from Paris, provided the security for the entire complex in Marseille, which now included a dozen letterboxes, transmitter sites, and hideouts.

After all the chaos of the previous six months, the network and its operations were not only back on an even keel but thriving. The Marseille-Madrid-London radio link was working well, and, every other week, Jean Boutron brought in other essential material from London in his mailbags.

But that sense of well-being did not last long. Once again, the network found itself at risk. This time, however, the problem was not the result of an agent's negligence or betrayal. This time the fault lay with Marie-Madeleine Fourcade herself.

CHAPTER 11

A GAME OF WITS

T HE ORIGIN OF ALLIANCE'S LATEST CRISIS COULD BE TRACED TO the previous November, when, in her rush to flee the Vichy net and travel to Madrid, Fourcade had left behind all her network records at the home of the couple who had briefly sheltered her in Tarbes.

The papers, deposited under the coal bin in the couple's cellar, contained information about the organization of Alliance, a chronology of its operations, and various messages to and from London, all in code. Jean Boutron, whom she'd consulted about what to do with them, later acknowledged that to keep such confidential and compromising notes was courting trouble, but worth the risk as long as they could be safely hidden. He admitted that it was not prudent to leave them in Tarbes with people whom neither he nor Fourcade knew well. At the same time, he added, it would have been far more dangerous to take the papers with them in the car to Spain.

When Fourcade sent an agent to retrieve the records after she returned from Madrid, the couple were evasive, telling her emissary that they had given them to another friend for safekeeping and would return them as soon as possible. In all the furor over Gavarni's machinations and Faye's reappearance, she had put off further efforts to get them back.

Thanks to a surprise visit from her brother-in-law, Colonel Georges Georges-Picot, in early March 1942, she realized the folly of her procrastination. Although Georges-Picot was a loyal Pétain supporter and had not followed Marie-Madeleine and other members of her family into resistance work, he had maintained a close relationship with his headstrong young sister-in-law. But when he confronted her on that chilly March morning, he showed few signs of affection. "Who is ASO 43?" he snapped. "Who is PLU 122?"

Marie-Madeleine was stunned. He was referring to the code names of Jean Boutron and another agent, Admiral Pierre Barjot, a former submarine commander whom Boutron had recruited in Marseille. Where could Georges have gotten such information? Almost immediately, she figured out the answer: from the papers she had left in Tarbes. She had rebuilt her broken network, and now, through her carelessness, it was once again in danger of collapsing.

After Gavarni's meeting with Henri Rollin, the head of the Surveillance du Territoire in Vichy, Rollin had ordered a more extensive investigation into Alliance, which led to the handing over of Marie-Madeleine's records by the couple who had hidden her. An old acquaintance of Georges-Picot, Rollin passed on to him the fact that Marie-Madeleine was involved in suspicious activities with England and advised him to bring her to Vichy to explain herself.

She had lost her mind, her brother-in-law exclaimed. For once she was going to follow his orders and accompany him by train to Vichy that evening. Marie-Madeleine, however, needed time to think about this bombshell—and to warn Faye, Boutron, Barjot, and other top Alliance operatives, as well as MI6. She asked Georges-Picot to give her two days. Then, she promised, she would go with him to Vichy. He grudgingly agreed, warning her that if she reneged, she would end up in prison and he could do nothing more for her.

Fourcade immediately convened what she called a council of war with Faye, Gabriel Rivière, Émile Audoly, and other key operatives in Marseille. Both Boutron and Barjot, who was now in Algiers, were alerted, as were MI6 officials, who urged her not to go. But she saw no alternative. Faye would follow her, ready to warn the rest of the network if she was unable to talk herself out of this latest predicament.

Two days later, accompanied by her brother-in-law, Fourcade was on her way to Vichy. As the train chugged along, she agonized again over how negligent she had been. If the network survived, she knew that at the very least, she would have to change the code names of its operatives. Her thoughts whirling, she closed her eyes, and while she dozed she had a dream in which she envisioned Alliance members as animals who were being hunted down by other predators.

In her mind, she began to assign animal names to agents. Maurice Coustenoble would be Tiger; Gabriel Rivière, Wolf; Émile Audoly, Fox; Jean Boutron, Bull. She herself would be Hedgehog. When she alighted from the train in Vichy, she saw Faye leaving a rear car and following her and Georges-Picot. He would be Eagle, she decided—"a sharp-eyed, fearless high flyer."

HENRI ROLLIN, FOURCADE'S ADVERSARY in Vichy, was a man of many contradictions. A career naval intelligence officer, he had worked closely with MI6 before the war and had stayed in contact with Stewart Menzies, the agency's head, after it began. Rollin was also noted as a staunch opponent of anti-Semitism in the French military and in 1939 had written a book that questioned the authenticity of the notorious *Protocols of the Elders of Zion,* a fraudulent document purporting to be the proceedings of an international Jewish conference plotting worldwide domination. After the German occupation of France, Nazi officials banned Rollin's book, and all remaining copies were seized and destroyed.

Yet at the same time, as chief of the Surveillance du Territoire, Rollin had led Vichy's crackdown against Alliance and other resistance groups in the free zone, as well as against anti-German forces in French military intelligence. He was in fact playing a double game. Loyal to Pétain and Darlan, Rollin and others in Vichy had persuaded Darlan to adopt a more sophisticated strategy in his suppression of dissidents. While remaining ruthless in crushing violent Communist

resistance, they said, Vichy should try to buy off more moderate re-
sistants, promising them protection from persecution and imprisonment if they agreed to cooperate with the government. Groups like
Alliance would even be allowed to provide the British with selected
bits of intelligence, as long as they were given to Vichy first.

Darlan liked the idea. By the spring of 1942, even though the
Nazis still had the upper hand in the war, a German victory was no
longer a foregone conclusion. Britain and the Soviet Union continued to hold out, while the United States, which had entered the war
in December 1941, was fast mobilizing its vast war machine. Ever the
opportunist, Darlan wanted to keep his options open. If Germany
started losing the war, it might serve him and Vichy well to have established various secret channels with the Allies. And even if the plan
did not succeed, the mere fact that Rollin had held discussions with
resistance leaders would serve to compromise those leaders in the eyes
of the British and members of their organizations. Gavarni was
one of the first to fall into the trap. Now Rollin would try his campaign of seduction on Fourcade.

She, for her part, entered his office determined to be the winner in
this cat-and-mouse game. As she sat down, joined by her brother-in-
law, she studied the short, thickset, graying man standing before her.
Rollin went on the offensive immediately, pointing accusingly at papers scattered all over his desk. They were, Marie-Madeleine realized,
her notes from Tarbes.

"We're going to arrest ASO 43 tomorrow morning," Rollin said.
"It's Jean Boutron, isn't it?"

Fourcade acknowledged she knew Boutron; he had been a merchant seaman for the same shipping company that had employed her
father. But she denied that Boutron had ever worked for her network.

"Then who is ASO?" Rollin asked. Fourcade parried the question, saying she had no intention of giving any names to him. She had
come to Vichy, she said, to see if she could find any "patriots" there.
Rollin retorted that he and others in Vichy were far more patriotic
than she, adding that he wanted to get rid of the Germans, too, but

not in alliance with the British. In response, Fourcade said he knew very well that her network had collapsed and that she no longer had any contact with Britain.

After another hour of questioning that went nowhere, Rollin abruptly broke off the session and ordered her to return the following day. "By the way," he said as she prepared to leave, "your friend the vegetable dealer is going to have an interesting awakening tomorrow morning." Fourcade hurried back to her hotel to warn Faye that ST officers were planning to arrest Gabriel Rivière the next day. Faye in turn dashed to a phone to tell Rivière of the raid and to order him to remove the transmitter and all other incriminating material from the shop.

After a restless night worrying about Rivière's fate and that of Alliance, Fourcade returned to Rollin's office. She found that the stern, threatening man she had encountered the day before had transformed himself into an avuncular, fatherly figure who invited her to have lunch with him and his wife at his country house.

There, Rollin seemed a different man, Fourcade remembered. His wife, a Russian Jew, expressed sympathy and understanding for Fourcade's anti-German views and activities and said to her husband that he should leave her alone. Appearing to yield to his wife's arguments, Rollin told Fourcade that his purpose was not to defeat her network but to make sure it was working in the best interests of the country. She was well aware that all of this—the lunch in the country, the display of sympathy by Rollin and his wife—were tactics meant to disarm her and to get her to do what he wanted. Nonetheless, she couldn't help liking him.

At the end of the lunch, he told her that her duty now was to her children. As long as she accepted that duty, he would protect her, even though that protection might not last long. He said that Darlan's position in Vichy was not as strong as she might think and that Pierre Laval, supported by Berlin, was angling to return to power. If he succeeded, Marie-Madeleine and the other resisters would lose any hope of protection.

That night, she decided to accept Rollin's proposal. She would assure him that her days as a spymaster were over and that if Alliance was ever resurrected, its new master would be Vichy. Of course, she meant none of it. Because she was a woman, she knew Rollin under-estimated her—a miscalculation on which she was determined to capitalize.

Rollin, meanwhile, had summoned Gabriel Rivière and Jean Boutron to Vichy for questioning. Thanks to Fourcade's warning, Rivière had had plenty of time to prepare himself for the interroga-tion. Yes, he told Rollin, he knew Marie-Madeleine Fourcade. She was an acquaintance who had lent him money to buy his vegetable business. When Rollin asked about his reported involvement in her resistance network, Rivière was aghast. Heaven forbid, he said, he would never get mixed up in anything like that! What about the use of radio transmitting sets? Again, Rivière was horror-stricken. Of course not, he declared. That would be sheer suicide. Was he involved in any resistance work? Heavens, no—he would never do something so dangerous! When Rollin's agents had arrested Rivière, they found nothing incriminating in his warehouse and shop. After several hours of protesting his innocence, Rivière was finally let go. He traveled back to Marseille that night.

Boutron was not as fortunate. For weeks, he had been aware that he was being followed in Madrid and other Spanish cities to which he traveled as part of his duties as Vichy's deputy naval attaché. Although he didn't know whether the men who shadowed him were French or German, he concluded that his cover had been blown.

When ordered to report to Rollin in Vichy, Boutron decided to end the charade. He denied that he was a member of Alliance but acknowledged he had been sending information to London about German military operations in the free zone. His action, he said, had been taken on his own initiative. Responding to accusations that he had handed over state secrets to the enemy, he said such a charge was ridiculous, pointing out that his reports on the German military in no way harmed the national security of France. In addition, he insisted, Britain was not France's enemy.

For nearly a month, the French admiralty, which was eager to keep quiet the fact that it had a pro-British agent in its ranks, debated the question of what to do with Boutron. In the end, it imposed the relatively lenient sentence that Rollin had recommended: separation from the navy, reduction in rank, and, instead of prison, an indefinite internment at a sixteenth-century fort in the Alps, where his fellow internees would be Communist activists and black marketeers.

Fourcade sent Boutron a message promising that Alliance agents in Grenoble would help him escape, although it might take some time to arrange. After agreeing to Rollin's terms for herself, she was free to go. As she left Rollin's office, she casually asked him about the 2 million francs that Gavarni had surrendered to him. "Rubbish," he snorted: Gavarni had given him only 80,000 francs.

Before she boarded a train for the Côte d'Azur and a reunion with her family, she tracked Gavarni down and told him about her meeting with Rollin. Now that she had reached her own agreement with Vichy, she said, she had no further need of his services. When he feebly accused her of ingratitude, she remarked that he had no reason to complain, given the fortune in francs that he had amassed for himself. His face turned a sickly green. She turned on her heel, confident that she needed to fear no more acts of betrayal from him.

ACCOMPANIED BY HER EVER-VIGILANT brother-in-law, Marie-Madeleine traveled to her mother's house overlooking the sea, near Mougins. She spent several weeks in that peaceful setting, ostentatiously cooking, tending the garden, playing with her children, mending their clothes, and engaging in other Vichy-approved "feminine" activities.

But that did not mean she had given up her leadership of Alliance. Once she was sure she was not being shadowed by Rollin's agents, she clandestinely reestablished contact with her headquarters and asked Maurice Coustenoble to act as her emissary between the Côte d'Azur and Marseille. During Coustenoble's first visit to her mother's house, Marie-Madeleine told him that in order to improve security and avoid the disasters of the previous year, several steps would have to be taken immediately: decentralizing the network, increasing the autonomy of individual sectors, and creating independent services for radio transmission, air operations, and sending mail. She also ordered Marseille to implement her decision to use animal code names for agents and sent, via Coustenoble, a list of names she had chosen thus far.

With the many problems facing Alliance that demanded urgent attention, she was eager to leave the Côte d'Azur to take up her work, but she was concerned that if she returned too soon to Marseille, Rollin would discover that the network was not only still alive but flourishing. A family emergency provided a solution to her problem. During Marie-Madeleine's stay at home with her family, a doctor had told her that her nine-year-old daughter, Béatrice, who suffered from a hip displacement like her mother, needed an operation to help correct the condition; the surgery, he added, would require a long period of convalescence. She was given the name of an eminent surgeon in Toulouse, a Dr. Charry, who reportedly was the only doctor in southwestern France who could perform the operation. She took Béatrice to see him, and he agreed to do it.

The surgery was a success, and Marie-Madeleine was allowed to stay in Béatrice's room at Charry's clinic while the child recovered. The room was a large one, with enough furniture in which to hide the voluminous diagrams, maps, and organizational charts that Marie-Madeleine created as she sat by Béatrice's bedside.

While Léon Faye ran Alliance's day-to-day operations in Marseille, Marie-Madeleine plotted its future. She worked on melding the new agents whom Faye had brought in with the network's remaining old hands. She also made plans for resuscitating bases that had been entirely blown and plugging the holes with newcomers. She examined the strengths and weaknesses of the individual sectors and their chiefs and devised ways that she hoped would enhance the strengths and minimize the weaknesses. She dealt with endless logistical details—authorizing a transmitter to be sent to one place and more money to another, and setting up new bases in Bordeaux, Brest, and Strasbourg, among other locations. In addition, she directed Faye to send to Toulouse any agents he thought she should meet.

During the several weeks that Béatrice and her mother spent at the clinic, Marie-Madeleine did her best to hide the documents on which she had been working before Dr. Charry and his nurses came into the room to tend to Béatrice. On a couple of occasions, however, Charry entered unexpectedly to find papers piled all over the floor.

He asked Marie-Madeleine if she was writing a book. Actually, she said, she was doing some research for one. Charry stared at her for a moment, and she realized he had figured out what she was doing. But he said nothing. The next day, he ordered that a large table be brought into the room, on which she could spread out her papers, and asked if he could be of any further help. She replied that she would greatly appreciate it if he would allow her to have visitors for the rest of her and Béatrice's stay. Charry readily agreed.

At one point, he told Marie-Madeleine that he'd like to take a more active role in her resistance activities, but she gently declined his offer. He had already provided an essential service by sheltering her, she said, adding that his work as a surgeon was far more important to France and its people than his joining her network.

Although she did not enlist Dr. Charry during her stay in Toulouse, Marie-Madeleine did not refrain from recruiting others. Toulouse—the fourth-largest city in France, with one of the oldest universities in Europe—was an important new base of operations for Alliance. To head the new sector, she named a married couple— Mouchou Damm, a local engineer of Polish descent, and his wife, Nelly. The Damms' teenage son would serve as their adjutant. Soon their home would also house a radio transmitter, along with an operator sent by MI6 from Britain.

The Damms were just one of dozens of married couples who worked for Marie-Madeleine and Alliance over the nearly five years of the network's existence. Others included Gabriel Rivière and his wife, Madeleine, and the Duke of Magenta and his spouse, Marguerite. Sometimes whole families were involved, among them eight close relatives of Maurice Gillet, the fearless leader of the network's sector in Brest, a key seaport in Brittany.

A police superintendent named Jean Philippe was another important addition to the Toulouse operation. Philippe had many informants in the area who in the past had provided him with intelligence about criminal activities. He now instructed them to focus on ferreting out information about German military operations. He also used his position to prevent the arrest of a number of resistance fighters and to provide false papers to Jews.

By the end of the war, more than 130 additional French policemen would join Philippe as Alliance operatives—proof that the much-hated French police forces, who were seen, quite rightly, as doing the Germans' dirty work for them, had their fair share of members who passionately opposed the idea of being Nazi collaborators.

AFTER TWO MONTHS IN the hospital, Béatrice was judged well enough to leave, and Fourcade rented a chalet in the foothills of the Pyrenees where her daughter could complete her convalescence in the company of Béatrice's brother, grandmother, and other close relatives. For the little girl, the idea of another long separation from her mother, after so many months of being together, was devastating. On the day they left Toulouse, both mother and daughter were in floods of tears. More than two years would pass before Béatrice saw Fourcade again.

Once again feeling profound guilt over her separation from her children, Fourcade returned to Marseille in June 1942. From the moment she arrived, she could see the progress that had been made in the reconstruction and expansion of the network. Her first stop was the Saint Charles bar, which was humming with activity. After meeting Faye there, she followed him back to the Alliance headquarters, a house at the highest point of the Corniche, a roadway that bordered the sea, with a panoramic view of the water. When they arrived, a servant in a white jacket appeared, bearing a tray of coffee and liqueurs. Faye introduced the man as Albert, a security man who doubled as a cook and butler. After taking a coffee and rejecting the liqueurs, Fourcade remarked tartly about how nice it was to have all these little luxuries, but what about the work of collecting intelligence?

With a grin, Faye pointed to a desk across the room, on which several tall piles of paper were neatly stacked. They contained messages and queries from London and information from the sectors. Combing through them, she realized that the network's day-to-day operations under Faye were very much under control. Indeed, the summer of 1942 marked the apogee of Alliance's wartime activity. Thanks in large part to Faye's assiduous recruitment work, the network now numbered almost a thousand agents and had sectors in virtually every region in France. Although the Paris sector was still being rebuilt, there were strong operations in, among other places, Normandy, Brittany, Vichy, the Dordogne, Lyon and the rest of the Rhône Valley, and Grenoble and the Alps.

Particularly vital was the information being gathered by Alliance spies in Marseille, Nice, and other locations on the Mediterranean coast of France and Italy. Such intelligence was of critical importance to the British, whose troops were then engaged in a desperate struggle with General Erwin Rommel's Afrika Korps in Libya. There were also rumors of an upcoming Allied invasion of North Africa in the fall of 1942, which, if true, would require as much information as possible about the strength of German, Italian, and Vichy French forces in the region.

Virtually every day, Alliance's headquarters was inundated with queries from MI6 about the movement of German and Italian land, sea, and air forces from their bases on the Mediterranean coast to North Africa. Émile Audoly, who ran the network's agents in Marseille, was in charge of supplying many if not most of the answers. According to Fourcade, Audoly and his operatives never missed anything to do with the shipping that went in and out of Marseille, such as German raiders sailing under neutral flags or consignments of arms and material loaded under French commercial labels but intended for the Afrika Korps. Thanks to Audoly's intelligence, the Royal Air Force and Royal Navy were able to intercept and destroy much of the shipping on which Alliance reported.

The network's sector in Nice, run by Colonel Charles Bernis, also provided invaluable information about the Mediterranean. Bernis,

Alliance's first supervisor of intelligence, had conquered his doubts about Fourcade's ability to lead the network and had been in charge of its operations on the Côte d'Azur for almost a year. He had reinforced its strength by working closely with an antifascist network just across the border in Italy, which gave him information about Italian troop, naval, and air force operations. Shortly after Fourcade returned to Marseille, Bernis passed on a report from his Italian colleagues that several of Mussolini's air force squadrons were about to be dispatched to Libya to reinforce the Afrika Korps. A day or so later, MI6 reported to her that the Italian planes had been intercepted.

Less well known than the agents but just as important to Alliance's success were its couriers, who crisscrossed the country carrying transmitters, diagrams, maps, photographs, and other documents between Marseille and the various sectors. They tended to be people whose occupations required them to travel, such as truck drivers and salesmen, and who thus were eligible for an *ausweis*. The risks they faced were enormous. Unlike the network's agents, couriers did their work out in the open, carrying incriminating information and material on trains and other public forms of transportation, all of which were heavily patrolled by German and French security officials.

In the spring of 1942, Fourcade needed a courier to transport several transmitters to the occupied zone. A teenager named Robert Lynen, who had just started working at the Marseille headquarters, volunteered for the job. As it happened, the nineteen-year-old Lynen had one of the most recognizable faces in France. A freckle-faced redhead, he had been known in the 1930s as the best and most popular child actor in French cinema. His first movie, *Poil de Carotte* (*Carrot Top*), which he made in 1932 at the age of twelve, was an international success, spawning Robert Lynen fan clubs across the Continent and as far away as Japan.

When the Nazis occupied France, Lynen, who had starred in nine films since his first hit, refused offers from a German film company to continue to make movies aimed at French audiences but under its auspices. Instead he became involved in resistance work in Marseille, where he came to the attention of Fourcade and her network.

ROBERT LYNEN
IN HIS ROLE IN
THE HIT FILM
POIL DE CAROTTE
(CARROT TOP)

Lynen, who had recently agreed to take part in a theatrical tour across France, said he would transport the transmitters and secret documents from one city to another in his costume trunk. He told Fourcade that his celebrity would be an advantage rather than a negative: No one would ever believe that the famous "Carrot Top" was a spy. It would be, he said with a grin, his finest role.

CHAPTER 12

"AN UNDISPUTED LEADER"

BUOYED AS SHE WAS BY ALLIANCE'S RESURGENCE, FOURCADE HAD very little time to savor its success. By the summer of 1942, Nazi officials in France, increasingly infuriated by what they saw as Vichy's vacillating policy toward resisters, had begun to strike back hard.

Returning to Marseille in early July after visiting several of the network's sectors, Fourcade was startled to see Léon Faye and three other Alliance agents positioned along the length of the platform as her train pulled into Saint Charles station. As she stepped down from the train, Faye was the first to spot her. Grabbing her arm, he hustled her to a car, which was waiting at the bottom of the station's steps with its engine running. As it raced off, he exclaimed, "They're after you again! And this time the Boches are handling the job."

In the late spring of 1942, German officials had pressured Admiral Darlan to step down as head of the Vichy government and engineered the reinstatement of their puppet, Pierre Laval. As the car carrying Marie-Madeleine sped through Marseille, she recalled Henri Rollin's warning that if Laval returned to power, she and other resisters would lose all hope of Vichy protection. Although a collaborationist himself, Darlan had shown occasional signs of ambivalence. Laval demonstrated no such vacillation: He was Hitler's man and proud of it.

One of his first acts after taking over the reins of government again was to push Rollin aside as chief of the Surveillance du Territoire.

During that same period, the SS in occupied France had wrested complete control of policing and security from the German military, thereby winning its ongoing power struggle with the Abwehr, the army's intelligence and counterintelligence operation. SS authorities regarded the Abwehr as being too weak and lenient in its dealings with French resisters. Now, with the SS unequivocally in charge, the Nazis set out to crush anti-German activity throughout the entire country.

Under the armistice, German security agents and police were barred from entering the free zone. In fact, they had been infiltrating the area since the French capitulated. Until mid-1942, most Vichy officials had closed their eyes to the fact, although some rebels in the government, notably army counterintelligence officials, continued to track the Germans down and arrest them. But with Laval back in power, Vichy now actively assisted the German security services in their hunt for resisters.

The Germans had long complained about the fast-growing number of radio transmitters in Vichy France being used by the resistance to communicate with the Allies. With Laval's approval, German officials in Paris dispatched more than 280 agents from the SS and Abwehr to the south, bringing with them cars and vans with direction-finding equipment to track the transmitters down. Vichy officials provided the German intruders with French identity cards and local license plates for their vehicles. The Germans were also allowed the use of Vichy police headquarters to send their reports to Hugo Geissler, the Gestapo's chief representative in the free zone.

In yet another egregious infringement of the armistice, dozens of Surveillance du Territoire agents were ordered to accompany the Germans and, under Abwehr and Gestapo supervision, to make the actual arrests of resistance members. When a French army counterintelligence official complained to his superior about the order, he was told that if Vichy didn't do what the Germans wanted, Hitler had made it clear he would occupy the free zone.

The main focus of the German dragnet was resistance activity in Marseille, Pau, Lyon, and Vichy—all areas in which Alliance had transmitters. After whisking Fourcade away from the Marseille station, Faye told her that he had ordered the network's radio operators in those sectors to drastically reduce their transmission times and to repeatedly change frequencies while sending messages, in an effort to prevent the Germans' direction-finding operation from pinpointing their locations.

Faye also insisted that it was not safe for Fourcade to return to her apartment in Marseille. When she protested, he was adamant, saying he had already found her another place to stay. She was driven to a house outside Le Lavandou, a small seaside village in the rocky, wooded headlands of the Côte d'Azur, some sixty miles east of Marseille. There she took refuge in a small villa surrounded by pine trees and overlooking the sea. It was owned by Marguerite Brouillet, a social worker whose husband was with the French army in North Africa and who served as an occasional courier for Alliance.

As was her practice wherever she went, Marie-Madeleine transformed Le Lavandou into an Alliance outpost. She enlisted Brouillet's two teenage sons and other local residents, among them a doctor, a schoolmaster, and a wine grower, in the network's cause. Couriers traveled daily between Alliance's Marseille headquarters and her new hideaway, carrying messages and documents.

MARGUERITE BROUILLET WAS THE LATEST in a widening circle of women whom Marie-Madeleine welcomed into Alliance and whom she considered friends. In the French resistance as a whole, women played crucial roles. Their effectiveness, in France and throughout occupied Europe, owed much to the Nazis' stereotypical view of them. Coming from a traditional, conservative society themselves, the Germans saw women chiefly in their conventional domestic roles as wives and mothers and, at least early in the war, rarely suspected them of being spies or saboteurs.

As the only female resistance chief in France, Marie-Madeleine made a special effort to surround herself with other strong women. Although Alliance began as an almost exclusively male organization, women accounted for some twenty percent of its agents over the five years of its existence. Like their male counterparts, they represented all classes of society, from maids and laundresses to Paris socialites.

Among Marie-Madeleine's female agents was Jeannie Rousseau, an impish, elegant young Parisienne whose reports on the development of Germany's terror weapons—the V-1 flying bombs and the V-2 rockets—turned out to be one of the greatest Allied intelligence achievements of the war. Another was Jeanne Berthomier, a high-level official in the Ministry of Public Works in Paris, whose access to top-secret information about the Germans' presence in the occupied zone proved invaluable to Alliance and the British. And then there was a young dressmaker (code-named Shrimp) who repaired submariners' life vests at the German base at Saint-Nazaire in Brittany. In the course of her work, she learned which submarines were coming in for repairs and which were headed out to sea. She passed on the information to Alliance, which in turn transmitted it to MI6.

Women also were numerous at Alliance's headquarters in Marseille. Its administrative head was the former historian Denise Centore, who oversaw the comings and goings of couriers and agents and monitored the flow of mail. In the spring of 1942, Marie-Madeleine brought in an intrepid nineteen-year-old blonde named Monique Bontinck—code-named Ermine—as her personal courier and assistant.

The eldest of seven children, Bontinck came from Doue, a village in northern France. She was strongly anti-German as a child, thanks to the stories her Belgian grandfather told her about German atrocities in Belgium during the 1914–18 war. When Germany occupied France in 1940, she left her family and traveled to Paris, determined to join the resistance. She met Edmond Poulain, a young lawyer who had recently joined Marie-Madeleine's network, and the two soon became engaged.

Poulain was one of the Alliance agents arrested in Paris in the fall of 1941 and sent to Fresnes prison. In a coded message smuggled out

MONIQUE
BONTINCK

of Fresnes, he wrote to Marie-Madeleine that he expected to be executed and appealed to her to save the girl he was to marry. But keeping Bontinck from harm was easier said than done. Her demure, shy appearance masked a fearless nature that bordered on recklessness. In her memoirs, Marie-Madeleine recalled that during Bontinck's three-year tenure with Alliance, she repeatedly went out on extremely dangerous missions without Marie-Madeleine's knowledge.

Ferdinand Rodriguez, a British radio operator assigned to Alliance later in the war, said of Bontinck: "She performed with an icy pluck the most mind-boggling acts. She had a candid face and a childish silhouette, with her fair hair falling to her shoulders, but she also had the spirit of a secret agent ready to do anything."

As was true of other French resistance networks, Alliance found that women were particularly successful when acting as couriers. Many, like Bontinck, were young and attractive—and used their charm and guileless appearance to talk their way out of ticklish encounters with German and French police and security officials. "I carried messages all over France, and sometimes radio transmitters, too," Bontinck later wrote in an unofficial account of her wartime activities. "You can't imagine what I went through trying to avoid police controls on trains and at train stations."

Among Alliance's other women couriers was a chic, well-connected Paris matron named Odette Fabius, whose background was very similar to that of her *patronne*. Like Fourcade, Fabius was thirty-two years old. The daughter of a wealthy lawyer in Paris, she had been tutored by a British governess and spoke English fluently. At the age of seventeen, she had married an affluent antiques dealer considerably older than she and a year later gave birth to a daughter.

But Fabius wanted more than marriage, motherhood, and a prominent position in Paris society. Shortly before the war began, she volunteered as an ambulance driver for the French army. After the armistice was signed, her restlessness returned, and she cast about for something else to do. In a chance encounter, a friend with ties to Alliance asked her if she would be willing to deliver a letter to Léon Faye in Marseille. Ignoring the objections of her husband, she did as her friend asked and was recruited by Faye as a full-time courier. Fabius embarked on her resistance career with zest, carrying letters and documents and escorting people across the demarcation line between the occupied and free zones. Her young daughter occasionally accompanied her, and on more than one occasion, Fabius hid incriminating papers in the girl's suitcase.

Having developed a taste for risk and adventure, Fabius was anxious to assume a more important role within Alliance. Fourcade taught her how to encrypt and decrypt coded messages, and she was occasionally given other duties at the Marseille headquarters. But she was never assigned weightier responsibilities or included in the long, conspiratorial closed-door meetings that Fourcade held with Faye, Maurice de MacMahon, and her other key agents. In Fourcade's view, Fabius was somewhat of a dilettante, focusing more on the excitement and drama of this deadly serious work than on the need for discipline and security.

Fabius, who eventually left Alliance and joined another network, clearly resented Fourcade's treatment of her, and after the war, she was the only Alliance operative to write negatively about her boss.

Idolizing Léon Faye as she did, Fabius believed that he, not Marie-Madeleine, should be leading Alliance, and she was scathing about his willingness to subordinate himself to a woman. "Faye is obsessed with the beauty and undeniable charm" of Fourcade, Fabius wrote in her wartime journal. "She exercises on him, as on everyone, a huge influence, and makes him accept without difficulty the role of assistant to the *'grand chef.'*"

Odette Fabius was hardly the only one to comment on Marie-Madeleine's striking good looks; many others—men and women—did the same. After the war, MI6's Kenneth Cohen noted that "fact had outpaced fiction in producing the copybook 'beautiful spy.' That was Marie-Madeleine." In Madrid, Cohen's deputy, Eddie Keyser, had been transfixed by her appearance when he first met her. In his old age, Chris Marker, a noted French photographer and documentary filmmaker who had joined the resistance in Vichy early in the war, told his biographer that he had done so in part because "he, like so many young men in Vichy, was madly in love with the fabulously beautiful Marie-Madeleine."

Unquestionably, Faye, like so many others, had been smitten by Fourcade's beauty and charm. As it happened, she was equally attracted to him, and the two had become lovers. But the jealous Fabius was wrong in her belief that Fourcade's allure was the main reason for Faye's willingness to subordinate himself to her leadership. When he had first approached Colonel Édouard Kauffmann, his old air force colleague, about joining Alliance in early 1942, Kauffmann had asked him who ran the network. "A woman," Faye responded. "But not just any woman! She's an indisputable and undisputed leader. Even the English have accepted her!"

His view was echoed by the British radio operator Ferdinand Rodriguez, who would later become part of Fourcade's inner circle. "She was young and very beautiful, but there was an unmistakable aura of authority around her," Rodriguez told an interviewer after the war. "She was definitely *la patronne par excellence*."

CHAPTER 13

SITTING ON A BARREL
OF GUNPOWDER

FOURCADE DID NOT STAY LONG AT MARGUERITE BROUILLET'S HOUSE in Lavandou. Soon after her move there, Gabriel Rivière arrived with yet another dose of bad news. Émile Audoly, the architect of Alliance's astonishingly successful intelligence gathering operation in Marseille, had been arrested by Vichy police. He'd been betrayed by a former Alliance radio operator who had gone to work for another network and then, having been caught by French security officials, told them about Audoly's operation in order to save himself. Fourcade had no time to properly mourn the capture of Audoly, one of the few remaining members of Alliance's first wave and a treasured associate. Her first priority must be to save his sector. She asked Rivière if he could take over from Audoly. He replied that he'd already begun to do so.

Worried that Vichy and German security forces were again closing in, Fourcade moved once more, this time to a spacious villa called La Pinède, perched on a hill outside Marseille and surrounded by lush gardens. The villa was rented in Marguerite Brouillet's name, and she and one of her sons moved in first, telling the landlord that several relatives of hers, refugees from the occupied zone, would be staying with her. Those "refugees" included Fourcade; her brother, Jacques Bridou; Léon Faye; and Monique Bontinck.

The villa's large drawing room was turned into an office and radio transmission center, where operators sent and received messages to and from London and the network's other sectors. In another room, Ernest Siegrist, the former Paris policeman who served as the network's specialist in forged papers, turned out a flood of false identity cards, ration books, and other documents needed by Alliance agents.

Acutely aware of the growing threat to the network, Fourcade felt as if she were sitting on a barrel of gunpowder. One of her greatest priorities now was to locate safe places in the countryside where Allied operatives on the run could hide and be evacuated to safety. One such agent was Audoly's radio operator, who had been captured with him but who had managed to flee while he was being taken to jail. Another was Jean Boutron, who had been interned for the previous three months at a fort in the French Alps and who was still waiting for Marie-Madeleine to fulfill the pledge she had made in Vichy to help him escape.

During her stay in Madrid, Major Eddie Keyser, her MI6 handler, had discussed with her the creation of a new air operation between England and France, using small planes called Lysanders to pick up and bring in her agents, mail, and other important material. Until then, Alliance and other French spy networks had been forced to rely on radio messages, unofficial shuttle services like Jean Boutron's mailbag scheme, parachute drops, and crossing the Pyrenees into Spain as the main ways to communicate with London and to bring agents in and out.

All those methods had major disadvantages. Mountain crossings into Spain, for example, were arduous and time-consuming, with a high risk of being captured by Vichy, German, or Spanish border police. Parachute drops were also problematic. To make one, an agent had to have special training. Even then, it was not uncommon to break a leg or suffer some other injury on landing. And of course parachute operations could only be mounted from England; there was no way to use parachutes to smuggle agents out of France.

In the summer of 1942, MI6 finally inaugurated the new plane service. In July, it dispatched an agent from London, whose real name was Arthur Gachet but who was known to Marie-Madeleine and her operatives by his code name, Arthur Crowley. Gachet was to teach network operatives the intricate and risky maneuvers necessary to bring in and send off the Lysanders.

His pupils were members of a small, recently created branch of Alliance called Avia, whose purpose was to handle the ground logistics of parachute drops and the new Lysander service from Britain. It was headed by Pierre Dallas, a twenty-six-year-old former air force pilot who had been one of the first fliers recruited by Faye. A native of Lyon, Dallas had already established a parachute dropping zone just south of that city, in a field near the Saône River. His house, which was located on the banks of the Saône, served as Avia's headquarters.

In the months to come, the field near Lyon would be used for Lysander landings, as would another site, discovered by Fourcade, that would prove to be even better for the new air operation. She learned about the location from an Alliance agent who before the war had been a gun runner in the Corrèze, a wild, rocky region in south central France. Set in the Massif Central, the third biggest mountain range in the country, the Corrèze was an area of steep peaks, deep gorges, and flat plateaus—the perfect setting for an emergency hideout. Alliance's new landing strip was installed on a wide, grassy former army airfield near the isolated town of Ussel.

The strip would play a key role in one of the least known yet most important RAF operations of the war. The pilots who ferried agents from Alliance and other French intelligence networks to and from their country were members of a special operations unit—161 Squadron—an elite all-volunteer group. The aircraft they flew—a tiny two-cockpit single-engine plane—had been designed as a reconnaissance plane, with the ability to rapidly land and take off in small, contained areas, which made it an excellent craft for pickup operations. But the Lysanders, affectionately known as Lizzies by their young pilots, had more than their share of problems. They were slow and carried no guns, which made them vulnerable to German fighter planes and antiaircraft batteries.

Before the war, the ungainly little Lysanders had been mainly used for patrolling coastal areas, towing targets, and spotting downed aircraft in the English Channel—unimportant duties in the eyes of most airmen in the RAF, who, completely unaware of the planes' new wartime function, looked down on their colleagues who flew them. In fact, the work of the Lysander pilots was top secret, highly dangerous, and essential to the war effort.

The squadron's flights, which lasted as long as eight hours round-trip, took place only at night. Since the Lysanders had no navigation equipment, the pilots had to rely on light from the moon to locate small landing fields that appeared no bigger from the air than a pocket handkerchief and to see the terrain clearly enough to make a safe landing, all the while looking out for enemy aircraft. The fields themselves were lit only by flashlights operated by members of the resistance networks' reception committees.

But the members of 161 Squadron enthusiastically embraced the difficult challenges they faced. An iconoclastic, buccaneering crew, few of them were regular RAF officers, and most had little use for military rules or discipline. One of the unit's top pilots, Peter Vaughan-Fowler—who joined the squadron as a nineteen-year-old and whom Marie-Madeleine would get to know later in the war—was known for his love of jazz and his penchant for performing daredevil acrobatic stunts over a village near the squadron's airfield.

"We were all different, and our greatest common factor must have been our individualism," said Hugh Verity, a French-speaking Oxford graduate who at the age of twenty-four was named 161's squadron leader. "I was rather pleased," Verity added, "to find myself in a job where I could make an operational contribution to the war without killing people. It was also much more satisfying to carry people than bombs—especially when the people one carried were such outstanding personalities."

As the war progressed, the Lysander pilots forged tight bonds with many of the French men and women they ferried between France and England. Of all the Britons based in England who dealt with the French during the war, the men of 161 Squadron developed arguably the most personal relationships with them, sharing their dangers, rejoicing in their successes, and grieving when they were all too fre-

LYSANDER PILOTS IN FRONT OF ONE OF THEIR AIR-CRAFT (NOTE THE FIXED LADDER BEHIND THE WING). SQUADRON COMMANDER HUGH VERITY IS SECOND FROM LEFT, AND PETER VAUGHAN-FOWLER, WHO FLEW MARIE-MADELEINE FOURCADE TO BRITAIN IN 1943, IS SECOND FROM RIGHT.

quently swallowed up in the Gestapo maw. But the closeness between the two groups could also be attributed to the great similarity in the personalities of their members. Like the Lysander pilots, *résistants* tended to be mavericks.

During and after the war, both groups expressed great esteem for the courage and dedication of the other. Speaking of the French with whom he worked, Verity wrote that while he and the other pilots "were only vulnerable to the enemy on the ground for a few minutes at a time, they were at risk for months and years on end. It was they and their invaluable work that justified this unusual type of air taxi service."

SHORTLY AFTER ARTHUR GACHET arrived in France, he launched a crash course to teach the Alliance aviation team how to work with the Lysanders and their pilots. On the night of each mission, he told the French, a strict routine had to be followed without deviation. When the plane approached the field, three team members were to position themselves on it in the shape of an inverted L. The pilot would be flying at a low altitude—usually no more than 1,500 feet—to enable him to make out the distinguishing features of the surrounding countryside. As he came near, he would flash a prearranged Morse code signal with his craft's signal light. If the head of the reception committee, using a flashlight, responded with a prearranged signal of his own, the pilot would prepare to land; if he didn't see the correct signal, he was under orders to return to base. Provided all went well, the other members of the team would then turn on flashlights mounted on sticks to guide the pilot in.

After touching down near the first light, the airman would make a turn at the second light, then stop his plane at the third, thus positioning himself to take off. At that point, any baggage aboard the plane would be thrown out, and its passengers—three at most—would quickly climb down a ladder fixed to the side of the Lysander. Outgoing sacks of documents, maps, samples of new weapons, oils, and gases used by the Germans, and any other material would be quickly loaded, along with the baggage of departing passengers. Then the passengers themselves would clamber up the ladder into the plane. To avoid enemy detection, the emphasis was on speed, and the operation usually lasted less than ten minutes from landing to takeoff.

Since moonlight was essential for the Lysander flights, they could be scheduled only two weeks a month—before, during, and after a full moon. The first Alliance pickup took place in early August 1942 on the field in the Corrèze. One of the passengers whisked away was Léon Faye, who was traveling to London for consultations with MI6. The agency's officials had wanted Fourcade to make the trip, but she declined, sending Faye in her place. The morning after the pickup, to her great relief, the BBC broadcast a prearranged coded message telling her that Faye was at that moment walking the streets of London. He was scheduled to return during the full moon period the following month.

For the September operation, the RAF decided to use Alliance's other landing ground, on the bank of the Saône River near Lyon. This time, Jean Boutron was scheduled to be one of the outgoing passengers. Earlier in the summer, Fourcade had finally made good on her promise to smuggle him out of the fortress where he had been held since April. A doctor who moonlighted as an Alliance agent injected him with a substance that produced symptoms of urinary disease, which, the doctor insisted to officials at the fort, must be treated at his hospital in Grenoble. Boutron was taken there and a few weeks later was spirited out by agents in Alliance's Grenoble sector and whisked off to a hideout in the town of Meyzieux, about eighteen miles from Lyon. There he received a message from Marie-Madeleine informing him of her decision to send him to London aboard the next Lysander flight.

The flight that would bring Faye back to France was scheduled for September 11. A worrier at the best of times, Marie-Madeleine was edgy from the moment she heard that the date had been fixed. She thought about all the dire possibilities: the Lysander shot down by enemy fighters or antiaircraft fire; a crash caused by bad weather; capture of the Avia reception crew and the outgoing passengers. But Marie-Madeleine's greatest fear, although she never specifically acknowledged it, was centered on the fate of Léon Faye.

Throughout the war and after, Marie-Madeleine was extremely discreet about her private life. She never discussed or wrote, for example, about her affair with Faye. But while she made no public mention of the intimate nature of their relationship, her comments about him in her memoirs left little doubt that she was deeply in love with him.

On the evening of September 11, she would later write, she was at her villa outside Marseille. Pierre Dallas called to tell her that despite wretched weather conditions in England, the Lysander carrying Faye had taken off and was on its way to France, where clouds and rain also predominated. As she knew, it was hard enough to conduct the missions in perfect weather. Having to fly through clouds, rain, or fog with no navigation aids was far more difficult, even for the most skilled pilots. She heard nothing more about the flight that night or the following day.

Finally, on September 13, Dallas informed her that his team had waited for the Lysander for several hours, but it had never shown up. With her anxiety, already sky-high, mounting even further, she finally got word that Faye was all right. His plane had been forced to turn back because of the bad weather, and another attempt would be made when the conditions improved.

For the next week, Dallas and his crew, along with Boutron, traveled to the landing ground every night, but the weather continued foul and the Lysander never appeared. Having waited in the cold and rain for several nights, Boutron came down with a bad case of the flu. On the evening of September 20, racked by fever and chills, he was in bed at a nearby inn when Dallas came to see him. He told Boutron that although he and his crew were going to make one final trip to the landing ground, the weather was still bad and he was sure the plane would not appear. He advised Boutron to stay in bed.

Unbeknownst to Dallas and the others, however, the sky had finally cleared in England and the Lysander was once more on its way to France. As it approached the coast of Normandy, the moon appeared from behind a bank of clouds. Heading southeast, the plane was caught in the beams of German searchlights, but the pilot, John Bridger, veered away, making a sudden dive, and the searchlights, unable to find the craft again, went out.

As the Lysander flew over the Loire River, the sky clouded over again, and the plane and its occupants were plunged into almost total darkness. They crossed over two mountain ranges, and Bridger struggled to stay clear of the ridges that were no more than vague outlines in the thick clouds veiling them. When the plane drew close to the Saône River, the rain was coming down in sheets, and, as Bridger approached the field, he was flying almost at ground level, trying to make out the landing ground's features. There were no lights to indicate the reception crew's presence, and he began to circle, looking for any sign of life below.

Suddenly he and Faye saw a jerky flicker of light. The plane's signal light blinked the prearranged Morse code signal, and the light from the ground blinked back with the correct response. Descending into the darkness, Bridger finally spotted the lights marking the inverted L of the flare path and touched down a few seconds later on the rain-soaked earth. When the Lysander made the turn to get ready for the takeoff, however, one of its wheels sank in the mud, and the plane tipped over on its right wing. Revving his engine, Bridger tried to free the Lysander, but to no avail. After throwing his luggage and bags of mail to the ground, Faye climbed out of the plane. He and the Avia crew loaded bags of outgoing mail into the Lysander and then, using their hands as makeshift shovels, dug a deep furrow in front of its mired wheel. The aircraft still refused to budge. In a desperate final effort to free it, the four Frenchmen clung to its fuselage while Bridger revved the engine to full throttle. Slowly, the Lysander began to move, heaving itself out of the muck and lumbering down the field. Faye and the others let go, and Bridger lifted the plane into the air and back into the storm.

There had been no time to fetch Boutron from the inn. Bridger's revving of the plane had been extremely loud, and he and the French reception committee feared that the noise might attract unwelcome attention from nearby farmers or, even worse, Vichy security officials. The unlucky Boutron would have to wait six more weeks for a new opportunity to escape.

In Marseille, meanwhile, Marie-Madeleine spent another agonizing night. Early the following morning, she heard a pounding at the front door of the villa. When she opened it, Faye, covered with mud, burst in with two equally muddy suitcases. "Well, I've got what you wanted," he exclaimed as he unlocked the luggage and revealed its contents—countless stacks of francs and piles of important documents.

Trying to control her emotions, Marie-Madeleine didn't say a word. Realizing that Faye was puzzled by her silence, she picked up what looked like a photo negative from one of the suitcases and peered closely at it. He stared at her for a moment, then began to laugh. "I see your imagination has run away with you again," he said. "When will you stop worrying for no reason?"

She laughed, too, although she knew how wrong he was; there was a multitude of reasons to worry. But for his sake, she would try to put her anxiety aside. All that mattered was that he was safe—at least for now.

CHAPTER 14

THE TRAITOR

O N A CHILLY AFTERNOON IN LATE OCTOBER 1942, ARTHUR GACHET, having overseen the first Lysander missions to Alliance, arrived in Marseille for a meeting with Fourcade. As he left the Saint Charles train station, he spotted a familiar face—someone he had met during an MI6 training course for radio operators a couple of years before in London. His former colleague recognized him, too, and seemed delighted to see him.

The man told Gachet that the resistance group to which he had been assigned had been destroyed by the Gestapo, that he had barely escaped, and was now looking around for another network to join. He mentioned the fact that the head of the defunct group had been a woman.

Gachet immediately realized to whom he was speaking: Arthur Bradley Davies, also known as Bla, the former Alliance radio operator suspected of selling out more than a dozen agents in Paris and Normandy to the Germans the year before. Even though MI6 had assured Fourcade in late 1941 that Bla had had nothing to do with the arrests, she believed otherwise and, with the help of some of her men, had set out to prove his guilt.

In the early spring of 1942, Maurice Coustenoble, Fourcade's adjutant at the time, had uncovered a key piece of evidence that supported her suspicion. He'd made the discovery during a trip to Paris to investigate the possibility of organizing an escape attempt by the jailed agents from Fresnes prison, a massive gray fortress-like structure near the French capital that held hundreds of resisters. After several days of casing it from the outside, Coustenoble gloomily concluded that unlike Vichy jails and prisons, whose guards often could be bribed or were anti-German themselves, Fresnes was so impregnable that a successful escape attempt was impossible.

But during his reconnaissance mission, Coustenoble also found that several of his imprisoned colleagues had smuggled out messages to their families, hidden inside parcels of soiled clothing that were laundered by family members and returned to Fresnes. Most of the messages detailed the extraordinarily harsh treatment the Alliance agents had received, including several instances of torture. But a message from Lucien Vallet, Fourcade's former radio operator, provided the first bit of concrete evidence of Bla's treachery. During an interrogation by the Gestapo, Vallet wrote, he had been shown the very radio set he had been using before his arrest—a set that had been spirited away by another Alliance agent before the Germans could find it and had been delivered by the agent to Bla.

Fourcade immediately passed on Vallet's report to MI6 headquarters, which replied that Bla was still sending excellent information from Normandy and reiterated that she was mistaken about his guilt. This time, however, she refused to give up and dispatched yet another message arguing her case. MI6 failed to respond for several days. Then one morning, a top-priority message landed on Fourcade's desk, with instructions to decode it at once. In it, MI6 officials acknowledged that Bla was indeed a traitor who had worked for the Germans. They ordered Alliance to execute him.

Not until months later did Fourcade find out that MI6, thanks to her pressure, had finally conducted an investigation into Bla's past. In doing so, the agency discovered that he had been a member of the British Union of Fascists, founded by Oswald Mosley, a former member of Parliament who'd been arrested and jailed by the British government in 1940. MI6 officials came to the conclusion that Bla had been working for the Germans the entire time he had been in France. They immediately sent a cable ordering him to hide his radio set and travel to neutral Spain or Switzerland, where he was to report to British authorities. He never responded. It was then that the agency decided that because he was personally acquainted with leading members of Alliance, the danger to the network was grave enough to warrant his execution.

Eddie Keyser suggested that Fourcade try to set up a meeting between Bla and one of her top agents in Lyon, with the idea of executing him there. She agreed, and a message was sent to Bla in Normandy telling him to appear at the rendezvous on a certain date. When the Alliance agent showed up at the appointed place, Bla was nowhere in sight; German military police, however, were there in force. The agent barely escaped.

For the next several months, Bla's trail went cold. There were reported sightings in Pau and Toulouse, but to Fourcade's frustration, no solid leads regarding his whereabouts—until Gachet's chance encounter with him in Marseille.

During their brief chat, Bla asked Gachet if he could help him get a job with another network. Gachet said he would see what he could do and arranged to meet him the following night at a bar in Marseille. The next morning, Léon Faye burst into La Pinède and told Fourcade about Gachet's spotting of Bla and the scheduled rendezvous. He insisted that she stay away, and she agreed to let him take charge of Bla's capture and interrogation.

At the bar that evening, Gachet told Bla that the head of his network was anxious to meet him and had asked Gachet to bring him to the network's headquarters. Shortly after they left the bar, two men in raincoats, their hats pulled down over their eyes, stopped them on the street. Identifying themselves as Vichy police, they asked both for their papers. Gachet strongly objected, but Bla readily handed over an identity card that bore his real name, an address in Paris, and his nationality as a British subject. One of the policemen said they needed to check out his story and ordered him to come with them.

Gachet again objected, but Bla told him to be quiet, then handed the policeman a piece of paper with a phone number scribbled on it, saying that if he called the number, he'd find out that everything was all right. The number, it later turned out, was that of the Abwehr headquarters in Paris.

The policemen hustled Gachet and Bla into a waiting car, which raced through Marseille's narrow streets, skirted the port, and headed along the Corniche for a mile or so before stopping at a building a few blocks from the coastal road. Once inside, the policemen's courtesy vanished; they shoved Bla into a brightly lit room, where Gabriel Rivière stood, pointing a gun at the Englishman. Léon Faye, who was next to Rivière, grabbed Bla by the lapels of his jacket and barked, "We've got you at last!" Bla looked around the room in panic. The two "policemen" had taken off their hats and coats, revealing themselves to be Alliance operatives as well. Bla told Faye he'd made a mistake, that he was not the man Faye thought he was.

For more than an hour, Faye battered Bla with questions, but he insisted again and again that Faye and his colleagues were mistaken. None of the Alliance agents in the room had been in Pau when Bla had arrived by parachute in the spring of 1941; Fourcade was the sole member of the network in Marseille who could positively identify him. Although Faye had wanted to keep her involvement in this whole sordid business to a minimum, he reluctantly asked her to come to the office where Bla was being held, saying she was the only one who might be able to get him to talk.

When she entered the bare, smoke-filled room, lit only by a single unshaded bulb overhead, Bla recoiled in shock. Earlier, Fourcade had told Faye that although Bla should not be mistreated during his interrogation, he should be forced to stand throughout. He continued to do so as she questioned him, with only one other agent, who kept a gun trained on him, in the room. Bla readily admitted to her that he had indeed been a member of Oswald Mosley's fascist party and had offered his services to the Abwehr in Paris shortly after leaving Pau. On the Abwehr's orders, he had infiltrated Alliance's sector in Paris, worming his way into its agents' confidence and setting up their arrests.

When Fourcade asked if he had ever been in Normandy, he replied that he had rarely gone there. His radio set, which MI6 believed was being operated from there, was in fact at the Abwehr's Paris offices. He did the actual transmitting himself, since each operator had his own distinctive style and he didn't want to arouse any suspicions within MI6. Much of the information he sent was genuine although relatively unimportant, he said. Occasionally, though, the Germans slipped in a bit of false intelligence to send MI6 on a wild-goose chase. He'd come to Marseille on behalf of the Abwehr, he added, to find out where she was.

As forthcoming as he was about his activities in Paris, however, Bla fell silent when Fourcade asked him about his contacts in London. When he had first come to Pau, he had boasted to her brother that he had a secret high-level connection in the British capital. But when she mentioned that, he refused to say anything more. Exhausted, Fourcade finally gave up. Finding Faye in an adjacent room, she said that Bla had confirmed everything they already knew but had revealed little else. He told her to go back to La Pinède, adding that what happened next didn't concern her.

Knowing that MI6 had confirmed the execution order for Bla earlier in the day, she asked Faye what he was going to do. He produced a packet of white pills from his pocket, saying he had been given them in London. Fourcade knew what they were: cyanide tablets issued to MI6 and SOE agents operating in occupied Europe to use in case of arrest and interrogation by the Gestapo. Faye said they worked very quickly. Nodding, she told him she didn't want Bla to know what was about to happen.

As the sun rose over the Mediterranean, she left the building and caught a tram back to La Pinède. Several hours later, Lucien Poulard, one of the agents involved in Bla's capture, rushed into the villa. He was distraught, and it took Fourcade several minutes to calm him down. Despite two separate attempts to kill Bla, Poulard told her, he was still alive. "You can't imagine what it was like," Poulard said with a shudder, as he described the macabre scene from the beginning.

After Fourcade had left, Poulard, on Faye's orders, had given Bla a bowl of hot soup in which he had dissolved a cyanide tablet. Also on Faye's orders, Poulard joined Bla at the table, eating from his own bowl of soup so that Bla would not suspect that his had been tampered with. They began eating, but nothing happened. Finally, Bla complained of a stomachache and asked to lie down. Poulard agreed. After three hours, Bla was still conscious.

Faye told Poulard to try again, this time with a cyanide tablet dissolved in a cup of hot tea. Bla swallowed a mouthful, grimaced, and asked, "Is this an order from London?" Then he finished the tea and handed the cup back to Poulard with the remark, "It can't be much fun for an officer to have to do this kind of thing." Another two hours went by, and Bla was still very much alive.

Once Fourcade heard the story, she returned to the building near the Corniche, where she and Faye reluctantly agreed to a proposal by Rivière to recruit several gangsters from Marseille's underworld, who were acquaintances of his, to help them dispose of the seemingly indomitable Bla. According to Rivière's plan, he and the Alliance operatives would escort Bla late that night down to a small, secluded beach near the city's Old Port, where the mobsters would meet them in a fishing boat. After boarding the boat, Bla would be taken several miles out to sea and then thrown overboard.

Again, Fourcade headed back to La Pinède, where she spent a sleepless night. Staring out a window early the following morning, she saw Faye's tall, slightly stooped figure approaching the door. Without a word, he opened it, flung himself down on a couch in the ground-floor office, and began to tell her the latest chapter in this ongoing ghastly comedy of errors. The gangsters had failed to show up, and Bla was still alive.

They had waited for hours on the beach, Faye said. As the time crept by, he began losing his resolve to get rid of Bla. When Rivière told Faye that the gangsters obviously weren't coming, Faye ordered everyone, including Bla, to return to the Corniche.

Fourcade realized that Faye was having a crisis of conscience, and she understood why. Like many of his Alliance colleagues, he was a career military officer, a toughened veteran of World War I who had never quailed at the thought of killing the enemy. But the cold, deliberate execution of a former colleague, even one who had admitted to betraying his comrades, was harder to stomach.

"You're exhausted, and your men are worn out," she told him. "To [them], this villain will soon seem like a nice person. They'll pity him, whereas he is in fact an enemy." Bla, she declared, must be put on trial for espionage: "We have the right to do so, and it's our duty."

A few hours later, she, Faye, Rivière, Lucien Poulard, and two other operatives sat around a large table in the room where Bla was being held. He was placed in a chair facing them. Faye, who presided over the improvised military tribunal, stood and read a lengthy indictment. When asked to respond, Bla said that all the allegations were true; he was indeed a German spy. Faye then condemned him to death. At that point, Fourcade left the room, returned to La Pinède, took a strong sleeping pill, and went to bed.

Bla's fate was never made public. There was some talk after the war that Faye had been unable to go through with the execution and allowed Bla to flee to North Africa, where he settled down with his wife and children. In fact, Bla's wife never saw him again. In late 1944, when she made inquiries to British authorities about his whereabouts, she was told that her husband had been turned by the Germans and, when found out, had committed suicide.

CHAPTER 15

A GENERAL ESCAPES

A S OCTOBER 1942 GAVE WAY TO NOVEMBER, FOURCADE'S NERVES were stretched tight. She was doing her best to keep up with MI6's incessant demands for intelligence while having to deal with Bla's capture and execution and Germany's crackdown against the resistance in the free zone. Rumors were spreading that German troops were on the verge of occupying all of France. Adding to the strain, MI6 had just catapulted her and Alliance into the midst of a political hornet's nest involving the Allies' top-secret planning for an invasion of North Africa.

Although she had no idea of its meaning, Fourcade had received the first hint of the coming operation six months earlier, when her daughter was convalescing at the clinic in Toulouse. Working one night by the dim light of the lamp in Béatrice's room, she was deciphering the latest messages from MI6 brought to her by a courier from Alliance headquarters. She was puzzled by the last one she read. Sent to her by Eddie Keyser and marked "strictly confidential," it noted the recent escape of a top French general from a German prison. Keyser wanted Fourcade to contact the general, who was believed to be in Lyon, to see if he would serve his country again.

The subject of Eddie Keyser's inquiry was General Henri Giraud, the highest-ranking French officer captured by the Germans during the 1940 fighting in France. Taken prisoner when his headquarters was overrun during the third week of the Nazi blitzkrieg, Giraud had been jailed at Koenigstein fortress, on the banks of the Elbe River near Dresden. One of the largest hilltop fortifications in Europe, Koenigstein was known as the Saxon Bastille.

In the early hours of April 17, 1942, the sixty-three-year-old Giraud had lowered himself down a sixty-foot rope in an extraordinary escape engineered by anti-German military intelligence agents in Vichy. They spirited Giraud out of Germany, through Switzerland, and into the free zone. An infuriated Hitler demanded his return, and Pierre Laval, who had just taken over again as head of the Vichy government, insisted that Giraud must give himself up to the Germans. But Marshal Pétain, to whom Giraud had sworn his allegiance, would not hear of handing the general over. Laval did not dare to arrest Giraud on his own, knowing that the French armed forces would revolt if he tried. Although Giraud and his family were kept under police surveillance, he led a relatively unrestricted life near Lyon, making clear his opposition to German occupation and the need to combat it.

From the moment she read Keyser's cryptic message about Giraud, Fourcade had misgivings about the motive behind it. Why were she and Alliance being asked to get involved in this? Clearly, MI6 officials had no intention of asking Giraud to gather intelligence for them. What, then, did the British government want from the general? Was Churchill thinking of setting up a rival to Charles de Gaulle?

Since the fall of 1940, Fourcade had resolutely avoided getting involved in issues relating to French politics, whether inside or outside the country. As she saw it, Alliance's only mission was to collect information about the German military presence in France. While she supported the efforts of de Gaulle and the Free French, her first loyalty was to MI6. She wanted no part of the rivalries and feuds bedeviling other French resistance networks or the constant, often violent intrigues and power struggles raging at the Free French headquarters in London.

As it happened, her suspicions about the motivation behind the British government's interest in Giraud proved to be correct. As a result of pressure from President Roosevelt, Churchill was reluctantly seeking another French general to work with the Allies in helping them win over Vichy French forces in North Africa.

In the spring of 1942, just four months after the United States entered the war, its military leaders had joined their British colleagues in preparing for the Allies' first joint offensive against Germany. U.S. generals had pushed for an invasion of the Continent, but the British protested that Anglo-American forces were not ready for such a high-risk campaign. The two sides finally compromised on an alternative proposed by the British—an amphibious invasion of North Africa, to take place in November.

From the beginning, however, FDR had been adamant that de Gaulle and the Free French must have no involvement in either planning or carrying out the attack. Filled with disdain for both the French general and his country, the president had little understanding of the complexity of the situation in France and scant sympathy for its citizens. All he knew or cared about was that France had failed the Allied cause by capitulating to Germany. As for de Gaulle himself, Roosevelt considered him insignificant and absurd, a British puppet with grandiose ambitions.

It didn't matter to Roosevelt that by late 1942, the Free French had recruited an army of more than a hundred thousand men, an air force exceeding a thousand pilots and crew, several dozen ships, and support from most resistance leaders in France. Roosevelt informed Churchill that the general and his followers "must be given no role in the liberation and governance of North Africa or France" and insisted that de Gaulle not even be told of the upcoming attack.

The president was far more cordial to Pétain and his government; unlike Britain, the United States had formally recognized Vichy as the legitimate government of France almost immediately after the country's capitulation to Germany. Convinced that America was popular with Vichy, Roosevelt told Churchill he was confident that

Vichy troops in North Africa would put up little or no resistance to the landings as long as U.S. soldiers took the lead and Free French troops were nowhere to be seen.

Churchill, for his part, was faced with an agonizing dilemma. In June 1940, he had made a solemn pledge to support de Gaulle, and he shrank from having to go back on his word. But he desperately needed Roosevelt and the United States to provide the manpower and industrial strength necessary for Britain to survive and, in tandem with Britain and the Soviet Union, to eventually win the war. Churchill considered himself FDR's lieutenant and told his staff that "nothing must stand in the way of his friendship for the President on which so much depended." The British ended up handing over all initiative for the invasion to the Americans.

To take charge of Vichy forces in North Africa once the attack occurred, U.S. officials wanted a French general who was anti-Gaullist but also anti-German and untainted by Vichy's collaboration with the Reich. Giraud, who outranked de Gaulle by two stars, seemed the perfect solution. Unlike many of his military colleagues in Vichy, he strongly believed that Germany was going to lose the war and that Vichy must ally itself with the Americans and reenter the conflict. The tall mustachioed general, who had distinguished himself in both world wars, was known for his courage and integrity. His remarkable escape from the Koenigstein fortress had been heavily publicized in newspapers around the world and had added even more luster to his already notable name.

Having designated Giraud as commander of French forces in North Africa, the Americans instructed the British to sound him out about the job and then find a way to smuggle him out of France. MI6, which was handed both tasks, turned to Alliance—its most effective French spy network—to carry them out. The selection of the network for this delicate, controversial mission showed how vital Alliance was to the British war effort. But it also thrust Fourcade and her agents into uncharted territory: They had never before been involved in this kind of operation. Although she continued to have grave doubts, she did what MI6 asked, later writing that it was not her job to think. Her job was to help Giraud return to the fight against the Germans.

She and Faye decided to send one of their top agents—Maurice de MacMahon, the Duke of Magenta—as their envoy to Giraud. The meeting between the two in Lyon, however, proved to be highly problematic. The general told the duke that while Giraud was willing to cooperate with the Americans, he was anti-British and had no interest in going to London. At the same time, though, he was prepared to accept British aid to help him achieve his primary goal: to become the leader of all resistance movements in occupied Europe. Giraud would consider leading French forces in North Africa, he said, as long as the invasion there was coordinated with an attack in France. If the Allies supplied him with enough arms and equipment, he added, he could lead France's armed forces to victory over Germany, accompanied by armed rebellions in other occupied countries, including Holland and Norway.

Marie-Madeleine was dumbfounded by Giraud's presumption. How could he possibly believe he could take charge of all of Europe's resistance movements from inside France? It was hard enough, as she knew from bitter experience, to lead a single network in one's own country. She also knew that French resisters would refuse to accept the leadership of a man like Giraud, who had never had any dealings with the resistance up to that point and who had pledged his loyalty to Pétain and Vichy. Resistance members who had already taken a political stand had, for the most part, thrown their support behind de Gaulle and the Free French. Courageous as Giraud obviously was, he was also clearly out of touch with reality, political and otherwise. One resistance leader later called him "idiotically self important." Another labeled him "delusional."

Knowing that British officials would be as nonplussed by Giraud's quixotic plans as she had been, she sent a brief, considerably watered-down version of his demands to Eddie Keyser. She told Keyser that Giraud wanted to stay in France for the moment and play a leading role in the resistance there.

Marie-Madeleine heard nothing more about Giraud until late September, when Léon Faye returned by Lysander from his month-long stay in London. During his time away, he had also made a brief trip to Algiers. From various sources, British and French, he had learned that the Allied invasion of North Africa was imminent and that planning was already well under way to spirit Giraud out of France. American officials had met with a representative of the general and promised him that Giraud would be given an important role in the invasion if he could persuade French commanders in North Africa not to oppose the Allied landings. While agreeing to work with U.S. forces, Giraud, according to Faye, was apparently still trying to induce the Americans to combine the attack on North Africa with a simultaneous landing on the French Mediterranean coast.

Although such a demand was obviously unacceptable, the Americans apparently believed they could bend Giraud to their will. They told the British to proceed with arrangements to retrieve the general from the south of France and bring him to Gibraltar, the forward-planning headquarters for what would be called Operation Torch. Instead of a Lysander, a submarine would be dispatched to help him escape. The submarine and its crew would be British, but the anti-British Giraud would not know that. Instead, he was to be informed by officials in London that the sub was American.

Alliance was put in charge of finding a secure embarkation site on the Côte d'Azur, as well as smuggling Giraud out of Lyon from under the noses of his Vichy and German watchers and transporting him to a safe house to await the submarine's arrival. Marie-Madeleine chose Colonel Charles Bernis, head of the network's Nice sector, and Pierre Dallas, chief of the Avia team, to handle the logistics of the escape, which the British christened Operation Minerva.

After scouting several possible embarkation locales on the French coast, Bernis recommended Le Lavandou, the village sixty miles east of Marseille where Marie-Madeleine had briefly taken refuge a few months before. The rocky, wooded terrain there, overlooking the sea, was quiet and secluded, with little sign of German or Vichy police activity. A local fisherman who was sympathetic to Alliance had agreed to take Giraud and his party from the coast out to sea to rendezvous with the submarine. Marguerite Brouillet's villa, where Marie-Madeleine had stayed, would be used to shelter the general and his retinue until the vessel came.

On November 1, Marie-Madeleine was notified that Operation Minerva must begin no later than November 4. Over the next three days, a flood of coded messages flew back and forth between London and Alliance headquarters in Marseille. Marie-Madeleine was uncomfortably aware of how dangerous these frequent, lengthy radio transmissions were to the safety of her network. With German radio-detecting vans and cars on the prowl in and around Marseille, it was essential to keep transmissions short and to a minimum. But when one was working out the details of a mission as complicated as the Giraud escape turned out to be, it was virtually impossible to do so.

MI6 informed Marie-Madeleine that Giraud would be picked up by HMS *Seraph,* commanded by the Royal Navy's Lieutenant Commander William Jewell. Giraud, however, would be told that the British sub was actually the USS *Seraph,* under the command of U.S. Navy Captain Jerauld Wright, who would greet Giraud as he boarded. As part of the charade, the *Seraph*'s forty-man British crew would pretend to be Americans as well. Once the submarine was several miles out to sea, Giraud would be transferred to a seaplane that would fly him directly to Gibraltar to meet with U.S. General Dwight D. Eisenhower, the commander of the North Africa invasion.

Two days before the *Seraph* was to arrive, Faye showed up at La Pinède with disconcerting news: Giraud had just told him that one submarine was not enough. He was now asking that a second one also be dispatched, to pick up a number of other French army generals from Vichy whom he had urged to accompany him to North Africa.

Marie-Madeleine couldn't believe it. This escape plan had already put her network and its operations in jeopardy, and now Giraud was making matters worse with his ridiculous new demand. She wasn't running a public transportation company, she exclaimed to Faye. Although she would do everything possible to smuggle out Giraud, the other generals would have to fend for themselves.

After calming down, she reluctantly agreed to pass on Giraud's request to the British, although she was convinced that no other high-ranking Vichy officers would break ranks and join the Allies. Just in case they didn't, she said, she wanted several Alliance agents who needed to be evacuated, among them Jean Boutron and her brother, Jacques, to be ready to board the submarine in the generals' stead.

The British agreed to the second submarine, and plans for Operation Minerva seemed back on track. Then on November 3, Giraud dropped another bombshell. He had changed his mind, he told Faye. He'd decided not to leave France after all; instead, he would take control of the country's resistance from there. When Faye told her of this latest turn of events, Marie-Madeleine exploded with rage.

She knew that the noose was already tightening around Alliance. In addition to the threat posed by the direction-finding vans, French and German police had somehow learned of Giraud's planned escape and were searching the coast for the general and those helping him. Faye urged her to calm down, assuring her that Giraud would change his mind again and decide to go. Faye's prediction proved correct. Late that night, Marie-Madeleine received confirmation from Giraud's representative that Operation Minerva was on track once more.

Early the following morning, she left Marseille with Monique Bontinck and several other headquarters staffers. She was determined that the network should not suffer because of the venture. If the escape effort failed, she wanted to make sure she was still free to oversee Alliance's continued operations. She and the others spent the next two days at the headquarters of the network's Toulouse sector.

With Faye taking her place at Le Lavandou, the stage was set for that night's embarkation attempt. Their nerves on edge, Faye, Colonel Bernis, Pierre Dallas, and the rest of Alliance's escape team spent the day at Marguerite Brouillet's villa awaiting the arrival of Giraud and his party. Brouillet had prepared a lavish meal for the general, but by dinnertime, there was still no sign of him, and the food went cold. Finally, at about ten o'clock, two cars arrived at the villa, and Giraud, his son, and several aides stepped out.

After Brouillet reheated the food and everyone sat down to eat, Faye was pulled away from the table by an incoming message from London. The submarine, it appeared, might not arrive in time that evening. If it didn't, another attempt would be made the following night—November 5.

While Giraud and his party were escorted to their rooms, the sixty-three-year-old Bernis and twenty-six-year-old Dallas scrambled down to the beach and for several hours used flashlights to send out prearranged signals to the submarine, scanning the horizon in vain for a response. Early the next morning, they gave up their watch and returned to the villa for a couple of hours of sleep before going back to the shore at dawn. The sea had grown considerably choppier, but the conditions were still good enough, they thought, for the embarkation to proceed that night.

As the hours dragged by, a strong wind began howling outside the villa, and the Alliance team's anxiety mounted, reaching sky-high levels when the fisherman who was to take Giraud from the coast to the submarine arrived. He said that at the moment, the wind was too gusty for him to take his boat out of the harbor, and if the gusts continued, the operation would have to be canceled.

A fierce debate broke out. Faye insisted that an attempt must be made, regardless of the weather, while Giraud's chief aide said that the decision must be left up to the fisherman. The general himself remarked that he was willing to take any risk necessary. Bernis, who was equally worried about the weather conditions and the security threat posed by Giraud's presence at Lavandou, settled the matter, declaring that the operation would proceed as planned if the boat could make it through the harbor entrance.

Near midnight, the wind began to die down. Giraud's son and aides left with the fisherman to help him load the party's luggage into his boat and get it in the water. Giraud and the Alliance team, meanwhile, set out on foot toward a rocky headland overlooking the sea. When they reached the headland, Pierre Dallas hurried to its tip and flashed a signal meaning "wait" to the submarine that he hoped was out there in the inky darkness.

Giraud and the others clambered down a narrow path to the beach. The fishing boat soon came alongside and took Giraud and Dallas on board. Standing in the bow, Dallas flashed a prearranged letter signal out to sea. After a few heart-stopping seconds, a light flashed back with the correct letter of response. A muffled cheer went up from those in the boat and on the shore. They could barely make out the dark mass of the *Seraph,* which had surfaced a few hundred yards away.

The rescue's only hitch came when Giraud tumbled into the water while trying to board the *Seraph* from the fishing boat, which was pitching and rolling in the ocean swells. His son and aides immediately fished him out, and he climbed aboard the sub with only minor injuries to his pride and the herringbone suit he was wearing. The American naval officer posing as the captain showed him to the captain's quarters, where he fell asleep without ever noticing the pronounced British accents of the crew.

Later that morning, an RAF seaplane rendezvoused with the *Seraph* in the Mediterranean, landing about thirty yards from the submarine. The transfer of Giraud and his retinue—from sub to rubber dinghy to plane—took more than an hour. Finally, after a bumpy takeoff in an increasingly rough sea, the seaplane flew west to Gibraltar, landing three hours later. Giraud was immediately whisked away for a meeting with General Eisenhower.

Meanwhile, after delivering the general to the *Seraph,* the fisherman and Pierre Dallas returned to shore, met by cheers and embraces from Faye, Bernis, and the rest of the embarkation team. The Alliance men all had mixed emotions: jubilation over their successful execution of an exceedingly difficult operation coupled with a lingering sense of regret that as former military officers, they were unable to emulate Giraud and return to actual combat against the enemy.

But they had little time to dwell on such things. It was time to get back to work. Another submarine was arriving in less than forty-eight hours.

CHAPTER 16

CAPTURED

FOURCADE RETURNED TO MARSEILLE IN THE EARLY MORNING OF November 6. She stopped first at the Saint Charles bar to make sure it was safe to go on to La Pinède, observing as she did so that none of the Vichy generals who were supposed to leave on the second submarine had yet shown up.

When she arrived at the villa, Faye described in detail the success of the previous night's mission. He emphasized the importance of the second submarine's arriving as planned on the night of the seventh, saying that the British had informed him that no submarines would be available after that date. Although London had not told him why, Faye had correctly guessed the reason: The Allies planned to launch their invasion of North Africa on November 8.

Fourcade pointed out that no generals had yet arrived. She didn't mention that she'd already arranged for Jean Boutron, Jacques Bridou, and two other Alliance agents to be at the bar the next morning, ready to take the generals' place.

Late that evening, Marguerite Brouillet phoned to say she had come down with the flu and couldn't host the guests who were attending the party the following night. Her message was a prearranged code for some very bad news: Lavandou could not be used as the embarkation site for the second submarine. Fourcade guessed that the Germans had been tipped off by the unusual comings and goings of the previous night and were roaming around the area. The submarine must be diverted to a backup site—Cros-de-Cagnes, another small fishing village on the Côte d'Azur, midway between Cannes and Nice. With the submarine due in less than twenty-four hours, it was crucial, she told the radio operator on duty at La Pinède, that MI6 be notified immediately about the change in plans. He assured her he would send out the alert in that night's transmission to London. But when she returned the next morning, she found the operator, un-shaven and red-eyed, still hunched over his transmitter. He told her he had tried to contact London repeatedly throughout the night, but there had been no response.

He added he was going to switch frequencies and try again. Re-trieving from his pocket the crumpled and stained message that she had coded the night before, he placed it on the table beside him and turned on the transmitter. At that point, Ernest Siegrist, Alliance's head of security, came in to give Fourcade more unsettling news: A friend in the Marseille police had warned him that German detector vans were on the verge of locating a transmitter in the area of La Pi-nède. After urging her to shut down the radio immediately, he left to try to ferret out more information. A few minutes later, Monique Bontinck and another agent, who had been out shopping for food, returned to the villa to report that several strange men were walking up and down the avenue.

Fourcade knew she should follow Siegrist's advice and halt the transmission. But as she and he were talking, her operator finally made contact with London and began tapping out her message. Since it was vitally important to keep the submarine away from Lavandou that night, she allowed him to continue. She walked into another room, listening to the Morse signals and begging him under her breath to work more quickly.

Finally the tapping stopped, and the operator switched over to receive London's reply. There was a moment or two of silence, then the front door crashed open and shouts of "Police" echoed through the house. Glancing out a window, Fourcade saw several police cars and vans haphazardly parked in the street and men swarming into the villa.

She ran into the office and saw her operator holding a cigarette lighter and trying to burn the message and his transmission schedules, while a man waved a gun in his direction and shouted at him to stop. Another man, dressed in a leather overcoat and speaking German, was rifling through the drawers of the operator's desk. In a fury fueled by two years of frustration, anger, and constant worry, Fourcade lost control. Screaming "Dirty Boche!" she threw herself at the German plainclothesman and clawed at his face. Astonished by her outburst, he shrank back and picked up a chair to fend her off, much like an animal trainer facing an enraged lion.

Suddenly she remembered a sheaf of incriminating notes from her recent travels that she'd stored in her purse. Rushing back to the other room, she retrieved the notes, wadded them into balls, and crammed them into her mouth. At that point, the man whom she'd assaulted burst in and ordered her to stop.

Another member of the police team—a short, wiry, dark-haired man—rushed in and grabbed her by the throat. She loudly swore at him while trying to swallow. When the German went back into the office, her assailant loosened his grasp and whispered in her ear that he was not German. He told her to continue shouting but to chew everything up as quickly as she could. She did as he instructed, but in between the insults and chewing, she asked him who he was.

A friend, he answered: a French policeman forced by Vichy to escort the Germans in their raids on the resistance. She turned her head and stared at him. She desperately wanted to trust him, but her two years in the spy business had taught her the importance of doubt. When she said she didn't believe him, he sighed and gave his name—Jean Boubil.

He was in fact who he said he was—Inspector Jean Boubil of the Surveillance du Territoire, who'd been placed in charge of a squad of four French policemen assigned to accompany German agents in their raid on La Pinède. He and his French colleagues, not the Germans, were supposed to take into custody any resistance members and material captured in the raid.

Fourcade decided she had no alternative but to trust him. She told him that she had a parcel of incriminating documents beneath her bed and that she was expecting visitors that day who must be stopped from coming in. Boubil retrieved the parcel from under the bed and stashed it out of sight atop a cupboard. He then summoned a young French policeman to the room and told him to go outside and stop anyone who wanted to enter the house.

Boubil whispered to Fourcade to keep on struggling as he pushed her into the office. To her horror, she saw that the German—an Abwehr agent, she discovered later—was closely examining a sheet of paper that he'd picked up from the table on which the transmitter sat. It was a diagram, made by her brother months before, that listed the locations, call signs, wave-length details, and transmission times of all of Alliance's transmitters in France. Waving it triumphantly at Boubil, the German exclaimed, "It's the plan of their whole radio circuit!" Fourcade grabbed the paper from him. As he lunged toward her to retrieve it, Boubil intervened. He took the list from Fourcade and stuffed it into his pocket, telling the German that he'd give it to him later.

At that moment, the network's radio operator began shouting, "QS5, QS5!" The Abwehr operative slapped him across the face and yelled, "The man is mad!" A slight smile flickered across Fourcade's face; he was agitated, certainly, but not mad. "QS5" was the code for a successful transmission: he was telling her that London had received his warning about the need to change that night's embarkation site.

Close to collapse from the high-wire tension of the last few minutes, Fourcade thought the day could not possibly get worse. And then it did. She looked up to see her brother, Jacques, who was due to leave that night on the British submarine, walk through the front door. In his hand was an old, muddy, moldy suitcase. He told her he'd come to say goodbye but that it hadn't been easy. Somebody standing near the door had shouted at him that the Gestapo was inside.

Her heart sinking, she stared down at the suitcase, knowing what it contained: the early records of Alliance, including the 1940 letter from Charles de Gaulle to Navarre, that she and Jacques had buried almost two years before in the pigsty at their mother's villa on the Côte d'Azur. In a faltering voice, Jacques said he thought the papers would be ruined if they stayed in the pigsty. His voice trailed off. Watching the interaction between the siblings, Boubil figured out what was going on. He put the suitcase in a corner and threw an eiderdown quilt over it.

It was at that point that a short, youthful, fair-haired Frenchman named Xavier Piani appeared on the scene and began to restore order to the chaos. Piani, a Surveillance du Territoire superintendent, calmly but firmly ordered the Abwehr agents to leave. He reminded them that under the terms of Germany's agreement with Vichy, they were obliged to leave these prisoners and all the incriminating material that had been gathered in the custody of the French police. The Germans did as they were told but made it clear that they would inform their superiors about the importance of the resistance members who had just been captured.

After the Abwehr men were gone, Piani formally arrested Fourcade and the other Alliance agents, telling them to pack overnight bags and accompany him and his men to the police headquarters in Marseille. Seven in all were taken to jail, including Fourcade, Faye, Jacques Bridou, Monique Bontinck, and the radio operator. As they emerged from the villa and were placed into police cars, Fourcade noticed Ernest Siegrist watching from across the street. Her heart lifted: He had undoubtedly already sounded the alarm of their capture.

As soon as they arrived at the headquarters, it became clear that Boubil was not the only French police official who secretly sympathized with Fourcade and the network. She and her staff were immediately given a good meal and then subjected to several hours of relatively gentle interrogation.

That night, they were escorted to L'Évêché prison on the outskirts of Marseille. Fourcade was taken to a cell containing a cot, toilet, and a naked lightbulb hanging from the ceiling. Sitting on the cot, she took a cigarette from the lining of her coat. As she lit it, she saw bugs and a few rats emerging from the cell's darkened corners. Wrapping her coat closely around her and shrinking back on the cot, she forced herself to focus on the rescue operations that her network had just overseen. "I only hoped that Giraud had arrived safely at Gibraltar and that the second submarine had managed to get away," she recalled. "Only that would justify our present plight."

GIRAUD HAD INDEED ARRIVED safely in Gibraltar, but nothing after his arrival had gone according to plan. Shortly after his seaplane landed, the French general had been escorted to a warren of tunnels that burrowed deep inside the Rock of Gibraltar. Excavated by the British army more than a century before, the tunnels were in effect a huge, dank underground fortress, housing barracks, offices, hangars, and stores of guns and ammunition. General Eisenhower had taken over one of the offices as his headquarters for Operation Torch. It was there that he and his deputy, General Mark Clark, welcomed Giraud.

The Americans were greatly relieved to see the Frenchman. They had hoped to have him in North Africa by the time of the invasion so that they could announce his appointment as leader of the Vichy forces there. But with the launch of the attack only eight hours away, that was clearly impossible; he would not be able to travel until the landing forces had captured an airport. In the meantime, the Americans planned to broadcast a statement to France's colonies in North Africa in Giraud's name, urging French troops to cooperate with the Allies. It would be transmitted as soon as word came that the landings had been successful.

Because time was short, Eisenhower and Clark had already written the statement for Giraud. It declared that the United States, in order to stop Germany from invading North Africa, had acted first. It then called on French officers and troops to join the Americans in their fight against the occupiers of France. The statement, ostensibly from Giraud, concluded by saying, "I resume my place of combat among you."

But before Eisenhower and Clark could explain the statement to

Giraud, he let them know what he expected from them. "As I understand it," he said, "when I land in North Africa, I am to assume command of all Allied forces and become the Supreme Allied Commander in North Africa." The two Americans were incredulous. "I think," Eisenhower said cautiously, "there is some misunderstanding."

Later, Clark would write that "Ike had never been so shocked and showed it so little. . . . There was no question in my mind that [Giraud] was stating what he believed to be in the agreement. Furthermore, he was under the impression that there would be an almost immediate Allied effort to invade France proper to forestall the German occupation of Vichy territory. Just how he had gotten this impression I was never able to clear up. . . . As we talked it over, it became obvious that we were in for some serious trouble."

The three generals argued for hours, with neither Eisenhower nor Clark able to change Giraud's mind that only a Frenchman could be in charge of an Allied assault on French territory. At his wit's end, Clark finally told Giraud that while he and Eisenhower were happy to have him commanding all the French forces in North Africa, they were not prepared to offer him anything more.

"Then I shall return to France," Giraud replied.

"How are you going back?" Clark asked.

"By the same route I came here."

"Oh, no, you won't," Clark snapped. "That was a one-way submarine. You're not going back to France on it." The Americans then accused Giraud of putting his personal ambition before the best interests of France. He answered the insult with a shrug.

Clark had had enough. Turning to the American colonel who was acting as translator, he snarled, "Tell him this. Tell him that if you don't go along with us, General, you're going to be out in the snow on your ass!"

AT THE SAME TIME that the generals were wrangling in Gibraltar, Jean Boutron arrived at the Saint Charles station in Marseille. He had been in hiding near Lyon since his failed attempt to escape by Lysander two months before. A few days earlier, Marie-Madeleine had sent a messenger to inform him that he was to leave by British submarine on November 7. The messenger told him to go to the Saint Charles bar that morning and await instructions.

When he arrived, Émile Hédin was standing behind the bar. The two, who had never met, introduced themselves by their animal code names. "Bull," Boutron said; "Beaver," Hédin replied. They grinned and shook hands. "In a second," Boutron later wrote, "two animals that did not know each other became fast friends."

Boutron and Hédin were expected at La Pinède at eleven o'clock that morning. After being briefed by Marie-Madeleine, Boutron, along with the other submarine passengers, was scheduled to travel to Cros-de-Cagnes late that afternoon. As she had predicted, none of the generals had shown up.

Shortly before they were to leave, the phone rang. When Hédin answered it, a male voice said hurriedly: "You were to come with someone at eleven o'clock for a rendezvous on the Corniche. Do not come at any cost! Do you understand, at any cost!" The caller abruptly hung up, and a shocked Hédin relayed the message to Boutron. "We looked at each other with anguish," Boutron recalled. He and Hédin had no idea what had happened, but "it clearly was a catastrophe."

Soon afterward, Ernest Siegrist hurried into the bar. It was he who had made the call. Siegrist, who had been outside La Pinède from the beginning of the raid, described to Hédin and Boutron what had happened. He then left to find out the latest news about his arrested colleagues.

Meanwhile, Pierre Dallas, who, together with Colonel Bernis was to direct the second submarine operation, arrived at the bar, along with the other passengers. After absorbing the shock of the arrests of Marie-Madeleine, Faye, and the rest of the Alliance headquarters staff, Dallas decided that the network must carry on with that night's operation. The Avia head had no way of knowing what had happened in the villa that morning, and, for him, the blow of the arrests was compounded by the fear that London had not been informed in time of the change in embarkation sites.

Late that afternoon, Dallas and seven passengers boarded a train to Cros-de-Cagnes. In addition to Boutron, the travelers included two other Alliance agents, two aides of General Giraud, and a friend of the general's who at the last minute had taken the place of Marie-Madeleine's brother. When they arrived, they were escorted to a small hotel near the sea, run by supporters of the network, where Colonel Bernis was waiting for them.

Bernis, too, was stunned by the news from Marseille and worried that the submarine might not show up at the new embarkation point. But he and Dallas shrugged off their concern and followed the same plan they had employed at Lavandou. Although it was cloudy, the weather was far better than it had been two nights before: There was no wind, and the sea was calm, almost flat.

A few minutes before midnight, Dallas and the seven travelers boarded a fishing boat and headed out to sea. Standing in the bow, Dallas flashed the prearranged signal. Consumed with anxiety, Boutron scanned the darkness. Would this be another fiasco, like the Lysander mission? He heard a muffled exclamation from one of his companions, who pointed his finger to the right and exclaimed, "There!" Turning his head, Boutron saw "a low, elongated mass that became more defined as the boat moved forward." Suddenly, he spied the vessel's conning tower. "The message had been received," he later wrote. "There was no trap. The submarine was there." His initial feeling—an enormous sense of relief—was followed by pure euphoria. After all the fears and disappointments of the last seven months, he was finally on his way to London.

A slight problem arose when the British submarine captain, who thought he was rescuing a group of distinguished Vichy generals, saw instead, as one observer put it, "a bunch of ordinary people in tattered old clothes and shivering with cold." Boutron told him he and several of the other travelers were agents of a French intelligence network working with MI6, mentioning the name of Major Richards as their main British contact.

Although he was clearly still suspicious, the commander brought everyone on board. As the sub headed out to sea, Boutron watched

Pierre Dallas, who was heading back to shore. "I was going toward freedom," he recalled, "while he was returning to the enemy and bondage."

Before retiring to the bunk to which he had been assigned, Boutron asked the captain to send a message to MI6 reporting the arrests of Marie-Madeleine and his other colleagues. As soon as the officials there received it, they sent a coded warning over the BBC to all of Alliance's sectors.

In addition to providing news and commentary to occupied Europe, the BBC also served as a conduit of information between the British secret services—MI6 and SOE—and the European resistance networks. The information was sent in the form of brief, cryptic coded messages whose meaning was known only by the networks to which they were directed. MI6's message to Alliance was succinct: "Be careful. In the south of France, the animals are ill with the plague."

AT DAWN THE NEXT day, Fourcade was awakened from a restless sleep by a police inspector who rushed into her cell with a big grin on his face and some "absolutely marvelous" news: The Allies had landed in North Africa. With a smile as wide as his, she embraced him.

When she and the others were taken back to police headquarters later that day for more questioning, they were greeted with even greater warmth by police officials than the day before. Everyone, she recalled, was celebrating the Allied landing.

Jean Léonard, who was the chief police commissioner in Marseille and the man in charge of the agents' interrogation, told Faye that the Allied landing had thrown the Vichy government into a state of turmoil and that police officials there had requested that Faye be brought to them. Buoyed by the enthusiastic response of the French police in Marseille to the Allied invasion, Faye told Fourcade he was sure that Vichy would be receptive to the idea of armed opposition to the Germans, especially in light of the rumors of Germany's imminent occupation of the free zone.

Remembering the disastrous outcome of Faye's earlier efforts to launch a mutiny of French military forces in North Africa, Fourcade urged him to try to escape during the trip to Vichy. A police inspector named Simon Cottoni, who had been assigned to drive Faye there, supported Fourcade's argument. Cottoni, as it turned out, was himself an Alliance agent, recruited by another of Fourcade's lieutenants, and was meeting her and Faye for the first time. He told them the Germans had been on a rampage since their capture and were determined to take them into custody. Cottoni offered to drive Faye to neutral Switzerland, a suggestion that Fourcade emphatically seconded.

She told Faye that his Vichy plan wouldn't work and that everyone there was "rotten to the core." She added that she herself was going to do everything she could to get away. Faye refused to listen. If he didn't at least try to persuade Vichy officials to do the right thing, he said, he would feel like a deserter. His departure with Cottoni, Fourcade later wrote, left her heartbroken.

The next morning, she saw from the pained expression on Jean Léonard's face that the news from Vichy was not good. Friends of Faye's had met with Marshal Pétain, pleaded Faye's case, and urged that Pétain and his government leave for Algiers before the Germans marched into the free zone, which was expected any day now. Pétain refused, and Faye was put in jail. The armistice army did nothing to prepare to resist a German incursion.

Meanwhile, the Abwehr and Gestapo had ordered the Marseille police commissioner to turn over all the papers captured at Alliance's Marseille headquarters, including the diagram with the locations and other details of the network's radio transmitters. Fourcade exclaimed that if Léonard did as the Germans ordered, he would in effect be surrendering all her network's radio sets to them, which would mean the destruction of Alliance.

Léonard responded that he had no option, although Fourcade could see that he was badly shaken by the order. She pleaded with him to allow her and her brother to make a copy of the diagram that would look like the original but with false information. After considerable argument, Léonard agreed, as long as the two documents appeared identical.

Accompanied by two policemen, Fourcade returned to La Pinède to pick up the same items Jacques had used to create the diagram, including squared paper, pens, and a variety of colored inks. Back at the police headquarters, as three inspectors looked on, she and another Alliance agent dictated to Jacques the apocryphal details, including hundreds of incorrect call signs and frequencies. The work was laborious and lasted throughout the late afternoon and well into the night. When it was done, Léonard looked closely at both documents, declaring admiringly that he couldn't tell them apart. To make sure there was no mixup of the two, he took out a cigarette lighter and burned the original in front of Marie-Madeleine and her brother.

On the morning of November 10, Léonard allowed Fourcade to sift through the other documents that had been removed from La Pinède and remove those that were particularly incriminating and would put the lives of agents in jeopardy. Those that were left would be handed over to the Germans, while the rest were burned. Also destroyed was the suitcase filled with documents that Jacques had brought from their mother's house on the Côte d'Azur.

Late that afternoon, however, her sense of relief was replaced by a feeling of panic. Jean Boubil, the inspector who had come to her aid at La Pinède, took her aside and whispered that the Germans had persuaded the Vichy government to send her and her agents to the prison in Castres, a town in Languedoc about 160 miles west of Marseille. From there they would be extradited immediately to Fresnes, the Gestapo prison near Paris.

A few minutes later, Jean Léonard informed Fourcade that she couldn't stay at the police headquarters that night but must return to L'Évêché prison, adding that he would retrieve her and her colleagues the following morning. Fourcade blanched. She told him she had intelligence that the Germans would invade the free zone the following day. They would find her and the other Alliance agents at the prison and take them into custody—so in effect Léonard would have handed them over.

Once again, Léonard gave in, assigning three inspectors to keep watch over her and the others from Alliance. She persuaded her guards to check periodically through the night with other police stations in the free zone to see if there were any signs of incoming German troops. At about midnight, the police in Moulins, a city in central France just south of the demarcation line, reported that German forces were marching in and fanning out through the countryside.

Early in the morning, Léonard came in, his head bowed, and without a word went into his office and shut the door. A truck pulled up outside and a squad of French policemen got out. Fourcade knew they were there to take her and her colleagues to Castres.

She burst into Léonard's office. "The whole police section was there, dismay written on their faces," she remembered. "I was conscious of their tragic role under the German jackboot. . . . I knew, however, for I had just been living in their company, that not one of them wanted to hand us over to the enemy and had done their best to save us."

Explaining that he was under orders from Vichy to transfer the Alliance group to Castres, Léonard assured Fourcade that she and the rest would be safer there than in Marseille. Did he really not know, Fourcade thought, that Castres was simply a springboard for extradition? Despairingly, she glanced at Léon Théus, Léonard's deputy, who had burned the incriminating suitcase and its papers, and at Xavier Piani. Both men, their eyes steady, gazed back at her.

A few minutes later, Fourcade saw Théus walk outside and talk to the head of the waiting police squad. They got back in the truck and drove away. Returning to the building, Théus pulled Fourcade aside. He whispered that he had arranged for Gabriel Rivière and several other Alliance agents to attack the police van taking her and the others to Castres. At that point, Piani joined them. He told Fourcade that he and two inspectors would be in the van and that they would make sure the rescue attempt succeeded.

At that point, Fourcade recalled, all the policemen in the room helped her and her comrades pack up their belongings. On their way out, several agents picked up revolvers and Sten guns lying around the room, as well as a sealed envelope containing eighty thousand francs that had been taken from the villa. While all that was going on, Théus grabbed a pile of paper—the transcripts of the interrogations of Fourcade and the other agents—and burned it. As she left, Fourcade shook hands with all those who had helped her and wished them luck. Two policemen whispered that they were leaving that night to join the Alliance sector in Nice.

Once in the van, she promised Piani that she would arrange for him and the two inspectors "guarding" her and the others to escape to London. She knew that if they did not leave France, the Germans would track them down and, in all likelihood, execute them.

At the rendezvous point agreed upon by Théus and Rivière, a swarm of Alliance agents stopped the van and liberated their colleagues. "Come on!" yelled Rivière. "We can't hang around here." The three French policemen joined their erstwhile captives aboard the large truck that Rivière had commandeered. As it sped along the road toward Avignon, a vehicle appeared in the distance, advancing slowly toward them. Fourcade stiffened. It was an open-topped German staff car—the vanguard of a flood of troops that was soon to follow. A Wehrmacht officer sat next to the driver, staring intently at a large map spread across his knees. They were completely unprotected.

Struck by the same thought, several agents in the truck took out the Sten guns and revolvers they had pilfered from the police headquarters. "No!" Fourcade shouted. "Don't move!" As tempting as the thought of killing the Germans was, "it would be too idiotic a risk after all our providential luck," she wrote. "Our duty was elsewhere."

She turned and watched as the German car passed by and disappeared down the road.

CHAPTER 17

OPERATION ATTILA

THE GERMANS CALLED IT OPERATION ATTILA.

On November 11, 1942, more than two hundred thousand Wehrmacht troops, armed with tanks and artillery, crossed France's demarcation line and flooded into the free zone. By nightfall, the army's panzers had reached the Mediterranean coast and were parading through Marseille. Italian forces, meanwhile, moved into Nice and other cities on the eastern edge of the Côte d'Azur.

The invasion prompted a few feeble protests from Vichy radio, but those broadcasts—and the scuttling of the remnants of the French fleet at their base in Toulon—were the only gestures of resistance made by Pétain's government. The armistice army was disbanded and its weapons confiscated.

Although the Germans retained Pétain and Laval at the top of the Vichy government, the illusion of power and authority that the two men had sought to project was brutally stripped away. In the aftermath of the occupation, they were exposed for what they were—figureheads who were there to serve their German masters. Members of the Vichy police were seen as Nazi henchmen who rounded up Jews for deportation, along with other French citizens who had been drafted by the Reich to serve as slave labor in Germany.

For Fourcade and others in the resistance, there would be no more safe havens, no buffers of any kind shielding them from Nazi fury. No longer could they count on sympathetic members of the Vichy police and other security forces to turn a blind eye to their activities or come to their aid.

As it happened, many anti-German policemen and security officials joined resistance networks after the occupation. The two inspectors who told Marie-Madeleine they were about to enlist in Alliance did so; one of them eventually became head of the Alliance sector in the northwestern city of Rennes. Superintendent Léon Théus, who had played a key role in Fourcade's rescue, cofounded a new resistance network called Ajax, whose members were largely former policemen. The Nazis would hunt down these new recruits as relentlessly as they did veteran Alliance operatives. Nowhere in France would any resister feel safe again for the duration of the war.

THE EVENT THAT TRIGGERED Germany's occupation of the free zone—the Allied invasion of North Africa—had not unfolded in the way that the U.S. government had hoped or expected. Contrary to Roosevelt's prediction that Vichy forces would welcome an assault by American troops, the French mounted stiff opposition at almost every landing site. General Giraud was finally airlifted to Algiers, but French troops didn't seem inclined to follow him. In any event, another candidate had already preceded him on the scene—none other than Admiral François Darlan, commander of the Vichy military, who happened to be in Algiers visiting his ill son at the time of the Allied assault.

In an effort to stop Vichy's armed resistance to the invasion, Americans offered a deal to the opportunistic Darlan: In exchange for his engineering a cease-fire, the Allies would appoint him high commissioner, or governor, of North Africa. For a time, Darlan seesawed back and forth on the deal, first accepting it, then reneging. Finally, under heavy Allied pressure, he gave in and ordered an armistice.

Darlan's appointment was one of the Roosevelt administration's most controversial decisions of the war and was greeted with a storm of protest around the globe. The president was unfazed by the criticism, telling a French resistance leader visiting Washington: "For my part, I am not an idealist like [Woodrow] Wilson. I am concerned above all with efficiency. I have problems to solve. Those who help me solve them are welcome. Today, Darlan gives me Algiers and I cry 'Vive Darlan!' If Quisling gives me Oslo, I will cry 'Vive Quisling!' Let Laval give me Paris tomorrow, and I will cry 'Vive Laval!' "

In the view of many, such cynical pragmatism undermined the lofty moral position of the Allied cause. Members of the French and other European resistance movements, whose lives were in constant danger due in part to collaborators like Darlan, were the most outspoken in expressing their dismay and anger. For Jean Boutron, who had been transported to Algiers by the submarine that rescued him, the news of Darlan's appointment "hit me like a bomb. I was stupefied. I had escaped Darlan's police in France so that I could deal with his police in Algeria? And the Allies were responsible for this? The thing seemed so absurd that all I could do was laugh."*

In France, meanwhile, the march to de Gaulle accelerated. On November 17, leaders of some of France's largest resistance movements issued a statement calling for de Gaulle, "their uncontested leader," to be named governor of North Africa. De Gaulle was supported as well by much of the British public, most members of Parliament, and the British press. Even some high-level British government officials, including several from the Foreign Office, joined the parade.

Like nearly everyone else, Winston Churchill, who had reluctantly supported Darlan's appointment, couldn't help knowing that it was a huge political mistake and that some corrective action was necessary. It wasn't long before the corrective occurred. On Christmas Eve 1942, a twenty-year-old French military trainee burst into Darlan's headquarters in Algiers and shot him dead. There were suspi-

---

* After a short stay in Algiers, Boutron made it to London, where he joined de Gaulle's staff. He later enlisted in the Free French navy and was appointed captain of a frigate.

cions that American and British secret services had arranged the murder, but nothing was ever proved.

To replace Darlan, the U.S. military turned to Giraud. But the general, who accepted the position, also turned out to be extremely unpopular and had little or no Allied support, except in Washington. "Between Giraud and de Gaulle, there is no real choice," a French resistance leader said. "Giraud is not a name at all in France. De Gaulle is more than a name, he is a legend."

FOURCADE WAS APPALLED BY the Giraud fiasco and the peril that now faced her network because of it. After more than a year of relative refuge and stability in Marseille, she and her staff were fugitives again. Following their November 11 escape, they were whisked off to Châteaurenard, a rural Provençal town about fifty-five miles northeast of Marseille. Like shadows, they crept down the streets in the dark to various hiding places. They would remain in those bolt-holes until false identity papers could be prepared for them.

The task was undertaken by the redoubtable Ernest Siegrist, who not only served as Alliance's chief of security but was also a skilled forger. After photographs were taken of Fourcade and the others, Siegrist inserted their names, descriptions, and fingerprints and pasted their photos onto false identity cards, complete with perfectly forged seals. According to her new card, Fourcade was now a vegetable and fruit dealer, born in North Africa, who had been cut off from her home by the American landings there. Siegrist also provided her and the others with false ration cards for food and clothing, along with driver's licenses and other documents appropriate for their new identities.

Plagued by worry about Faye and his fate in German-controlled Vichy, Marie-Madeleine left immediately for the Alliance sector in Toulouse. When she arrived, Jean Philippe, the police superintendent who moonlighted as the network's security chief there, told her that the Germans and Vichy police were scrambling to find her. But the Toulouse sector, at least for the moment, appeared quiet, and Fourcade decided to stay there long enough to draw a breath and assess the network's status.

She was joined by a new addition to her team—a twenty-seven-year-old British radio operator known as Edward Rodney. He had been dispatched from London on October 26, 1942, landing by Lysander at the field in Ussel and taken to Toulouse to await further orders. The newcomer could not have been more different from the first radio operator sent by MI6—Arthur Bradley Davies, the infamous "Bla." Tall and fair-haired, with pale blue eyes and a lively sense of humor, Rodney "looked terribly British, with his blond hair and Burberry trench coat," Monique Bontinck remembered.

It was not until the end of the war that Bontinck and Fourcade discovered that Edward Rodney was a *nom de guerre*. In reality, he was Ferdinand Edward Rodriguez, a young Briton with a pedigree as exotic as his name. At the turn of the century, just a few years before the Bolshevik revolution, Rodriguez's father, a Spaniard, had been the secretary to a high-level Spanish diplomat in the Russian capital of St. Petersburg. There he met Rodriguez's mother, a young Englishwoman who served as a companion to the wife of the British ambassador. The two fell in love and were married.

Not long afterward, they moved to Paris, where they had four children—three girls and Ferdinand, who was the baby of the family. Rodriguez's father died when Ferdy, as he was called, was a boy, and his mother remained in Paris with her children. After high school, Rodriguez attended the École Supérieure de Commerce de Paris, France's foremost business school, and became an accountant.

When the war broke out, he tried to enlist in the French army, but because he was a British citizen, he was rejected. He promptly went to London and joined the British army's Royal Signal Corps. In 1941, he was attached to the British Eighth Army in Egypt, serving as a signals officer in a reconnaissance group that slipped behind enemy lines at night to collect intelligence on German positions.

The following year, Rodriguez, who spoke flawless French without an accent, was recruited by MI6 and, during his training, met Léon Faye during Faye's trip to London that August. "I was looking

FERDINAND RODRIGUEZ (LEFT) WITH THE BRITISH EIGHTH ARMY IN EGYPT

for a network to serve," Rodriguez recalled, "and he was looking for an agent who knew his country as well as he knew it himself." Impressed by Faye's passion and charisma, he expressed interest in joining Alliance, although he later acknowledged he was a bit skeptical when told that the leader of the network was a woman. But the moment he met Fourcade, he later said, he was won over. She was just as impressed with him, citing, in a later message to MI6, his "constant good humor, unfailing loyalty, intelligence, courage, and calm." He was given the code name of Magpie—Pie for short—and swiftly became one of the most important members of Fourcade's team.

After handing Rodriguez a message to send to London assuring MI6 that she was safe, Fourcade began picking up the threads of her operation. Weeks before, in preparation for the possible destruction of Alliance's headquarters in Marseille, she had arranged for Colonel Charles Bernis, head of the Nice sector, to take over command of network activities in the southern zone and Maurice de MacMahon, who led the Paris sector, to do the same in the north. The preparation had paid off: With the exception of Marseille, everything was still running smoothly.

In the north, all sectors had escaped German detection thus far and were operating at peak efficiency. Bernis, who had come to report to her in Toulouse, said that Alliance's key agents in Marseille—Gabriel Rivière and Émile Hédin among them—had managed to escape and were being assigned to new sectors. The stations in Grenoble, Vichy, Nice, and other locations in central France were all still functioning well.

Then Fourcade received the best news of all: Léon Faye had escaped from the Vichy prison to which he had been confined since his abortive attempt to persuade Pétain to fight the Germans. Faye's escape was as dramatic as that of General Giraud: He had lowered himself down a rope from the fourth floor of the prison, followed by General Gabriel Cochet, the former head of the French army's intelligence branch, who had been imprisoned in 1941 for his repeated calls for resistance against the Germans. The two men's escape was organized by members of Alliance's Vichy and Grenoble sectors, who immediately spirited them away.

While all this was taking place, Fourcade made good on her promise to Superintendent Xavier Piani and the other two French policemen who had helped engineer her own escape from Marseille. On the night of November 25, a Lysander that she had summoned from Britain arrived at the field in Ussel. When she had asked MI6 officials to send the plane, she didn't tell them who the passengers would be. Increasingly anxious about her safety, especially in light of her recent capture, they had repeatedly appealed to her to come to London and obviously believed, as she well knew, that she would be one of the Lysander passengers leaving France.

Early the next morning, an MI6 welcoming party, headed by Kenneth Cohen, the official in charge of Alliance operations, waited on the tarmac at an RAF base near London. After the Lysander taxied to a stop in front of Cohen and the others, they were astonished to see three unknown French policemen extricate themselves with difficulty from the cockpit. At the time, MI6 higher-ups were less than thrilled by Fourcade's small deceit, but they forgave her when told the reason for the unexpected passengers.

These various successful escapes had given her a sense of well-being, but that feeling quickly vanished after a surprise visit from Colonel Édouard Kauffmann, the leader of Alliance's Dordogne sector. Kauffmann, who had traveled to Paris to see what he could find out about the fate of the network agents betrayed by Bla, returned with horrific news: They all had been executed on November 30.

Closing her eyes, Fourcade could see them in her mind: Antoine Hugon, leader of the Brittany sector, who had triumphantly arrived in Pau in the summer of 1941 with the cloth map of the Saint-Nazaire submarine base wrapped around his middle; Lucien Vallet, her light-hearted, charming radio operator in Pau who had first warned her about Bla; Edmond Poulain, who had been engaged to Monique Bontinck. Nine agents in all had been executed. Consumed with grief and rage, Fourcade struggled to regain control of her emotions. The only way to do that, she concluded, was to continue working to eradicate the "monsters" who had murdered her friends.

Believing that her continued presence in Toulouse was putting the agents there at risk, she, along with Bontinck and Rodriguez, slipped away to the Corrèze, the wild, rocky region in south central France where the Ussel landing field was located and where, because of its isolated location, she felt particularly safe. She had a joyous reunion with Faye there on December 17.

The two of them, along with Bontinck and Rodriguez, would remain near Ussel through the holidays, gathering for Christmas dinner with other agents at the house of Jean Vinzant, the leader of the sector there. A year earlier, she noted, Alliance had boasted about one hundred members. Now there were nearly a thousand. Each of them was part of this special family that she had helped create, including those who had disappeared and whose legacy she and the others had inherited.

CHAPTER 18

"DOWN GO THE U-BOATS"

HROUGHOUT THAT YEAR'S CHRISTMAS HOLIDAYS, FOURCADE AND
Faye pored over a backlog of intelligence sent to London that, because of the chaos of the previous six weeks, they had not yet had a
chance to carefully examine. The reports revealed that despite growing threats to Alliance's survival, its agents were still producing a
flood of vital information.

The messages and other materials touched on a wide array of subjects, among them the antiaircraft defenses and types of planes on
airfields throughout France, German troop movements toward the
Russian front, and samples of synthetic fuels and a new type of gas
mask. But the most important reports, as had been true since 1941,
focused on the German submarine bases near Bordeaux and on
France's Atlantic coast.

Thanks in part to the intelligence provided by Alliance and other
French spy networks, Britain had become considerably more effective in combating the depredations of German submarines on its
shipping in the Atlantic. Supplies transported from North America
were still scarce, yet more were getting through. But there was another reason why intelligence about the U-boats' movements and positions remained crucially important.

By the end of 1942, the Allies were on the verge of halting Germany's seemingly unstoppable momentum. The Red Army was close to defeating the Wehrmacht at Stalingrad—a five-month bloodbath that would produce more than a million casualties. American and British forces, meanwhile, were slogging their way across North Africa. Although many punishing battles lay ahead, the Western Allies would wrest the region from Germany in the early spring of 1943.

In January 1943, Winston Churchill and Franklin Roosevelt met at Casablanca to plot future offensives in the European theater. Among their key decisions was a massive buildup of U.S. forces in England to prepare for the upcoming invasion of Western Europe. The two leaders noted the obvious: In order for American troop convoys and war matériel to make their way safely to Britain, the Atlantic must be cleared of German submarines. If the U-boats continued to pose a danger, D-Day might be rendered impossible.

By late 1942, dozens of Alliance agents and subagents had infiltrated all the ports and U-boat bases in the west of France, from Bordeaux and La Rochelle on the southwestern coast to Lorient, Saint-Nazaire, and Brest in the northwest. The leaders of these sectors, most of them in their twenties, were an impressive group.

One of them was twenty-four-year-old Philippe Koenigswerther, the slight, blond, boyish head of Alliance operations at the submarine base at La Rochelle and the inland port near Bordeaux, located on the Gironde River. The Bordeaux port was particularly important because of the number and variety of vessels it housed, from submarines and warships to mine-laying boats, torpedo transports, and blockade runners. Bordeaux was a major destination for goods to support the German war effort, and cargo ships bringing those goods headed there, provided they were successful in slipping through an Allied naval blockade in the Atlantic.

A member of a prominent, wealthy Jewish family in Paris, Koenigswerther had escaped to Britain in a sailboat at the time of France's occupation. His parents were also able to flee, spending the rest of the war in New York. In London, Koenigswerther joined the Free French and was recruited by BCRA, its intelligence and sabotage service,

PHILIPPE
KOENIGSWERTHER

which trained him in the specifics of gathering information about the German navy. In 1941, he was parachuted back to France, where he was captured by the Germans in Bordeaux. After escaping to Britain, he returned to France in September 1942 but was dropped by parachute in the wrong location in the Dordogne and was unable to make contact with BCRA. After meeting an Alliance operative, he asked for a job with Fourcade's network. MI6 checked him out and urged her to take him on.

Koenigswerther, who, according to Marie-Madeleine, looked more like Little Lord Fauntleroy than an intelligence agent, proved to be a brilliant organizer, recruiting a wide-ranging group of informants. As was true throughout Alliance, they came from all classes of society—regular and reserve naval officers, workmen, secretaries, shopkeepers, priests, and at least one Protestant pastor. One of Koenigswerther's key operatives was the former mayor of La Rochelle, who was dismissed by the Germans in 1940 for refusing to lower the French flag at the city hall after his country's capitulation. Another was Franck Gardes, a crane operator at the La Rochelle submarine base, who used his lofty vantage point in the crane's cab to monitor the comings and goings of U-boats. In August 1943, after Gardes reported the departure of five subs from the base, the RAF sank all of them in the Bay of Biscay.

One of Koenigswerther's greatest successes was providing the information that led to Operation Frankton, arguably the most daring British commando raid of the war. In the late fall of 1942, he had sent intelligence to MI6 about the location of six cargo ships anchored in the Gironde. Based on that knowledge, a small group of Royal Marine commandoes, using canoes, paddled up the river on December 11 and placed limpet mines on the hulls of the ships. The resulting explosions caused heavy damage.

In Brittany, another young agent—twenty-four-year-old Lucien Poulard—had been praised by the British for his own stellar work and that of his operatives. One of the air force pilots recruited by Léon Faye for Alliance in early 1942, Poulard had worked for several months as Faye's adjutant, which, among other things, involved his reluctant participation in the execution of Bla. In early November 1942, Poulard was sent back to his native Brittany to form subnetworks to spy on the submarine bases at Saint-Nazaire and Brest.

At Brest, Poulard oversaw the efforts of Maurice Gillet, a maritime broker who headed the Alliance group scouting out information at the base there. Eight members of his own family were in the group. Another was the young seamstress, code-named Shrimp, who repaired the life vests of the submariners. They usually brought the vests to her as they were getting ready to leave on a patrol, and by listening carefully to their chatter, she often learned the times and dates of their subs' sailing. Thanks to the information provided by the Brest crew, several submarines based there were sunk by the RAF and Royal Navy shortly after they left the port. As Poulard delightedly reported to Marie-Madeleine, "A word from us to London, and down go the U-boats."

There was yet another outstanding subnetwork in Brittany on which Marie-Madeleine could depend. It had considerably more autonomy than the others, as a result of her determination to begin decentralizing Alliance's operations. The group, called Sea Star, was headed by a twenty-eight-year-old former naval officer named Joël Lemoigne.

Soon after Marie-Madeleine's escape from Marseille, Lemoigne paid her a visit. He brought with him a large amount of information about the Lorient base, including a sheet of paper that listed the exact number of U-boats based there, giving their fleet numbers and individual call signs as well as their operational rosters and any damages or losses they had sustained. It was, Marie-Madeleine noted, a complete picture of the entire base. She asked Lemoigne who had written the report. He said he couldn't tell her. He did, however, give her a few details about his source, including the fact that he was a naval engineer, but said he had promised the man he would not reveal his name.

That wasn't good enough for Marie-Madeleine. She told him she had to know the identity of the report's author before she could vouch for its authenticity to the British. The two sparred verbally for a few more minutes, then Lemoigne scribbled something on a scrap of paper and got up to leave. As he shook her hand on his way out, he slipped her the paper. After he'd gone, she looked down. On it was written "The engineer is Jacques Stosskopf."

FOR MORE THAN TWO YEARS, Admiral Karl Dönitz had ruled his submarine kingdom from a stately, elegant seaside château overlooking the huge base at Lorient. The twenty-room mansion, built in the nineteenth century by a French tycoon who had made his money in the sardine trade, boasted an unobstructed view of the harbor and of the massive fortress-like concrete bunkers that housed Dönitz's U-boats.

The commander of the Reich's submarine fleet took great pride in all his bases, whose close proximity to the Atlantic killing grounds had made life so much easier for his crews. But the crown jewel was Lorient, a once quaint and peaceful fishing village on the Bay of Biscay that Dönitz had transformed into the largest submarine base in the world.

From the château's grand salon, which he had turned into his command post, Dönitz monitored the operations of his "gray wolves." On nice days, the salon's lofty windows were opened, and the admiral inhaled the sea air as he dispatched orders to his submarines by radio, "moving them like chess pieces," in the words of one historian, and overseeing their attacks. He and his staff kept track of the wolf packs' positions on a huge map of the Atlantic hung on one of the salon's walls.

Dönitz was known for his paternal attitude toward his crews, who knew that if they got into trouble at sea, an SOS to him would bring immediate help from other submarines. In the evenings, the admiral, over dinner with his staff in the villa's baronial dining room, would lift a glass of Bordeaux and toast his U-boats' successes.

Submariners considered themselves the royalty of the German navy, and when they returned from successful patrols, their reception, especially at Lorient, was regal indeed. Dönitz himself was on hand to greet them, as was a brass band and a crowd of welcomers, including a number of attractive young German women who would bestow flowers and kisses on the victorious sub commanders. Medals would be awarded, speeches made, and triumphant anthems played.

The backdrop for the celebrations were the gigantic submarine pens, nineteen in all, each connected by its own channel to the main harbor. Beneath the cavernous, vault-like structures, with their fifteen-feet-thick concrete walls and roofs, was an enormous underground city, replete with offices, workshops, guard rooms, living spaces for crewmen and key workers, a hospital, electrical and water purification facilities, and vast storage spaces for fuel, explosives, and spare parts. Although defended by batteries of antiaircraft guns that ringed the town, the U-boat pens, which were built in late 1940 and early 1941, didn't really need them. Their thick concrete shells proved largely impenetrable to the bombs that rained down on them during frequent RAF bombing raids in 1942 and 1943. The raids, in fact, did far more damage to the town of Lorient and its residents than to the base itself. "It was a great mistake on the part of the British not to have attacked these pens from the air while they were under construction," Dönitz later observed, "but Bomber Command preferred to raid towns in Germany. Once the U boats were in their pens, it would be too late."

Yet although he was confident that his base could survive any aerial assault, he was less sure of its security on the ground. Dönitz was well aware of the problem posed by the infiltration of Allied spies in Lorient and the other French bases. But he remained convinced that the Abwehr and Gestapo would root them out and that his beloved submarines would go on to help win the war for Germany.

To limit the pilfering of secrets, the Lorient base was heavily guarded. Nonetheless, there remained an insoluble problem: Dönitz was forced to rely on French tradesmen, technicians, dockyard hands, construction workers, and others to do much of the labor in and around the facility. "From an operational point of view, Dönitz gained a great deal by moving his bases six hundred miles closer to his hunting grounds," U.S. Rear Admiral Daniel V. Gallery noted. "From a security point of view, he lost."

Even if the base itself had been impenetrable, keeping all its secrets would have been impossible. While the U-boats were in the pens being readied for the next patrols, their young crewmen, recuperating from the stress of their last mission, indulged in a great deal of hard partying. They were given the run of the town of Lorient, frequenting the many bars, brothels, cafés, and gambling clubs that catered to them.

In turn, the employees of those businesses—prostitutes and bartenders prominent among them—took advantage of the submariners' binges to ferret out details of submarine arrivals and departures, along with other vital bits of intelligence. "Anyone who kept his ears open after the first five or six rounds of drinks could pick up many items of secret official information," one observer remarked.

For the Germans, such problems were exacerbated by the fact that Lorient, along with Brest and Saint-Nazaire, was located in the northern French province of Brittany. While German security officials viewed every French citizen as a potential enemy of the Reich, they were uneasily aware that Bretons were more hostile than most of their compatriots.

A craggy, starkly beautiful, wind-swept peninsula that extends into the stormy North Atlantic, Brittany seemed to many to be a land apart from the rest of France. Likewise, its people regarded themselves as a race quite different from the residents of other parts of the country.

Known for their independent, passionate, rebellious spirit, Bretons were descended from Celtic settlers who had populated the area in the sixth century. In many ways, the residents of Brittany seemed more like the citizens of Celtic lands like Ireland and Wales than to the rest of the French. Indeed, as they pointed out, their native Breton language had more in common with Gaelic and Welsh than it had with French. Bretons never lost sight of the fact that Brittany was an independent kingdom until it was absorbed by France and became a province in 1532.

"In Breton eyes, if your family hadn't lived in Brittany for generations, you were new here," the novelist Jean-Luc Bannalec wrote. "Even if [a Parisian] married a Breton woman, had Breton children and spent his twilight years here, he would always remain an 'outsider.' After two or three generations, his great-grandchildren would be sure to hear murmurs of 'Parisian.'"

If Bretons thought of Parisians as outsiders, it's not hard to guess what they thought of the Germans. On the surface, most residents of Lorient and elsewhere in Brittany might have seemed submissive, but underneath was a simmering hatred that, for more than a few, manifested itself in resistance work.

The Germans' worst enemy in Lorient, however, was not one of the town's natives. It was a Frenchman trusted by Dönitz and despised by the Bretons—the naval engineer Jacques Stosskopf.

ON OCTOBER 24, 1942, a contingent of French workers at Lorient was dispatched to Germany to serve as forced laborers there. As they trudged past a crowd of fellow workers on their way to the railway station, several in the crowd shouted, "Death to Stosskopf!"

The epithets were aimed at a man who, in the words of one historian, was the most hated Frenchman in Brittany during the war. The deputy chief of naval construction at the Lorient shipyard, the forty-three-year-old Stosskopf was a native of the French region of Alsace, which borders Germany. He spoke fluent German and was regarded by the occupiers and by his countrymen as a diehard collaborator.

Dönitz and his staff were so dependent on Stosskopf that he was given the run of the shipyard and base. A cold, formal perfectionist, he meticulously inspected the work of French laborers to make sure they were living up to his and the Germans' exacting standards. He also had access to top-secret information—everything from operational orders and U-boat movements to debriefing reports of submarine crews after their missions. His French colleagues loathed him not only because he used his technical expertise for the Germans' benefit but also because he socialized with Dönitz's staff and even invited them to his home.

In fact, the "traitor Stosskopf" turned out to be one of the most brilliant, audacious Allied spies of World War II. Since the fall of 1940, he had been providing a treasure trove of intelligence about German submarine operations at Lorient, first to high-ranking anti-German naval officers at Vichy and then to Fourcade's network.

Stosskopf had fought in World War I and won a Croix de Guerre. After the war, he studied maritime engineering at the prestigious École Polytechnique near Paris, which produced elite technocrats to run French industry and the government. In 1938, he had been brought to Lorient to help monitor the construction of new ships. He was soon promoted to chief engineer. As part of his job, he worked closely with French naval intelligence officials in Paris.

When the Germans arrived in June 1940, the word spread that Stosskopf had heartily welcomed them. In fact, he hated the intruders and initially had tried to avoid any contact with them. But his friends at naval intelligence, who were now in Vichy but who remained resolutely opposed to German occupation, persuaded him that with his knowledge of German, he could provide them with invaluable information about the enemy's activities at the base. He agreed.

Stosskopf then launched a campaign to win the Germans' trust. It proved so successful that when the submarine base became operational, he was one of the few Frenchmen in a high-level position to be allowed to enter it. Under the pretext of supervising French workers, he could come and go as he wished without arousing suspicion.

Stosskopf regularly traveled to Vichy to hand over the fruits of his labor: details about the submarine pens, the number and identification of the U-boats housed there, the names of their captains, the dates of their missions. In addition, he noted the technical innovations in submarine warfare made by the Germans.

His reports also contained details of the homecoming ceremonies of subs returning from their missions, to which he was always invited. When a sub entered the harbor, it displayed victory pennants on its forward stay, one for each ship the crew had sunk. A white pennant signified a merchant ship, a red pennant meant a warship,

JACQUES
STOSSKOPF

and a red-and-white pennant was a cruiser. Stosskopf noted the number and color of the pennants and cross-checked them with the insignias painted on the submarines. Instead of a number, each sub was identified by a distinctive emblem, such as a bull's head, cupid, fish, iron cross, heart, or four aces. In that way, he could identify the U-boats and the precise successes—or failures—of their missions.

His friends at naval intelligence, meanwhile, passed on all this information to the British, who were anxious to learn as much about Dönitz's operation as they could. Shortly before the Germans occupied the free zone, Stosskopf began working for Joël Lemoigne and Alliance's Sea Star group. As the war progressed, he also transmitted information from a group of young French engineers who worked for him and whom he recruited as subagents.

For Marie-Madeleine and the British, Stosskopf was a gift from the gods. Their constant worry was how long he could continue this extraordinarily risky double life before the Abwehr and Gestapo finally caught up with him.

1943–1944

AFTER GERMAN TROOPS OCCUPY ALL OF FRANCE IN NO-
VEMBER 1942, MARIE-MADELEINE FOURCADE IS CON-
STANTLY ON THE RUN, JUST ONE STEP AHEAD OF THE
GESTAPO. DURING THE NEXT EIGHT MONTHS, SHE MOVES
HER HEADQUARTERS TO EIGHT DIFFERENT PLACES, START-
ING IN MARSEILLE AND ENDING IN PARIS.

CHAPTER 19

ON THE RUN

FOR THE REST OF HER LIFE, MARIE-MADELEINE FOURCADE WOULD refer to 1943 as "the terrible year."

Faced with the looming Allied triumphs in North Africa and Stalingrad, the Reich, once seemingly omnipotent, was under threat and on the defensive, which made life even more perilous and menacing for those under its thumb and especially for those who actively resisted it.

The Reich's military defeats in 1943 coincided with a sharp increase in resistance activity in France, sparked primarily by Germany's decision to draft hundreds of thousands of French citizens to work as forced labor in its industrial war effort. Initially, Pierre Laval had called on the French to volunteer, but when few responded, he issued an order requiring all Frenchmen between the ages of eighteen and fifty and all unmarried women between twenty-one and thirty-five to give two years of service to German war work. The Service du Travail Obligatoire (or STO, as it was commonly known) was in effect a national draft for slave labor—imposed by the French government itself.

Until the work draft, the lives of most of the French had not been deeply affected by German repression. STO, however, hit home in the most literal way: Virtually every family had a loved one in danger of being rounded up. For many, enduring the occupation was now no longer an option; it was time to work toward ending it. As a result, the resistance finally became a true force in French society. Clandestine newspapers called on all French citizens to refuse to obey the order. Worker strikes and protests multiplied. More important, tens of thousands of men left their homes and went underground. The lightly populated, heavily wooded French countryside, along with mountainous regions in the east and south of the country, became favorite hiding places; in those out-of-the way places, members of newly formed quasiguerrilla groups, called *maquis,* lived off the land and began to plot sabotage and subversion.

Once it had wrested control of policing and security from the German military, the SS set out to destroy the increasingly audacious resistance networks and movements. "If there had been any bridle upon the terror before 1943, it was swept away now," recalled Pierre de Vomécourt, a prominent resistance leader.

From mid-1942 to mid-1943, German security forces, along with French police, arrested some sixteen thousand resistance members, many of whom were tortured and put to death. Also taking part in the purge was a brutal new French paramilitary force called the Milice, whose members, according to Vomécourt, were, "almost to a man, thugs on the make."

For the Abwehr and Gestapo, the Alliance network was a key target. In late 1942, a suspected French spy was arrested in the Alsatian city of Strasbourg. Under harsh interrogation by the Gestapo, he revealed he had been recruited to collect information in Alsace by "an important British intelligence network" and had met its two leaders, whose code names were Aigle (Eagle) and Hérisson (Hedgehog). The Strasbourg Gestapo reported to its headquarters in Paris that it had opened a full investigation into this clandestine organization whose members took the names of animals as pseudonyms. The Germans began referring to the group as Noah's Ark.

WHILE MARIE-MADELEINE LOVED THE peace and security of Ussel, she knew that her presence there was putting at risk the clandestine Lysander landings at the nearby airfield. So two days before the 1943 New Year, she, together with Faye, Bontinck, and Rodriguez, moved to an abandoned château on the outskirts of Sarlat, a medieval town in the Dordogne, about ninety miles to the southwest.

The capital of the Dordogne in the Middle Ages, Sarlat looked, in the words of one writer, "as if it had been preserved in aspic since the 16th century, a glorious jumble of medieval houses, narrow alleyways, dank tunnels, and grand Renaissance townhouses." But Fourcade was in no mood to appreciate the beauty of the town, with its honey-colored stone buildings, gracious central square, and imposing cathedral. She was gloomy and on edge, a state of mind not helped by her stay in the dark, dusty, neglected château that had become her new headquarters.

Her spirits rose briefly on New Year's Day when the château's ancient stove rumbled to life and more than a dozen Alliance agents and staff members came together again to enjoy a holiday feast. She, Faye, Bontinck, and Rodriguez were joined by, among others, Maurice Coustenoble, Philippe Koenigswerther, Lucien Poulard, Ernest Siegrist, and Colonel Édouard Kauffmann, the head of the Dordogne sector. The dinner was made even more cheerful by the largesse of Kauffmann, who owned a farm near Sarlat. He had brought with him a cornucopia of foods that were unavailable even on the black market, including a ham and some of the famous Dordogne truffles, along with a selection of wines from his extensive cellar. As Fourcade listened to the laughter, lively conversation, and clink of glasses, her eyes filled with tears at the sight of her veteran agents and newcomers celebrating together.

But when they left the next day, her distress returned. In her increasingly unsettled and dangerous life, she was now forced to deal with yet another complication: She was expecting Faye's child. Her pregnancy could not have come at a more inopportune time, but it did not deflect her from her commitment to Alliance. Faye knew about the pregnancy, as did Bontinck and Rodriguez, but it's unclear how many others were aware of her condition. Fourcade, who was extremely slender, likely did everything she could to conceal it, keeping it a closely guarded secret both during the war and afterward. In her memoirs, she made no mention of it, just as she never discussed the nature of her relationship with Faye.

Her emotional state, already fragile, suffered another blow when on January 13, Faye left for Ussel, where he would board his second Lysander flight to London. While she knew it was important, for the network's sake, that he go, his departure hit her hard. She couldn't rid herself of a sense of impending danger, and, on the night he left, she wrote to Mouchou Damm, the leader of Alliance's Toulouse sector, asking him to find her a new, less isolated headquarters as soon as possible. Unable to sleep that night, she barricaded herself inside the château.

Before dawn the next morning, she heard the crunch of tires on the gravel drive outside. Turning out the light, she hid behind the massive front door, a small revolver in her hand. To her relief, the door opened to reveal Ferdinand Rodriguez, who had driven Faye to Ussel. He walked in, carrying a suitcase, and told her to relax: Everything had gone as planned.

After giving her a British cigarette from a cache in his pocket, he opened the suitcase, which the Lysander had brought from London, and took out a tin of powdered coffee, one of the many small gifts that the British routinely included when they sent questionnaires, along with thousands of francs in brick-like bundles plus letters, reports, and various other items. For the next hour or so, Fourcade smoked, slowly sipped her coffee, and read the piles of papers which she had been sent, most of them dealing with top-secret problems on which information was urgently needed. Later that morning, she summoned Colonel Kauffmann and told him she was leaving early the following day. Damm had found her a house in Cahors, another charming medieval town, about thirty miles south of Sarlat.

At first light, the two vehicles sent by Kauffmann to take her, Bontinck, Rodriguez, and Ernest Siegrist to Cahors, along with all their papers and equipment, stood waiting outside the château's front door. Once again, Fourcade had not slept, and she knew from experience that her insomnia often presaged imminent peril.

Before she and the others left, Rodriguez tapped out some last-minute messages to London. The reception was excellent, and he wanted to continue for another few minutes. Gripped by a premonition, Fourcade demanded that he stop immediately and told Siegrist to turn off the power. The network's security chief did so. Rodriguez folded his aerial and put his transmitter into its case. As they hurried out the door, he shot her a doubtful look that she interpreted as questioning her nerve.

The next day, Siegrist returned to the château to retrieve a reserve transmitter that Rodriguez had hidden in a small copse of trees at the back of the garden. Two peasants who lived nearby stopped his car before he reached the château. They said that several Germans, their guns drawn, had surrounded the place right after Siegrist and the others had left. The Germans said they were after a "Mrs. Harrison" and were furious to find out she had vanished.

When Siegrist told Fourcade about the raid, she laughed. The Germans clearly didn't know who she was. Someone had told them her alias of "Hérisson" and they interpreted it as "Harrison." They thought she was an Englishwoman.

Deep down, however, she knew this was no laughing matter. Her pursuers were closing in on her.

FOURCADE's NEW HIDING PLACE was in another jewel of a medieval town, tucked into a bend of the Lot River and almost completely surrounded by water. Cahors was known not only for its dramatic setting and distinctive historic buildings but also for the dark red wines it had produced since the Middle Ages.

Again, none of that meant anything to Fourcade. All she cared about was the security offered by the house in which she and her staff took refuge. Located on a hill, it had several exits and overlooked all the roads approaching it.

As soon as they moved in, she imposed strict security measures. Rodriguez's radio transmitter was hidden in a secret space behind a dining room wall. A twenty-four-hour guard was mounted, with everyone, including herself, taking turns keeping watch. Any visitor to the house could be observed while still a long distance away, and if an unfamiliar car should appear, she and the others would have time to escape into the countryside from a rear door.

They had been in Cahors for two weeks when Fourcade received an anonymous warning that the Gestapo was on the trail of her agents in Toulouse. She dispatched Rodriguez there to tell Mouchou Damm and his family to leave their house immediately and go into hiding. When Rodriguez returned the following morning, he was furious. He had passed on Marie-Madeleine's orders to Damm and his son, but they had insisted on staying one more night.

A few hours later, an agent arrived with the news that the Damms had been arrested at their house at dawn and that several other agents in Toulouse had also been rounded up. Then word came that Jean Philippe, the police superintendent who covertly oversaw Alliance intelligence operations in Toulouse, had also been taken. Just a few days before, Philippe had resigned from the Toulouse police after he'd received orders from the Vichy government to turn over local Jews for deportation. "I refuse to persecute Israelites who, in my opinion, are as much entitled to happiness and life as Mr. Laval himself," he wrote in his letter of resignation. "I believe that . . . any Frenchman who is complicit in this infamy acts as a traitor."★

Late that afternoon, the cascade of horrific news continued: Colonel Bernis and several of his men in Nice had been captured by Italian secret police. Just before midnight, Fourcade learned by phone that a number of Alliance agents in Pau had been taken into custody. In less

---

★ After the war, Yad Vashem, Israel's official memorial to the victims of the Holocaust, honored Philippe for his efforts to save French Jews.

JEAN
PHILIPPE

than a day, three major Alliance sectors—Toulouse, Nice, and Pau—
had been wiped out.

Fourcade told Rodriguez and Bontinck they all must leave the
house immediately. Some of the arrested agents had been there, and
the Gestapo would torture them to make them talk. She sent a message to MI6 officials detailing the disaster and asking them to pass on
the news to Alliance's other sectors. She also urged them to send Faye
back as soon as possible. Once Rodriguez had finished his transmission, he, Fourcade, and Bontinck hurriedly packed their belongings
and papers. Then, as Marie-Madeleine remembered, "we marched
off into the cold night and its army of hostile shadows to catch the
dawn train."

The next stop for the three fugitives was the town of Tulle, about
sixty miles north of Cahors. Louis Lemaire, the head of the Alliance
sector there and a close friend of Jean Vinzant in Ussel, had readily
agreed to Vinzant's request to find a new hideout for them. A fifty-
year-old plumber and the father of five, Lemaire installed the three in
a hotel for the night after instructing the owner not to list their names

on the hotel's register. Emotionally and physically exhausted, Marie-Madeleine retreated to her room and collapsed, fully clothed, on the bed. She knew, she later said, how an ant felt when a boot came down on its nest.

How had the Gestapo known where everyone was? Fourcade acknowledged—then and later—that lax security was undoubtedly a key reason. Like most other French resistance groups, Alliance was hardly known for its obsessive attention to safety. With the exception of Colonel Bernis and a few other senior agents, the men and women of the network, most of them young, were amateur spies, including herself. They had joined this clandestine world with little idea of what was required for success or even simple survival. Few of them copied the tactics of French Communist resistance groups, which were organized into cells of a few men, with each cell having minimal contact with one another. Members of the cells had to abide by strict rules, including not sleeping in the same place for more than two or three nights in a row and not gathering together in public places like bars and restaurants.

As much as Fourcade tried to combat it, she was well aware that indiscretion was endemic among members of Alliance, as it was among most of the resistance rank and file in France. She found it impossible to prevent her agents from getting together and telling each other about their discoveries.

As the French American historian Ted Morgan saw it, this type of secret work was not something that his French compatriots were very good at. Morgan wrote that the French "have a hard time taking security measures seriously because they interfere with their social habits and natural garrulousness."

But Fourcade knew that there was another reason for the trouble in which Alliance found itself: its extremely rapid growth. "For a clandestine network to work well, one must understand that two agents are weaker than one, three are weaker than two, four are weaker than three," she told an interviewer after the war. "Each one that you take on is an additional security risk, an additional person who can betray you all." It was particularly vexing, she added, when an operative who had been carefully vetted and trained proudly announced later that he had brought in several new agents who had not been properly scrutinized before joining the network. Such casual recruitment made Alliance vulnerable to being infiltrated by Frenchmen acting as German informers.

At the same time, as she later noted, what was the alternative? As deficient as their sense of security undoubtedly was, she and her agents were living in the reality of an extremely dangerous and unpredictable world, risking their lives every day to foil the Germans and help the Allies win the war.

AFTER A COUPLE OF DAYS at the hotel in Tulle, Fourcade, Rodriguez, and Bontinck moved to a small château outside the town that had been turned into a kind of boardinghouse for French refugees. But Rodriguez, fearing that the noise of his transmitter would alert the château's owners and other inhabitants to the true activities of the newcomers, decided he could not safely send messages to London from there. It was Louis Lemaire who came up with an ingenious solution.

The next day, Lemaire went to confession with Abbé Charles-Jean Lair, the vicar of the Tulle cathedral. A majestic Gothic structure built in the twelfth and thirteenth centuries, the cathedral was particularly noted for its lofty bell tower, boasting the highest spire in the region. During his "confession," Lemaire persuaded the abbé to allow Rodriguez to install his transmitter in the belfry.

On the evening of January 31, Rodriguez spread his transmitter's antenna out in the bell tower, turned on his set, and made immediate contact with London, while Abbé Lair kept guard. After his transmission, he returned to the château with alarming news he'd just been given by MI6. Alliance's transmitters in Marseille, like those in Pau, Toulouse, and Nice, had fallen silent, and no one knew what had happened to the sector's agents. Faye had gone from London to Algiers on a mission for MI6 and could not return to France until March. London concluded its transmission with a personal message to Fourcade from her main MI6 contact, Eddie Keyser, telling her that he feared her immediate arrest and ordering her to take the next Lysander to Britain.

Fourcade had no intention of escaping to London or anywhere else, but her intuition told her she had to leave Tulle as soon as possible. It was clear, she later said, that Alliance was the target of a major Gestapo operation. With all her network's sectors burned in the southwest region of France, she decided to move more than two hundred miles east to Lyon, the country's third-largest city. She had no idea if the network's operations there were still intact, but it was a gamble she felt she must take.

For the fourth time in less than a month, she and her small headquarters staff were on the run. Before they left to take the night train to Lyon, a courier from Tulle arrived at the château to tell her that the Gestapo had just descended on the house of Louis Lemaire but couldn't find him. He had gone into hiding at a friend's house in a nearby town.

It wasn't until weeks later that Fourcade learned what had happened next. After a week, everything seemed quiet again, and Lemaire returned home. On February 19, he was at his shop in Tulle when three members of the Gestapo burst in and arrested him. With surprising calm, Lemaire told them, "You forget that we are here in the former free zone and you cannot arrest me without the authorization of the prefect of the region and the assistance of the French police."

As Lemaire argued with the Gestapo, his wife, who was working in a back room of the shop, slipped out a rear entrance and alerted Abbé Lair and the deputy mayor of Tulle. The deputy mayor hurried to the shop and told the Gestapo plainclothesmen that Lemaire was correct: They did not have the right to arrest and question him without the permission of French authorities. Meanwhile, the abbé had spread the news among residents of Tulle, who converged on the shop and surrounded the Nazis' car. Faced with a hostile crowd and an obdurate city official, the Germans retreated. When they returned the next day with the proper authorization, Lemaire had disappeared again. Fourcade wanted him to take the next Lysander to London, but he refused to abandon his wife and five children, even if he could only keep watch on them from afar. He joined another resistance organization that specialized in sabotage.

Abbé Lair was also urged to go into hiding, but he refused to do so, saying he would never desert his parishioners. He was arrested by the Gestapo agents who had come back for Lemaire. He was later deported to a German concentration camp, where he was executed on May 25, 1944.

CHAPTER 20

THE TINDERBOX
OF LYON

W HEN FOURCADE ARRIVED IN LYON, SHE DISCOVERED A CITY
of vast contradictions. On the surface, it was a sober, stolid, conservative place, full of successful and prudent inhabitants who prided themselves on their bourgeois values and disdained any form of excess. To some people, particularly those from Paris or Marseille, Lyon seemed more Swiss than French in its outlook. One observer described it as "a citadel of old money that was never flaunted."

But there was another Lyon, one that boasted a tradition of sedition and insurrection. In 1793, for example, the people of Lyon revolted en masse against the radical government that had seized power after the French Revolution. The revolt was violently quashed, but it left behind a residue of antigovernment sentiment in the city, as well as a taste for rebellion and independence.

That tradition of insurgency was one reason why so many members of the French wartime resistance were drawn to Lyon. There was another, more practical explanation: It was a big, sprawling city, with a multitude of warehouses, cellars, and other potential hiding places. It also was the hub of several major rail lines and highways, making it easier, if under threat, to move in and out of it.

Whatever the reason, Lyon became known as the capital of the French underground because so many resistance leaders congregated there. "You couldn't go ten meters without running into an underground comrade whom you had to pretend not to know," one leader noted. Among them was Jean Moulin, the former French official who would become known as the greatest figure of France's wartime resistance. More than any other person, Moulin would be responsible for bringing together a wide array of fragmented movements and welding them into a relatively cohesive body.

Not surprisingly, Lyon also became a hotbed of Gestapo and Abwehr activity. The major figure of Nazi repression was Klaus Barbie, the local Gestapo chief, who gained notoriety as "the butcher of Lyon." Barbie's four-year campaign of terror and death, which eventually extended beyond the boundaries of the city, claimed more than twenty thousand victims, most of them resistance members and Jews. He personally tortured many of those whose arrests he had ordered, including a thirteen-year-old girl whose parents had been taken into custody as both Jews and resisters. Trying to get information from the girl about her parents, he came "at me with his thin smile, like a knife blade," she testified after the war. "Then he smashed my face. He kept doing that for seven days."

Fourcade had no illusions that she would be safe in Lyon, but she had run out of hiding places. As her pregnancy advanced, she also was in need of help and support. She had several close women friends in the city whom she was sure would shelter her while she tried to figure out how to save her network. The first friend she approached—Anne de Mereuil, a writer for *Marie-Claire*, the French fashion magazine, whom Fourcade had known in Morocco—warmly welcomed her. Mereuil's apartment in the center of Lyon was tiny, but she invited Marie-Madeleine, Bontinck, and Rodriguez to share it with her. The three women slept in the bedroom, while Rodriguez bedded down on cushions on the floor of the small drawing room.

The day after Mereuil took Fourcade in, the Lyon Gestapo arrested two Alliance couriers—Madeleine Crozet and Michèle

Goldschmidt—who had reported to her just days before. They were taken to the Hotel Terminus, the Gestapo's headquarters in Lyon, for interrogation by Klaus Barbie.

For more than a week, they endured various kinds of torture at Barbie's hands as part of his effort to get them to talk. They were punched, beaten with riding crops, and given electric shocks. When they continued to deny any knowledge of Alliance and its leaders, they were stripped naked, and Barbie burned their breasts with lighted cigarettes. Nothing worked. Crozet and Goldschmidt repeated their claims that they had never heard of Hedgehog, Eagle, Magpie, or any of a dozen other animal names hurled at them by Barbie. And since they didn't know them, they said, they obviously had no idea where they were.

During and after the war, Fourcade paid tribute to the remarkable courage of many of her agents, but she made special note of the women. "In my network," she said, "no woman ever faltered, even under the most extreme kinds of torture. I owe my freedom to many who were questioned until they lost consciousness, but never revealed my whereabouts, even when they knew exactly where I was."

The news of the two young women's arrests was swiftly followed by a report confirming that all the agents in the Marseille sector were also in the hands of the Gestapo, including Robert Lynen, the young movie star turned courier. As she stood in Anne de Mereuil's drawing room listening to the news from Marseille, Fourcade was overwhelmed by the fast-mounting wreckage of her agents' lives.

Rodriguez, who failed to notice her despair, summoned her back to reality. He asked if she planned to let MI6 know that she and the other Alliance agents in Lyon were still free. She glanced at him, then at Bontinck, de Mereuil, Colonel Kauffmann, and the other operatives who were standing around her. The second wave had been largely destroyed, she later wrote, but she could not allow the sacrifice of its members to be in vain. She repeated the four words that had become her mantra: "We must carry on."

As Fourcade began assessing the network's status, she realized that although the situation was bad, Alliance was far from dead. Granted, its principal sectors in the southwest and Nice had been wiped out, but the stations in Vichy, Grenoble, and some parts of central France remained intact. Those in the northern part of the country, including Paris, were still operating well, as were the crucial stations at Bordeaux and on the Atlantic coast. Although a sizable number of her senior agents had been arrested, many of them, including most of her top lieutenants, were still free.

In response to Rodriguez's cable to London that Fourcade was safe, she received an effusive message of relief from Eddie Keyser, who said he and the others at MI6 had been sure she'd been caught up in the Gestapo raids. He renewed his appeal to her to come to London, but she again turned him down, saying she must begin rebuilding the collapsed sectors before she could even think of leaving. She presumably also had no intention of letting MI6 know about her pregnancy.

At the moment, Fourcade's first priority was to find a larger headquarters for herself and her staff. Once again, one of her female friends came to the rescue. Marguerite Berne-Churchill, a physician who was already involved in resistance work, invited her to share her apartment. Berne-Churchill's teenage children volunteered as Alliance couriers.

Berne-Churchill also introduced Fourcade to a French industrialist who had headed a branch of a resistance network in the southwest that had recently been annihilated by the Germans. He placed himself and his agents at Fourcade's disposal. Four of them became part of a new protection team, whose role was to guard her and other high-level Alliance operatives.

IT WAS NOW EARLY MARCH. As a result of the chaos of the previous six weeks, there had been no Lysander landing since Faye had left in January, but one was definitely needed now. A flood of detailed intelligence reports, including Jacques Stosskopf's information about the Lorient submarine base, was waiting to be sent. And Fourcade felt an equally urgent need for the return of Faye.

The RAF scheduled the flight for March 8, saying it preferred to use the landing ground near Ussel. Fourcade was assured by Jean Vinzant that the field was still secure despite the German raids in nearby Tulle in early February. For the first time, she decided to be present at a Lysander landing, presumably because of her eagerness to have Faye back.

Rodriguez had gone to Ussel before her and installed his radio set in the attic of Vinzant's house, where he, she, and the agents scheduled to leave on the Lysander would stay for a few hours before the plane landed. The outgoing passengers were to arrive at the Ussel train station on the night of the eighth.

When she arrived earlier in the day, she met Rodriguez at a safe house near the landing field. While there, she received word that German security forces had surrounded Vinzant's house, barricaded the roads leading in and out of Ussel, and were driving stakes in the landing field to prevent its use. Dumbfounded by this latest disaster, Fourcade had no idea how she was going to extricate herself and her network. She reckoned without the ingenuity of Vinzant's elderly maid, Marie.

Marie had been snapping string beans for dinner when the Gestapo pounded on Vinzant's front door. She answered it, clutching her apron, which was piled high with the beans. Apologizing to the Germans for his "simple-minded" maid, Vinzant ordered her to leave the room. She trudged up the stairs, still holding up her apron and muttering about the nerve of *"les Boches."*

The Gestapo officers told Vinzant they had been informed he was hiding a radio transmitter in his house. Ignoring his protests, they began ransacking the ground floor. When they found nothing, they stormed upstairs and again came up empty-handed. As they climbed the stairs to the attic, Vinzant behind them, they passed Marie, still holding the edges of her apron high, coming down. To Vinzant's astonishment, their search again turned up nothing.

Drenched with sweat, Vinzant collapsed in a chair after they had left. Marie entered the room. "Have they gone?" she asked. Then, with a grin, she lifted up her apron: "Your radio, it's very heavy, Monsieur."

She told Vinzant she had heard strange tapping sounds coming from the attic the night before, and, when the Gestapo came, she figured that the source of the noise might be the reason *"les sales Boches"* were there. Years after the war, Vinzant would tell an interviewer: "I had always thought she was a simple country woman. Thank God she knew about the radio and had the wit to go to the attic, to get it and clean up the mess we had made. She saved my life, as so often the lives of many of us were saved by simple, brave citizens everywhere in France."

Although Marie's quick-wittedness had indeed saved Rodriguez's transmitter and Vinzant, the situation was still dire. German forces had set up checkpoints on every road out of Ussel and were conducting extensive searches of the trains leaving and entering the town. Somehow Fourcade had to warn the three London-bound agents, who were scheduled to arrive in Ussel by train that evening. One of them was Pierre Dallas, the head of Alliance's transportation unit, who was heading to Britain for a month of advanced training.

After sending a terse message to London canceling the Lysander flight, she told one of Vinzant's agents—a country doctor—about her dilemma. He replied that he had an *ausweis* allowing him to transport patients in his car at any time of the day or night. He would tell the Germans that she was a patient of his, whom he was taking to the city of Clermont-Ferrand for an immediate operation. Rodriguez would pose as her husband. After they'd cleared the roadblock, he would drive them to the railway station closest to Ussel so they could catch the next train and try to intercept the inbound agents at a station hub where they would change trains.

Fourcade had no trouble appearing ill when the doctor's car was waved over by a German sentry at one of the checkpoints. She was trembling with fear and her face was bathed in sweat as the German guard's flashlight swept over her in the car's backseat. The doctor explained the urgent reason for his travel and produced his *ausweis* and identity papers.

After a few excruciating moments, the guard removed the roadblock, and the doctor drove off at top speed. When he pulled up at the station, their train had just left, and their rescuer again pressed down on the car's accelerator, shouting that they would catch it at the next station. After a few nail-biting minutes, Fourcade and Rodriguez did get to the second station just a few seconds before the train pulled out. As they jumped from the car, Fourcade hurriedly thanked the doctor for saving their lives. Shrugging, he replied, "That's what doctors are for, madame."

Once aboard the train, she and Rodriguez anxiously checked their watches, agonizing over whether they would make it to the junction in time. When their train finally pulled in, they got off and hurried into the buffet, squinting through the smoky haze to try to locate their colleagues. Fourcade was the first to spot them, sitting uncomfortably at a table with a group of German soldiers on leave. As the three looked up in surprise, she walked past them without a sign of recognition and murmured under her breath, "Back to Lyon."

"*Merde alors,*" Pierre Dallas muttered back.

AFTER HER RETURN TO LYON, Marie-Madeleine looked so ill that Marguerite Berne-Churchill summoned a doctor. When he asked how she felt, she told him she suffered from chronic insomnia, and that when she did grab a few hours of sleep, she was plagued with nightmares. She ate very little. Every time she tried to do so, she said, she was racked with stomach pains. She didn't tell him that she also smoked three packs of cigarettes a day.

After examining her, he announced that she was suffering from a severe case of nerves: Marie-Madeleine made no mention in her memoirs of any discussion of her pregnancy. According to her, the doctor prescribed plenty of sleep and a respite from the stress of whatever she was doing. Staring at him in disbelief, she struggled hard not to laugh. He was talking sheer fantasy! After docilely agreeing to do as he said, she sent a message to London rescheduling the aborted Lysander landing for the night of March 11 at Alliance's other landing field, near the banks of the Saône River outside Lyon.

She stayed up the entire night of the eleventh, waiting for news of the landing and Faye's safe return. But instead of Faye, her first visitor the following morning was Pierre Dallas, who was supposed to have been on the Lysander flight back to Britain. He and his crew had waited all night, he said, but the plane didn't come, even though the weather was perfect. Marie-Madeleine felt faint. Had the plane crashed? Had she lost Faye when she needed him most? Throughout the rest of the day, she tried to focus on her work, with little success.

Late that evening, she received word from London that Faye was all right. The pilot of his plane had gotten lost the night before and had been forced to return to his base in Britain. The plane had already taken off again and would be at the Saône airfield early in the morning. Dallas and the other passengers were alerted, and they, along with the reception crew, headed for the field.

When Faye walked in the following day, Marie-Madeleine broke down, her body shaking with the convulsive sobs she'd been suppressing for days. Faye stared down at her. "Marie-Madeleine, there's nothing left of you!" he said. "I don't recognize you anymore." She responded with a tremulous laugh. He was referring not only to her thinness but to the color of her hair, which was now bright red. (As part of an ongoing effort to change her appearance, she would dye her hair a total of five times during the war.)

But just as she was rejoicing in Faye's return, the Germans struck again. In Paris, Gestapo agents rounded up several Alliance radio operators and couriers. The Duke of Magenta, head of Alliance's operations in the northern part of the country and the main target of the Gestapo raid, managed to escape and headed back to the Château de Sully, his grand ancestral estate in the heart of Burgundy.

The Gestapo tracked him there, and a few days later, several German plainclothesmen crossed the moat in front of the château and pounded on its door. The duke's wife, Marguerite, ushered them in. The château contained dozens of rooms, which the ducal couple used to their advantage. The duchess, who was pregnant with her fourth child, allowed the Gestapo to inspect all the rooms, knowing that her husband was "dodging from room to room, using secret doors and odd recesses known only to him." After searching for hours the Germans finally gave up, saying they would return. Before they did so, Alliance agents spirited the duke, the duchess, and their three small children out of France and into Switzerland.

That good news, however, was overshadowed by the fact that the Germans had captured the entire Alliance network in Vichy—thirty-five operatives in all. Among others caught up in this new onslaught of raids were members of Marie-Madeleine's own family. Her elder sister, Yvonne, who had been tangentially involved in the network, was arrested by Italian secret police in Nice. Although Yvonne's husband, Georges Georges-Picot, had stayed aloof from resistance work, he was warned that as Marie-Madeleine's brother-in-law, he was on the target list, too. Friends helped him escape to Spain.

Also on that list, to Marie-Madeleine's horror, were her own two children. She received a message from the head of her son's boarding school that the Gestapo had ordered him to turn Christian over to them as a hostage, in order to force her to give herself up. He had refused. Marie-Madeleine's mother, who had been caring for Béatrice at her villa on the Côte d'Azur, worried that the Germans would make the same demand of her.

Marie-Madeleine made arrangements to bring both children to Lyon and hand them over to Amitie Chretienne, a Lyon-based organization run by two Catholic priests that had helped save hundreds of Jewish children and others at risk by hiding them in private homes or Catholic institutions like convents and schools. The group promised to smuggle Christian and Béatrice out of France and into Switzerland, where her mother owned a chalet.

During her brief, clandestine stay in Toulouse in January, just three months earlier, Marie-Madeleine had managed to see Christian. But she had not been with Béatrice for almost a year, ever since she had stayed with her during her hospitalization at the Toulouse clinic. She desperately wanted to see her son and daughter now, if only for a few minutes, to explain what was happening and to kiss them and say goodbye. But she remembered how Navarre had been arrested in 1941 after making arrangements to see his family before attempting to escape from France. She decided that for the children's safety and that of the network, she could not risk a meeting.

Monique Bontinck had taken care of the children since their arrival in Lyon. Shortly before they left, Marie-Madeleine asked Bontinck to walk them past the window of Marguerite Berne-Churchill's apartment. She looked down at her son and daughter, who appeared lost and helpless, with no idea of what was happening to them. "As I watched them walk past me," she recalled, "I had the feeling of being buried alive."

She was not informed until much later that the children's escape route to Switzerland had been blocked and that the French-Swiss border was bristling with German patrols. Just before their party reached there, the French peasants to whom the children had been entrusted refused to go any farther and simply pointed to the barbed wire marking the frontier. Christian and Béatrice were forced to evade the patrols and cross the border alone. "My son came through the test with flying colors and saved his sister," Marie-Madeleine noted. "He was 12 and she was 10."

ALTHOUGH DEEPLY WORRIED ABOUT her children, Marie-Madeleine had little time to focus on their departure and uncertain fate. Her most immediate concern now was the safety of the agents who were with her in Lyon. As she knew, the Gestapo noose was fast tightening around her and her headquarters. To strengthen security, she split up her staff and sent them to new locations. She and Rodriguez left Berne-Churchill's apartment to take cover in a private clinic on the outskirts of Lyon, where a nurse involved in the resistance, known to Marie-Madeleine as Madame Prudon-Guenard, watched out for them and also likely monitored Marie-Madeleine's last weeks of pregnancy.

Faye and Bontinck, meanwhile, moved to an apartment in downtown Lyon, joined by Marguerite Brouillet, Marie-Madeleine's friend from Le Lavandou, whose house had been the base for Alliance's rescue of General Giraud the previous November. Also sent to new quarters were the security chief Ernest Siegrist and Pierre Dallas's Avia team.

The increasing worry over security affected Rodriguez most directly. In an attempt to keep German direction-finding vans from zeroing in on him and his radio set, he roamed around the countryside near Lyon, transmitting from various places. As he noted in a letter to MI6 early that spring, his peripatetic travel was mostly on foot, meaning that he had to carry his heavy, bulky set from place to place. "Last Sunday," he wrote, "I had to walk 9 miles carrying the set and the aerial—you can guess what a sport that is. Incidentally, the handle of the case is not strong enough—mine has broken twice—and I can tell you it is not very easy to carry without a handle."

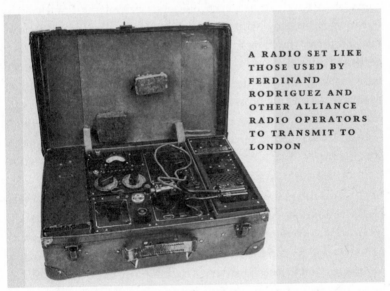

A RADIO SET LIKE THOSE USED BY FERDINAND RODRIGUEZ AND OTHER ALLIANCE RADIO OPERATORS TO TRANSMIT TO LONDON

Rodriguez proposed that MI6 provide him with additional transmitters that could be left in various locations, so that he would not have to put himself constantly at risk by carrying his only set. Commenting on Rodriguez's letter, Kenneth Cohen noted that the network "had been more or less on the run during the previous two months" and urged that more sets be sent to Rodriguez immediately.

But none had yet arrived by early April, and Rodriguez was still carrying around his case. In the late morning of April 7, he transmitted from Meyzieux, a small town near Lyon. London had demanded several repetitions of one of his messages, and realizing that he had been on the air for a dangerously long period, he abruptly cut off contact, retrieved his antenna, and set off by foot back to Lyon.

As he walked past the town's central square, he noticed a black car, whose rear windows were shielded by dark blinds, pull up behind him. Two men got out and hurried toward him. Rodriguez knew instantly who they were—Gestapo agents—and approached a priest who was in the square. "Act as if you know me," he murmured to the priest. "Talk to me as if we're old friends." The startled priest did as he was told, and the two men were chatting when the plainclothesmen approached them, one with a revolver in his hand. "Police!" the man with the gun yelled in German. "Show us what you have in your suitcase."

Rodriguez hurled his set at the head of the agent and sprinted across the square. He was chased by his pursuers, both of whom began shooting at him. Bullets crashed into the windows of nearby shops, and customers took cover.

A champion sprinter in high school, Rodriguez lengthened his lead, dashing down one street and then another. When he reached the outskirts of the town, he saw an open gate that fronted a large vegetable garden. He darted in, observed by an old gardener, whose bald head was shielded from the sun by a large straw hat. Trying desperately to catch his breath, Rodriguez asked the bewildered man if he had fought in the 1914–18 war. "Of course," the gardener replied. "Then please hide me," Rodriguez panted. "I'm being chased by the Germans." Without hesitation, the man escorted him to the back of the garden and hid him behind a woodpile. Then he went to summon the mistress of the house.

Within a few minutes, he returned with a woman in late middle age who introduced herself as Madame Clément. In a ragged voice, Rodriguez explained who he was and what had happened. He asked her if she knew a man named Mathieu, an Alliance agent who lived in the area and who had selected the places from which Rodriguez transmitted. Once again, luck was with him: Madame Clément's husband, as it turned out, was also in the resistance and had worked with

Mathieu. Madame Clément went back to her house and soon returned, a glass of red wine in her hand. "Drink it," she told Rodriguez. "It will do you good." She had contacted Mathieu, and he was sending someone to take Rodriguez away. She warned him that the Germans were searching the town but added that its postmaster, whose office was next door and who had seen him enter the garden, had directed them to the other end of Meyzieux.

Rodriguez waited for what seemed an eternity. Finally, a teenage boy—Mathieu's son—arrived, bringing with him two bicycles. After Madame Clément inspected the road and gave an all-clear signal, the boy, followed by Rodriguez, bicycled to a small house outside the village. He told the elderly woman who lived there that Rodriguez was an escaped French prisoner of war and asked her to hide him for a couple of days. She agreed. When Rodriguez finally returned to Lyon, the Nazis had embarked on an intensive citywide search for him, and Marie-Madeleine knew she had to get him out of there as fast as possible. He was soon spirited away to Paris.

For Marie-Madeleine, Lyon had become a tinderbox. The Germans had on their payroll dozens of French informers, whose job was to loiter in cafés and on street corners, eavesdropping on conversations and taking note of anyone they found suspicious. Marie-Madeleine's concern was not eased by an MI6 radio message that strongly urged her to leave the city.

On the morning of May 16, Monique Bontinck failed to show up as scheduled at the clinic where Marie-Madeleine was hiding. In midafternoon, the phone rang at the clinic, and Madame Prudon-Guenard, the nurse who acted as Marie-Madeleine's protector, handed it to her. Bontinck, her voice trembling, told her that she had badly hurt her foot and couldn't come that day, and neither could the others. She abruptly hung up.

Marie-Madeleine instantly understood the meaning of Bontinck's message: Her staff in Lyon had all been caught. Whom could she turn to now? She wanted to rush out and find out what had happened, but Madame Prudon-Guenard gently told her she couldn't appear on the street. "Sit quite still," she said, "and tell me what to do." Marie-

Madeleine asked her to warn Anne de Mereuil and Marguerite Berne-Churchill, her previous hosts in Lyon, that they were in great danger, and to tell them to alert other members of the network.

Finding it hard to breathe, Marie-Madeleine waited for further news. Early in the evening, the door to her room in the clinic abruptly opened and Faye rushed in. Struggling to catch his breath, he exclaimed that he had just escaped. When she saw him, she later noted, "the blood flowed to my heart again." She fetched him a glass of water, and after he'd drained it, he told her what had happened.

He, Bontinck, Brouillet, and three male agents had been having lunch at their apartment when four French police inspectors burst in. Faye told the police he and the others were Vichy secret agents working for Marshal Pétain. Perplexed by his claim, two policemen took Faye and his male colleagues to the central police station for questioning, while the other two inspectors remained in the apartment to guard Bontinck and Brouillet. When the car reached the station and all the men got out, Faye and the other Alliance agents broke free from their captors and sprinted down the crowded street, melting into a throng of pedestrians and disappearing from view.

Meanwhile, at the apartment, Bontinck managed to evade her guards' attention long enough to warn Marie-Madeleine. When the two policemen began searching the living room and bedrooms, Marie-Madeleine's assistant sneaked into the kitchen, rolled up a pile of coded messages into a paper log, lit a flame on the gas stove, and burned the paper. "My guards burst into the kitchen, but it was too late," she recalled. "There was nothing left but ashes." They were, she noted in a masterpiece of understatement, "in a pretty bad mood."

Bontinck and Brouillet were forced to stay at the apartment for several days as bait for a "mousetrap"—a common Vichy police and Gestapo tactic of lying in wait in the house or apartment of an arrested résistant to see if other members of his or her network would show up. But no other Alliance agents appeared, and Brouillet was taken away to jail. Bontinck, for her part, was told she would be turned over to the Gestapo that afternoon.

With the saddest expression she could muster, Bontinck asked her captors if she could first take a bath, saying that it probably would be her last. They agreed but told her to hurry. She went into the bathroom, turned on the taps of the tub full blast, and then retraced her steps. It was a beautiful spring day, and her guards had gone out for a smoke on the balcony. Taking off her shoes, she tiptoed down the hallway, quietly opened the front door, and raced down four flights of stairs. By the time she got to the ground floor, she could hear shouts from the policemen in the stairwell.

Knowing that the front of the apartment building was under police surveillance, Bontinck ran into the courtyard, climbed atop a trash can, scaled a wall next to it, and yanked open the back door of an adjacent building. She made her way to its entrance, which faced a parallel street, and, as calmly as she could, put on her shoes, walked out, and caught a passing tram. Within a few minutes, she was at the office of a Lyon lawyer and part-time Alliance agent, who found her a hiding place.

The Gestapo, informed by the French police about the various escapes of the Alliance agents, began conducting house-to-house searches. Marie-Madeleine was taken from the clinic by Madame Prudon-Guenard and hidden in a seamy hotel frequented by prostitutes. Faye and the other agents found their own temporary hideouts. Thanks to Marguerite Berne-Churchill, who had close contacts with the French Red Cross, several of the fugitives—including Faye, Bontinck, and Brouillet, who was rescued from jail—were soon spirited out of Lyon in Red Cross ambulances.

With the exception of Ernest Siegrist, Marie-Madeleine was the last member of the Alliance headquarters left in Lyon. About to give birth, she was hidden away by her female friends and guarded by Siegrist. Her baby, a boy, was born in June.

But she had very little time with her newborn son. He was entrusted to the care of Monique Bontinck, who whisked him away to an Alliance hideout in the south of France. Meanwhile, Marie-Madeleine, with new identity documents forged by Siegrist, left to join Faye and Rodriguez in Paris, the most Gestapo-ridden part of the country.

CHAPTER 21

HIGH ANXIETY

H ER ENERGY DEPLETED BY CHILDBIRTH AND THE CHAOS OF THE previous six months, Fourcade took the overnight train from Lyon to Paris, accompanied by Madame Prudon-Guenard. When German police entered the women's compartment to inspect their papers, Fourcade pretended to be asleep. Prudon-Guenard, who introduced herself as Fourcade's nurse, told them in a hushed voice that the patient was suffering from a serious illness that might be infectious. She then handed them a sheaf of medical documents that Ernest Siegrist had forged. After a cursory glance at the papers, the Germans quickly backed out of the compartment.

Early the following morning, the train rolled through the drab gray suburbs of Paris. "Barricade" was the code name Fourcade had given to the French capital, and when she arrived at the Gare de Lyon, the cavernous station seemed as "forbidding as fortified battlements." She knew that legions of people in the city, both German and French, were plotting the destruction of her network and others like it. By 1943, the Paris operations of the Gestapo and the Sicherheitsdienst (SD), the SS's counterintelligence unit, had grown exponentially. Both agencies had established multiple substations there, with armed guards, thousands of French informers at every level of society, and fleets of black cars, ready to sweep up their quarry at any hour of the day or night.

Although still anxious and depressed, Fourcade felt a bit better when she saw a smiling Ferdinand Rodriguez waiting for her at the station. Since escaping to Paris in mid-May, he had become head of Alliance's radio operations nationwide. Prodded by Kenneth Cohen, MI6 had finally done as Rodriguez asked, dispatching more than a dozen new radio transmitters to the network. It now had at least thirty sets scattered throughout the country, a number of them in the all-important sectors of Bordeaux and the Atlantic seacoast towns of Lorient, Saint-Nazaire, and Brest. Paris alone had six. Rodriguez called the transmitters his "orchestra" and gave each one the name of a musical instrument.

Having come so close to being captured, he was extremely careful with his own transmissions and preached to his two assistants in Paris and the network's other radio operators about the importance of tight security. He had secreted the six Paris radios in different locations, as far away from each other as possible, and when he and his assistants went from place to place to communicate with London, they took with them only microfilmed operating schedules and the sets of crystals they needed to operate the sets. They also frequently changed their daily transmission times and frequencies.

As Fourcade often noted, radio operators had the most perilous jobs in the network because they were so highly vulnerable to detection. "They were on the front lines, in the line of fire," she said. "It's as if they were manning the cannons." And now, with Germans' detection techniques growing increasingly sophisticated, heightened safeguards were essential. In a secret headquarters in Paris, dozens of German clerks worked around the clock to monitor radio frequencies in the area. When they found signals they considered suspicious, they would often cut off the electricity supply to the neighborhoods in which the transmitter was thought to be operating. If the transmission stopped when the current was cut and started again when it was restored, the headquarters would alert agents who were cruising nearby in unmarked vans containing sophisticated direction-finding equipment. As Alliance operators knew only too well, the longer the transmission continued, the easier it was to find the exact location. Once a van arrived near the transmission site, German agents, carrying portable detectors, would get out and, with few exceptions, could easily pinpoint the apartment in which the radio set was operating.

After collecting Fourcade at the Gare de Lyon, Rodriguez took her with him on his transmission rounds to show her how the new system worked. Traveling by vélotaxi, they proceeded from one apartment to another. As she kept watch from the apartment's balconies to spot any suspicious vans or cars on the street, Rodriguez transmitted that day's messages to London. At one of the stops, Fourcade heard him cursing under his breath. It had taken him ten minutes to raise the London operator, and he was now approaching twenty minutes on the air—the limit he had given himself and his operators. He abruptly cut off the transmission, and he and Fourcade moved on to the next apartment.

After a reunion with Faye, she and he joined Rodriguez for a celebratory dinner at a black-market Paris restaurant, whose other patrons were mostly uniformed German officers. Even though all three had bounties on their heads, none seemed bothered that they were flirting with danger. Indeed they seemed to revel in the fact. "Who would ever think we three were being hunted by the Gestapo?" Faye murmured, as he smiled and raised a glass of Beaujolais in the Germans' direction. "To your health, gentlemen!" he called out.

But for Fourcade, such displays of audacity were increasingly rare. Keenly aware of the peril surrounding her, she traveled around Paris with a personal bodyguard—her old police friend Pierre Dayné, who had helped her hide during her first trip to occupied Paris in early 1941. He was still a member of the city's police vice squad and, as such, was authorized to carry a gun. When they went out together, he and Fourcade had agreed that at the first sign of danger, she would pose as his prisoner. As part of that plan, she had, thanks to Ernest Siegrist, a complete set of false papers under the exotic-sounding name of Pamela Trotaing.

Yet, for the moment at least, things seemed to have quieted down in Paris and elsewhere. After the debacle in Ussel, Alliance had found a new Lysander landing site, set amid sprawling cornfields near the village of Nantheuil-le-Haudouin, less than thirty miles from Paris. The RAF was thrilled with the new location, which was considerably closer to England than the ones near Ussel and the Saône River. The first landing on the new field, in early June, went perfectly.

Also seemingly working well was Alliance's new headquarters, housed in a luxury apartment on the rue Raynouard, in Paris's elegant 16th Arrondissement. The apartment, with its thick pile carpets and expensive furniture and art, had been loaned to the network by Alliance's new treasurer, a wealthy Paris businessman.

During Fourcade's first visit, the headquarters was bustling with activity. A constant flow of staff members and agents from Alliance's fourteen sectors came and went. In its intelligence center, workers collected, sorted out, cataloged, and analyzed incoming messages, reports, and other documents. A duplicate of each was typed out, then kept until the network received word that the documents, sent by Lysander, had arrived in London. Once that occurred, the copies were burned.

Yet as professional as the operation on rue Raynouard obviously was, Fourcade felt alienated by it. To her, the headquarters and its staff had become too bureaucratic, impersonal, and centralized. There was little of the warmth and camaraderie she had treasured in Alliance's early years—the laughter and conversation at the many meals she and her agents had shared, the fellowship that bound them together.

Soon after she arrived in Paris, she noticed a distinct unraveling in those ties of fraternity. Agents were arguing among themselves about political matters, including which wartime general they should support: de Gaulle or Giraud. They're thinking of the future, Faye said when she expressed her worry about these emerging rivalries. The future? she thought to herself. Which of them will actually see the future? Alliance operatives who had already been swept up in the German net were certainly not debating the future. The first priority of those still free must be to concentrate on their intelligence work and avoid getting caught. When she said as much to Faye, he replied that she had become overly gloomy and desperately needed a rest.

As it turned out, she was just being realistic. In late June 1943, the Gestapo resumed its orgy of arrests. Among those captured was Ernest Siegrist, Alliance's indispensable chief of security. Just days before he was to come to Paris, Siegrist, along with his deputy, was seized in Lyon. The news was brought to Alliance headquarters by Jean-Philippe Sneyers, one of the four young agents who had joined Alliance in Lyon as members of the network's new protection team.

Devastated by Siegrist's capture, Sneyers, who was the team's leader, admitted to Fourcade that he had assigned a newcomer to the squad, a former railway worker from Alsace named Jean-Paul Lien, to guard Siegrist, instead of doing it himself. Lien had bungled the mission.

Fourcade blamed herself for the debacle. Sneyers was too young and inexperienced to be in charge of this kind of dangerous, delicate work, she concluded. Also of concern was the incompetence of Lien, whom Sneyers had recruited and whom she had not yet met. Who was he? Why had he joined Alliance? When Sneyers told her that Lien wanted to meet her to apologize for what had happened, she snapped that Lien was either a fool or a traitor and must be kept away from Alliance headquarters.

The day after Siegrist's arrest, Jean Moulin, the movement's most important and powerful figure, was captured by the Gestapo, along with six key resistance leaders with whom he was meeting at a safe house in a Lyon suburb. Less than two weeks later, during what would become the worst month of the war for the French resistance, Francis Suttill, a British lawyer who headed SOE's largest network in France, was arrested in Paris, together with his courier and radio operator. Within days, the Gestapo had slashed through Suttill's network, arresting hundreds of local resistance members and seizing dozens of arms caches throughout central and northern France.

For Alliance, there were near escapes as well. Lucien Poulard, the young head of the network's Brittany operations, had returned from Brest to the village of Redon, where his parents lived, carrying reports detailing the identities of ships and submarines at the port there, along with coastal defense plans. Early the next morning, he heard a car pull up outside his parents' house and had just enough time to climb out a window in the back, clutching his documents, when Gestapo agents began pounding on the door. Neighbors across the street took him in.

Fourcade suspected that Poulard had been betrayed. But by whom? The latest round of arrests strengthened her conviction that Alliance had grown too large and that its agents, some of whom had not been carefully vetted, were spending too much time together. She was haunted by the fear that this intricate spiderweb of a network she had woven might be swept away in an instant.

Fourcade had been living in a state of high anxiety for the previous two and a half years, and the constant tension and dread, coupled with the stress of her pregnancy and childbirth, had exacted a significant physical and emotional toll. Long plagued by nightmares, she began having a new, recurring one. In it, a Lysander landed in a field surrounded by pink heather. Faye and Rodriguez emerged from the plane and were greeted by a group of fellow agents. As the Lysander flew away, a throng of Gestapo agents, waving guns, suddenly appeared and grabbed her two top lieutenants. "We have gotten Faye!" one of them crowed. "We are delighted."

The first time she had the dream, she called Pierre Dallas, who had just returned from London, to ask him if any of the Lysander landing fields had heather in bloom. After thinking for a moment, Dallas answered no. Fourcade asked if he was sure. Yes, he said. She then made him promise never to schedule a landing on any field containing heather. Fourcade knew what he was probably thinking: that she'd lost her mind. She wondered if he was right.

For more than a year, MI6 had been urging her to go to London for a respite. Now Faye pressed her to do so as well. Before, she'd always refused, arguing that she could not leave her agents. But now she wondered whether she should follow MI6's and Faye's advice. It was not because she feared, as they did, that her luck was bound to run out and that she would be captured. It was more a realization that for her own well-being, she needed a break from the ceaseless strain. She also recognized the importance of face-to-face meetings with MI6 officials to discuss the future status and activities of the network. She decided, albeit reluctantly, to leave on the next Lysander flight, scheduled for the next full moon period, in mid-July.

Before her departure, she installed an interim leader for the network to run it while she was gone. Faye, of course, was the logical choice, but he was focused almost exclusively on operational activities and was not eager to assume the administrative burdens of the top post. Her choice was fifty-one-year-old Paul Bernard, an old friend of Fourcade's and the managing director of the French and Colonial Financial Society, a leading investment bank with major holdings in businesses in French possession in Asia, notably Indochina.

From the first days of Alliance's existence in 1940, Bernard had expressed interest in joining it, but Fourcade had told him that the important position he held would make him more useful to the network at a later date. In early 1943, he had taken over responsibility for running the network's intelligence center in Paris, and, when she suggested to him that he succeed her temporarily as Alliance's head, he readily agreed.

But, as she discovered at a meeting of her top agents two days before her departure for London, some of the others did not share her enthusiasm for Bernard's selection. As armed sentries stood guard on the street outside, more than a dozen key figures in Alliance gathered around a large table at the Paris headquarters. A few operatives from its first wave, Gabriel Rivière and Faye among them, were joined by representatives of the second wave, including Édouard Kauffmann, Lucien Poulard, Émile Hédin, and Ferdinand Rodriguez. Also present were Bernard and a few new recruits from the third wave.

Fourcade explained what she hoped to accomplish in London: improve the security of radio communications between MI6 and Alliance, secure more financial aid and equipment, and discuss changes in the network's structure to increase the safety of its people. She reaffirmed her "total solidarity with the English," a statement that was greeted with raised eyebrows by a few of those present.

At her behest, Faye introduced a motion calling for Alliance to remain united and to work as a group to continue intelligence activities for the benefit of Allied troops until the end of hostilities. Several of those who thought the network should align itself with either Giraud or de Gaulle objected to the motion, but Fourcade insisted that the vote must be unanimous, and it finally passed.

At that point, she announced that Paul Bernard would take over her duties as Alliance chief while she was gone. Several of the veteran operatives greeted the news with frowns. No one said a word, however, and a second motion, to approve Bernard's promotion, was adopted.

After the meeting, Colonel Kauffmann reproached her for choosing a newcomer, rather than one of the old hands, to take control of the network. She watched sadly as the old colonel, whose direction of the Dordogne sector had been stellar, stalked off. Would internecine quarrels and rivalries accomplish what the Gestapo had yet failed to do—tear apart this group before the final Allied victory?

In the hubbub of her preparations for London, however, she had little time to dwell on this latest worry. The day before her departure, she gave Marguerite Berne-Churchill, who also had fled from Lyon to Paris, instructions about providing aid for the families of arrested agents. In addition, Berne-Churchill and her sister, who lived in Paris, had assumed responsibility for watching over Alliance's safe houses in the French capital, as well as monitoring the apartments in which the transmitters were kept and the locations, used as letterboxes, where intelligence material was stored for other agents to collect.

Before Fourcade left, the wife of Paul Bernard, who acted as a courier for the network, insisted that she needed some stylish new clothes to take with her to London. Although Marie-Madeleine had not thought much about fashion for the past three years, she accepted with guilty pleasure the offerings of Bernard's wife, which included a tailored suit and an outfit designed by the popular couturier Maggie Rouff.

The night before she left, a small group of Alliance agents, including Faye and Rodriguez, held a farewell party for her at a fashionable Paris bar, which was a favorite hangout for German officers. It was owned by Bernard de Billy, who occasionally provided bits of intelligence to the network that he had picked up from his German customers.

After the party, she and Faye strolled down the Champs-Élysées in the golden twilight of what had been a beautiful, clear summer day. The unaccustomed drinks had induced in her a state of well-being, and when she and Faye stopped at the Arc de Triomphe to take in the view, she gave Paris an appreciative smile. But the sight of the ubiquitous swastika flags flapping in the breeze swiftly dimmed her sense of elation.

That exhilaration had vanished altogether by the next morning. When Faye came by to confirm that the Lysander operation was on for that night, he sensed the shift in her mood. "Be brave," he said. "You know perfectly well that you must go." She did know—but at the same time, she later noted, she could "not bear the thought of cutting the umbilical cord between Alliance and myself." Left unsaid was her sadness over yet another separation from Faye.

A few minutes before seven that evening, Fourcade put on her hat and trench coat, grabbed her suitcase, and walked down the street to meet Pierre Dayné, who accompanied her in a vélotaxi to the railway station. On the way, she saw Faye standing on a street corner to watch her go by.

At the Gare de l'Est, she spotted Pierre Dallas, who carried the case containing the intelligence reports she would take on the Lysander, and the two agents who would accompany her, one of them Lucien Poulard, whose near capture in Brittany had convinced her he must leave France for a while. None showed any recognition of each other. While Fourcade and Dayné took their seats in a first-class carriage, the others split up and occupied nearby compartments. After getting out at the stop for Nanteuil-le-Haudouin, about thirty miles from Paris, they walked separately from the little station and followed Dallas by foot for a mile or so, until he reached a large ditch by the side of the road. They would wait there until dark.

When night fell, they set out again and were picked up by Dr. Marcel Gilbert, an elderly country physician who moonlighted as an Alliance operative. After driving for several miles, Gilbert turned down a narrow side road and then bumped his way onto a newly threshed cornfield, stopping his car behind a huge pile of cornstalks, which was, he told his passengers, less conspicuous than parking on the road.

Next to the corn rick was the landing strip. As she crouched beside Dr. Gilbert under the rick, Fourcade watched Dallas and the other members of the aviation crew mark out the strip for the incoming plane. Looking up at the brilliant full moon, Gilbert murmured to her about how lovely and peaceful the evening was. She glanced at him. He had an intellectual manner and appearance—spectacles, a mane of gray hair, and bushy eyebrows and mustache—but his clothes were threadbare. Dallas had earlier told her that he had spent his life ministering to the poor.

Impulsively, she asked Gilbert if there was anything she could do for him when she got to England. After thinking a moment, Gilbert replied that he'd love to have some English toilet soap so that he could clean his hands really well before treating the sick. Fourcade promised she would send the soap to him by the next Lysander.

Shortly after midnight, Dallas and two other members of the crew took their places on the field in the shape of a large L, pointing to windward. They switched on their flashlights. A few minutes later, Marie-Madeleine heard a sputtering sound that reminded her of the noise made by a motorcycle. As the hum grew louder, the three men aimed their flashlights in its direction, and Dallas began flashing the letter *M* in Morse code. In a moment or two, Fourcade could make out an approaching shape in the sky, coming in from the northeast. The Lysander blinked back its own code letter—*R*. With the signaling completed to everyone's satisfaction, the little plane swooped down, came to a stop and taxied toward Dallas, who swung it around and readied it for takeoff.

As he did so, the rear cockpit popped open, and three Alliance agents jumped out, pulling their luggage out after them. They then grabbed the bags and cases of the outgoing passengers and placed them in the tiny cubbyhole where their own had been moments before. Fourcade had just enough time to hug each of her arriving operatives before she was hoisted up into the plane, along with Poulard and the other outbound agent. Pierre Dallas, meanwhile, exchanged greetings and small presents with the twenty-year-old Lysander pilot, Flight Lieutenant Peter Vaughan-Fowler, who had befriended him during Dallas's stay in London two months before. Moments later, the plane was airborne. From the time it touched down to when it took off, less than seven minutes had elapsed.

Seated facing backward in their cramped cabin, Fourcade and her fellow passengers were separated from Vaughan-Fowler's cockpit by a bulky fuel tank. He could see only straight ahead, and a sign in French in the passengers' compartment instructed them: IF YOU SEE AN ENEMY AIRCRAFT, PRESS THE BUTTON BELOW TO ALERT THE PILOT. Another sign read: YOU WILL FIND HOT COFFEE IN THE THERMOS PLACED TO THE RIGHT OF YOUR FEET, A BOTTLE OF WHISKY TO THE LEFT. After fortifying themselves with cups of whisky-laced coffee, Fourcade and her colleagues spent the rest of the trip anxiously scanning the night sky for Messerschmitt fighters. She occasionally looked down as the Lysander passed over the lightless towns and cities of France. The darkness below matched her own bleak mood.

Less than two hours after takeoff, Fourcade heard a burst of voices from the front cockpit. Vaughan-Fowler had made contact with his base. As the plane began its gentle descent, she spied the white cliffs of Dover and then a succession of fields, roads, and villages. Suddenly she saw the RAF airfield, with its "flood of beacons" and "festival of lights," welcoming her to Britain.

CHAPTER 22

"HERE YOU ARE AT LAST!"

As soon as Fourcade climbed down from the Lysander, she was surrounded by a crowd of men in British army and air force uniforms. At the back of the group, she spotted a familiar face—Eddie Keyser, her main link to MI6 since their meeting in Madrid more than two years earlier. "Here you are at last!" he said as he clasped her hand. "We were terribly worried about you. Why didn't you come before this?"

After a flurry of introductions, Keyser and the other officers took her and her two agents, accompanied by Peter Vaughan-Fowler, to a small seventeenth-century cottage opposite the gates of Tangmere RAF station. Entrance to the cottage, which served as the headquarters for the top-secret Lysander operation, was restricted to pilots, crew members, MI6 staffers, and French intelligence agents.

At two in the morning, the officers' mess was jammed. There was no pause in the cheerful buzz of conversation when the newcomers walked in; indeed, as a bemused Fourcade noted, no one even looked up. It was clear that the arrival of foreign civilians in the middle of the night was not an uncommon occurrence.

Fourcade was offered a choice from what seemed a vast array of different kinds of cigarettes and alcoholic drinks. Sitting at a table, she took pleasure in watching Lucien Poulard, a former fighter pilot himself, sprawled in an easy chair and eating a ham sandwich with gusto, all the while observing Vaughan-Fowler and his RAF comrades with wide-eyed admiration.

After about an hour, she, Keyser, and her French colleagues were taken by car to their quarters for the night. Fourcade expected the lodging to be a barracks on the base. Instead, she and the others were driven to a small stone manor house, surrounded by a garden that, in her words, looked like it had been lifted from the nursery rhymes of her childhood.

The house was leased to Major Anthony Bertram, a French-speaking liaison officer between MI6 and the agents from Alliance and other intelligence networks who flew back and forth from France. Bertram, an Oxford graduate who'd published several novels before the war, lived there with his wife, Barbara; two small sons; and a menagerie of animals that included Duff the dog, Peter the cat, Caroline the goat, and an assortment of unnamed rabbits and chickens.

Set well back from the road, the Bertrams' home—with its glorious view of the South Downs, a range of chalk hills in Sussex—was as enshrouded in secrecy as the cottage adjacent to Tangmere. To the outside world, it was billed as a hostel for Free French officers. Few people knew its true purpose—a way station for French spies, who stayed there when they first arrived in Britain and then just before they returned to France. To keep the house's secrets safe, Barbara Bertram did all the cooking and cleaning herself; no servants were allowed on the premises.

To the two-hundred-plus French men and women who visited the Bertrams' home during the war, it was an oasis of gaiety, caring, and warmth, thanks in large part to Barbara Bertram's extraordinary hospitality. "A delightful hostess, she was . . . first up in the morning and last to bed at night, looking after her guests and her family . . . but always with time to spare for a hand of bridge, a walk, or that favorite diversion of the British, a game of darts," one of the Bertrams' French guests recalled. He added that Bertram's efforts to soothe and distract were especially important for the agents about to go back to France: "They were nervous, short-tempered, impatient, and let's face it, scared stiff. . . . But so good was she with them that I have often heard them say, 'Our best memory of England was the time we had to spend in Mrs. Bertram's house.' She won the hearts and the gratitude of all the French who passed through it [and] many left her with their courage renewed."

Among the many ways in which Barbara Bertram endeared herself to her guests was her habit of collecting the dried mud that the agents scraped off their shoes and boots when they first arrived. Like Marie-Madeleine, many had tramped through muddy French pastures to get to their Lysander's landing field. After they'd removed the mud outside her front door, Bertram would use it in her garden to grow mustard greens and watercress, so that she could offer a salad grown in French soil to the next group of Frenchmen that arrived.

As it happened, Bertram felt as strongly about her guests as they did about her. After the war, she noted the bonds of "intimacy and love" that had grown up between them and her family. "When they arrived, I always went to the front door to greet them," she recalled. "It was lovely to welcome old friends who had been to the house before, and I prided myself on always remembering them. The men would call me 'Madame Barbara' and would ask after the boys by name."

Bertram grew particularly fond of "the beautiful Marie-Madeleine," as she referred to the Alliance leader. "She came several times," Bertram said, "and never looked the same twice running—sometimes red-haired and sometimes black—but always elegant and lovely." Fourcade felt warmly toward Barbara Bertram, too.

But when she first arrived at the Bertrams' home, the only thing she cared about was sleep. She had trouble keeping her eyes open during an early morning breakfast of scrambled eggs and bacon; when she was finally shown to a room, she collapsed, fully clothed, into bed. She was awakened late that morning by a loud rapping on the bedroom door. "The Gestapo!" she thought—and jumped out of bed, her heart pounding. After a few seconds, she remembered where she was and opened the door. It was Keyser, who told her it was time to go to London.

BARBARA AND
TONY BERTRAM

Later, as their car sped toward the British capital, Fourcade stared out the window at the English countryside. Here she finally was, in the nation that had been the focus of her attention and work for the past three years. But all she could think of was the people she had left behind in France.

To Keyser's consternation, she burst into tears. When he said he had thought she'd be happy to be there, she replied that she wished her friends could be with her. She should never have left them, she declared, and she had a terrible feeling she would never see them again. With that, the tears flowed once more, despite her efforts to stop them.

To the great relief of the bewildered Keyser, they soon arrived at the posh hotel near Buckingham Palace where Fourcade was to stay. The young major announced he was going for a doctor and after an hour or so he returned with one, who prescribed vitamins, a sedative, and plenty of sleep. Keyser insisted on filling the sedative prescription himself. When he came back with the bottle, she thanked him politely, and after he'd gone, relegated it to the back of a bathroom shelf.

Before he left for the evening, Keyser told her that *"le grand patron"*—Claude Dansey, the deputy head of MI6—would pay a call on her at eleven the following morning.

PRECISELY AT 11:00 A.M, a balding, bespectacled man in his late sixties, bearing a bouquet of flowers, rang the bell at the flat. When Fourcade opened the door, the man put the flowers down on a table, took both her hands in his, and gazed at her paternally. "So this is the terrible woman who has had us all scared!" Claude Dansey said. "I've often wondered what you were like, Poz. It's good to have you safely here."

When Fourcade told him that she couldn't stay in London for long, Dansey replied that for her own safety, she needed to remain there. She had been head of Alliance for two and a half years, he noted, pointing out that most leaders of French resistance networks were caught by the Gestapo within six months of assuming command.

"You mean you're not going to let me go back?" she asked, an edge of anxiety in her voice.

Not immediately, he said. Swiftly changing the subject, he told her how important her network's intelligence had been for British military planning and operations. Then he asked her if he could do anything for her in return. Encouraged by his solicitousness, she asked him to help her get in touch with her children in Switzerland. He promised to do so.

Later, Fourcade referred to Dansey at their first meeting as "a charming older gentleman." For those who knew Dansey well, "charming" and "gentleman" would hardly be the first—or last—words they would use to describe him.

Although Stewart Menzies was the official head of MI6, Dansey, in the opinion of most of his colleagues, was the man who really ran the service. A shadowy, ambiguous figure well versed in stealth and deceit, he was, in the words of the writer Ben Macintyre, "a most unpleasant man and a most experienced spy."

An anomaly in MI6's upper-crust world, Dansey—who, according to Macintyre, had the sharp, penetrating "eyes of a hyperactive ferret"—had not gone to Eton or served in one of the army's posh regiments. Instead, he had spent much of his early career as a military intelligence officer in Africa, where he ran spy networks that gathered information on and helped put down rebellious native groups. During World War I, he worked for British intelligence in London, where his myriad duties included rounding up suspect aliens and engaging in counterespionage in Britain and Western Europe.

"Everyone was scared of him," said the journalist and author Malcolm Muggeridge, who worked for MI6 during the war. "He was the only real professional there. The others at the top were all second-rate men with second-rate minds." The eminent historian Hugh Trevor-Roper, who was also at MI6 then, was far more jaundiced in his view of Dansey, describing him as "an utter shit; corrupt, incompetent, but with a certain low cunning." Patrick Reilly, a young diplomat who worked temporarily as Stewart Menzies's assistant, remembered Menzies's deputy as being "consumed by hate of everything and everybody."

Although Fourcade apparently never knew it, one of Dansey's greatest antipathies was the idea of women playing any kind of leadership role in public life. A thoroughgoing misogynist, he never let on to her how appalled he'd been when he first learned that the leader of MI6's most successful French network was a beautiful young mother of two.

She also had no idea that Dansey had been responsible for dispatching the traitor Arthur Bradley Davies, also known as Bla, to Alliance. Anthony Read and David Fisher, who wrote a largely sympathetic biography of Dansey, called the Davies/Bla affair "one of Dansey's most serious mistakes"—a blunder that "brought almost total disaster to the Alliance network." Read and Fisher added, "It's hard to explain or understand how Dansey could approve sending him. But send him he did."

In the days and weeks ahead, Fourcade would come to realize that her views on how to run her network were often in sharp conflict with those of Dansey and MI6. One of her first frustrations came when Major Keyser, her longtime MI6 liaison whom she considered a friend, was suddenly reassigned. His successor was an officer whom Fourcade identified only as Tom and who was a thorn in her side from the start. He ignored her questions and advice and kept from her much of the material sent by Alliance to MI6.

Another early source of vexation was her visit to MI6's radio transmission center—a Tower of Babel in which hundreds of operators received the coded messages streaming in from Alliance and the other intelligence networks in France and elsewhere in Europe. She was there to pass on a request from Ferdinand Rodriguez that MI6 stop the practice of requiring radio operators in the field to initiate contact with London; instead, he said, MI6 should call first. One of the main reasons for the arrest of so many operators in Alliance and other networks, Rodriguez told Fourcade, was having to be on the air for long periods waiting for London to respond.

She agreed. "The unnecessary risks run by our operators, crouching in the front line, seemed to me utterly cruel," she wrote. "I had so often heard them sending out their desperate calls and saying 'They don't answer, the sods!' " Still fresh in her memory was the police raid on her Marseille headquarters the previous year, after her operator had been up half the previous night trying to raise London. But the head of the MI6 center was hostile to her suggestion and adamantly refused to do as she asked.

AS SHE TRIED TO NAVIGATE the shoals of British bureaucracy, Fourcade was also caught up in the poisonous quarrels and rivalries of her countrymen in London. Her first inkling of the situation came when, a few days after she arrived, she hailed a taxi and gave the driver the address of her destination. Turning around, he asked her if she was French. When she nodded, he asked, to her astonishment, which side she was on—de Gaulle or Giraud.

By the summer of 1943, despite continuing opposition from the American and British governments, Charles de Gaulle clearly had the edge in his leadership battle with his fellow general Henri Giraud.

Thousands of Vichy French soldiers in North Africa had switched sides, joining the Free French and making de Gaulle's movement a much more potent military force.

Finally bowing a bit to what most people saw as inevitable, President Roosevelt acknowledged that de Gaulle could not be wholly excluded from the North Africa government and authorized his association with Giraud. In June 1943, the French Committee of National Liberation was formed in Algiers, with Giraud and de Gaulle as co-chairmen. Within weeks, however, it became apparent that a struggle for power was taking place within the committee and that de Gaulle was winning it.

The feud between the two sides was as vitriolic in London as it was in Algiers, where Giraud supporters accused the Free French intelligence agency of ordering its agents there to spy on Giraud and his men. Giraud's adherents, meanwhile, were suspected of hatching a plot to kidnap de Gaulle and hold him hostage.

A number of those backing Giraud in Algiers were anti-German military officers who'd served in the Vichy government and had fled to North Africa when the Germans invaded the free zone. While they were eager to take up arms again against Germany, they refused to have anything to do with de Gaulle. The Free French leader, in turn, rejected the idea of cooperation with anybody who had worked in Marshal Pétain's regime.

Fourcade and her network were caught in the middle of this bitter power play. Because of Alliance's help in arranging Giraud's escape from France, many in both camps considered it a Giraud ally. Some in Alliance, including Léon Faye, were in favor of that idea and advocated that their group become affiliated with the general's military command in North Africa.

Determined as ever to stay out of politics, an exasperated Fourcade wanted nothing to do with the scheme. In France, supporters of both generals were active in the resistance, risking arrest, torture, and execution for their efforts to rid France of its occupiers. In London and Algiers, they treated each other as enemies.

Announcing her intention to work with both sides, Fourcade

agreed to be at the disposal of the French military command, headed by Giraud, while insisting that the intelligence generated by her network be shared with de Gaulle and the Free French. At the same time, she made it clear that Alliance's first loyalty was to MI6 and the British.

IN THE MIDST OF ALL these distractions, Fourcade never lost sight of her main focus: her agents back home. Early in her London stay, she made the rounds of the big department stores there to buy gifts for them—kilos of hand soap for Dr. Gilbert; Ceylon tea for Marguerite Berne-Churchill; sweaters, stockings, blouses, and underwear for her other female operatives. She packed these presents, along with "surprises of every possible kind" for her male agents, in a large suitcase, to be carried by Lucien Poulard when he returned to France at the next full moon.

During her first month in the British capital, Fourcade frequently saw Poulard, who loved everything about his time there. He told her with boyish enthusiasm how, during intensive debriefing sessions with the British Admiralty and War Office, he had spent hours describing in detail the coastal terrain and enemy defensive positions of Brittany. He also had given the British information about his various agents and their methods of operation.

At the end of one of the young agent's visits, she told him she wanted to buy him some new clothes before he returned to France. When she asked what he'd like, his answer was immediate: a dressing gown. When she laughingly said that he wouldn't be able to wear a dressing gown in his secret work, he said he didn't care. Giving in, she took him to one of London's poshest stores, where "under the astonished but discreet eyes" of the saleswomen, he tried on dressing gown after dressing gown. His final choice, according to Fourcade, was the longest and most English-looking of all of them.

Poulard was scheduled to return to France on August 15. The night before his departure, he and Fourcade discussed in detail MI6's new assignments for his subnetworks in Brittany. She gave him a

LUCIEN
POULARD

sheaf of reports for the network's headquarters staff, along with the large suitcase filled with the gifts she had bought.

The two incoming passengers aboard the Lysander that would take Poulard to France had been specifically requested by Fourcade. One was Ferdinand Rodriguez, whom she wanted to bring in so he could discuss with MI6 officials his proposal for ending the requirement that radio operators initiate contact with London. The other was Léon Faye.

From reports Faye had sent, she knew that Gibbet—the code name that Alliance had given to the Gestapo and Abwehr—had rounded up several more of the network's agents in Paris and elsewhere. Among them was Pierre Dayné, the redoubtable Paris policeman who served as her personal bodyguard. In his messages, Faye had connected the latest arrests to the capture of Ernest Siegrist in Lyon. According to Faye, the Gestapo had found a notebook in Siegrist's pocket with the code names of a number of agents, including those just arrested. She had asked him to come to London so that the two of them could come up with a comprehensive plan for tightening the network's security to prevent such lapses from happening again. But she also just wanted to be with him again, even if only for a month.

In the late afternoon of August 15, Fourcade accompanied Poulard to Tony and Barbara Bertram's cottage to see him off and to welcome Faye and Rodriguez. "Barbara did her best to cheer me up by chatting gaily away," she recalled, but, haunted by her perpetual fear of losing Faye aboard a Lysander flight, she failed to respond. It was not until Tony Bertram called from Tangmere to tell his wife to "put the kettle on for tea"—a code message that meant the Lysander had arrived—that Marie-Madeleine came to life. Jumping up, she embraced Barbara and helped her set the table for the light meal she had prepared for the travelers.

Faye's and Rodriguez's arrival was boisterous. Both had stayed with the Bertrams before, and they greeted Barbara with exuberant hugs, kisses, and gifts. In her wartime memoirs, Barbara recalled all the presents Faye had showered on her in his several visits, among them oranges from Algiers and a large bottle of Schiaparelli perfume. Rodriguez, meanwhile, spent his first few minutes at the cottage entertaining the others with an off-key rendition of the song "Home, Sweet Home."

Later that morning, Fourcade, Faye, and Rodriguez traveled to London. There she and Faye examined the rich bounty of intelligence reports he had brought with him. One of them immediately caught her eye. She skimmed its contents, then looked at Faye in astonishment. "I see it's made the same impact on you that it did on me," he said.

Faye had received the document from Georges Lamarque, a

GEORGES LAMARQUE

twenty-eight-year-old native of Paris who, in the eleven months he'd been with the network, had become one of its top agents. Before the war, Lamarque had distinguished himself as a brilliant up-and-coming mathematician, writing his doctoral dissertation on the calculation of probabilities and making plans to create an institute for the study of public opinion in Paris.

When the Germans invaded France, Lamarque had fought in the Battle of Samaur, a last-ditch stand by French forces along the Loire River. Wounded in the fighting, he was awarded the Croix de Guerre. He refused to accept Pétain's capitulation to the Germans and joined a fledgling resistance network, which was soon decimated. Not long afterward, he took a position with the Compagnons de France, a scouting movement sponsored by the Vichy government and aimed at teenage boys. The group's members, thirty thousand in all, worked on farms and were assigned to construction projects, such as rebuilding roads and bridges that had been damaged by the fighting. They also participated in cultural and social activities.

Although Vichy had putative control of the youth organization, its head was an anti-German liberal who had already joined the resistance and who saw the Compagnons de France as a possible vehicle for such work. He enlisted Lamarque as its inspector general; his job was to travel around the country and keep an eye on the group's young members, as well as on the activities of German forces in the various places he visited.

Lamarque joined Alliance in August 1942 and was initially assigned to distribute new radio transmitters to its sectors around France and to recruit and train their operators. Four months later, he came to Fourcade with a startling proposal: He asked to be put in charge of an autonomous group within the network, which would draw its agents from the Compagnons de France.

At first, Fourcade regarded the idea as an implicit criticism of Alliance and its operations, which Lamarque insisted was not the case. He told her that granting autonomy to this new subnetwork would create protective walls for both it and Alliance. She promised to think about the plan, and as she grew more convinced over the next few months that the network needed to decentralize, she decided to approve it.

While Alliance provided financial and other resources, Lamarque, whose code name was Petrel, was solely responsible for recruiting agents and administering his new organization, which he called the Druids after the Celtic priesthood in the pre-Christian British Isles. The new subnetwork immediately proved its value following the mass Gestapo arrests in the early months of 1943 that decimated many of the Alliance sectors in southern France. At Fourcade's urging, Lamarque recruited from the Druids new sector leaders who were dispatched to rebuild the devastated areas. The result was the rebirth of sectors in Lyon, Nice, Vichy, Toulouse, and other cities, "conjured into life as if by magic."

Fourcade was so impressed by Lamarque's organizational skills that she had sent him to London in June 1943 for advanced training by MI6. He returned to France in July, aboard the same Lysander that then flew her to Tangmere. Now, less than a month later, Marie-Madeleine had in front of her, thanks to Lamarque, a report that was better than anything she had read in more than two years. In his foreword to the document, Lamarque had written, "This material looks preposterous. But I have total faith in my source."

Marie-Madeleine asked Faye who the source was. A young woman with the code name of Amniarix, Faye replied. Lamarque had refused to divulge her real name. All he would say was that she was a gifted linguist and that she had acquired all the intelligence firsthand.

In less than a week, the voluminous report would be on Winston Churchill's desk. Not long afterward, it and its author would help determine the course of the war.

CHAPTER 23

"THE MOST REMARKABLE GIRL OF HER GENERATION"

WHEN WORLD WAR II BEGAN, TWENTY-YEAR-OLD JEANNIE Rousseau had just graduated at the top of her class at the École Libre des Sciences Politiques, an elite institution credited with producing some of France's most distinguished intellectuals, government leaders, researchers, and scientists. Adept at concealing her brilliance beneath a disarmingly guileless exterior, Rousseau took advantage of the fact that most men, while beguiled by her effervescent charm and pert good looks, failed to take her seriously. Such was the case in June 1940 when she went to work for the Germans in the seaside town of Dinard, in the northwest corner of Brittany.

Rousseau and her family were there because her father, a former high-ranking civil servant in Paris, had decided to move them out of the capital when the Germans invaded France, thinking that such a remote place would be safe from the occupiers. To his chagrin, Field Marshal Walther von Reichenau, whom Hitler had put in charge of planning a possible invasion of Britain, established his headquarters in Dinard, and Wehrmacht troops poured in by the hundreds.

The mayor of the town, who lived next door to the Rousseaus, told Jeannie's father he needed someone to serve as a translator and

JEANNIE
ROUSSEAU

interpreter for the German high command. Rousseau suggested his precocious daughter, who was fluent in five languages, one of them German. She got the job and soon was a favorite of von Reichenau and his staff. "The Germans still wanted to be liked then," Rousseau later recalled. "They were happy to talk to someone who could speak to them." Her new employers spoke openly in front of her about military tactics and strategy—"all the things that older men imprudently let themselves discuss with a pretty young girl who speaks such good German," the *Washington Post* journalist David Ignatius wrote years later in a profile of Rousseau.

A few months after the Germans arrived, a man from a nearby town who had heard about Rousseau's new job paid a call on her at home. He asked if she would be willing to share with him any interesting information she picked up from the Germans. He, in turn, would relay it to the British. Rousseau immediately agreed.

Not long afterward, Berlin began to notice that the British seemed to know a great deal about military operations in the Dinard area; officials suspected a spy at work there. In January 1941, Rousseau was arrested by the Gestapo and sent to prison in the city of Rennes, but the officers with whom she had worked protested, adamantly insisting that their lovely translator was incapable of espionage. With no concrete proof against her, the young freelance spy was released and ordered to leave the coastal area. She traveled to Paris, where she looked for another post that would give her access to sensitive information, a job "that would take me into the lion's den, which was where I wanted to go."

The news of Rousseau's arrest apparently was never passed on to the Gestapo in Paris, and soon after she arrived, she found the kind of work for which she had been searching. She was hired as an interpreter for a syndicate of French industrialists who often met with the staff of the German military command in Paris to discuss commercial issues, such as the placing of German orders with French firms. In time, Rousseau became the syndicate's chief staff person and met almost daily with German army officers at their headquarters at the Hotel Majestic. "I knew all the details about the plants and commodities in Germany," she recalled. "We were building up knowledge of what they had, what they did, and we could keep an eye on what they were doing—'we' being me."

As it happened, some of the officers Rousseau met at the Majestic were old friends of hers from von Reichenau's headquarters in Dinard, who worked in a different office than the ones she frequented. Delighted to see her, they took her out for drinks one evening, and in the course of it, dropped hints that their work involved a top-secret weapons project.

Having acquired a great mass of intelligence about German industry, not to mention the tantalizing possibility of information about a new weapons program, Rousseau grew increasingly frustrated about her inability to pass on such vital material to the British. Then Georges Lamarque appeared on the scene.

One night in early 1943, Rousseau, as part of her work, took a train from Paris to Vichy. Soon after she boarded, she spotted a familiar face. It was Lamarque, an old friend of hers from her university days in Paris. They hadn't seen each other in years, and, finding no empty seats on the train, they stood in the corridor and caught up on each other's lives.

Rousseau told him about her job with the syndicate and her constant contact with German officers. She also mentioned the secret work being done in other offices at the Majestic. In turn, Lamarque told her about his job. He had created "a little outfit" that was gathering intelligence for the British, he said. It was called the Druids. He asked her if she would like to work for him, and she enthusiastically agreed. He gave her the code name of Amniarix.

Rousseau's German friends from Dinard began inviting her to their evening social gatherings at a house on the avenue Hoche, near the Arc de Triomphe, where they ate, drank, and talked freely about their work, including frequent mentions of secret weapons being developed on Germany's Baltic coast. She never used sex—what she called "Mata Hari games"—to get information, she later said. What she did do was listen. "I had become part of the equipment, a piece of furniture," she remembered. "I was such a little one, sitting with them, and I could not but hear what was said. And what they did not say, I prompted."

Rousseau "teased them, taunted them, looked at them wide-eyed, insisted they must be mad when they spoke of the astounding new weapons that flew over vast distances, much faster than any airplane." Over and over, she exclaimed: "What you are telling me cannot be true!" Finally, one of the officers had had enough of her playful skepticism. "I'll show you," he said, pulling from his briefcase drawings of a huge rocket and a map of an experimental testing station, called Peenemünde, on an island off the Baltic coast. He also showed her documents detailing, among other things, how to enter the testing site, the passes that were needed, and even the color of each pass.

After each evening with the officers, Rousseau, who had a photographic memory, went to a Druids' safe house on the Left Bank and wrote down what she had heard, word for word. "I would absorb it, like a sponge," she said. "I wasn't asked to paraphrase, or to understand." As it turned out, she didn't understand most of it. When the Germans talked about *raketten,* for example, she hadn't the slightest idea what they meant. What she did know was that this purloined information was "very serious." She suspected it might be one of the top secrets of the war.

EIGHT MONTHS EARLIER, on October 3, 1942, a gleaming black-and-white rocket, nearly five stories tall, sat on a launchpad in a clearing surrounded by a dense thicket of pine trees. German scientists and engineers, watching tensely from the assembly building at Peenemünde, could see clouds of vapor streaming from the missile. There was the sharp scream of a siren, then the beginning of a ten-second countdown.

As the countdown ended, flames shot out from under the rocket, and, with a thunderous roar, it slowly rose from the pad and began to accelerate. Within seconds, it thrust itself into the stratosphere, broke the sound barrier, and then, exactly as planned, veered to the east and traveled 120 miles before crashing into the Baltic.

When he heard the news, Luftwaffe General Walter Dornberg, the director of the Peenemünde center, exultantly crowed to his staff, "This afternoon, the spaceship was born." But, as Dornberg knew, this first successful test flight of the V-2 rocket—the world's first long-range ballistic missile—had a much more immediate importance. He told Wernher von Braun, the young director of the V-2 project, that "the new superweapon must be put into production as soon as possible for the Führer and victory."

It had been six years since the German military had taken over the Baltic island of Usedom, a popular summer retreat for Berlin's upper crust, then torn down its tiny village, called Peenemünde, and created the world's largest missile testing center and launch site. It was there that von Braun and other top German scientists and engineers worked on the development of new aerial weapons, particularly the long-range rocket, dubbed the V-2, and a pilotless jet aircraft armed with bombs, known as the V-1.

The success of the V-2 test flight came at a particularly crucial moment for Hitler and his generals, who were soon to face two major military disasters—the defeats at Stalingrad and in North Africa. Hoping that the V-2 and V-1 would help Germany regain the initiative in the war, Hitler gave top priority in early 1943 to their mass production, pouring huge amounts of money and assigning thousands of slave laborers to the task. Calling the missiles "the new weapons that will change the face of the war," he told his top military officials that by the end of 1943, London would be leveled, Britain forced to capitulate, and any planned invasion of the Continent rendered impossible. The attacks would begin on October 20, 1943, he declared. The V-2 rocket would be the first to launch.

Even though security was extremely tight at Peenemünde, small amounts of information about the test site had been leaked to the British by resistance members from various countries who had worked as slave laborers there. British officials knew that the Germans were conducting experiments on guided bombs and building launch sites along France's Atlantic coast. But they lacked specific details of the missiles and their tests.

And then, unexpectedly, Jeannie Rousseau's report turned up in London. Providing a wealth of detail, she described what she called the "stratospheric bomb," including its size, launch speed, range, fuel supply, deficiencies, the locations and other information about its launching sites, and even the sound it made during launch—"as deafening as a Flying Fortress." According to her sources, "50–100 of these bombs would suffice to destroy London" and would be aimed at "most of Britain's large cities during the winter."

After her report had been sent, Rousseau wondered whether British officials would ever actually receive it or put it to any use. Years later, she would describe the loneliness that she and other intelligence agents felt—"the chilling fear, the unending waiting, the frustration of not knowing whether the dangerously obtained information would be passed on—or passed on in time." In her case, she need not have worried.

Marie-Madeleine Fourcade immediately sent the document to MI6, which passed it on to Dr. Reginald V. Jones, a young physicist from Oxford who served as assistant director of scientific intelligence at the Air Ministry and unofficially as Winston Churchill's chief adviser on scientific warfare. Jones, who instantly grasped the implications of what he called "this extraordinary report," asked who the source was. Fourcade told him only that she was *"une jeune fille la plus remarquable de sa génération"* (the most remarkable girl of her generation). The information provided by Rousseau reached Churchill the following day.

Along with the other material received by the British about Germany's new terror weapons, Rousseau's document, described years later by one historian as a "masterpiece in the history of intelligence gathering," convinced Churchill and his team that a large-scale attack must be launched as soon as possible against Peenemünde.

SHORTLY AFTER 11:00 P.M. on August 17, 1943, Wernher von Braun was going to bed after attending a party with some of his fellow scientists at the officers' club at Peenemünde. It had been a beautiful, clear evening, and a few of the partygoers were still outside, enjoying the balmy air and star-filled sky.

As von Braun began to drift off to sleep, the air raid sirens began to wail. After quickly dressing, he hurried to the testing station's communications center to get a status report. He was told that several waves of bombers from England were now over Denmark and approaching Germany but that they were believed to be on their way to Berlin.

Walking back to his quarters, von Braun noticed that an artificial fog system in the complex had been activated, and a heavy mist now enshrouded nearby buildings. Looking up, he saw what he and his colleagues called "Christmas trees"—red and green marking flares dropped by RAF advance bombers. A thunderous roar filled the sky, and antiaircraft guns bellowed into action. As von Braun and dozens of other Peenemünde workers raced to the main air raid bunker, the first bombs were already falling.

Almost six hundred British aircraft, comprising virtually all of RAF Bomber Command's frontline units, swept over the island, dropping a lethal mix of high explosive and incendiary bombs. Before they took off from England, the air crews had been told that the raid's outcome "would affect the whole course of the war." In an attempt to destroy the brains behind the weapons, the first wave of bombers targeted the scientists' and engineers' living quarters. Succeeding waves were aimed at laboratories, production plants, and testing facilities.

When the raid finally ended and a dazed von Braun left the shelter, he gazed out at a nightmarish landscape of splintered trees and burning buildings. "It was like hell," one of his colleagues recalled. Another Peenemünde worker described the scene as "a veritable sea of flames."

Accompanied by his secretary, von Braun rushed into the blazing building containing his office to try to salvage key documents and plans. They were able to collect a few piles of paper before the flames and extreme heat forced them out. Overall, the raid exacted a heavy toll: Most of the blueprints and model devices of the V-2 were destroyed, many key installations were heavily damaged, and an estimated 180 scientists and engineers were killed.

In a poignant irony, several of the workers who had earlier reported to the British about the V-1s and V-2s at Peenemünde also died during the bombing. "A substantial proportion of our bombs fell to the south of the establishment itself," Reginald Jones recalled, "and particularly on the camp which housed foreign laborers, including those who had risked so much to get the information through to us."

As Winston Churchill later noted, the raid "had a far-reaching influence on events." Workers were evacuated from Peenemünde, and research there was halted. The production and testing of both weapons were pushed back several months, long enough to prevent an attack from interfering with the June 1944 Allied invasion of France, which had been a main goal of German officials.

Initially, the V-2 was to be used almost simultaneously with the V-1, which could have had calamitous consequences for Britain. But thanks to the raid on Peenemünde and to difficulties with the V-2's production and testing, the Germans repeatedly had to postpone its use. Instead, as Churchill and his men discovered from reading later reports from Jeannie Rousseau, the V-1 was to be deployed first. It was finally fired at Britain on June 13, 1944, eight months after Hitler's planned launching date and one week after the Allies successfully landed on the beaches of Normandy.

"Were the Germans able to perfect these new weapons six months earlier, it was likely that our invasion of Europe would have encountered enormous difficulties and, in certain circumstances, would not have been possible," General Dwight D. Eisenhower, supreme commander of the invasion forces, later wrote. "I am certain that after six months of such activity, an attack on Europe would have been a washout."

For nearly three months, thousands of these pilotless missiles—called buzz bombs because of the noise they made—showered down on London and its outskirts, killing more than 6,000 residents, injuring some 16,000, and destroying about 23,000 houses. But while losses were heavy and the fear and worry excruciating, the damage caused by the V-1s was considerably less than it might have been. The British could not prevent them from being launched, but in the fifteen months that they had known about the weapon's existence, they had been able to plan countermeasures, such as improved antiaircraft defenses, to greatly lessen its impact.

Of the more than 8,500 V-1s fired at London, fewer than thirty percent overall reached their targets. By August, less than one bomb in seven—about fifteen percent—got through to the London metropolitan area. Early in September 1944, the V-1 campaign came to an abrupt end when Allied troops fighting in France overran the areas containing the buzz bombs' launching sites.

Londoners, however, enjoyed only a few days of relief. On September 8, from sites in still-occupied Holland, the Germans unleashed the V-2 rocket, which tormented the British capital until just a few months before the end of the war. To most people, the V-2s—which traveled faster than sound and approached their targets in total silence—were even more terrifying than their predecessors. More than five hundred of them exploded in and around London, rocking the city like an earthquake and killing nearly three thousand people.

Again, though, the death toll and scale of damage were far less than they would have been had Germany been left unhindered. Without the delays caused by the Peenemünde raid, the rockets would have been fired months earlier and from shorter ranges. "Although we could do little against the rocket once it was launched," Churchill observed, "we postponed and substantially reduced the weight of the onslaught."

Jeannie Rousseau, meanwhile, had no knowledge during the war of the astonishing impact that her report had had. By the time the V-1s and V-2s were launched, she was in a German concentration camp, struggling to remain alive.

CHAPTER 24

PINK HEATHER

FOR MARIE-MADELEINE, THE MONTH SPENT IN LONDON WITH LÉON Faye and Ferdinand Rodriguez was a cherished interlude in a difficult time. Thanks to Jeannie Rousseau's astonishing report about the new German terror weapons, Alliance's standing with the British had never been higher. And under the direction of Paul Bernard in Paris, key intelligence continued to pour in from network agents throughout France.

During a visit to MI6's communication center, Rodriguez proved his point about the importance of initiating broadcasts from London when he used a transmitter at the center to call several Alliance sectors. They responded with more than fifty intelligence messages within a few hours. Impressed, Dansey decreed that London would now originate calls, at prearranged times, to the network's highest-priority sectors, including those covering the ports and submarine bases at Caen, Brest, Saint-Nazaire, and Bordeaux. Meanwhile, Fourcade and Faye worked out a plan to increase the network's security by further decentralizing its operations.

In the evenings, her English friends occasionally took her, Faye, and Rodriguez to some of London's most popular nightclubs. She loved to dance and spent considerable time on the clubs' tiny dance floors as the orchestras played such wistful hits of the day as "A Night-ingale Sang in Berkeley Square," "I've Got You Under My Skin," and "I'll Be Seeing You." Yet although she enjoyed the evenings out, she couldn't rid herself of a lingering sense of melancholy. As cigarette smoke spiraled to the ceiling, she watched the other dancers—the bomber and fighter pilots in RAF blue who might soon be killed in action and the agents from European countries who would be heading back to highly uncertain futures on the Gestapo-infested Continent. She was clearly thinking about Faye and Rodriguez.

Fourcade's gloom increased as the September full moon approached and her two colleagues prepared to return to France. A week before they were scheduled to leave, Claude Dansey treated Fourcade and Faye to lunch at Brown's, one of London's most luxurious hotels. The meals there were lavish, Fourcade remembered. Also on offer was a dazzling array of the finest French wines.

But thanks to an announcement by Dansey, she found herself unable to enjoy any of this bounty. He told her with an air of great satisfaction that she soon would move out of the hotel where she'd been staying into a house of her own in west London. Stunned, she exclaimed that she didn't want a house; she wanted to go back to France.

Impervious to her outburst, Dansey responded that it was more important for MI6 to have her in London than in Paris. Her network was the largest and most important French spy organization reporting to his agency, he went on, and it was vital for her to stay in Britain so she could have a bird's-eye view of Alliance's far-flung operations. When she failed to accept his reasoning, Dansey said bluntly that the Gestapo was stepping up its campaign against the French resistance and that only by staying in London would she be able to survive.

A few nights later, Fourcade, her mind awhirl, dreamed again of the landing field surrounded by pink heather. In her nightmare, she saw the Lysander touching down, Faye and Rodriguez getting out, the Gestapo closing around them as the plane took off, and the German voice saying, "We have gotten Faye! We are delighted."

The next morning, Dansey paid her a visit. This time, he insisted that both she and Faye must stay in London. The network was running well without them, he said. Why not let Paul Bernard take charge for a little longer? There was an advantage, he added, in dividing the direction of the network between France and England. Rumors were swirling that the Allies would soon mount an invasion of Western Europe, with France as the odds-on favorite landing site. It was far better, Dansey argued, for Alliance's two top leaders to remain in London to help plan their network's role in the attack.

Fourcade didn't deny the logic of what he said but insisted that if she were to extend her stay, she must first go back to France to explain in person to her headquarters staff and agents why she was doing so. Dansey curtly replied that her job was to give orders, not explanations. That might be true in the military but not in the resistance, Fourcade retorted. Her agents were volunteers, not soldiers subject to military discipline.

Then changing the subject, she asked Dansey why he didn't want Faye to leave. Because, he said, Faye would surely be captured if he returned to France; he was already living on borrowed time. When Marie-Madeleine said Faye would never agree to stay, Dansey replied, "If you order him not to return, Poz, we won't provide him with a Lysander. I'm putting his fate in your hands."

Marie-Madeleine's nightmare, coupled with Dansey's warning, made her sick with anxiety. At lunch with Faye that day, she repeated word for word her conversation with Dansey. Then she told him she agreed with their MI6 boss. He leaped to his feet, his eyes blazing. "Damn their law of averages!" he shouted. "Tell them that I've got fifty bombing missions to my credit and that I was a volunteer at the age of seventeen in the trenches. According to their calculations, I should have been dead long ago!" He could not allow the agents he had recruited for Alliance, particularly his former air force comrades, to be caught in his place, he said.

Realizing that no argument would dent Faye's intense sense of honor, Fourcade backed down. She wouldn't force him to stay in London, she said, but he must agree to take special care the moment the Lysander arrived in France. This would be the first landing operation not directly supervised by either her or him, and she was concerned that the inexperienced Bernard would not insist on the strictest possible security. She would let him go back only if he promised to travel to Paris as soon as he landed in France. After finding out what was going on in the network, he would return to England by Lysander in October, and she would fly to France in November. In that way, they would alternate direction of Alliance until the invasion.

After Faye promised to do as she said, she phoned Dansey to explain how passionately he had fought the idea of his staying. She had agreed to his return, she added, but with two conditions—he must come back to London after a month and take exceptional precautions while he was there. "It's up to you, my dear," Dansey replied with a sigh. "You've made a very grave decision."

The final few days before the September 13 Lysander flight passed in a flurry of last-minute consultations with British military officials, who outlined the specific information they needed most urgently. Many of the requests, Fourcade noted, focused on the German defenses on Normandy's Cotentin Peninsula. She speculated to Faye that the peninsula might be the landing site for the long-awaited Allied invasion.

When they were not in meetings, Fourcade, Faye, and Rodriguez packed up cases with a profusion of supplies—crystals and operating codes for the radio operators; dozens of questionnaires; millions of francs; new directives for agents; a variety of equipment; and material needed for the forging of documents, including rubber stamps, Red Cross cards and armbands, and identity and ration cards. Faye and Rodriguez would take a couple of the cases with them on the plane, while the others would be dropped by parachute over a new Alliance landing ground in Normandy.

All the while, Fourcade's mind kept returning to Dansey's statement—"It's up to you." Her intuition, which had saved her from disaster again and again, was working overtime now. Why was she so loath to obey it? Was she a coward for not stopping her two closest associates from going back?

September 13 dawned cool and clear—perfect weather conditions for that night's flight. Early in the evening, just before sunset, Fourcade, Faye, and Rodriguez, accompanied by an MI6 liaison officer, set out for Tony and Barbara Bertram's cottage. With everyone lost in his or her own thoughts, it was a silent, somber trip.

As the rolling, wooded countryside flashed by, Fourcade suddenly spotted a field filled with heather. The pink rays of the setting sun shone down on the pale purple of the heather bushes that spread as far as the eye could see. Her nightmare had come to life, and she sat frozen in shock. Should she order the driver to turn around? Should she explain the dream to Faye and Rodriguez and tell them that because of it, they could not go? And if they were going to their deaths, how could she not stop them?

In the end, she said nothing. When the group arrived at their destination, Barbara Bertram had a light supper ready, but it went mostly untouched. At ten o'clock, Faye and Rodriguez, together with Tony Bertram, left for the airfield. Arriving on that night's Lysander were two key Alliance agents—Maurice de MacMahon, who had eluded the Gestapo and escaped to Switzerland in the spring, and Philippe Koenigswerther, the head of the network's operation in Bordeaux. Bored by the peace and quiet of Switzerland, MacMahon had left his wife and children there and slipped back into France, where arrangements were made to fly him to London as soon as possible. As for Koenigswerther, the British Admiralty was anxious to quiz him about the current status of German submarine bases on the Atlantic coast.

The next few hours seemed like an eternity to Marie-Madeleine, who stayed behind at the cottage with Barbara Bertram. Finally, at about two in the morning, the phone rang. "Tea for the same guests," Tony Bertram told his wife. The flight had been aborted and Faye and Rodriguez were back at Tangmere.

Marie-Madeleine was as jubilant as Faye was furious. He growled that even though the moon was full, there were no signals from the reception team on the landing field. Tony Bertram speculated that the brightness of the moon had prevented the pilot and passengers from seeing the flashlight signals below them—a guess that was validated later that day when Pierre Dallas, in a message to London, confirmed that the team had indeed been in place and had seen the plane but received no response when they signaled.

Marie-Madeleine didn't care what had prompted the Lysander's return. All that mattered was that Faye was back. In the previous seventeen months, he had flown three times from London to France aboard a Lysander; each time, the aircraft had had to return. For Marie-Madeleine, this third return was confirmation that her premonition was right. Pleading with Faye to stay, she argued that the plane was refusing to take him back and that he should heed its warning.

He would not reconsider. Two nights later, the Lysander, with Faye and Rodriguez on board, took off again. Marie-Madeleine watched Faye go with the "absolute conviction" that she would never see him again. After their wrenching farewell, she helped Barbara change the sheets on the beds that her lieutenants had vacated. Then, as Barbara remembered it, the two women sat talking for hours, with Marie-Madeleine opening up to Barbara in a way she had never done before. Among other things, she confided that Faye was her fiancé.

Shortly before 3 A.M., the phone rang. "Tea for our new guests," Bertram told his wife. Faye and Rodriguez had landed in France, and MacMahon and Koenigswerther were on the return flight. When they walked in a few minutes later, Marie-Madeleine embraced MacMahon, then asked him how the landing had gone. Very badly, he replied. Even before he and Koenigswerther had arrived at the landing field, he'd had misgivings about the area. His father had fought in a bloody battle there during World War I and later had told his son that it was "cursed ground." The situation was made worse, MacMahon added, by the confused and disorderly scene at the landing ground. With the exception of Pierre Dallas, the members of the reception team were all new. He also thought there were far too many people milling around on the field before the Lysander arrived.

After Faye had jumped out of the plane, MacMahon had only enough time to embrace him and whisper in his ear to get out of there as soon as he could. Koenigswerther echoed MacMahon, telling

Marie-Madeleine that the scene was chaotic on the ground and that he had the feeling they were being watched.

Marie-Madeleine struggled to keep her emotions under control. All she could think of was Rodriguez's next transmission from Paris, scheduled for one o'clock that afternoon. Its purpose was to let her know that he and Faye were safe.

LATE THE PREVIOUS NIGHT, as Rodriguez removed his bags from the Lysander, he overheard MacMahon's whispered message to Faye. Already uneasy about returning to France, Rodriguez became even more anxious, not only because of MacMahon's warning but also because of the sight of unfamiliar faces in the crowd at the landing site.

Faye, too, was troubled. After everyone had piled into Dr. Gilbert's car for the short trip to the farm that served as the reception center, he sharply quizzed Pierre Dallas about the reason for the presence of so many people. The Avia chief replied that he'd brought reinforcements because of the growing danger posed by the Gestapo. Dallas added that instead of following the usual procedure of an immediate departure for Paris, everyone would spend the night at the farm and catch the early morning train, which, he assured Faye, would be perfectly safe.

When the travelers arrived at the farm, they discovered that Dallas's "reinforcements" included two members of the network's protection team—its head, Jean-Philippe Sneyers, and Sneyers's assistant and friend, Jean-Paul Lien. The security team had never been part of a Lysander landing before, and there was no reason for two of its members to be there now. Faye was particularly concerned by the presence of Lien, whose carelessness had been responsible for the capture of Ernest Siegrist in Lyon.

The owners of the farm had laid out an early morning feast of roast chicken and wine for the throng of agents, more than a dozen in all, who gathered around their kitchen table. Faye seemed to be the only one not enjoying the meal. He brusquely asked a number of questions about what had gone on in his absence and showed particular irritation when Lien spoke boastingly about his own activities. Faye again chided Dallas for the size of the crowd on the field and rejected his argument about the need for reinforcements.

Yet although he clearly sensed danger, Faye did not leave immediately for Paris, as he had promised Marie-Madeleine. Rodriguez would later speculate that as one of Alliance's leaders, Faye felt that if he saved only himself, he would be abandoning his fellow operatives. Whatever the reason, he spent the night at the farmhouse, sharing a bedroom with Rodriguez, although neither was able to sleep.

At a quarter past five the next morning, Faye, Rodriguez, Sneyers, Lien, and three other Alliance operatives set off by foot for the train station at the village of Nanteuil-le-Haudouin. Walking in groups of two and three, with several hundred feet between each group, they were followed at one point by a car with its headlights out. Dallas dispatched Lien to find out the identity of the car's occupants, while he and the others hid in a ditch. When Lien returned, he said the driver had told him he was lost and had asked for directions to Paris. The car then sped away.

At the station, each man bought his own ticket, then waited on the platform several feet away from each other. As Rodriguez lit his first cigarette of the day, a tall, stocky man in a trench coat and felt fedora approached him and asked for a light. The train steamed in, and the Alliance group, at Lien's direction, entered a first-class carriage and took seats throughout the car. Although riding together in one compartment was another violation of network security, Lien insisted that it would enable him and Sneyers to protect the others more easily in case of a problem.

Rodriguez, his hands in the pockets of his raincoat, slouched down in his seat and, lulled by the rhythm of the train, drifted off to sleep. A few minutes later, the train jerked to a stop, a movement so abrupt that he nearly fell off his seat. The door of the compartment opened with a crash, and a throng of men, wearing trench coats and armed with machine guns, burst in. One of them was the man who'd asked Rodriguez for a light.

Shouting "French police," they ordered the car's occupants to put their hands up. Like everyone else, the network's security men—Sneyers and Lien, who were both armed—obeyed. Two of the intruders headed straight for Faye, pulled him out of his seat, and dragged him out of the compartment. The other Alliance agents were handcuffed and hustled from the car. As he left the train, a gun pointed at his back, Rodriguez had no doubt that their assailants were members of the Gestapo.

He and his colleagues were herded along the platform of the station—Aulnay-sous-Bois, the last stop before Paris—as dozens of travelers waiting on the platform nervously looked on. Four black cars, their engines idling, waited in front of the station. Approaching Rodriguez, one of the Germans said in fluent English, "Good work, don't you think?" Shrugging his shoulders, Rodriguez instantly understood the man's underlying message: They already knew he was an Englishman.

Faye was put in the first car, Rodriguez in the third. The Gestapo man in the front passenger seat of Rodriguez's vehicle slapped the driver on the back and told him in fluent French, "We will have champagne tonight."

In less than half an hour, the cars pulled up in front of 11 rue des Saussaies, a massive gray building that served as the Paris headquarters of the Gestapo. Before the war, it had housed the French secret police, the Sûreté Nationale. Rodriguez and the other Alliance operatives were pulled from the cars and taken to a bare fourth-floor room, where they stood for hours, guarded by two gun-toting German soldiers.

Léon Faye was not among them. Veering off, his car had headed to 84 avenue Foch, the headquarters of the Sicherheitsdienst (SD), the SS's counterintelligence unit, which also served as a jail for the Reich's most high-profile French prisoners. Armed guards pulled back the ornate iron gates, and the car disappeared into the darkness of an underground tunnel.

CHAPTER 25

CALAMITY

F OR TWO DAYS, FOURCADE WAITED. THERE WAS NO WORD FROM Ferdinand Rodriguez on September 16, nor did he send a message the following day. Adding to her worry was the failure of any of the seven radio sets in Paris to transmit during that time.

Alliance's chief tried to convince herself that the situation wasn't as dire as she feared. It wasn't uncommon for a radio operator to have problems establishing contact. But how did one account for the silence of all the transmitters in the capital?

Finally, on the evening of September 18, she received a black leather briefcase from MI6 containing the latest messages from France. Although most of them came from Paul Bernard, she saw to her surprise that they'd been sent from a transmitter in Le Mans, a city in the northwestern part of the country. As she read Bernard's reports, she understood why.

The network's interim head informed her of the capture of Faye and Rodriguez on the train to Paris, along with Jean-Philippe Sneyers, Pierre Dallas, Jean-Paul Lien, and two other agents. On the same day, four Alliance radio operators had been arrested in Paris and all their sets confiscated.

Bernard and the rest of the headquarters staff, meanwhile, had had a narrow escape of their own. On the morning of September 18, they had been waiting in their office for the arrival of Faye, Rodriguez, and the others who had taken part in the Lysander landing. At mid-morning, Marguerite Berne-Churchill spotted more than a dozen Gestapo agents swarming into the building and sounded the alarm. Everyone there—including Bernard; Berne-Churchill; Joël Lemoigne, head of the Sea Star subnetwork; and Lucien Poulard, who was now Bernard's top lieutenant—managed to flee before the Germans made it to their floor. Jean Raison, a former Vichy police superintendent who had replaced the captured Ernest Siegrist as the network's expert in forged papers, unwittingly walked into the building during the Gestapo raid but was saved by its concierge, who threw her ams around him, called him her nephew, and exclaimed how happy she was to see him. He realized what was happening and got away, too.

As she struggled to absorb the calamitous news, Fourcade came close to breaking down. She had barely slept for a week, and the reflection of her pinched, haggard face in the bathroom mirror frightened her. She said out loud, "I'm going mad. I have no right to go mad." Spying the liquid sedative prescribed by the MI6 doctor two months earlier, she opened the bottle and gulped its contents down.

The next thing she knew, it was morning, she was lying on her camp bed, and the phone was ringing. When she finally picked it up "with a hand as heavy as a block of stone," she heard Claude Dansey on the other end, saying he had been on the verge of sending someone to break down her door. Within minutes, Dansey was there. When he saw her, he said, in a failed attempt at lightheartedness, that the London air didn't seem to agree with her. What she needed was French air, she exclaimed. She had to go back to France.

Shaking his head, he said he could not authorize her return. Alliance was far from the only French resistance network currently under brutal German attack. Throughout the autumn of 1943, the Gestapo, like a giant scythe, had swept through dozens of resistance groups—some supported by MI6; some by the BCRA, de Gaulle's intelligence and sabotage department; and others by SOE. A number of intelligence networks were totally wiped out, among them the Confrérie de Notre Dame, which, next to Alliance, was the largest and most important spy group in France.

With the Allied invasion of Europe looming, it was vital for the British that Alliance—and Marie-Madeleine—survive. If she went back now, Dansey argued, she would be immediately arrested and the network she had so painstakingly built would be destroyed. But if she remained in London, she could help guide it through the extremely difficult months that lay ahead.

As she always did when facing such crises, Marie-Madeleine finally pulled herself together and doggedly got on with her work. She sent an urgent message to all her sectors not to communicate with one another by radio and ordered radio operators in the critical areas on the Atlantic coast to strictly limit the number of their messages to London. She told Paul Bernard via Le Mans that he and the others in Paris must go into immediate hiding until they received further instructions.

On September 19, word reached her of yet another hammer blow in Paris: the arrests of two of her most trusted veterans—Gabriel Rivière and Alfred Jassaud. The loss of the burly, jovial Rivière, recruited by Henri Schaerrer in Marseille in 1940, was especially devastating. "Good God, a woman," he had shouted when he first met her, yet in time, he had become not only one of her most loyal lieutenants but an extremely close friend and adviser.

On the same day, a Gestapo raid in central France netted Colonel Édouard Kauffmann, Léon Faye's former air force colleague, and more than a dozen of his agents. In Autun, a town in eastern France, sixteen Alliance operatives were also captured. The deputy head of the sector, a banker, was taken away in chains, with two machine guns that had been found in his bank hanging around his neck.

Less than a week later, one of Fourcade's favorite young operatives—the boyishly enthusiastic Lucien Poulard—was taken by the Gestapo while walking down the Champs Élysées, only six weeks after he had returned to France with the dressing gown that she had bought him in London. The capture of the twenty-four-year-old

Poulard was immediately followed by the collapse of the Brest sector and the arrests of most of its agents, including its head, Maurice Gillet, and seven members of his family. Also captured in Brest was Joël Lemoigne, who had hidden there after escaping the mass arrests in Paris ten days before. The network's sector in the town of Rennes, in eastern Brittany, was decimated, too. Among those caught was its head, Pierre Le Tullier, one of the Vichy policemen in Marseille who had helped Fourcade escape after her arrest at La Pinède in November 1942.

In little more than a week, Alliance's operations in Paris, central France, and eastern Brittany had been annihilated, with dozens of agents swallowed up in the Gestapo maw. "Since September 16, Eagle, my magnificent Eagle, had fallen, and with him more than 150 members of my beloved network," Fourcade wrote. How many of her agents were now in the Gestapo's clutches? Three hundred, perhaps four hundred?

Throughout all of France, only six Alliance transmitters had not been shut down, and just a few of Marie-Madeleine's major operatives remained at large. Besides Paul Bernard, they included Georges Lamarque, head of the Druids; Jean-Claude Thorel, who replaced Joël Lemoigne as chief of Sea Star; Henri Battu, a businessman from Lyon, in southwestern France; and Count Helen des Isnards, who headed the network's activities in the southeast. A former air force pilot, the twenty-eight-year-old des Isnards was the scion of a prominent aristocratic family with centuries-old roots in Provence. His region was considered the most secure of all, and his radio transmissions from Aix-en-Provence were so regular and frequent that MI6 dubbed his operation "the post office."

And although Brittany had been badly hit, key operatives continued their work there, among them Jacques Stosskopf, Alliance's uberspy in Lorient, and André Coindeau (Urus), an engineer from Nantes who was in charge of intelligence gathering at the port of Saint-Nazaire. (Coindeau was also known as Nero because he carried on his work seemingly heedless of the fires consuming the other sectors in Brittany.)

In a message to Marie-Madeleine, sent this time via Aix-en-Provence, Paul Bernard begged her to dispatch new transmitters, money, and other urgently needed material to a new landing field near Verdun, in eastern France. Marie-Madeleine was as desperate as he to reestablish the air link between Britain and Alliance. She assured him that help would soon be on the way.

But the full-moon period in October came and went with no RAF operation to the Verdun landing ground, to the anger and dismay of Bernard and his reception committee who waited there for several nights. Bernard directed his wrath at both Fourcade and MI6, blasting what he called "the indifference . . . the unexpected and disappointing attitude of London." Bernard thought she had deserted him, Fourcade recalled, and she couldn't tell him the truth—that the RAF had cut back on its commitment to ferry Alliance agents and supplies to and from France. Fourcade was aware that the Lysander operation had recently experienced a number of losses, but she also worried that British air force officials considered Alliance on the verge of extinction.

PAUL BERNARD

With the Lysanders unavailable, at least for the moment, Fourcade decided that her only option for forging a new link to Bernard was to send an agent by sea to the coast of Brittany, which was closed to all small craft and heavily guarded by German patrols. André Coindeau, in Nantes, was tasked with finding a location and organizing the reception committee for this extremely difficult mission.

As the landing place, Coindeau chose a cove near Cape Frehel, a cliff-lined peninsula in northern Brittany. The British Admiralty agreed to provide a torpedo boat for the operation, and Marie-Madeleine appointed as her emissary Philippe Koenigswerther, the young head of the Bordeaux sector, who had spent the last two months in London.

Because of bad weather, the initial landing attempt, in early November, was a failure, and Marie-Madeleine was informed that another one couldn't be staged for several weeks. In the meantime, she appealed to the RAF to consider a myriad of other possible operations, including parachute drops in three areas: Aix-en-Provence, Brittany, and near Verdun. She also came up with another idea for a sea operation, this one on the Mediterranean coast, to pick up a huge backlog of agent reports and other crucial mail.

All the while, she attempted to fend off a growing sense of despair. As she learned of the capture of more agents and crossed off their names on her network chart, she said, "I experienced the feeling of having wielded the executioner's axe. . . . I was dying of grief."

In late September, Fourcade had moved into a stately four-story townhouse that MI6 had found for her in Carlyle Square, in the fashionable London borough of Chelsea. The house's interior was painted pale green, and its more than a dozen rooms were filled with flowered chintz furniture. Fourcade, however, spent virtually all her time in her ground-floor office, sleeping on a camp bed next to her desk so that she could be close to the phone, with its direct line to MI6.

From there, she fought to keep her network alive. Despite the wholesale pillaging of Alliance, intelligence reports from surviving agents kept trickling in. As she read the messages, she often thought of something Colonel Bernis had once told her, that each bit of information, dry as it appeared on paper, "represented a wealth of suffering."

It troubled her that some of the French and British officials whom she encountered in London seemed to have little concern for the human tragedies behind the intelligence they so eagerly sought from France. One evening in late November, she was reminded of the chasm between London officialdom and her colleagues back home when a London-based agent for BCRA surreptitiously came to see her at Carlyle Square. The operative, who had met Fourcade in Lyon in the spring of 1943, handed her a radio message sent to BCRA that he had just found in its files.

The cable, sent from Paris, informed BCRA that Léon Faye had been arrested on a train with Pierre Dallas and "a British radio operator," along with Jean-Philippe Sneyers and Sneyers's lieutenant, whose first name was Jean-Claude. The message went on to say that Jean-Claude was a German collaborator and had been released by the Gestapo after the others were imprisoned. BCRA had received the message in mid-October.

Marie-Madeleine felt a chill. The Alliance protection team had no member named Jean-Claude. But it did have a Jean-Paul—Jean-Paul Lien, who was Sneyers's deputy. More than a month had passed since the Free French received this report, and they had not seen fit to forward it to her. In the meantime, Lien had been free to continue his work of betraying his colleagues.

She suspected that the oversight was a deliberate act on the part of BCRA officials, particularly the agency's icy young chief, André Dewavrin. Free French officials had long fumed about Alliance's close ties with MI6, criticizing the network and Fourcade for sending their intelligence to the British rather than to de Gaulle's intelligence operation. Ever since she'd arrived in London, those attacks, particularly by the BCRA, had grown noticeably sharper.

To prove themselves to the Allies, the Free French needed to produce as much information as possible about German military activities in France, as well as to establish themselves as a significant presence on the battlefield. But the BCRA's obsessive quest for intelligence was also part of its struggle to win its brutal internecine war with the secret services of de Gaulle's archrival, General Henri Giraud.

By November 1943, de Gaulle was firmly in charge of the French Committee of National Liberation, the political entity set up in North Africa earlier in the year. Yet although Giraud no longer was co-chairman of the committee, he still retained some authority as head of French military forces there. Both in Algiers and London, a ruthless fight for power continued to rage between Giraud's supporters, many of them former Vichy officials and military officers, and the backers of de Gaulle.

Having long refused to take part in that political clash, Fourcade now found herself and her network caught in the middle of it. Soon after learning of the BCRA's withholding of information about Jean-Paul Lien, she discovered that MI6, without her knowledge, had been turning over to Giraud's secret service all the intelligence reports from her network. When she confronted Dansey with that fact, he blandly told her that the British had an agreement to exchange intelligence with the French military; since Giraud was commander-in-chief of the military, he was entitled to receive all of MI6's information, regardless of its source.

WHILE ADHERENTS OF GIRAUD and de Gaulle battled for power and influence, a similar fight was raging between Gaullists in London and Algiers and the leaders of France's major resistance movements. Earlier in the war, thanks to Jean Moulin, those leaders had been of inestimable help in de Gaulle's fight for Allied recognition of him as leader of Free France. In the spring of 1942, Moulin had succeeded in extracting pledges of support for the general from the resistance heads; later, he forwarded to Churchill and Roosevelt a statement from the resistance movements calling for de Gaulle, whom they called "their uncontested leader," to be named governor of North Africa.

Yet as the war continued, these proclamations of unity proved to be a veneer that barely concealed the resistance chiefs' increasingly deep suspicions of de Gaulle and his postwar ambitions. The more influence he acquired, the more suspicious they became.

From the beginning, a gulf of understanding had divided the Gaullists and the leaders of the resistance movements, who risked their lives daily and who greatly resented their compatriots in London who, in their view, had lived out the war in comfort and safety, with none of the daily tension, terror, and privations of occupation.

As the war progressed, the belief grew among some resistance leaders that de Gaulle was interested in their work only for what it could do for him and his forces. "The Resistance, for him, was one pawn among others," Henri Frenay, the head of the Combat movement, wrote after the war. "The devotion and courage of its members, the dangers, the arrests, the executions were for him only an inevitable tithe paid to the gods of war."

As the war advanced, Frenay added, the rapid growth of resistance activities, which at first had been encouraged by the Free French, began to alarm them. "Despite our proven loyalty, they were afraid that a new force was on the upswing in France, a force with a will of its own and capable of open defiance of de Gaulle. In this view we were no longer friends but rivals—admissible rivals but rivals just the same. We were to be carefully watched and strictly controlled."

At the same time, as Fourcade knew only too well, the French were not the only ones caught up in the brutal feuds and infighting that raged in London and elsewhere. The British secret services had also erupted in what one historian called "full-scale and dangerous brawls the likes of which Whitehall bureaucracy had rarely if ever seen before." MI6 and SOE were the major antagonists, and Claude Dansey was arguably the principal instigator in this "viciously petty, infantile, and time-wasting" vendetta, as the journalist and historian Tom Keene put it.

Dansey and his boss, Stewart Menzies, were both highly skilled bureaucratic infighters, and they used every trick they could think of in their five-year attempt to bring SOE under their control or, failing that, to kill it outright. "Though SOE and MI6 were nominally on the same side in the war, they were, generally speaking, more abhorrent to one another than the [Germans] were to either of them," noted the journalist Malcolm Muggeridge, who was a bemused witness to the bureaucratic mayhem.

In his memoirs, Dr. Reginald Jones, Churchill's chief adviser on scientific warfare, recalled being summoned to Dansey's office to find the MI6 deputy chief "almost incoherent with indignation about those buggers in SOE." Patrick Reilly, the young diplomat who served as Menzies's assistant, meanwhile, had a vivid memory of his own. One day in June 1943, he wrote, a beaming Dansey marched into his office and exclaimed, "Great news! Great news!" Reilly expected to hear a report about "some splendid intelligence coup." Instead, the source of Dansey's glee was the complete destruction of the SOE Prosper network in France. "Misery, torture and death for many brave men and women, British and French—and Dansey gloated," Reilly observed. "I remember feeling physically sick."

Reilly, who served as British ambassador to France and the Soviet Union after the war, called Dansey "an evil man—fierce, ruthless, venomous . . . I have often asked myself how it was possible that this wicked man . . . could hold a key position in [MI6] for the whole of the war."

The question then arises: How does this sinister depiction of Dansey by Reilly and others square with Fourcade's warm memories of him as sensitive, kind, and understanding toward her and her network? She frequently bridled at his refusal to allow her to return to France, but there was no question, then or now, that he did this to save her life.

In his unpublished memoirs, Reilly did acknowledge that Dansey "was said to be responsible for an occasional kind act." He also observed that his MI6 superior was noted for his flashes of charm, especially toward attractive women like Fourcade. But far more important in Dansey's eyes was the vital intelligence she and Alliance had provided MI6 throughout the conflict, not only significantly aiding the war effort but also his agency's struggles for influence in Whitehall.

Nonetheless, there were limits to Dansey's sympathy. While he was caring and solicitous in Fourcade's presence, he often referred to her behind her back as "Cohen's bitch," according to Reilly. Dansey was referring to Kenneth Cohen, the head of MI6's intelligence operations in France, who, with his wife, Mary, became very close to Fourcade during the last months of her stay in London.

There's no evidence that Fourcade ever knew of Dansey's duplicity toward her. But she repeatedly made clear how much she hated being enmeshed in the bureaucratic rivalries and feuds that were taking place around her—"all these cumbersome cliques and criminally childish antagonisms of the Secret Services!"

CHAPTER 26

CAPTIVES

O N THE SAME DAY THAT MARIE-MADELEINE LEARNED ABOUT THE treachery of Jean-Paul Lien, Ferdinand Rodriguez marked the seventy-first day of his nightmarish new life in a Nazi prison cell. Like his Alliance boss, he struggled not to give in to despair.

For the first two weeks of his captivity, Rodriguez had been transported daily in handcuffs from Fresnes prison near Paris to the Gestapo headquarters on rue des Saussaies for interrogation. From the beginning, he was stunned by how much his questioners knew about Alliance.

Rodriguez's first inkling of the depth of their knowledge came when he was asked his name. Pierre Thomas, he replied, using his network cover name. One of his interrogators, however, addressed him as Edward Rodney. "A snake sliding along my vertebra could not have caused me greater surprise," Rodriguez later observed. MI6 had given him the pseudonym of Edward Rodney in February 1942, and he was convinced that no one in France knew it, with the exceptions of Marie-Madeleine and Léon Faye. Lien had never heard it, he was sure, and Faye would never have revealed it to the Gestapo.

Finally, he acknowledged that Edward Rodney was indeed his name—the Germans apparently had not yet heard of Ferdinand

Rodriguez—but he dodged most of their other questions. When ordered to give them the names of his Alliance colleagues, he said he only knew their animal code names. He insisted he was an ordinary radio operator, not the chief of the network's radio service, as his interrogators claimed. When they told him to hand over his code, he responded that he didn't have one, adding that the messages he sent had already been encoded. "I do not believe that you became an envoy from London without a code," one of his questioners remarked. Rodriguez replied, "It was not necessary to possess a code as radio operator. I had a code operator who did that."

When he was sent back to Fresnes in the evenings, he worried that his continued silence would soon result in the torture he was sure was coming.

THE WHOLESALE CAPTURE OF Alliance agents sparked by Rodriguez's and Faye's arrests was the latest chapter in a sophisticated and ruthlessly efficient SS counterintelligence operation against the network that began in November 1942. It was then that a French spy arrested by the Gestapo in Strasbourg revealed he had been recruited to collect information by "an important British intelligence network," whose two leaders were called Aigle (Eagle) and Hérisson (Hedgehog). The Strasbourg Gestapo reported to Paris and Berlin that it had launched an extensive investigation into this clandestine organization, whose members took the names of animals as pseudonyms.

In January 1943, the Germans realized that the group was in fact a far-flung military intelligence network working with the British and mostly operating in the free zone, with strong points in Marseille, the Dordogne, and the Corrèze area. Both the Strasbourg Gestapo and the Paris SD, the SS's counterintelligence branch, were placed in charge of the investigation.

The first arrests began at the end of January, when Maurice Grapin, who had taken Gabriel Rivière's place as the regional Alliance head in Marseille, was captured, along with his wife. When he was promised his wife's release in exchange for his cooperation, Grapin gave his interrogators the information they wanted, including the identifications of other agents in his region. The copious information he provided the Germans, along with a number of agent reports they found on their own, led in the late winter and early spring of 1943 to the annihilation of the network's sectors in Marseille, Toulouse, Tulle, Nice, and Lyon, among others. Because of the Strasbourg Gestapo's early involvement in the probe, most of the agents arrested in the first part of the year were transported in the late spring, following their initial interrogations in Paris, to prisons near Strasbourg in northeastern France.

To the frustration of the Germans, the heads of Alliance—"Hedgehog" and "Eagle"—were not swept up in this first wave. Thanks to the rogue agent Jean-Paul Lien, however, the German secret services were soon able to launch a new operation that they labeled Alliance II. A former railway worker from Alsace, Lien had earlier worked for Combat, one of the country's largest resistance movements. Pierre Frenay, the former Vichy military intelligence officer who founded Combat, later wrote that he had had misgivings about Lien from the start. The Alsatian had been assigned to head Combat's organization in Toulouse, but according to Frenay, he "had done absolutely nothing. He didn't even try to excuse his idleness. . . . I was dealing with an incompetent, shallow, characterless man who lacked any convictions." Frenay eventually replaced Lien in Toulouse but never passed on his misgivings to other resistance groups.

Lien then settled in Lyon, where he befriended Jean-Philippe Sneyers, whose small resistance organization had joined forces with Alliance. When Sneyers became head of Alliance's protection team, he named Lien as his deputy, although he knew little or nothing about Lien's background. No outside check was made.

By then, Lien was firmly in the pocket of the Germans. With his help, the Gestapo arrested Alliance security chief Ernest Siegrist and his deputy in Lyon on June 11, 1943. During searches of the men and their apartments, a wealth of reports and other documents were seized, which included boxes of letters and the addresses of almost one hundred Alliance agents. According to a joint Gestapo/SD report, this bounty gave investigators "a much more complete overview of the organization."

That summer, Lien moved to Paris, where he cozied up to Pierre Dallas. Lien persuaded Dallas to include him and Sneyers in the planning and carrying out of future Lysander landings, arguing that protection must be increased because of a metastasizing Gestapo threat. That was how he learned the date of Faye and Rodriguez's return from London—information that he immediately transmitted to the Gestapo. Other information that Lien supplied to the Germans, coupled with the documents they had recovered from Siegrist, led to the arrests of more than 150 additional Alliance agents in the months following Faye and Rodriguez's capture. For his services to the Germans, Lien was awarded 2 million francs.

KEPT IN SOLITARY CONFINEMENT at Fresnes, Rodriguez had no knowledge of any of this. His fears of torture were apparently never realized, and his interrogations stopped at the end of September. His only human contact from then on was with the German guards who brought him what constituted his daily food ration: a blackish, lukewarm liquid that was supposed to be coffee, a piece of wormy bread, and two bowls of watery soup.

Feeling himself fading into nothingness, he struggled hard to resist such ennui. "I walk constantly in my cell, riveted by the concern of not letting go," he wrote. "Five meters back and forth, back and forth. I have to stay alert." Every morning, he exercised for twenty minutes.

To impose intellectual discipline on himself, Rodriguez obsessively read and reread two prayer books, one in English and the other in French, given to him by the prison's military chaplain. Memorizing the texts, he recited them over and over as he paced around the cell.

Every few days, the soulless quiet of the prison was broken by the noise of other cell doors crashing open and the cries of fellow *résis-*

tants, a few shouting *"Vive la France,"* as they were taken away, some for deportation to Germany, others for immediate execution. As agonizing as they were, "these separations, these amputations of our community, do not destroy me," Rodriguez wrote. "They encourage me not to falter.

"I count the steps, count the days, count the nights," he added. "I pray, I think, and I count."

FOR LÉON FAYE, NOVEMBER 24 was also spent in Nazi captivity. His place of confinement was a small attic room at 84 avenue Foch, the SD headquarters in Paris, where he'd been held since his arrest. But unlike Rodriguez, Faye did not view this day as just another in a seemingly endless chain. Later that night, he planned to break out of avenue Foch and, in a matter of days, be back in London.

The house's top floor had been set aside for the SD's VIP prisoners, most of them British agents from SOE. Faye was the only opera-

84 AVENUE
FOCH

tive there who worked for MI6. He and the other inmates were held in twelve rooms directly above the office of Josef Kieffer, the chief of SS counterintelligence in Paris.

During his lengthy interrogations, Faye was as aghast as Rodriguez had been by the extent of the Germans' knowledge of Alliance's workings. His questioners boasted to him about the three-hundred-plus network agents they'd arrested and the mountains of documents they'd acquired, as well as the information provided by informers and by agents who'd broken down under torture.

As they did with other prisoners at avenue Foch, the SD interrogators repeatedly insisted to Faye that since they already knew everything about his network and its people, it made no sense for him not to cooperate. What they didn't share with Faye and their other captives was that they had yet another valuable source for their information: a highly successful radio playback operation located on the building's fourth floor.

After extracting codes and other transmission-related information from captured radio operators, the SD "played back" the operators' wireless sets, which meant that it sent messages to London as if the operators were still free. The "radio game," as it was called, was aimed for the most part at SOE, which blithely accepted the bogus messages as valid, despite doubts raised by some within the agency. Thanks to this communication, the Germans were the recipients of a flood of valuable intelligence about the workings of SOE, including the arrival of new agents and equipment.

Faye's interrogators tried to persuade him that a leak from a traitor in London had resulted in his arrest, but he told them he knew that the traitor was their informer, Jean-Paul Lien. Their next ploy was to agree to one of his demands—to recognize Alliance as part of the French army and to treat its members as prisoners of war rather than enemy spies, which meant that their lives would be spared. But even this seeming concession, which had worked with other Allied agents, had no effect on Faye. He still refused to talk.

The skillful mind games played by the Paris SD on its prize prisoners were encouraged by its chief, the wily Josef Kieffer, who believed that treating them well would yield far better results than threats or torture. Although some prisoners were certainly tortured at avenue Foch, Kieffer decided who would be spared. He occasionally brought his favored captives, usually British, to his high-ceilinged office with its Louis XV furniture for a meal, a drink, or a chat. The conversations often focused on England's public schools and its officer class, both of which Kieffer said he greatly admired. He suggested to the agents that instead of fighting each other, British and German officers should be working together to combat their real enemy: communism.

Lulled into a sense of security, a number of them began to trust and cooperate with their captors. Faye did not, and as a result, never received favorable treatment. During his first few days at the mansion, he thought about killing himself, believing that he soon would be tortured for refusing to say anything that might lead to the capture of his fellow operatives.

But, when no torture occurred, he dropped the idea of suicide and began thinking about escape. His tiny room, which used to be a maid's room, contained only a bed and a chair. A six-foot-tall ventilation shaft, looking like a square chimney, was topped by a large skylight that opened onto the roof. The bottom of the shaft was barred.

Faye had already proved to be a master of escape. He had done so twice before, including his dramatic flight from a Vichy prison in late 1942 in which he climbed down a sixty-foot rope to the ground. As he examined his room on avenue Foch more closely, he realized that with a screwdriver or other simple tool, he could probably loosen and remove the bars covering the ventilation shaft. Once that was done, he was physically fit enough, he thought, to stand on a chair under the skylight and hoist himself up to the roof.

Even if he got that far, however, other obstacles awaited him. Because he had refused to cooperate with the SD, he had never been allowed into other parts of the house, with the exception of the interrogation room, so he had no idea of its layout. Nor did he know anything about the neighboring houses and streets, including how heavily they were guarded.

Deciding he needed partners to help with his escape plan, he found two SOE agents who were interested. The first was in the room next to his—a young woman with whom he communicated by tapping out messages in Morse code on the wall separating them. She was Noor Inayat Khan, a twenty-six-year-old former Women's Auxiliary Air Force (WAAF) officer who, after the war, would be one of SOE's most celebrated operatives.

Petite and slender, with a soft, high-pitched voice, Noor was the offspring of an American mother and a father who came from Indian Muslim nobility. She grew up in Paris, where she studied piano at the Paris Conservatory under the famed composer and teacher Nadia Boulanger. But her great love was writing, and by the time the war broke out, she had begun to make a name for herself by creating and broadcasting children's stories. In 1940, she and her brother left Paris for England to join the war effort.

NOOR INAYAT
KHAN

By all accounts, the quiet, gentle Noor was an unlikely secret agent. An SOE colleague who trained with her described her as "a splendid, vague, dreamy creature, far too conspicuous—once seen, never forgotten," who had "no sense of security" and should never have been sent to France. In a fitness report, one of her instructors wrote that she "tends to give far too much information. Came here without the foggiest idea what she was being trained for." The officer in charge of instructing her and other would-be operatives in survival tactics wrote that she was "temperamentally unsuitable" to be an agent and would be a major security risk in the field. He based that judgment in part on a mock interrogation of Noor by a Bristol police superintendent, whose force worked with SOE. After the interrogation, the superintendent informed the agency that "if this girl's an agent, I'm Winston Churchill."

Despite all the warnings, Noor's training was cut short, and she was dispatched to France on June 16, 1943, as a wireless operator—the most dangerous job an agent could have. Her superiors acknowledged that she didn't measure up in many ways but that it "was necessary, for overriding reasons of shortages of specialists—particularly wireless operators—to stretch a point in favor of a candidate."

She arrived in Paris just days before the Gestapo roundup of hundreds of resistance members belonging to the Prosper network. Noor eluded the German dragnet, and, as one of the few SOE agents still free, she became virtually overnight one of its foremost operatives and the Gestapo's most wanted British agent in Paris. Even though her sense of security had not noticeably improved, she managed to remain free throughout the summer and early fall, transmitting regularly to London. Then, in early October, SOE instructed her to link up with a circuit that was actually being run by the Germans. When she did so, she was promptly arrested by Gestapo agents, who acquired not only her transmitter but a notebook on her bedside table in which she had recorded every message she had received and sent since arriving in France.

Once in custody, however, she showed far more courage and mental toughness than most of her male counterparts. Within hours of her arrival at avenue Foch, she tried to escape by climbing out a bathroom window but found herself on a narrow ledge with no place to go. Her guards located her within minutes and dragged her inside. During her interrogations, she refused to cooperate, refusing all Kieffer's blandishments and remaining stubbornly silent. "She told us nothing of value," Kieffer told Allied officers after the war. "We could not rely on anything she said."

Although Faye had no knowledge of her background, he was impressed by how fearless Noor seemed to be in her communication with him. When he told her about his plan to escape, she replied that she had already attempted to do so and couldn't wait to try again. She suggested that they recruit another prisoner, an SOE agent named John Starr, whose room was opposite hers and with whom she was also communicating. Starr had heard her crying soon after she arrived and slipped a note under her door saying that if she wished to get in touch with him, she could do so through messages hidden in certain places in the communal lavatory.

Noor said that Starr, who had been a graphic artist before the war, would be helpful because he was doing some work for Kieffer as a draftsman, which allowed him to move freely about the house. As a result, he was familiar with its layout and perhaps that of surrounding buildings.

As it happened, Starr's cooperation with the Germans extended far beyond drafting work—a fact that Noor did not know. Arrested in Dijon during the roundup of the Prosper network, he had spent several weeks in prison there and then at Fresnes before being sent to avenue Foch. Having experienced brutal treatment and near-starvation rations at both places, he was delighted by the leniency he found in Paris.

Starr showed his willingness to cooperate during his first interrogation by Kieffer, who showed him a large map of all the SOE circuits in France and asked him to outline on the map the area covered by his section in Dijon. He did so with what Kieffer thought was great precision and artistry, and the SD chief asked him to redraw the entire map. Starr readily agreed, and after he'd finished, Kieffer assigned him more graphics work. In effect, said the historian Sarah Helms, he became "Kieffer's artist in residence," which included painting the portraits of top-ranking SD officials, including Kieffer himself.

Starr's cooperation became outright collaboration when he agreed to copyedit the English text of the false messages being sent to SOE as part of avenue Foch's "radio game." "It was he who corrected various spelling and editing mistakes for me and showed me the proper [English] way to write a technical report," noted Josef Goetz, who headed avenue Foch's radio playback operation. Starr also translated BBC French news reports for the Germans.

SOE agents who arrived after Starr at avenue Foch were astonished by his obvious friendliness with his captors. "The Gestapo boys are quite decent when you get to know them," he told Brian Stonehouse, an agent who'd been arrested in Lyon. Another colleague, Harry Peulevé, later said of Starr, "His presence was unfortunate in that it may have been used to give confidence to newly arrested agents that they would be well treated. In fact Starr was used by the Germans as a living example of the way in which they would keep their word." His cozy relationship with the Germans prompted newcomers to cooperate as well. To other SOE operatives, Starr justified his work with the Germans by saying he planned to escape at some point and was collecting intelligence about SD activities, including the radio game, to relay to London once he was free.

Léon Faye knew nothing about Starr's collaboration. All he cared about was the SOE agent's apparent familiarity with the mansion's floor plan and his potential access to a screwdriver and other supplies needed for the breakout. At Faye's suggestion, Noor sounded him out. Initially, Starr rejected the idea of an escape attempt, saying he saw no chance of its succeeding. But he changed his mind when Noor told him Faye had promised to arrange a Lysander to pick them up and take them to Britain. When she asked Starr, at Faye's behest, to tell her what he knew about the neighboring houses and streets, he said it was possible to reach the nearest street, rue Pergolese, through the adjoining houses.

With Starr on board, Faye decided to go ahead with the plan. He knew it was exceedingly risky, even for him—a seasoned, tough-minded *résistant* who had been matching wits with the Vichy police and Gestapo for three years. His partners, on the other hand, were a children's book writer and a graphic artist who had only been in France for a few months and whose training for underground work had been minimal. As it turned out, neither was prepared, either physically or mentally, for what lay ahead of them. But Faye felt he had no choice now but to include them.

Using Morse code and notes hidden in the lavatory, he explained to the others how to loosen the bars across the ventilation shaft. Starr found a screwdriver in a maintenance closet, and the three surreptitiously passed it among themselves. The rope needed to rappel from the roof of the mansion would be made by tearing their bedspreads into strips. Starr promised to collect and bring with him a flashlight, additional tools, and, if possible, another rope.

The preparations took three weeks. On the morning of November 24, Starr left a note for Faye saying he had removed his bars and was able to get up to the roof. But from the tone of the note, Faye detected an increasing doubt on Starr's part regarding the escape. For it to succeed, Faye felt, it was imperative that he not back out; Faye and Noor needed his knowledge of the area, along with the supplies he was bringing. Fearful that the SOE operative would abandon the idea if they waited any longer, Faye decided they would make the attempt that night.

He informed the others that he and Noor would climb out on the roof at 9:30 P.M. and wait for Starr, who, because his room was next to the guardroom, could not leave until 1:30 in the morning, when the guards on the current shift went off duty. At 9:30, Faye hoisted himself up through the ventilation shaft and onto the roof, carrying with him the rope he had made from his bedspread. Once outside, he became "drunk with happiness" when he looked up at the night sky and stars—the first time in more than two months that he had seen them—and deeply inhaled the cold, fresh air. But his euphoria began to fade when he realized that the neighboring roofs and buildings bore no resemblance to Starr's description of them.

His worry increased when he approached the skylight over Noor's room and heard a loud scraping noise below. He realized she had not yet fully loosened the bars over the shaft in her room and was working frantically to do so. "This girl is crazy," he thought; it was doubtful that she'd be done before daybreak. Opening the skylight, he advised her to stop, put everything back the way it was, and go to bed. He added that Starr's information about the surrounding area seemed to be worthless and that he was going to take a look around for himself. He promised that he would come back to tell her whether he was going to try to escape on his own or whether he would wait for Starr.

He then made his way to the side of the roof away from avenue Foch, which was narrow and sloping, with no ledge. With considerable difficulty, he reached a slightly wider space that overlooked a terrace of the house next door. According to Starr's information, he would be able to see a street from there, but there was no sign of it.

Faye spent the next few minutes catching his breath and deciding what to do. Although he couldn't see the street, he was sure that the house below must open onto it. Once he reached the street, he could make his way to the apartment of friends who lived nearby. They would help him contact Alliance, and with any luck, he could be smuggled out of France and be back in England within a week.

Should he leave now, or should he wait for Starr, who, notwithstanding his faulty intelligence thus far, might know who occupied the adjoining house? After several minutes of examining the pros and cons of each move, Faye decided to play it safe and wait.

Retracing his steps, he again heard Noor fiercely working on the bars. When he begged her to be more quiet, she failed to respond and redoubled her efforts, clearly determined to finish by the time Starr was ready to leave. Faye admired her "magnificent courage" but was concerned about what he considered her foolhardiness. Two more hours passed, and the noise of traffic died down in the streets, with the only sound coming from Noor's implacable scraping.

At 1:30, he opened the skylight to Starr's room and helped haul him up to the roof. Faye was tempted to leave immediately but decided they couldn't abandon Noor. If she had stopped working on the bars when he first suggested it, she could have covered up what she had done. Now that was impossible: Her efforts would be immediately noticed by the guards when they entered her room later that morning.

From their brief conversation on the rooftop, Faye realized that Starr was fast losing his nerve and was no longer positive about anything. He led him to the other side of the roof to inspect the house next door. Starr told Faye he had no idea who occupied the house or, in fact, if it was occupied at all.

Finally, at 3:30 A.M., Noor was finished. Faye helped lift her out of the shaft, and moving in single file, the three fugitives clambered across the roof to the spot overlooking the neighboring house. Tying his makeshift rope to a pole, Faye threw it over the roof and climbed down to the terrace. The other two followed him. As Faye caught Noor at the bottom, he was horrified to see that her watch had a luminous dial that shone like a flashlight. Yet even then he couldn't contain his joy. They had escaped from avenue Foch and with any luck would soon be back on the streets of Paris and on their way to freedom.

He turned the knob of the terrace door and found it locked. Then he noticed that one floor below, there was another small terrace with glass-paned French doors that could easily be broken. He debated whether he and the others should use the rope Starr had said he would provide and shinny down three stories to the ground, or jump to the terrace, then go through the house and down the stairs to the street. As it turned out, there was no choice: Starr hadn't brought the rope or any of the other items he had promised.

As Faye considered this latest problem, he heard the roar of aircraft engines and looked up to see a large force of American Flying Fortresses flying directly overhead on their way back to England from a raid on Germany. Suddenly a loud voice rang out, complaining in German about a light, and a flashlight beam from a window at 84 avenue Foch was aimed toward the terrace on which they crouched. Faye believed their unseen challenger, probably an SS guard, had spotted the lighted dial of Noor's watch, but he didn't think the German could see them in the corner of the terrace in which they had taken cover. If they remained perfectly still and let things settle down, he whispered to the others, he thought they'd be safe.

Fifteen minutes passed. Starr, who had grown increasingly agitated, abruptly jumped to his feet, saying he had to leave now. Before Faye could stop him, he rushed to the center of the terrace, with Faye and Noor pursuing him. Just then, another flashlight beam from the window at 84 avenue Foch swept over them.

Quickly dashing to the edge of the terrace, Faye leaped onto the one below, followed by Starr and Noor. He smashed a pane in the French door, reached through and unlocked it, then groped his way through the darkened house until he found the stairs. With the other two behind him, he raced down the three flights and reached the ground floor hall. He cautiously opened the door to the street and peered out. An SS sentry was patrolling just a few feet away.

Faye quietly shut the door and waited. Starr and Noor crouched behind him. After a few minutes, Faye cracked open the door again and saw no sign of the sentry. He darted out and ran down the street in the opposite direction from the SS man, only to find that it ended in a cul-de-sac. He retraced his steps, but the sentry was waiting for him. A second guard appeared, followed by Gestapo agents in civilian clothes, all with revolvers in their hands. They backed Faye up against a wall and clubbed him repeatedly with the butts of their guns. He fell to the ground, unconscious.

JOSEF KIEFFER WAS INCOHERENT with rage when he learned of the escape attempt. Not only had the fugitives showed their ingratitude for his lenient treatment of them, but the SD's "radio game" would have been destroyed if Starr had managed to get away and inform London what was really going on.

Ordering the three to line up against a wall on the fourth floor of avenue Foch, he shouted that he was going to shoot them on the spot. After a few minutes, he calmed down. If they gave their word of honor that they wouldn't try to escape again, he told them, he would allow them to return to their cells. Starr immediately did as he was asked. Faye and Noor refused. That same day, the two were deported to prisons in Germany.

Classified as "a very dangerous prisoner," Noor spent the next ten months in solitary confinement, subjected to near-starvation rations and frequent torture. For the last four months of her life, her wrists and ankles were shackled. In September 1944, she was sent to Dachau concentration camp, where she was executed. She was thirty years old.

Faye, meanwhile, was transported by convoy to a grim prison fortress outside Bruchsal, a city in western Germany. Labeled as *"Ein Wichtiger Terrorist, ein Spezialist des Entfliehen"* (an important terrorist, an expert at escape), he was dragged in handcuffs out of the car and thrown into an underground dungeon, where his ankles were chained to the foot of an iron bed. There was no heat in the bare, unlighted cell, and the extreme cold was exacerbated by the fortress's penetrating dampness. "Water remains permanently on the ground, and everything is soaked," Faye wrote in a surreptitious journal. "My hands and feet are frozen all the time."

The rest of the fortress's basement was occupied by a factory whose machinery roared night and day, adding to Faye's sense of being in Dante's Inferno. Because of the horrific noise, sleep was virtually impossible, and he spent most of his time in the early days at Bruchsal replaying the failed escape in his mind.

As he knew, there was a bitter irony attached to the fiasco. For years, Fourcade had chided him for his rashness. To her chagrin, he had never given much thought to his safety or security—until the night of November 24. If he had not waited for Starr on the roof that evening, if he had escaped on his own as soon as he'd left his room, he might well be back in London now.

WHEN JOSEF KIEFFER ASKED John Starr why he had tried to escape, the SOE agent replied that he felt he had no choice. If Noor, a woman, had managed to get away, he told Kieffer, "she would have made it impossible for him in England had he, as a man, not displayed the same courage."

For several weeks, Kieffer refused to have anything to do with Starr. Eventually, however, he forgave his protégé when Starr not only renounced any plans to escape again but also pledged he would never work against the Germans in any way.

Nonetheless, his charmed existence at avenue Foch was fast drawing to a close. Despite Kieffer's promises that his VIP prisoners would be treated as prisoners of war, Starr and the others were sent in July 1944, a month after D-Day, to two of Germany's most brutal concentration camps—Sachsenhausen and Mauthausen. Starr was one of a handful to survive the war.

Although he was never prosecuted for his collaboration with the Gestapo, he was regarded as a traitor and shunned by virtually all his former colleagues for the rest of his life.

CHAPTER 27

THE MAP

F OR A FEW DAYS NEAR THE END OF 1943, MARIE-MADELEINE HAD a flicker of hope that Alliance, like a phoenix, was again rising from the ashes. Philippe Koenigswerther had finally made it back to France on November 25—the first Alliance agent to do so in more than two months.

The late-night sea operation that delivered Koenigswerther to the coast of Brittany was a close-run thing. When the Royal Navy torpedo boat approached the designated rendezvous point, its captain failed to spot a prearranged signal from the reception committee and concluded, correctly, that the boat was at the wrong place. But Koenigswerther, still fuming over his failed attempt earlier in the month, was determined to land, regardless of the consequences. When the captain ordered his crew to turn back, the agent pulled out a revolver and waved it at the British sailors, shouting he'd had enough and was going ashore. The MI6 liaison man accompanying him begged Koenigswerther to wait. But he jumped overboard, found his footing in the shallow water, and splashed off into the darkness.

Carrying 2 million francs and a sack of mail, Koenigswerther remained on the rocky beach, dodging German patrols until daylight, when he made his way to an inn in a nearby village. Serendipitously, he found there members of the Alliance reception committee, who, following their vain wait for him the night before, had retreated to the inn to get some sleep. Two days later, an anxious Fourcade finally heard from Koenigswerther. He had safely returned to Bordeaux and soon was sending a stream of messages about submarine and shipping traffic at the port. In Saint-Nazaire, André Coindeau (Urus), who had helped arrange Koenigswerther's return, was equally prolific, reporting not only on activity at the submarine base there but also giving locations and descriptions of newly constructed V-1 rocket launching sites nearby.

From Lille, in the far north of France near the Belgian border, Henri Fremendity (Osprey) was also providing plentiful intelligence about the rocket sites in his sector. On November 26, Fremendity signed off his latest report with "More follows . . ." But for several days afterward, there were no further transmissions from him. Then Koenigswerther's transmitter went quiet, too. In his last message, sent December 5, he had requested an emergency parachute drop of three additional transmitters, as well as a variety of weapons that included Sten guns, revolvers, and knives. In his dispatch, he mentioned that the Germans had embarked on an intense radio detection campaign in the area.

As the silence from both agents continued, Fourcade was forced to conclude that the Gestapo had launched yet another wave of arrests in the north. She sent out an urgent message to the operatives still at large in the region to stop all transmissions and go into hiding. André Coindeau's operator replied that Coindeau would obey her order but only after presiding over an RAF parachute drop that had been scheduled for his sector. When the drop took place, the pilot ferrying the supplies reported to MI6 that he'd seen "a lot of activity" in the landing zone. Coindeau had been arrested, and Alliance's only operation in December ended with all the equipment sent by the British falling into enemy hands. This time, the man known as "Nero" was unable to escape the flames.

At a time when the British military command was particularly avid for intelligence about coastal defenses and rocket launch sites in the north of France, Alliance once again had suffered crippling losses there. Fourcade wondered if the British had decided to end their support for her network, even though she was sure that Alliance would revive if given help. But at least for the moment, the RAF and MI6 seemed loath to continue that assistance, despite repeated urgent requests from Paul Bernard and other Alliance operatives. "We have the impression London is losing interest in us," Bernard said in one message. "We are now being exposed to exceptional new risks, and in order for us to continue, we must receive more aid immediately."

Fourcade asked herself if she had the right to force the network to carry on when there seemed to be nothing she could do to help her agents. She decided that if the situation did not improve soon, she would consider shutting it down.

On Christmas Eve 1943, she attended midnight mass in the basement of her house in Carlyle Square. It was the saddest Christmas of her life. Once again, on this holiest of days, she was separated from her children, now including her infant son, who was still in hiding with Monique Bontinck in the south of France. As Fourcade listened to the priest read the liturgy, she thought back to the year before, when she had celebrated the holidays with Faye and other cherished associates—Gabriel Rivière, Ferdinand Rodriguez, and Lucien Poulard among them. All of them now were gone.

On that melancholy night, she derived some comfort from the fact that her closest friend from Paris, Nelly de Vogüé, was at her side. A few weeks earlier, Nelly, who had been with Antoine de Saint-Exupéry in Algiers, had made her way to London. Determined to raise Marie-Madeleine's spirits, she insisted that the two of them attend a New Year's Eve party to which Nelly had been invited at the home of William Waldorf Astor II, the son of Viscount Astor and his flamboyant wife, Nancy.

Marie-Madeleine reluctantly agreed, but from the moment she entered Astor's house, she was sorry she had. It was like an evening before the war, she recalled. The long tables, set with the finest silverware and crystal, sparkled in the candlelight. Equally glittering were the diamond necklaces and tiaras of many of the female guests, who sipped champagne as they laughed and chatted with their equally well dressed male companions. Instead of lifting Marie-Madeleine's depression, the gala scene only deepened it.

Just before midnight, she wandered over to a window and gazed at the dense fog that hid Astor's garden from view. What would 1944 bring? she wondered. Would it result in the liberation of France? Or would it merely continue the sadness and suffering of the "terrible year" of 1943? As she stared out at the fog, a wave of pain washed over her.

A FEW WEEKS LATER, however, her anguish began to recede a bit, thanks to the entrance of Kenneth Cohen into her life. Cohen, who was now the head of all MI6 operations in France, had been the British official who'd met with Navarre in Lisbon in 1941 and authorized the partnership between MI6 and Alliance. Since November 1941, he had been very much aware of Fourcade and her importance to the network; he had sent Eddie Keyser to meet her in Madrid and had overseen the relationship between MI6 and her group until mid-1943.

Shortly before Fourcade arrived in London, Cohen had been assigned to organize Operation Sussex, a mission to parachute dozens of two-man French intelligence teams into France before D-Day. They were to provide the Allies, both during and after the invasion, with information about the movements, communications, and supplies of the German army, particularly its panzer divisions. After the teams were dispatched to France in January 1944, he returned to MI6 headquarters.

Known for his warmth and sensitivity, Cohen deeply cared about the French agents with whom he associated, which made him a rarity in the bureaucratic confines of MI6. In his memoirs, Patrick Reilly noted how Cohen "won the lasting respect and affection of the Resistance leaders with whom he came to work."

His relationship with Marie-Madeleine was particularly close; indeed, in many respects, they were kindred spirits. For one thing, they both came from families that placed great value on culture and the arts. Cohen's maternal grandfather, Meyer Salaman, was a wealthy businessman who made his fortune in the late nineteenth century importing ostrich feathers from South Africa. The feathers, worn on hats and in women's hair, were so highly prized by the fashionable elite in Britain and the rest of Europe that their value per pound at the turn of the century was almost equal to that of diamonds.

A voracious reader, whose favorite authors were Shakespeare and Dickens, Salaman opened his country house to young writers, actors and painters, among them Augustus John and William Orpen. Several of his fourteen children also turned to painting, including Cohen's uncle, Michael Salaman, who was a good friend and associate of Augustus John. Cohen's first cousin, Merula Salaman, was both a painter and actress—and the wife of the actor Alec Guinness.

There was yet another renowned artist in Cohen's family: his wife, Mary. The daughter of a prominent London architect, she had trained at the Slade School, arguably Britain's most prestigious art academy. Her work—mostly landscapes, portraits, and still lifes—was displayed in a number of private and public collections.

Shortly after Cohen's first meeting with Fourcade, he and Mary took her under their wing. The Cohens, who had a young daughter, invited her often to their home and made her, in effect, a de facto member of their family.

Yet as important as Cohen was to Fourcade personally, he had an even greater impact on the fortunes of her network. Strongly affected by the massive losses suffered by Alliance, he broke up the bureaucratic logjam preventing it from getting what it needed, insisting that top priority be given to restoring the broken link between London and the network. After Fourcade told him that because of the stoppage of the Lysander flights, she had received no intelligence reports or any other mail since August 1943, he asked the Royal Navy to authorize a sea operation to pick up the reports.

A naval torpedo boat was sent on January 27, 1944, to a rendezvous point on the Côte d'Azur, near Saint-Raphael, to retrieve more than ninety pounds of mail collected by Helen des Isnards, head of the southeast region, from the other sectors. Dubbed Operation Popeye, it was far from an easy mission. As an icy rain pelted down, an Alliance operative spent three hours clinging to two enormous mail-bags while perched precariously on a rocky jetty. The agent was Count Élie de Dampierre, the twenty-six-year-old scion of one of France's oldest and most distinguished aristocratic families, who happened to be des Isnards's best friend and brother-in-law. When Dampierre had told his father the year before of his decision to join Alliance, Guy de Dampierre stiffly responded, "We Dampierres are not spies"—a dictum that Élie promptly ignored. He and the mail were plucked off the rock by the British just minutes before a German patrol, alerted by the noise of the torpedo boat's motors, arrived on the scene.

In London, Fourcade avidly read through the massive backlog of letters and reports, much of it containing the heartbreaking human details of the disaster that had struck the network the previous fall, as well as the desperate efforts to survive it. The most agonizing news came from a letter informing her of the death of Maurice Coustenoble, the young pilot who had been one of her first recruits in Vichy and who, along with Henri Schaerrer, had served as her most devoted and trusted lieutenants in the early years of the network. Coustenoble, who had been based in the north of France since the summer of 1943, suffered from tuberculosis and had been in increasingly poor health. Tracked down by the Gestapo in October 1943, he died before he could be arrested, fulfilling his vow to Fourcade that "the Boches shall never get me alive." Shattered by his death, she remembered what Coustenoble had repeatedly told her: "Little one, a soldier does not cry." This time, however, she could not hold back the tears.

THANKS TO COHEN'S DETERMINED prodding of the RAF, a Lysander operation on behalf of Alliance was finally scheduled for March. Élie de Dampierre and another network agent were to return to the south-west of France, carrying with them an enormous amount of material, including mail, questionnaires, money, equipment, and other supplies.

On the evening of March 3, the Lysander took off—and never returned. Again, Fourcade's emotions ricocheted between hope and despair. After a couple of days, MI6 and the RAF gave up the plane and its occupants for lost. But this time, a seeming disaster had a happy ending. Word came that the Lysander had indeed crashed but that its passengers and pilot were alive, although the pilot had been injured. A new Lysander operation was immediately scheduled to retrieve him.

On March 16, another plane was dispatched to a new landing ground in the Loire Valley. It returned with the flier, marking the first successful Lysander operation for Alliance in six months. The air link between France and Britain had finally been restored.

Also aboard the plane was an unscheduled passenger who had been added at the last minute. He was Jean Sainteny, who headed Alliance's sector in Normandy. Sainteny left the aircraft tightly clutching a large, bulging sack. It contained arguably the network's most vital document of the war.

ONE OF ALLIANCE'S MOST skilled and daring agents, the thirty-six-year-old Sainteny was a native of Normandy and had run a thriving banking and insurance business in Paris before the war. He owned a farm near the Normandy coast, overlooking what would later become known as Omaha Beach.

By all accounts, Sainteny was a natural-born spy. After taking part in the 1940 fight for France, he had set up his own personal intelligence network in the northwest region of the country, recruiting a number of his childhood friends, several of them seamen, to collect information about the burgeoning growth of German shipyards, submarine bases, and defense emplacements.

After first making contact with Alliance in late 1940, Sainteny combined his group with the larger organization a few months later. He was captured by the Germans four times during the war, the first in September 1941. After several weeks in a prison in Caen, he was released for lack of evidence. His second arrest came in September 1943 during the massive Gestapo roundup of Alliance agents, but unlike most of his colleagues, the swashbuckling, dark-haired Sainteny managed to escape.

In the fall of 1943, his informants had distinguished themselves with their detailed information on the construction of rocket launching sites. Late in the year, MI6 asked them to switch their focus to ferreting out intelligence for the American and British military commanders who were planning the upcoming invasion of Western Europe.

Operation Overlord, as it was called, would be the most complex, fateful, and massive military venture in history. In less than twenty-four hours, hundreds of thousands of troops and their equipment, including some fifty thousand vehicles, would have to be transported across the English Channel, land on a heavily defended shore, and secure a bridgehead.

Many of those involved in the planning of D-Day, including its commander, General Dwight D. Eisenhower, were consumed with worry that the Allies were not ready for the operation and that it would end in utter failure—a "disaster," as one British general put it, "of the most crushing dimension." With Overlord, Eisenhower knew, there would be no second roll of the dice. "In this particular venture, we are not merely risking a tactical defeat," he wrote, "we are putting the whole works on one number."

There were doubts about virtually every aspect of the operation, from insufficient numbers of landing craft to the notoriously fickle weather over the Channel to a shortage of supplies. But what most concerned the planners were the fearsome defenses that awaited them on the other side.

Known as the Atlantic Wall, a formidable string of fixed fortifications—concrete gun emplacements, bunkers, beach obstacles, barbed wire, observation posts, and mine fields—stood guard over 2,800 miles of coastline in occupied Europe, from Norway to Spain. The most heavily defended shores, not surprisingly, were those of France and the Low Countries, viewed by the Germans as the likeliest targets for an Allied invasion. In Normandy alone, almost eight thousand Wehrmacht troops manned its fortifications.

D-Day's planners originally considered six possible landing areas, including the North Sea beaches of Holland and Belgium and beaches in Brittany, all of which were rejected because they were beyond the reach of Allied fighter planes. That left the coast of the Pas de Calais, opposite the cliffs of Dover, and the Normandy coast from Caen to Cherbourg.

The D-Day architects eventually decided on Normandy, whose beaches seemed more suitable for the prolonged unloading operations that would be required. They also appeared to have adequate roads leading inland, which would allow for a swift and massive deployment of troops. The U.S. 4th Infantry Division would land on what was dubbed Utah Beach, while the U.S. 29th and 1st Infantry divisions would go ashore at Omaha Beach, less than a mile from Jean Sainteny's farm. British and Canadian troops, meanwhile, would land on beaches with the code names Sword, Juno, and Gold.

Having made their choice, the planners had to find out everything they could about the area—not only its coastal defenses but also troop deployments and the status of German communications and transport. In late 1943 and early 1944, high-altitude reconnaissance planes flew over the beaches to photograph their terrain. But the planners needed much more minute detail of the German fortifications than what was evident in the aerial photos.

For months, the operatives of dozens of networks—the largest of which were Alliance, Confrérie de Notre Dame, and Jade Amicol— had been collecting such information. But the Gestapo's savage crackdown in the fall of 1943 had taken a huge toll on most of these groups. Indeed the Confrérie de Notre Dame was virtually wiped out in November 1943. Such losses threatened the flow of vital information on which the success of D-Day depended.

Serendipitously, although Alliance had been hit extremely hard, too, the subsector responsible for information about the D-Day beaches remained relatively unscathed. The extraordinary fruits of the work of that group and its leader—a sculptor and artist named Robert Douin—were stuffed into the cumbersome bag that Jean Sainteny had lugged with him from Normandy.

ON THE SURFACE, ROBERT DOUIN seemed an unlikely spy, especially if one believed the maxim that spies should never call attention to themselves. Douin, by contrast, drew attention like a magnet, in large part because of his appearance. Tall and dark-haired, he sported a bushy mustache and goatee and was usually seen in a velour suit, cra-

ROBERT
DOUIN

vat, and large, wide-brimmed felt hat. Reminding some of his acquaintances of the playwright Edmond Rostand's great literary creation Cyrano de Bergerac, Douin had a personality as outsized as his looks. He was gregarious, witty, and opinionated and had legions of friends.

In 1930, he had succeeded his father, also an artist, as director of the École des Beaux Arts in Caen, a bustling city eight miles inland from the Channel coast. But since the fall of France, Douin's main obsession had been to rid his country of the Germans. He was furious when Pétain capitulated and considered the marshal a traitor— opinions that he was not shy in expressing.

In November 1940, Douin joined one of the first resistance groups in Caen. Contacted by Sainteny at the end of 1941, he enlisted in Alliance in February 1942 and soon became head of its Caen subsector, which had some forty members, among them fishermen, teachers, shop owners, and a blacksmith.

In August 1943, MI6 asked Sainteny to provide maps as detailed as possible of the German defenses on the Normandy coast—a request that Sainteny passed on to Douin. After mobilizing his agents, the art school director embarked on what he viewed as the master work of his life.

Aided by his fourteen-year-old son, Rémy, Douin walked and cycled up and down the coast, from the mouth of the Dives River east of Caen to the Cotentin peninsula, sketching in detail all the fortifications he saw and taking copious notes, all the while keeping a wary lookout for German sentries. He had restored a number of local churches in the past, which gave him an entree to their bell towers and the towers' sweeping views of the countryside and coast—vistas that helped him in his work.

Joining his father on the days he wasn't in school, Rémy was passed off by Douin as his apprentice. The boy made significant contributions to Douin's efforts, spotting antitank trenches as well as access paths from the beaches that would later be used by Allied troops. Another important contributor was a member of Douin's group, a fisherman, who noticed that whenever Wehrmacht officials installed a new coastal battery, they scheduled a practice bombardment over the Channel. Before doing so, they posted flyers warning fishermen and ship captains to keep away from the practice areas. The fisherman stole the flyers, which included the batteries' locations, and passed them on to Douin.

As he worked, Douin was well aware that the tentacles of the Gestapo were closing in on him and his group. The house of one of his key lieutenants was searched by German police in late 1943, and two other members of the subsector went into hiding after being warned their arrests were imminent. In early 1944, the Gestapo in Normandy intensified their crackdown. Sainteny offered to evacuate Douin and his family to London by Lysander, but knowing the importance of the map on which he was working, Douin refused to leave until it was done.

Finally, after six months, the map was finished. In early March 1944, Douin dispatched a long, rolled-up canvas by courier to Sainteny. When the Normandy chief unrolled it, he knew he had to get it to London as quickly as possible. When he learned about the March 16 Lysander operation to pick up the injured pilot, he made sure that he and the canvas were on the plane.

After landing at Tangmere, Sainteny immediately brought his precious cargo to Marie-Madeleine. As he pulled it out of the bag and unfurled it, her astonishment matched his. On the floor before her was a fifty-five-foot-long map of the beaches and roads on which the Allies would land on June 6. It showed every German gun emplacement, fortification, and beach obstacle along the coast, together with details of German army units and their movements. As one military historian wrote, Douin's masterpiece was "the most complete, detailed military picture of the landing sites" that the Allied command would be given in the course of the war.

CHAPTER 28

GOING HOME

MARIE-MADELEINE WAS TRANSFIXED BY DOUIN'S MAP. EVEN though the location of the D-Day landing was a closely guarded secret, she had long suspected it would be Normandy. If that indeed were the case, her agents there had seemingly provided the Allied chiefs with every detail they could possibly need.

The young MI6 officer who served as her liaison wanted to rush the map immediately to the War Office, but she told him to wait a few minutes so she could savor it. She later asked Sainteny for a list of those who had been involved in its making.

The map, as she would learn, had been whisked away to London just in time. On March 17, as she was admiring it, its creator was being rounded up by the Gestapo in Caen, along with fifteen members of his group.

Two more Alliance agents who, like Robert Douin, had provided vital intelligence to the Allies—Jacques Stosskopf and Jeannie Rousseau—were also swept up in early 1944 in the latest paroxysm of Gestapo raids in the north of France. Stosskopf, who had reported on German submarine operations at Lorient since the fall of 1940, finally saw his luck run out. A German officer at Lorient who was secretly anti-Nazi warned a subordinate of Stosskopf's that he was in imminent danger of arrest. When the subordinate passed the word on to his boss, Stosskopf replied, "I can't stop now. I'm the head of a sector that could not exist without me, and my desertion would have serious consequences for my agents." In early February 1944, his name was found on a list of agents in the pocket of a captured Alliance operative, and he was immediately seized. When Stosskopf disappeared from the Lorient base, there were rumors that he had been promoted to a better job elsewhere. In fact, he had been deported to Germany.

Jeannie Rousseau was captured in April. She had become so important to the Allied scientific intelligence effort that British officials decided to bring her to London for an extensive debriefing. She was to be picked up by a Royal Navy boat off the coast of Brittany, but the operation went awry and she, too, was taken by the Gestapo and dispatched to a German concentration camp.

Just as devastating for Fourcade was the news that Paul Bernard, her replacement as Alliance's chief in France, had been arrested in Paris on the same day as Douin and his group. Nine other agents in the French capital, including her close friend Marguerite Brouillet, had been captured as well. Fourcade would not learn until near the end of the war that Bernard had been subjected to intense torture, including waterboarding, to force him to divulge the whereabouts of other agents. He remained silent.

Her mind reeling from these latest calamities, Fourcade forced herself to focus yet again on saving her network. She would send Jean Sainteny to Paris to replace Bernard and resuscitate Alliance in the north. She would also call on the resources of the three leaders whose operations were still functioning well and whom she said were her last hope: Helen des Isnards in the southeast; Henri Battu in the southwest; and Georges Lamarque, who covered all regions of the country with his Druids. Each of them would be given money and autonomy over their own regions. She hoped to rejoin them in France as soon as possible.

Determined to circumvent Claude Dansey's adamant refusal to send her back there, she found an unlikely ally in her campaign to return—none other than the BCRA, the Free French intelligence service. By 1944, Charles de Gaulle had won his political battle with Henri Giraud and was widely regarded as the sole leader of Free France. He and his lieutenants were anxious to bring all French intelligence networks into the Gaullist camp in order to present a united front to the British and American governments.

Although Fourcade had long had a testy relationship with André Dewavrin, the head of the BCRA, both realized the importance of their organizations joining together. In exchange for Alliance becoming part of the Free French, Fourcade was promised continued autonomy for her network and independence for its air and radio links. The BCRA also agreed that Alliance could still send MI6 the intelligence it had gathered for as long as the war lasted.

Now that she was no longer subject to Dansey, she began getting ready for her return. MI6 provided her with a new false identity as Germaine Pezet, the wife of Raymond Pezet, an Alliance agent and former air force pilot. She changed her appearance as well, complete with dyed-black hair, a pair of round spectacles, and a "dental masterpiece" concocted by an MI6 dentist—a yellow plastic prosthetic that fit over her own teeth.

On April 11, Jean Sainteny flew back to France by Lysander. He more than lived up to Fourcade's expectations, restoring radio transmissions between Paris and London as soon as he returned. He also recruited a wave of new agents, including several radio operators. Within weeks, nine transmitters were operating in northern France.

As Fourcade made preparations to join Sainteny, she couldn't help but be aware of the growing carnival atmosphere in London over the long-awaited invasion. For anyone living in the south and east of England in the spring of 1944, there was little doubt that it was imminent. Truck convoys, tanks, and speeding jeeps choked roads and lanes in the south, while camouflaged artillery and weapons, along with millions of crates of supplies, were piled high in woods, fields, playgrounds, village greens, and along roads. The docks of the country's southern ports were crowded with seagoing vessels of all descriptions—British and American warships, landing craft, and merchant freighters from around the world. London, noted Marie-Madeleine, was like "a boiling kettle." Traffic was gridlocked, and restaurants were packed. Rumors about the invasion's date and destination swept through the city like a virus.

She expected to return to France during June's full moon period—probably June 9 or 10. As she was finishing some final paperwork late on the evening of June 5, she heard a humming noise outside that grew increasingly loud. When she opened a window in her Carlyle Square house, the humming became a thunderous roar, sounding, as one observer put it, "like a giant factory in the sky." Looking up, she saw fleets of Allied bombers flying wing to wing and heading east—toward France. The long-awaited invasion was about to begin.

The following night, Kenneth and Mary Cohen invited her to their home to celebrate what Fourcade later called the greatest event of the century. Cohen opened a bottle of vintage Bordeaux that he had been saving, and the three toasted the apparent success of D-Day. By day's end, some 150,000 Allied troops, along with their vehicles, equipment, and munitions, were on French soil and heading inland. When Fourcade wondered if it weren't a bit too early to celebrate, Cohen shook his head. The hardest part was over, he said. From then on, everything would go smoothly.

But as it turned out, he was far too sanguine about the future. After leaving the beachheads, Allied forces found themselves in an intractable battle against a still deadly foe. It would take them another two months to pick their slow, bloody way across Normandy and finally break out into the heart of the country.

The invasion, meanwhile, only increased the ferocity of the Gestapo's vengeful campaign against the French resistance. Early in the morning of June 6, as the Allied invaders neared the Normandy beaches with detailed maps of German fortifications in their hands, Robert Douin and the rest of the group that had provided much of that intelligence were rousted out of their jail cells in Caen. Along with some sixty other resistance members, they were taken down to the prison yard and shot. Their bodies—eighty in all—were loaded into trucks and taken to an unknown location. They were never found.

Six days later, Fourcade received word from Helen des Isnards that Sainteny and most of his agents in Paris had been arrested the day after the landing. Shortly after Sainteny's capture, Claude Dansey appeared in her office. If she insisted on returning, he said, she wouldn't last more than six days before being arrested herself. She paid no heed to his warning. As it happened, she had had few dealings with him since Cohen's return. It may well have been out of pique over her close relationship with Cohen that Dansey had begun referring to her as "Cohen's bitch."

While Fourcade was thrilled that the liberation of France had finally begun, the invasion, to her great frustration, had scotched the possibility of any Lysander flights in June. The earliest she would be allowed to travel was during the next full moon period, to take place in early July. As she waited, she wrestled with the question of where she herself should land in the tinderbox that France had become. She finally decided on the southeast, which, under the direction of Helen des Isnards, was the most stable and secure Alliance operation in the country. The heads of the network's other sectors were sending most of their radio messages and mail to des Isnards in the hope and expectation that he and his astonishingly productive radio operator could relay them to London. To reinforce the region, Fourcade persuaded MI6 to schedule a massive parachute drop of radio transmitters, arms, money, and supplies near des Isnards's headquarters, just outside the city of Aix-en-Provence.

On July 5, after nearly a year away from her homeland, she was told by the BCRA that her return flight was imminent; in fact, she was given just two hours to get ready. After packing her clothes in a light fiber suitcase, she placed transmitter crystals, codes, money, and her dental prosthetic in the false bottom of a small holdall bag. In her purse were her papers, including her false identity card as Germaine Pezet, and a packet of what looked like large aspirin tablets but were in fact cyanide pills.

A few days before, she had gone to confession and told the priest about the poison she was taking with her and her concerns about being damned in the eyes of the church if she used it to kill herself.

She hoped she would have the courage to resist torture, but she worried that she might not be able to do so and might, in the end, inform on her colleagues. The priest allayed her fears, saying her death would not be a suicide but rather a necessary means of resisting the enemy. He gave her absolution in advance.

Early on the evening of her departure, she headed for the airfield with her MI6 liaison officer and Raymond Pezet, the agent posing as her husband who would accompany her back to France. To her surprise, she discovered they were not going to the RAF base at Tangmere, where the Lysander operation had been based. Instead, she and Pezet would fly out of the Tempsford base, which lay a little farther north. The plane that would carry them back to France was a larger aircraft—a light bomber called a Hudson—which would also transport several BCRA agents heading home. As the car passed through the English countryside, Marie-Madeleine felt a deep nostalgia for this nation that she was eager to leave but that had done so much to give refuge and assistance to her and tens of thousands of others in occupied Europe when they needed it most.

Instead of Tony and Barbara Bertram's cozy manor house, she was taken to Farm Hall, a grand country mansion commandeered by the RAF near Tempsford, where she and the others were ushered into a baronial dining room that had been converted into a mess. After drinks and dinner, served by waiters in white jackets, she was escorted to the bedroom where she would spend the night before her flight.

The following afternoon, Kenneth Cohen, dressed in his naval uniform, came to escort her to the airfield. Before they left, he took out of his pocket an exquisite ring with a heart-shaped stone and handed it to her. It was a family heirloom, he said, and he and Mary wanted her to have it as a memento of them. Her voice choked with emotion, she protested that it was too valuable for her to keep. But Cohen insisted she take it, saying it would bring her luck.

As they approached Tempsford, Marie-Madeleine witnessed an extraordinary sight: row upon row of bombers on the runways as far as the eye could see. Cohen told her that they were heading out on raids to Germany that night and that her plane would take off immediately after them so that enemy radar would think it was one of the raiders.

As the sun began to set and the first wave of bombers headed eastward, Marie-Madeleine and Pezet were driven onto the tarmac and dropped off at the side of a Hudson. After bidding farewell to Cohen with a kiss and hug, she made her way up the ladder, followed by Pezet and half a dozen other agents, none of whom she knew. There was no attempt to provide any passenger comfort aboard the plane: Marie-Madeleine and the others had to sit on their luggage or on the floor, with their backs against the sides of the fuselage.

After a huge mound of baggage had been loaded and the door shut, she stood up and looked out a window, trying to catch a final glimpse of Cohen. Seeing her, he stood stiffly at attention and snapped off a smart salute. As her eyes filled with tears, the Hudson rumbled down the runway and lifted off, on its way to France.

1944–1945

THE LOCATIONS OF THE GERMAN PRISONS AND CAMPS IN
EASTERN FRANCE AND WESTERN GERMANY IN WHICH ALLI-
ANCE AGENTS WERE IMPRISONED AND EXECUTED

CHAPTER 29

CAUGHT IN THE NET

A S THE HUDSON FLEW ACROSS THE NORTH OF FRANCE, MARIE-Madeleine Fourcade remembered how dark and lifeless the country had appeared from the air during her Lysander flight to London the year before. Now she could see pinpricks of light below, which she realized were flashlight signals, blinking out letters in Morse code. She assumed they came from groups of resistance members who were awaiting RAF drops of weapons and other supplies.

The Hudson made a perfect landing on a brightly lit field in north-central France, about forty-five miles southeast of Paris. The BCRA had handled all arrangements for the flight, including organizing the reception committee. When the bomber door was opened, Fourcade was surprised to hear someone on the ground shout up, "Where's the lady?" As she was helped out of the plane by the committee's chief, she was even more shocked when he casually said, "Hello, Marie-Madeleine."

For her safety, both the BCRA and MI6 had insisted that no one in France, with the exception of Helen des Isnards, be told of her return. When she quizzed the young reception leader about how he knew who she was, he replied that the BCRA headquarters in London had sent him a cryptic but revealing telegram informing him that a network leader would return to take command of Alliance during the next moon period. He assumed it was she—an assumption that was confirmed when he saw her emerge from the plane. He had been in London a few months before, he explained, and someone had pointed her out to him. So much for BCRA security, she thought grimly. She urged him not to tell anyone else, emphasizing that no one must know she was in France.

Her unease increased when she and Pezet were taken to a nearby farmhouse, where they were joined by more than twenty resistance members for a late supper. As the eating and drinking continued, Fourcade, obsessed by what had happened to Léon Faye and Ferdinand Rodriguez, pulled Pezet aside and told him they must leave immediately. He tried to convince her to rest for a few hours, but she sharply reminded him of Faye's capture after he failed to leave the landing ground as quickly as possible. She wanted them on the road now.

Pezet, not surprisingly, shot her a look of disbelief. Their destination was Aix-en-Provence, more than four hundred miles away. "Do you mean to tell me we're going to walk?" he asked. She nodded: at least, for the moment, until they were well clear of the farmhouse and landing area.

After saying goodbye to the reception committee, the two, carrying their suitcases, set off along a road heading south. They passed cottages, fields, market gardens, roads, all shrouded in darkness. At one point, Fourcade reached down, picked up a handful of soil, and rubbed it between her fingers. The gesture brought it home to her: She was finally back in France.

After three miles or so, the two hitched a ride in the cart of a peasant, who, for a hefty sum of money, took them to the next town. That was just the first leg of an exhausting, three-day hegira during which they walked; hitched more rides, usually in trucks and wagons; and traveled on slow-moving, packed trains, whose schedules were frequently disrupted by sabotage and Allied bombing. They stayed in hotels crowded with German soldiers and endured several inspections of their papers by German patrols. Although others were taken away during these random searches, which occurred most frequently in railway stations, Fourcade and Pezet escaped unscathed.

On July 10, they arrived in Aix-en-Provence. Fourcade found herself a little nervous at the prospect of meeting Helen des Isnards, the French count whose skills as a resistance leader had so greatly impressed her and the leaders of MI6. Having corresponded with him for fifteen months, she wondered how she would get along with him in person.

Tall, fair-haired, and dressed in denim, des Isnards made a striking first impression. After kissing her hand, he rattled off several sentences in machine-gun fashion. Why had it taken her so long to get there? He had sixty pounds of correspondence and reports waiting for her to see. And Sainteny had escaped in Paris. . . .

She stopped him and asked for more details about Sainteny. He had been tortured by the Gestapo, des Isnards said, and had been sent for a few days to the hospital. Shortly after being returned to Gestapo headquarters, he managed to escape by sawing through an iron bar in his cell.

Then des Isnards put aside Sainteny's escape for the moment and escorted Fourcade to the hideout he had arranged for her—a flat in a small apartment house in the middle of Aix. After he showed her around, he took from a cupboard several huge stacks of documents and papers—intelligence reports from the surviving Alliance sectors throughout France.

As she began sorting them, she caught up on other network news from des Isnards, whom she quickly came to regard as a friend. She expressed her delight to him about the quality and diversity of the intelligence she was examining and about the large number of agents who seemed to have survived the relentless Gestapo dragnet.

For six days, Fourcade worked virtually nonstop on the mass of documents, encoding the most important reports, including information on the Germans' secret terror weapons and Wehrmacht troop movements on the Normandy front, for transmission to London.

Nearly every day, des Isnards picked her up at the flat and brought her to his headquarters, located at the farmhouse in which he lived with his family just outside Aix. There she handed over the messages to his radio operator and stayed for lunch with des Isnards, his pregnant twenty-three-year-old wife, Marie-Solange, and their two-year-old daughter, Catherine.

A graduate of Saint-Cyr, des Isnards had joined Alliance soon after the German invasion of the free zone. Taking a leave from the air force, he had been hired as an engineer by a regional electric company, which gave him a car, coveted gasoline allotments, and an official pass to travel—all invaluable tools for a spy.

Marie-Madeleine was impressed by des Isnards's daring, toughness, and steely nerves—qualities shared in equal measure by his petite, slender young wife, who was the sister of Élie de Dampierre. Marie-Solange and Élie's father was a prominent figure in French horse racing circles, and the siblings had grown up in Paris and Deauville, an exclusive resort catering to France's wealthy elite on the Normandy coast.

Notwithstanding her privileged upbringing, Marie-Solange des Isnards was as cool, unassuming, and committed to her husband's resistance work as he was. "She would accompany my father—no questions asked—when he went through German checkpoints, often with incriminating documents and other material stashed in the car," said their son, Charles-Helen des Isnards. "She told us later that for her, what she did was 'only normal.'"

As Fourcade sat outside under the hot sun, talking to her hosts and watching Catherine play, she found herself unwinding for the first time in years. If there was a paradise on earth, she decided, it was this Provençal farmhouse, with its masses of geraniums blooming everywhere. But while it may have seemed a little bit of heaven to her, it wasn't exactly an oasis of peace, disrupted as it was by the constant comings and goings of Alliance agents from sectors throughout the country. The security and reliability of des Isnards's operation had made it the unofficial hub of the network, and streams of operatives—from Marseille and Pau, Brittany and Paris, Lyon and Verdun—reported to him from morning to night.

Her confidence about Alliance's survival came surging back.

HELEN AND
MARIE-SOLANGE
DES ISNARDS

SINCE DES ISNARDS OBVIOUSLY had things well in hand in the south, Fourcade, after a week in Aix, decided it was time to move on to Paris to help Sainteny and her other beleaguered agents in the north. Georges Lamarque, who was then in Marseille, made arrangements to pick her up in Aix on July 17 and escort her to the French capital.

On the afternoon before she was to leave, she stood at an open window in her flat and gazed out at the narrow street below, watching housewives come back from their daily food shopping trips. The day was hot and humid, and the scent of the roses that grew everywhere in the city was particularly intense. Lulled by the peaceful scene and the heat, she was startled by a knock at the door.

When Fourcade opened it and saw the grim expression on des Isnards's face, her lethargy instantly vanished. He'd just been informed, he said, that the Germans were planning to raid Aix the following morning. They were apparently trying to track down a group of *maquis* that had set up camp nearby. He urged her to pack up all the reports, and he would take them and her back to his farmhouse. She argued against leaving, noting that the raid wasn't scheduled until the next day and that he could pick her up early in the morning. When she made clear that further arguments would not change her mind, des Isnards reluctantly agreed.

After closing the door behind him, Fourcade went into the kitchen to get something to eat. Once she'd finished, she returned to the sitting room to tidy it up in preparation for her departure. At that moment, she heard a loud crescendo of voices speaking German in the stairwell. Realizing she hadn't locked her door's dead bolt after des Isnards's departure, she rushed to push it into place, to give her time to escape out the back door and into the courtyard. Try as she might, though, she couldn't resist the force of the men pushing in on the door from the other side.

It crashed open, and well over a dozen gun-waving Germans rushed in, all but four of them in gray-green army uniforms. "Where's the man?" they shouted at Fourcade, a couple of them pushing her back against the wall with their revolvers. Her heart thudding, she replied that no man was there; she was on her own. Then she went on the offensive, just as she had done during the Germans' search of her Marseille headquarters almost two years before. Why did they think the man was in her apartment? There were plenty of other apartments in the building.

Her playacting was convincing enough that the leader of the raid, dressed in mufti and clearly Gestapo, ordered all but one soldier to search the entire building. With the lone guard training a machine gun on her, Marie-Madeleine wandered around her sitting room, waiting for a moment when she could move a stack of intelligence reports from the table on which they were piled. When the man turned his head for a moment, she scooped up the papers and pushed them under a divan.

Now that they were out of sight, she asked the guard to describe the man they were seeking. He was tall and fair, the guard said, and the Gestapo called him Grand Duke. Fourcade's heart skipped a beat. So the Germans' quarry wasn't the *maquis*. It was des Isnards himself.

After a few minutes, the rest of the raiding party returned, disgruntled over their failure to find the man they were after. They began searching the flat, turning over the mattress in the bedroom, pulling out the contents of the closets, and rummaging through the cupboards, bureaus, and her suitcases. She had wadded up and hidden much of the intelligence material inside two padded footstools in the sitting room, which the Germans ignored. They also had shown no interest, at least so far, in looking under the divan.

As the search continued, Fourcade vigorously protested her innocence. She was Germaine Pezet, a native of Marseille, who had come to Aix to get away from the Allied bombing raids of her hometown. They were driving her mad, she said. She hated the war, and all she wanted was a little peace and quiet.

The Gestapo leader of the group told her the man they were looking for was an important member of a terrorist resistance organization called Alliance. They obviously didn't realize that the head of the network was standing right in front of them.

No, she said, no one answering the man's description had come to her door. In fact, no one had visited her at all since she'd arrived in Aix. She rambled on and on, continuing her complaints about the bombing and the war and trying to make herself sound as stupid as possible.

Finally, after what seemed an eternity, the leader seemed convinced that she was telling the truth. He ordered her to let him know if she came in contact with the man they were seeking, and when she agreed, he motioned the other members of the raiding party toward the door. As they picked up their guns and headed out, one of them casually glanced under the divan. He looked again, and with a shout, sank to his knees and pulled out a large handful of coded messages on grid paper, holding them up in triumph.

With his discovery, the others went berserk. They ripped open the upholstered furniture in the sitting room and found the papers hidden in the footstools. Several of them advanced menacingly toward Fourcade with their revolvers and machine guns, and for a moment, she was afraid they were going to shoot her on the spot. At that moment, her only thought was that at last, her turn had come—like Navarre, Faye, Schaerrer, and the hundreds of others who had come before her.

Incandescent with rage, the Gestapo leader violently shook her.

"Who are you?" he roared. She replied that she was a spy sent by London to meet some agents in Aix. The man for whom they were searching had indeed come to her door, but she didn't know who he was. He was simply an emissary who was there to arrange an appointment between her and the operatives she was to meet the following day.

When the German ordered her to give him her real name, she coolly responded that he was far too unimportant for her to tell him. She would speak only to the senior Gestapo officer in the region. The leader snapped an order to a subordinate, who ran off. In a few minutes, he returned and whispered in his boss's ear. The leader told Fourcade that the senior Gestapo official in Marseille had agreed to come to Aix the following morning to question her. He ordered her to pack a suitcase, then hustled her down the stairs and into a black car that drove off at top speed, two Gestapo men flanking her in the backseat and the leader in the front.

She was taken not to a prison but to an army barracks in downtown Aix, where she was pushed into a punishment cell for soldiers. The several men in the cell were rousted out, and she was left alone in the small, bare space that stank of urine, sweat, and tobacco. Sinking down on a cot covered with a filthy gray blanket, Fourcade glanced despairingly at the cell's heavily bolted door.

She suddenly felt sick to her stomach and ran to the corner of the room to vomit. Notwithstanding her outward composure in front of the Germans, she was in fact mortally afraid. Exhausted and gasping for breath, she returned to the cot and ordered herself to try to get some sleep, to be better able to stand up to the ordeal that assuredly would face her the following morning. By then they would have combed through her mail and found out who she was.

Would she be able to remain silent and withstand the beatings and other forms of torture that would surely follow? She remembered confiding her fears about a Gestapo interrogation to the priest at confession and his response: Taking cyanide in such a situation would not be suicide but a necessary way of resisting the enemy.

Marie-Madeleine found her handbag and opened it. Perhaps she should take the cyanide now in order to make sure she would never talk. But then she realized that if she did so, the Gestapo would be waiting the following morning for des Isnards to arrive at her flat. He and his operation, the bulwark of Alliance, would be wiped out, and almost certainly the entire network as well. Before she took that irreversible step, she must explore every possibility of escape.

Feeling faint in the hot, stuffy cell, she walked over to the barred window to get a breath of air. As she stood there, she took a more careful look at the window, which was large and had no glass panes. A thick, horizontal wooden board was screwed into the window frame and blocked more than half the opening, leaving a relatively small space at the top to allow in air and a bit of light. There was also a space between the board and the bars covering the window.

Without the right tools, it would be impossible, she knew, to remove the board and one or more of the bars. But could she possibly slip between the board and the bars and ease her body out? Marie-Madeleine remembered her father telling her how robbers in Indochina would oil their bodies to squeeze through the bars of the gates and windows of houses they had chosen as targets. Thanks to fear and the stifling heat, her own slight, slender body was slick with sweat. Could she follow their example? She decided to try.

She waited until about 3 A.M., when the guards outside her cell went off duty. Pushing the cot under the window, she picked up a large washing basin, turned it upside down, and put it on the cot. After taking off all her clothes, she climbed onto the basin, a light summer dress clenched between her teeth.

She managed to pull herself up and over the board. With her body tightly pinned between the board and the bars, she began trying to ease her head between the gaps. The first two were far too narrow. The next one was wider, and she thrust her head as hard as she could through the opening. Although extraordinarily painful, the maneuver worked, and her head popped through.

Just then, a German truck convoy lumbering down the street stopped outside the barracks, directly opposite Marie-Madeleine's window. She quickly pulled her head back through the opening, with a pain so fierce she feared her ears had been torn off. It was the

Gestapo, she thought. They'd come early, and they would find her pinned like a bug between the wooden board and the bars.

An officer emerged from a staff car and shouted something at a sentry standing in front of the barracks, a few hundred feet from her window. With a great rush of relief, Marie-Madeleine realized he was asking for directions. The convoy was not Gestapo, as it turned out, just an ordinary army unit that had gotten lost. After the sentry responded, the officer got back in the car, and the line of trucks disappeared down the street.

After the convoy had gone, she again forced her head through the bars, an effort even more excruciating than before. With her body slick with perspiration, she squeezed one shoulder through, then her right leg. The most searing pain came when she began easing her displaced hip through; as she worked at it, she told herself that the agony of torture would be far worse than what she was enduring now.

Miraculously she succeeded and found herself out on the ledge, with her dress still gripped between her teeth. As she jumped to the ground, the soft thud of her feet alerted the sentry, who clicked on his flashlight and shouted, "Who's there?" She lay flat, and the beam of the flashlight passed above her. When the sentry finally turned it off and moved away, she wrapped her dress around her neck and scuttled on her knees, like a crab, across the street.

On the other side, she jumped up, put on her dress, and ran off, stumbling in the darkness. After a few minutes, she spied a cemetery that was dotted with white family mausoleums, some as big as chapels. There she could hide for a moment and figure out what to do next. She found a crypt with a broken door and crept inside. Sinking down to rest, she examined the damage to her body from the escape: her face was bruised and bloodied, her knees badly skinned, and the soles of her bare feet shredded from running through brambles and on the stony streets.

She knew she couldn't stay there for more than a few minutes. She had to reach des Isnards's farm no later than seven, to stop him from going to her flat in Aix and walking into the Gestapo trap. But first she had to thwart the efforts of the German searchers and dogs that soon would be on her trail. Remembering a book she had read as a child about an escaping officer who had eluded search dogs by washing off his scent in a stream, she found a trickle of a creek nearby and bathed her injured face, knees, hands, and feet. As she did so, she tried to remember how to get to des Isnards's farm.

She was appalled when she realized that to reach the road leading to the farm, she would have to retrace her steps through town, past the barracks from which she had just escaped. And she had to do so as soon as possible. Dawn was breaking, and before long, the guards would open the door to her cell and find her missing.

Trembling with fear and pain, she walked back the way she had come. Everything was quiet in the golden early-morning light, and although a few passersby looked at her curiously, the sentry in front of the barracks paid her little heed. But just a few minutes later, as she turned onto the road leading to des Isnards's farm, she heard in the distance the sounds she had feared: the barking of dogs and the unearthly din of sirens. They had discovered her escape.

Mechanically, she kept walking as her mind scrambled to come up with a way to dodge the roadblock that would soon be set up on this road, as well as on all the others leading out of Aix. Leaving the road, she headed into the field that stretched beside it, where a number of old peasant women were gleaning stray ears of corn left on the ground from the previous harvest. Marie-Madeleine joined them, stooping over and picking up an ear or two as, from the corner of her eye, she saw soldiers halting foot and motor traffic on the road and checking papers. None of them paid attention to the women in the field.

Marie-Madeleine continued gleaning for several more minutes— until the soldiers and roadblock were well in the distance. Joining the road again, she finally found des Isnards's farmhouse. The front door was unlocked, and Marie-Madeleine limped inside. As she did, she called out the names of des Isnards and his wife. She opened their bedroom door, and they sprang from their bed, their eyes wide with surprise. "I've just escaped," she said. "I've saved your lives."

And then she collapsed.

CHAPTER 30

LIBERATION AND BEYOND

WITHIN AN HOUR AFTER FOURCADE'S ARRIVAL AT THE FARM-house, she and the des Isnards family were gone. Putting two-year-old Catherine on the back of her bicycle, the pregnant Marie-Solange cycled about twenty miles to a château owned by members of her husband's family north of Aix-en-Provence, where she and Catherine stayed for the rest of the war. Helen des Isnards, meanwhile, whisked Fourcade off to a hideout he shared with other local resistance groups in the hills near Aix.

According to an Alliance operative who brought her a change of clothes, the Germans were rampaging through Aix in a door-to-door search for her and des Isnards, but thus far his headquarters had not been touched and all his agents were in hiding. Des Isnards's radio operator, Michel Lévêque, brought his transmitter to the hideout, where Fourcade and des Isnards would stay a day or two to give her a little time to recover from her ordeal. Then they would move on to a *maquis* camp in the foothills of Mount Victoire, the limestone peak overlooking Aix.

After what she'd been through, Fourcade couldn't bear the thought of being confined indoors, and she insisted on sleeping outside. Look-

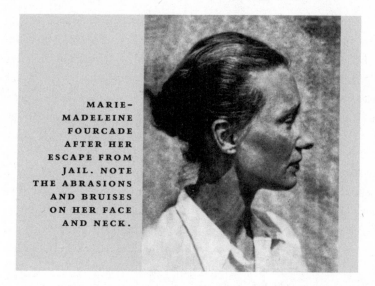

MARIE-MADELEINE FOURCADE AFTER HER ESCAPE FROM JAIL. NOTE THE ABRASIONS AND BRUISES ON HER FACE AND NECK.

outs were posted, with machine guns at the ready, and Fourcade, overcome with exhaustion, slept in the garden until dawn.

Later that day, Lévêque set up his radio outside, hitching his aerial to a cypress tree. Among the messages he transmitted to London were an account by Fourcade of her arrest and escape and an appeal from her for an immediate parachute drop for des Isnards, his agents, and the *maquis*. As Lévêque worked, a stream of operatives came and went, bringing food, supplies, and news of the manhunt for the two fugitives. It was too dangerous to remain where they were, des Isnards decided. Even though Fourcade's lacerated feet were still raw, he, she, and another agent would hike that night to the *maquis* camp, some twelve miles away.

Over the previous few months, the *maquis* had become a major force in the French resistance. Most of them were young Frenchmen who had left their homes and gone underground to avoid being sent to Germany as forced laborers. But the *maquis* with whom des Isnards cooperated were mostly Spaniards who had fought on the Republican side in the Spanish Civil War and had fled to France after General Franco's fascist forces took control of the country in 1939.

Late that evening, Fourcade and her two companions, carrying bags and weapons, set out for the camp. For her, the hike, which was uphill and took all night, was both painful and terrifying. At the slightest sound, the three took cover in the underbrush bordering the rock-strewn road. Such interruptions were frequent, as a seemingly endless parade of German patrol vehicles passed by. Fourcade found it increasingly difficult to walk, and des Isnards and the other agent had to help carry her.

As they approached the camp at daybreak, she collapsed, and a mule-driven cart was summoned to take her the rest of the way. The camp was well protected: Sentries stood guard in a stand of juniper trees on a small bluff overlooking the road, and the camp itself was tucked away in a clearing surrounded by dense thickets of under-brush. Thanks to des Isnards and Alliance, the *maquis,* as well as other resistance groups in the area, were well supplied with weapons, other military gear, and food.

In a corner of the clearing, Lévêque set up his battery-powered transmitter, with its aerial wrapped around a pine tree. Fourcade im-mediately set to work encoding the messages that continued flooding in from Alliance sectors around the country, containing intelligence about subjects ranging from the movement of German units on the Normandy front to the results of Allied bombing raids.

Fourcade loved everything about her days at the *maquis* camp, par-ticularly the experience of working and sleeping outdoors in the cool, drier air of La Victoire's foothills. At night, she lay on her back in the clearing and gazed up at the stars in the brilliantly clear sky, remembering how, as a child in China, she and her father had done the same thing—she with her head on his chest as he pointed out the various constellations.

She particularly enjoyed the camaraderie of the *maquis,* and one night she joined several of them around a small brushwood fire. A member of the group asked about her escape and how she came up with the idea of slipping through the bars of her cell. She told them about the example of the Indochinese robbers and noted how surprised she was that one of the gaps between the bars was actually wide enough for her to force her head through.

One of the *maquis* laughed. He was a mason, he said, and, having installed bars in many prison cells, he knew how she was able to escape. While the cement was still wet and after prison officials had checked the gap between the bars, he would push one of them an inch or two to widen the gap. That was the bar that allowed her head to go through, he said. He and his fellow masons called it "the bar of freedom."

After more than a week in this idyllic setting, Marie-Madeleine decided that with her feet almost completely healed, it was time to move on to Paris. She dyed her hair yet again and had a new photograph taken. Armed with a new name and forged identity papers, she left the camp on July 29, riding pillion on a motorcycle behind one of the *maquis,* her arms clasped tightly around his leather-jacketed middle.

He took her to Marseille, where she was met by Georges Lamarque and some of his Druids. They gave her a disguise for the next part of her journey—a full set of mourning regalia, including a black dress and woolen coat, hat with a black crepe veil, black stockings, and patent leather shoes. Even though the idea of wearing heavy black clothing in the July heat was unappealing, to put it mildly, Marie-Madeleine accepted the role of grieving widow and played it to the hilt when she boarded the train to Paris that night. Accompanying her were Lamarque and another of her regional chiefs, Henri Battu.

As a result of frequent air raid alerts, the tortuous journey took two days. A few miles outside Paris, the tracks had been destroyed by an Allied air raid and the train could go no farther. Lamarque and Battu flagged down a truck loaded with sacks of charcoal to take them the rest of the way. Marie-Madeleine was sitting atop the charcoal sacks when she caught her first glimpse of Paris, after more than a year away.

It was early August 1944, and Paris was gripped by a feverish energy. Allied troops, after a long, bloody summer of slogging across Normandy's hedgerow country, had finally broken through and were now slicing through the heart of France. Rumors had it that they were closing in on Paris, with liberation only a matter of days away.

After being taken to an apartment near the Eiffel Tower, Fourcade began recovering her former self. There were no more drab, dour disguises: If she was going to live in Paris, she had to look the part of a chic Parisienne. After having her hair newly colored and styled at a proper salon, she bought an elegant beige Hermès suit and a large rectangular shoulder bag that was currently in fashion.

Within days of her return, Fourcade tracked down Jean Sainteny, who was hiding out in an apartment in the middle of the city. She told him that he was still in danger and that MI6 wanted him in Lon-

JEAN
SAINTENY

don as soon as possible. She offered to have him evacuated by sea or Lysander. Sainteny suggested another possibility—crossing enemy lines to join the Allied forces closing in on Paris, who would then help him get to Britain.

When she asked him how he planned to do that, he replied, "By motorcycle." His friend Bernard de Billy—the owner of a popular bar near the Arc de Triomphe and a part-time Alliance operative—

had offered to take him. But he did not want to travel empty-handed; he would carry with him the most vital of the latest Alliance intelligence reports from around the country, as well as information for the Allies regarding German activity and positions in Paris itself.

Under Fourcade's direction, Alliance operatives in and around the city put together reports about the German presence there. Contrary to rumors that the Germans were preparing for a last-ditch stand, it appeared that the defensive measures they were taking were meant only as a maneuver to allow a massive retreat by their troops from north and central France. For days, entire Wehrmacht units had marched through or near Paris on their way east, requisitioning every kind of vehicle they could lay their hands on, from trucks to farm wagons to bicycles.

On August 16, the intrepid Sainteny set out on the back of Bernard de Billy's motorcycle, its saddlebags stuffed with material about the headlong German flight from Paris as well as a raft of other intelligence. Disguised as telephone engineers, the two made it to Le Mans, 130 miles to the southwest of Paris, where General George Patton's Third Army had established its temporary headquarters. There Sainteny turned over to Patton's intelligence chief the information that Alliance agents had collected, as well as his own observations about the state of German defenses between the capital and Le Mans. At Sainteny's request, the radio operator at Patton's headquarters passed on Fourcade's other intelligence reports to MI6.

Believing that Sainteny was now safely ensconced in London, Fourcade was startled when he called her from a Paris café two days later. Why was he back in the capital? Didn't he know how dangerous that was? Interrupting her scolding, Sainteny said the Americans had been so impressed with the intelligence he had brought that they wanted additional information, as detailed and specific as possible. They particularly needed to know which, if any, of Paris's bridges had been mined and more about German troop concentrations in the Bois de Boulogne and Bois de Vincennes.

Once again, Alliance agents set to work to gather the details. Only the day before, most high-level German civilian officials, including the chiefs of the SD and Gestapo, had fled the city, along with a bevy of monocled generals. The bulk of the German forces stationed in and around Paris pulled out, too. Fourcade was informed that General Dietrich von Choltitz, the German commander of Paris, had pledged to the Swedish consul Raoul Nordling that he would do everything possible to save it from damage and destruction.

She told Sainteny that the Germans apparently had only one aim—to retreat to the Rhine and save what they could. The German troops crossing the capital needed the Paris bridges because those farther downstream had been destroyed. The Allies could use them to enter Paris. But, she added, they must do so as quickly as possible because Communist members of the resistance, who had become the chief rivals of de Gaulle in the ongoing struggle for postwar control of France, had set in motion an uprising against German forces still in the city. Its purpose was to cement the Communists' authority and power before de Gaulle could return to Paris.

In mid-August, a series of Communist-inspired strikes had been launched in the capital; railway men, police officers, and postal and telegraph workers, among others, walked off their jobs. On the day Sainteny called Fourcade from the café, small bands of resistance fighters throughout Paris, most of them Communists, had begun to attack German patrols.

Fearful that internal French political divisions would result in an unnecessary bloodbath, Fourcade urged Sainteny to impress on Patton and his generals the importance of immediate action to liberate Paris. On August 20, he set off through enemy lines, again on the back of Bernard de Billy's motorcycle.

This trip, however, was considerably more eventful than the first. Some forty miles from the capital, four gun-carrying German sentries standing at the side of the road ordered Billy to stop. After he did so, he and Sainteny were led to a small house that doubled as a sentry post. The two men showed their papers and explained that they were telephone engineers who'd been sent to repair phone lines damaged in a recent battle. Apparently unsure what to do with them, the Germans rummaged through their bags, missing an intelligence report hidden in the pocket of a pair of Sainteny's trousers. Then the soldiers locked the two in the house while they went to confer with senior officers. The motorcycle was left outside. As soon as the four were out of sight, Sainteny and Billy broke a window, scrambled through it, and hopped on the motorcycle. By early evening, they were back at Patton's headquarters.

On August 25, the Second French Armored Division, part of Patton's Third Army, entered Paris.

MARIE-MADELEINE FOURCADE WAS NOT in the capital for the delirious celebrations that followed. A few days earlier, MI6 had asked her to send patrols to northeastern France to scout out information about German positions for the Third Army as it continued its dash toward the German border. Its next major objective was to liberate the eastern French provinces of Alsace and Lorraine, which had been claimed by the Reich as German territory at the beginning of the war.

In early August, Marie-Madeleine had rejected an appeal from Kenneth Cohen to return to London by Lysander during the next full moon. She would not leave France until it had been fully liberated, she told him. Now she decided to take personal charge of the final patrols. With Paris and much of western France now free, she did not think it right to assign operatives who had gambled with their lives for years to this new mission. She would send only those who volunteered, herself among them.

Marie-Madeleine had another, more personal reason for assuming responsibility for these last reconnaissance operations: The more intelligence she and her agents could supply to the Allied forces, the sooner the troops could cross the German border and, with any luck, save the lives of Faye, Rodriguez, and the hundreds of other captured Alliance operatives who she hoped were still alive in German prisons and concentration camps.

Georges Lamarque volunteered to take charge of the area around Nancy, the capital of Lorraine, while Marie-Madeleine headed toward Strasbourg, the capital of Alsace. As her deputy, she chose Pierre Noal, a young doctor who, although a fairly recent recruit, had already distinguished himself with his toughness and daring.

Carrying a new identity card as a secretary/nurse named Marie-Suzanne Imbert, Marie-Madeleine and Noal borrowed a Red Cross ambulance and, with a radio transmitter hidden under blankets in the

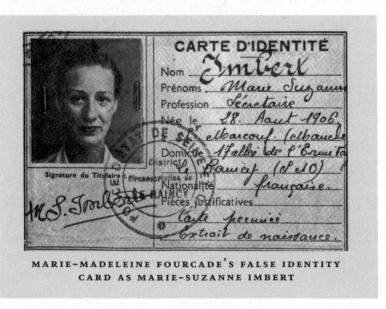

MARIE-MADELEINE FOURCADE'S FALSE IDENTITY CARD AS MARIE-SUZANNE IMBERT

back, drove it east through German roadblocks. At every stop, they told the guards that they were French collaborators traveling with the fleeing troops to aid the wounded—a story that won them plaudits and permission to continue.

Their first stop was Verdun, the site of one of the bloodiest battles of the Great War, located less than eighty miles from the German border. When they arrived at the house of the chief of Alliance's sector there, he informed them that the top leaders of the Paris Gestapo had just taken up temporary residence in the hotel across the street. Marie-Madeleine and Noal quickly returned to the ambulance and pushed on a few more miles to the little village of Brabant-au-Argonne.

Unable to make contact with London by radio, the two sent one of Alliance's local agents, who owned a motorcycle, to make contact with the Third Army, which having helped liberate Paris was swiftly advancing from the west. The agent carried intelligence reports on enemy activity, which alerted Patton and his men to mined roads and possible ambushes by German troops while also making clear that Verdun and the surrounding area were only lightly defended and could be taken with little trouble.

In mid-August, Georges Lamarque made an unexpected visit to Marie-Madeleine's base in Brabant-au-Argonne. He and his radio operator had made it to Nancy and set up a post there. Now, he told her, he wanted to continue his advance, heading for the Rhine and then entering Germany, with the aim of establishing an intelligence operation in the Reich itself.

His sense of urgency, he made clear, was fueled by a deep feeling of guilt over the arrests of several young women agents, particularly Jeannie Rousseau, whom he had recruited. Marie-Madeleine felt the same urgency and guilt, but she cautioned him not to push into Germany on his own. He didn't respond. When she begged him to stay another day or two, he declined, bidding her farewell with a cheery, "See you soon."

In the last days of August, so many German troops were seeking temporary shelter in Brabant-au-Argonne that Marie-Madeleine and Noal moved their base again, this time to a newly established *maquis* camp in a dense forest a few miles away. Most of its occupants were young resistance fighters from Verdun and the surrounding area.

Soon after they arrived, an Alliance courier told them that the Third Army had received the intelligence they had sent and had changed its route as a result of their warnings about possible ambushes. Now army intelligence officers wanted more information about German defenses in the nearby Argonne forest. The Allies, the courier added, were less than a day's march away.

After Marie-Madeleine and Noal ferreted out the status of the Argonne defenses, they dispatched another courier to Patton's forces. The next evening, they heard a dull roar coming from the west, and at daybreak, Noal left to find out what was going on. He returned an hour later, his face pale and his voice trembling. He told her Patton's troops had liberated Verdun.

That afternoon, she and Noal drove their ambulance to the nearby village of Recicourt, whose residents, gone mad with joy, were drinking, laughing, dancing, and singing. When they caught sight of the ambulance, they pulled Marie-Madeleine and Noal out, embraced and kissed them, and handed them glasses of wine. As the celebration continued around her, Marie-Madeleine couldn't hold back her tears. After Noal made a toast to victory, she shot back that "victory" was a meaningless word, when so many of those who had won it were still missing.

AS IT HAPPENED, a final Allied victory was still more than eight months away. There was no doubt, however, that after four terrifying years, the Germans had finally relinquished their iron grip on most of France. After a seemingly endless time suffused with secrecy and fear, it seemed surreal to see uniformed soldiers on the streets and know that they were liberators rather than persecutors. At first, Fourcade didn't know how to react. How long would it take, she wondered, before she felt comfortable using her real name instead of a false one? Or to realize that a knock on the door was not the Gestapo but the postman delivering mail? One of the first steps she took to emerge from the shadows was to attach a sign to the front door of the house of Alliance's Verdun sector leader that openly proclaimed the various intelligence organizations that she and her agents represented: ALLIANCE—BCRA—INTELLIGENCE SERVICE.

In early September, she briefly returned to Paris, which was filled to bursting with its Allied liberators. The Allies had taken over hundreds of hotels for their own use, and the city's best restaurants, which had served members of the Wehrmacht and Gestapo just two weeks before, were now welcoming the hordes of American and British officers and journalists who flocked to them.

Alliance set up an office in a building on the Champs Élysées, and dozens of agents streamed in from around the country to celebrate their network's survival, as well as their own. There were joyous re-unions of old friends and first-time introductions to colleagues previously known only by their code names. As Fourcade put it, "the animals of Noah's Ark were becoming people again."

Soon after her arrival in Paris, she had a happy reunion of her own with Kenneth Cohen, who had come to the French capital with a specific purpose in mind. On a beautiful early fall day, he and a throng of British military and diplomatic officials—some, like Cohen, in naval uniform, some in RAF blue, and others in army khaki—arrived at the Alliance office to pay tribute to the extraordinary achievements of the network and its leader. Surrounded by his compatriots and Alliance agents, Cohen called Fourcade to his side and presented her with the Order of the British Empire, one of his government's high honors for acts of gallantry and meritorious service.

She tried to respond but was so overcome with emotion that she couldn't utter a word until the champagne reception that followed, when Cohen asked her what else MI6 could do for her. She requested two immediate parachute drops, one at Verdun and the other at what Fourcade learned was Georges Lamarque's latest headquarters—near the village of Luze, about twenty-five miles from the German border. And then she asked him to get her children back from Switzerland.

Fourcade already had been reunited with her fourteen-month-old son. Soon afterward, she had an emotional reunion with Christian, now fourteen, and Béatrice, twelve, whom she had not seen since the summer of 1943, when she had viewed them from the window in Lyon before they were smuggled out of the country. She did not know until months later that they had been forced to cross the border into Switzerland on their own and had ended up in a refugee camp. Thanks to an Alliance agent who had been tipped off about their presence there, they were taken to their grandmother's chalet in the Swiss village of Villars-sur-Ollon, where they stayed until they were brought to Paris.

The two had been apart from their mother for almost all of the previous four years. The last time Fourcade had spent time with Béatrice was in the spring of 1942, after the little girl's surgery in Toulouse. In her memoirs, Fourcade was extremely terse about her reunion with her children, saying only that they had "returned, miraculously unaffected, bigger, of course, but also above all enriched by a flame that would make them forever different from many others." A reader might be forgiven, however, if he or she took this observation with a grain of salt. It's difficult to believe that Fourcade's offspring had not been greatly affected by their long separation from their mother, not to mention their traumatic escape. But Fourcade, who elsewhere in her memoir confessed to a sense of guilt about her failure to be with them, clearly did not want to deal any further with the issue, at least in public.

KENNETH COHEN LIVED UP to the other promise he'd made to Fourcade. On September 7, he came to Verdun to observe the parachute drop he'd arranged—and the first he'd ever witnessed. As dozens of parachutes floated down from RAF bombers, Alliance agents, joined by members of the nearby *maquis* group, hurled themselves on the containers as they landed. Fourcade helped unpack and distribute the containers' contents, which included radios, food, Sten guns, grenades, and revolvers.

As she worked, she thought of Lamarque, who was due to get his parachute drop that night. The following day, however, she received terrible news from London: The pilots of the bombers dispatched to his drop zone had spotted a village in flames and aborted their mission. MI6 had also lost contact with Lamarque's radio operator.

Fourcade never heard from Lamarque again. She later discovered that the SS had tracked down his radio transmissions and had captured him, along with his radio operator and adjutant. Lamarque had been tipped off about the raid but refused to flee for fear that the SS would take retribution against the residents of Luze. Several hours after his arrest, villagers had witnessed armed SS troops pushing him and his two colleagues toward a nearby orchard, where they were summarily executed. As it turned out, Lamarque's act of self-sacrifice was not totally in vain. Although the SS set afire the homes and farms of the villagers, they spared their lives.

Once again, Fourcade mourned the loss of a key agent. But her grief for Lamarque was especially intense. His work had been crucial in reviving the network in its darkest days, and the intelligence contributions made by his Druids, particularly Jeannie Rousseau, had been inestimable. With his boundless energy and enthusiasm, not to mention his keen wit, he had endeared himself to Fourcade, and the thought that this brilliant young mathematician, who had so much to offer postwar France, had been struck down with the war drawing to a close was particularly painful.

Fourcade's sorrow over his death was matched by her growing anxiety about the slowness of the Allied advance and the fate of Faye and her other imprisoned agents in Germany. After marching virtually unchecked across northern and central France, the Third Army had come to a sudden stop just thirty-five miles west of the Moselle River, near the German border.

This was not what Patton had had in mind. Determined to attack the Germans without letup, he was anxious to sweep across the border and smash into the German heartland. After liberating Verdun, he had immediately dispatched scouts to the Moselle, to prepare for its crossing by his troops.

But at that crucial moment, his army ran out of gasoline, as did other Allied forces making their way east. The port of Cherbourg in Normandy was the only source of gas and other supplies for the entire Allied Expeditionary Force, and the farther away Allied forces moved from Cherbourg, the more difficult it was to keep their supply lines open.

Fourcade was stunned when she was told the reason for Patton's sudden halt. When she argued that the pause would allow the Germans to regroup in Lorrain, U.S. Army officials told her that the German troops were finished. In fact, she was correct: The Germans took advantage of the halt to move in infantry and panzer forces to defend the Moselle.

Thus began what Fourcade would later call the longest winter of the conflict for her and Alliance. Doing her best to hurry the Allied forces along, she ordered her agents to continue probing the terrain in eastern France and report back to Patton's intelligence chief on the whereabouts of German forces. At one point during the winter, Alliance operatives alerted the Third Army to a planned attack by a German panzer division from Luxembourg, giving the Americans time to thwart the assault.

In early November, an Alliance patrol led by Pierre Noal clandestinely crossed the Moselle to scout out the territory behind German lines as far as the border. During their seven-week mission, Noal and his men sent fifty-four messages about enemy activity—reports that guided the late-December offensive launched by the Third Army and General Alexander Patch's Seventh Army that finally pushed German troops out of eastern France and back into their own country.

In the south of France, meanwhile, Helen des Isnards and his agents provided vital intelligence for Operation Dragoon, the landing of Allied forces on the beaches of the Côte d'Azur in mid-August. After helping to liberate Aix on August 21, des Isnards joined American troops in their drive up the Rhône Valley toward the Alps.

By early January 1945, all of France had been liberated except for pockets of German resistance in La Rochelle, Saint-Nazaire, Lorient, and other coastal redoubts in Brittany. A new generation of Alliance agents, replacing those who had been swept up in the Gestapo dragnet, provided intelligence from those places until their German defenders finally surrendered in May 1945.

No other Allied spy network in France had lasted as long or supplied as much crucial intelligence over the course of the conflict. "By their work and sacrifice," the historian and journalist David Schoenbrun later wrote, "the agents of Alliance saved thousands of Allied lives and speeded the victory over Hitler."

DURING THE WANING MONTHS of the war, Fourcade was overjoyed when a scattering of Alliance agents, who had disappeared into the "night and fog" of German prisons and concentration camps, turned up alive. One night in late 1944, she walked into the Alliance office in Paris and saw what she thought was an apparition. Standing with his back to her was a short, slender, older man with close-cropped gray hair, who was examining a large wall map of eastern France bearing little flags that marked the whereabouts of Alliance agents and Allied troops.

"Colonel Bernis," she murmured. He turned around. It was indeed Colonel Charles Bernis, the former Deuxième Bureau officer who had taught her the basics of intelligence gathering but who all the while seemed to doubt her ability as a woman to run a major spy network. She had never been sure she had had his approval. When he turned back to the map on the wall, her fears were finally allayed. "It's my finest intelligence map, my dear," he said. "Thank you."

As Allied forces headed farther into Germany in early 1945, word came of others who had miraculously survived the hell of German captivity. Among them were several female agents who had been liberated from the infamous Ravensbrück women's camp north of Berlin. They included Madeleine Crozet and Michèle Goldschmidt, who, before being sent there in the spring of 1943, had been personally tortured by Klaus Barbie, the infamous Gestapo commandant in Lyon.

Another survivor of Ravensbrück was Jeannie Rousseau, who owed her life to bureaucratic bungling by German officials. When Rousseau was arrested by the Gestapo, she was identified as Madeleine Chauffour, her code name. But when she arrived at the three camps in which she was incarcerated, she gave her real name to officials at each, none of whom ever made the connection between her and the official dossier, sent separately to all the camps, identifying her as Madeleine Chauffour, a dangerous Allied spy.

When Rousseau arrived at Torgau, a camp in Saxony attached to a munitions and explosives factory, she told the camp commander that she and the other Frenchwomen there were prisoners of war and under the Geneva Convention could not be forced to manufacture weapons. She was quickly dispatched to a punishment camp and then to Ravensbrück, where, weighing only seventy pounds and close to death, she was evacuated in the waning days of the war by the Swedish Red Cross.

Navarre came back, too. Almost two years after Georges Loustaunau-Lacau's arrest in July 1941, the Vichy government had turned him over to the Gestapo. He was deported to the Mauthausen concentration camp in Austria, where the vast majority of inmates died in unspeakable conditions. When he was liberated by American troops, the emaciated Navarre weighed less than one hundred pounds.

There was yet another astonishing piece of good news. In late January 1945, Kenneth Cohen's assistant called Fourcade to tell her that Magpie had just been released in a prisoner exchange. Marie-Madeleine's heart skipped a beat. Ferdinand Rodriguez, otherwise known as Edward Rodney, was alive! The news nourished her still flickering hope about the fates of the man she loved and the hundreds of other missing Alliance agents. Could Léon Faye have cheated death, too?

CHAPTER 31

"HAIL MARY, FULL OF GRACE"

O N JANUARY 14, 1945, THE 453RD DAY OF FERDINAND RODRIGUEZ'S captivity, he lay on a straw pallet in a fortress prison in Sonnenburg, Germany. Rodriguez knew the date and the number of days he'd been confined thanks to his obsessiveness in keeping track of both, jotting them down on scraps of paper with a tiny pencil he'd hidden from his guards. It was one of the methods he used to keep himself sane.

He was well aware of another consequential period of time. For 160 days, he'd been under a death sentence for espionage, a verdict imposed on him in June 1944 by the Reich's highest military court. During that same month, dozens of other Alliance agents had also been put on trial and condemned to death. He was sure that the sentence for most of them had already been carried out. Yet he and Léon Faye, who had also been tried and sentenced, were still alive.

Until two weeks earlier, Rodriguez had had no inkling of what had happened to Faye. The two had not seen each other since they'd been captured by the Gestapo outside Paris in September 1943. As the New Year dawned in 1945, Rodriguez was being held in yet another fortress—Schwabisch Hall—deep in the heart of Germany. It was the fourth prison he'd been in since his arrest.

Early on the morning of January 2, he'd been rousted from his cell there, and with chains shackling his hands and feet, hustled down several flights of stairs and pushed into a large room smelling of mold, sweat, and dirt. Milling around were dozens of haggard prisoners with shaven heads, many so weak they could hardly walk. To Rodriguez, they looked like ambulatory skeletons; he knew he appeared the same to them. "There is no personality here, no glimmer of life," he remembered thinking. "There may be, in this mass of humanity, military officers, engineers, craftsmen, professors, clergymen. But not one of them has any distinguishing feature."

"Where are we going? What's happening?" he whispered to a cluster of inmates. After a few moments of silence, one whispered back, "We are being transferred."

Rodriguez scanned the crowded room for a familiar face. He had done so every time he had been in the presence of other prisoners—occasions that had been extremely rare. Only twice in the last fifteen months had he caught a glimpse of other Alliance agents.

Here he saw only strangers. And then, across the room, he spotted someone who looked vaguely familiar—a stooped old man with sunken eyes and white stubble on his face and scalp. Peering more closely, Rodriguez recognized the man's aquiline nose and strong jaw. Hobbled by his chains, he shuffled over. "Commandant!" he cried. Léon Faye's eyes widened in disbelief, and his face lit up with a smile. Unable to embrace because of their chains, the two men put their cheeks together and clutched each other's hands.

"*Raus, raus,*" a guard shouted, pointing a machine gun at them and motioning them to separate. But as they and the other inmates formed lines to leave the prison and board a waiting train, Rodriguez kept an eye on Faye. Aboard the train, he maneuvered himself next to his old friend and boss. For the next several hours, they related, in low whispers, the hellish experiences each had endured over the previous fifteen months.

Faye told Rodriguez about his imprisonment at avenue Foch and his failed escape, followed by his solitary confinement in the freezing, damp underground cell at Bruchsal, where, from his first day there, stagnant water had covered the floor and oozed out of his straw mattress. Winter or summer, his hands and feet were raw with chilblains. The ceaseless noise from the factory next to his cell had damaged his hearing and led to an incessant buzzing in his ears. His daily food ration was one bowl of soup, and he was limited to ten minutes of exercise a week, always away from other prisoners.

The forty-six-year-old Faye was still considered a dangerous escape artist—so much so that the Gestapo refused to let him leave the prison for his trial, and the Reich's military court had come to Bruchsal in June 1944 to judge him. He had planned his defense carefully. When he was called before the tribunal, composed of two generals, three colonels, and a captain, he insisted that Alliance was not a terrorist spy group as charged but an official military organization defending its country. He noted the pledge of his SD interrogators at avenue Foch that he and his fellow agents would be treated as prisoners of war.

But the judges were having none of it. Faye was startled by the visceral rage expressed by the tribunal's chief judge as he accused Faye and Alliance of the mass murder of German sailors, citing the information the network had passed on to MI6 about the movements of German submarines and ships that were later sunk. The judge also noted the stream of Alliance intelligence about coastal fortifications on the beaches of Normandy, which he said had contributed to the killing of thousands of German troops. It was Faye's first inkling that D-Day had occurred.

As he listened to the judge's fulminations, Faye realized that the verdict against him was a foregone conclusion. At the trial's end, after the court pronounced him guilty and condemned him to death, Faye stood as straight as he could in his weakened state and loudly declared, *"Vive la France!"* He was sent back to his cell, where he stayed until September 1944. He was then transferred to Schwabisch Hall.

Before he left Bruchsal, he told Rodriguez, he had used a pencil and paper that he'd squirreled away to write an account of what had happened to him from the time of his arrest. After rolling up the bits of paper, which included his last will and testament, he had thrown them behind the grille of the defunct radiator in his cell, with the hope that they'd be found after the war and given to Marie-Madeleine.

When Faye had finished his story, he asked Rodriguez for his. The British radio operator recounted his time at Fresnes prison near Paris, then his transfer in January 1944 to a prison in the German city of Kehl, just across the Rhine from Strasbourg. Three months later, he was dispatched to a fortress in Fribourg-im-Brisgau, some fifty miles southeast of Strasbourg, where most of the trials of Alliance agents had been staged.

"And our friends?" Faye asked. "Have you news of any of the others?"

He had seen Paul Bernard at a distance at Kehl but did not get a chance to talk to him, Rodriguez replied. That was his sole contact with their former comrades until one morning in May 1944, shortly after he arrived at Fribourg. Taken to a courtyard for exercise, he was stunned to see several of his oldest and closest friends from the network in a group of prisoners circling the yard. Pierre Dallas, the head of the Avia team, was there. So was Lucien Poulard, the fun-loving chief of the Brittany sector; Ernest Siegrist, the former policeman who'd been in charge of producing false papers and documents; Joël Lemoigne, the head of the Sea Star subnetwork; and the incomparable Gabriel Rivière, longtime leader of the Marseille operation.

Rodriguez had laughed out loud, not only from the sheer joy of seeing them but also because of the motley outfits they were wearing, "like something out of a Laurel and Hardy movie." Poulard's was the oddest of all. Clad in the long, checked dressing gown that Marie Madeleine had bought him in London shortly before his arrest, he walked around the circle as if he were a gentleman taking a morning stroll. Although Rodriguez's colleagues were prevented by the guards from talking to each other or to him, their broad smiles expressed their delight at seeing him.

A week later, when Rodriguez was brought his morning ration of watery soup by another inmate, the prisoner whispered that the Allies had landed at Normandy. That afternoon, when Rodriguez was escorted to the courtyard for exercise, he noticed that his friends and the other prisoners there were in a tighter circle than usual, giving them the opportunity to whisper to each other. "They've landed," one of them said. "We're saved!" said another. A third burst out, "They'll be here in fifteen days."

The men's optimism pierced Rodriguez's heart: If only they were right! But he was not one to believe in miracles. Neither was Gabriel Rivière, who quietly engaged him in a brief conversation. Rivière asked if he had had his trial yet. When Rodriguez said he hadn't, Rivière made clear that he and his other Alliance comrades—more than twenty of them—had already been judged and been condemned to death. With his index finger, Rivière imitated the shooting of a gun.

Rodriguez's turn in court came on June 24, 1944. Before the trial began, he asked the attorney assigned to his defense if the death sentence had yet been carried out against any of the Alliance operatives being held at Fribourg. The answer was no: After a sentence was handed down, the case had to be sent to Berlin for review, which meant a delay of at least three weeks between the verdict and its execution.

On the day of his trial, Rodriguez was taken to a large courtroom in the shape of an amphitheater, with the five judges sitting on a raised platform covered by a dark green carpet. The name under which he was tried was his code name, Edward Rodney. The Germans still had not discovered his real name.

Like Faye, Rodriguez argued in his defense that Alliance was a military organization and its agents should be treated as prisoners of war. The court's response was the same: Because of the information supplied by Alliance, German sailors had been murdered in the Atlantic and German troops were being killed in Normandy. Rodriguez remembered with pride that just before he had left France for London in August 1943, he had installed a chain of transmitters from Bayeux to Cherbourg in Normandy, which undoubtedly had been used during and after D-Day to pass on the information to which the judge referred.

Although a guilty verdict was never in doubt, Rodriguez still felt a jolt when the sentence was pronounced. He ordered himself to stay calm; when he was asked if he had any final words, he declared, "God save the king!" As a guard led him from the courtroom in handcuffs, the thought came to him that he'd never be free again but that at least he'd lived long enough to learn about D-Day and know that he and his comrades had helped make it possible. He also knew that he had at least twenty-one more days to live.

Two days after the trial, he and the others from Alliance were loaded onto a train and taken to Schwabisch Hall, a massive fortress in south central Germany. As the days ticked by, Rodriguez tracked them with increasing dread. On July 3, his head was shaved, along with his beard and mustache. Shackled all the time now, he found it almost impossible to eat and dress himself, much less perform the physical exercises he had used over the past fifteen months to keep up his strength. There were no more courtyard promenades, no more sightings of his friends. The twenty-one days had passed, and he was living on borrowed time. All he could do was pray, as he had done from the beginning of his confinement.

On August 18, he heard rapping on the water pipe in his cell. It was Morse code, coming from several of his Alliance comrades, all of whom, as it turned out, were on the same floor. They apparently believed that he had not yet been sentenced to death because they asked him to seek out their families after the war and pass on their love. He promised to do so, deciding not to tell them that he, too, had been condemned and would never have a chance to fulfill his pledge.

Two days later, in the late afternoon, two jailers entered Rodriguez's cell. One removed his chains and placed a set of handcuffs around his wrists. Draped over the other jailer's arms were more than twenty additional sets. As Rodriguez silently held out his wrists, he was aware that fifty-seven days had passed since his verdict was pronounced.

He opened his mouth to ask the jailers what was happening but was unable to utter a word. As the cell door closed behind them, he was sure that the day he had feared since his capture had finally arrived. Several hours went by, and he fell asleep on his pallet. In the middle of the night, he was awakened by footsteps. He heard a nearby cell door creak open.

He lay there, clutching his rosary and telling himself that he must remain strong and continue to say his prayers until his own door was unlocked. Heavy footsteps descended the iron staircase, and then another door opened. Images of his friends—Rivière, Dallas, Siegrist, Poulard, and the others—flashed through his mind.

Every time another door swung open, his heart skipped a beat. Three . . . four . . . five . . . six. There were no words or cries, nothing but the sound of footsteps trudging down the stairs. Rodriguez began reciting the rosary out loud: "Hail Mary, full of grace, the Lord is with thee . . ."

Seven . . . eight . . . nine . . . ten.

"Blessed art thou among women, and blessed is the fruit of thy womb, Jesus."

Eleven . . . twelve . . . thirteen.

"Holy Mary, mother of God, pray for us sinners, now and at the hour of our death. Amen."

The sound of creaking doors came closer. Fourteen . . . fifteen . . . sixteen.

Hearing a guard stop outside his cell, Rodriguez, struggling for breath, began another Hail Mary. The guard passed by, and the door of the cell next to him swung open, then closed.

Determined to show no emotion when they finally came for him, he tried to control his shaking hands.

Seventeen . . . eighteen . . . nineteen . . . twenty.

How many more until his turn came?

Twenty-one . . . twenty-two . . . twenty-three . . . twenty-four.

"Hail Mary, full of grace, the Lord is with thee . . ."

His face bathed in sweat, Rodriguez pulled a coarse gray blanket tight around him. The sounds slowly died away. There was no more clanking of doors or steps on the stairs. As silence returned to the prison, he yearned to run after his companions and join them, shouting that he was there, too.

The next day, he was moved to a cell on another floor. When he was served his morning food ration, he asked the prisoner who brought it if he knew what had happened to the inmates who'd been moved the night before. "Your friends . . . all gone," was the reply.

Summer faded into fall, then into winter. For Rodriguez, every day was the same. Covering his shoulders with his blanket, he immersed himself in prayer. He celebrated Christmas Day by singing carols in a faltering, cracked voice. He would never see a Christmas tree again, he thought, nor celebrate the holiday with his mother, sisters, and friends.

Then, a week later, he was pulled from his cell, herded down the stairs, and reunited with Faye. When, during their whispered conversation on the train, he told his friend about the deaths of their old comrades, Faye sank into a deep depression. It was not right, he told Rodriguez, that they should be shot before him, their military leader.

Faye had touched on the question that had puzzled Rodriguez. "Why are we still alive?" he asked. "What are they going to do with us?" Faye said he thought they were being kept as hostages, in the event that the Germans wanted to trade for German spies being held prisoner by the Allies.

Rodriguez could understand why Faye—a major leader of Alliance—would be chosen as a hostage. But why him? In any event, he thought, the odds of a hostage exchange were so small as to be infinitesimal. When so many others had been killed, why would they be spared?

Their train journey took three days, covering almost four hundred miles from Schwabisch Hall to the Sonnenburg fortress, just north of Berlin. Before Hitler had come to power, Sonnenburg had been a penal colony. When the Nazis took over, they turned it into a concentration camp for their political opponents, one of whom described it as a "hellhole of torture." During World War II, many if not most of its inmates were members of the French, Dutch, and Belgian resistance.

At Sonnenburg, Rodriguez and Faye were assigned adjoining cells. On the other side of Rodriguez was an Alliance agent he'd never met before—a young Irishman named Robert Vernon, who'd worked as a courier in the Marseille sector and had been captured with the actor Robert Lynen and other sector members in the spring of 1943.

The cell was the smallest Rodriguez had been in—no more than three feet by six feet. It was unheated, and there was no electric light. But knowing that Faye and Vernon were next to him, he realized he was the happiest he'd been since his capture. The three were not prevented from talking, and he and Faye conversed constantly, mostly about faith and religion. If he survived the war, Faye said, he wanted to spend some time in meditation every year at a monastery he'd discovered in Algiers before the war.

Rodriguez continued his daily practice of saying the rosary and reciting from beginning to end the prayerbooks he had memorized. Occasionally, Faye asked him to sing hymns so that he could sing along. Rodriguez did so with the ironic thought that he had become "a choirmaster in a crypt."

On January 13, eight days after they'd arrived at Sonnenburg, Rodriguez heard a jailer slide open the small square hatch in the door of Faye's cell. A minute later, he did the same to the hatch in Rodriguez's door. He pointed his right index finger at Rodriguez, then curled it to imitate the shooting of a gun. "Tomorrow!" he barked. Then he moved on to Vernon's cell.

Rodriguez stood stock still. "Am I mistaken about what just happened?" he shouted to Faye, who answered no. He then asked Vernon, "Were you told it was tomorrow?" The response was affirmative.

If this was the end, Rodriguez thought, he would spend the last hours in prayer with Faye and Vernon. "Our three lives are no longer separate," he thought. "We will pray together, leave together, and die together." When Vernon asked him in a quavering voice if it would hurt when the bullets struck him, Rodriguez responded that it would be over in an instant and that he would support him until the end.

Throughout that interminable night, the three repeatedly called out to each other. As Rodriguez recited rosary after rosary, his thoughts flickered back to his mother and three sisters and to his childhood in France. Through the tiny window of his cell, he observed the coming of dawn. Minutes crawled by, then hours.

In midafternoon, he heard the sound of approaching footsteps. They stopped in front of his cell. Mechanically, he rose, watching as a key turned in the lock. When the door opened, three men were standing there—a jailer, the prison's warden, and an unknown man in a gray suit. The jailer signaled him to leave the cell; unsteady on his feet, he did so. The warden ordered him to come with them. In a low voice, he added, "You are being exchanged."

Rodriguez almost collapsed. He couldn't believe the callousness of this perverted practical joke. Staring at the warden, he said, "It's not true. This is just another of your methods of torture." The man returned his gaze. "Come with me to my office," he said. "You are going to Switzerland."

As Rodriguez and the others passed Faye's cell door, he wanted to call out but didn't know what to say. Dazed and shaken, he was taken to an office with a large desk, green-shaded lamp, bookshelves, and two leather armchairs. The warden motioned him to an armchair and took his seat behind the desk. He introduced the civilian, who sat in the other chair, as a member of the Gestapo from Berlin who, along with a prison guard, would escort Rodriguez to the Swiss border.

He was then taken to another cell, where his chains were removed. Left alone, he fell to his knees and thanked God and the Blessed Mary for sparing his life. That evening he received two helpings of a thick soup and for the first time in months slept free of nightmares.

The following day, he was allowed to take a bath, his first since his capture. Viewing his wasted body in the hot water, he was reminded of a plucked chicken. A guard brought him the wrinkled, dirty clothes he'd been wearing when he was arrested in 1943: a raincoat, shirt, slacks, and blue-and-green club tie. As he put them on, he thought of Faye and Vernon. Were they to be exchanged, too? He refused to think about the alternative.

A few hours later, accompanied by the Gestapo officer and a guard, Rodriguez walked, handcuffed, out of Sonnenburg. It was freezing outside, but he was so euphoric that even in his light summer clothing, he didn't feel the cold. The three took a train to Berlin, where they were to transfer to another train that left later in the day. With several hours to kill, Rodriguez's companions decided to have lunch at a nearby beer hall. Outside its entrance, they conferred with each other, then motioned him to follow them inside. After a waiter escorted them to a table, Rodriguez nudged the guard and indicated his handcuffs. His meaning was clear: Did his escorts really want the attention that the handcuffs would attract in the noisy, crowded hall? The guard took him behind a screen and removed the cuffs.

Ordering choucroute for themselves, the Germans asked the waiter to bring a sausage in a bun for Rodriguez. It was his first taste of meat since the ham sandwiches he'd been served at the RAF base at Tangmere before he and Faye flew back to France in 1943. As he ate the sausage and sipped from a small glass of beer, he couldn't help but think how surreal this experience was—sharing lunch with a Gestapo officer in a Berlin beer hall just a couple of days after he fully expected to die.

Once the meal was finished, his handcuffs were put back on and the three returned to the station. When their train arrived, they sat in a compartment occupied by three German civilians—an old man and two women—who stared at Rodriguez and his handcuffs but, to his surprise, not in a hostile way. Several hours later, one of the women offered Rodriguez part of a sandwich she was eating. He declined, but she insisted and he finally gave in. Then she handed him pieces of an apple—the first fruit he'd had since his arrest. Through it all, he thought of Faye and Vernon and how every revolution of the train's wheels was taking him farther away from them.

Late that night, the train stopped at what looked like a deserted station. Rodriguez and his keepers were the only passengers to get off. About half an hour later, another train approached. When it screeched to a stop, the Gestapo officer removed Rodriguez's handcuffs and turned him over to a tall, angular man in civilian clothes, who escorted him aboard. The train, it turned out, was a Swiss Red Cross convoy for British prisoners of war who were to be traded for wounded German POWs.

His escort, who was in charge of the convoy, took him to a compartment filled with uniformed British soldiers. A hush fell over the car when they saw the cadaverous Rodriguez in his shabby civilian clothes. After about ten minutes, he broke the silence, saying, "So, you're all prisoners of war?" One of them nodded: "We come from different POW camps in Germany." "Well then, I'm like you," Rodriguez responded, "only in plain clothes."

That was the extent of the conversation. He wanted to tell his countrymen what it was like to have been in the French resistance, to describe, for example, the extraordinary experience of transmitting military secrets to London from a beet field in the Corrèze. But after so many years of secrecy, he couldn't bring himself to do so. An enormous gulf existed between him and them, and he doubted it could ever be bridged.

After traveling only a short distance, the train came to a stop. The leader of the convoy came back to tell Rodriguez they would proceed no farther that night. The convoy had made the brief journey from the last station, the leader said, because "we thought you would prefer to be on the right side of the border." Leaning closer, he added, "We are in Switzerland."

Before those on the train settled down for the night, they were warmly greeted by a bevy of Red Cross workers, who offered them white bread and hot tea. One of the workers gave Rodriguez a thick beige wool sweater and warm pants to replace the grime-caked clothing he was wearing. When he stammered his thanks, the man replied that he was sorry the clothes were not new. Rodriguez wanted to tell him that he had never received a more generous gift. "Life was worth living, after all," he later wrote about the man's kindness. "The physical warmth from the sweater matched the warmth I felt in my heart, which just a few days earlier had despaired about my fellow men."

The next day, the train proceeded on. At every stop, the passengers were greeted by Red Cross volunteers, who gave them tea, bread, chocolate, and other sweets. When the train finally arrived in Geneva, Rodriguez was met by the military attaché of the British embassy, who told him the details of his exchange.

Faye had been right. On the orders of SS head Heinrich Himmler, Faye, Rodriguez, and Vernon were among a handful of captured Allied intelligence agents who had been held as hostages for a possible exchange. Rodriguez's status as a Briton and MI6 agent had helped his case. Pressured hard by Kenneth Cohen, Stewart Menzies, the head of MI6, had ordered his agency to do everything in its power to save him. After months of negotiations involving MI6 and the Foreign Office, the Germans had agreed to swap him for Berthold Schulze-Holthus, an Abwehr spy who had been caught by the British in Persia.

After thanking the attaché for his help, Rodriguez asked him to send a telegram to the War Office urging it to take immediate steps to arrange similar exchanges for Faye and Vernon. The officer agreed to do so but cautioned that the chance of more exchanges was extremely slim. He also told Rodriguez that he was not to return to Paris right away but was to be sent directly back to Britain. Accompanied by a British colonel, he was to take a train to Marseille, then board a hospital ship for home.

For Rodriguez, a delayed return to the real world seemed heaven-sent. Overwhelmed by what had happened to him over the past few days, not to mention the previous seventeen months, he needed a period of quiet to come to terms with all of it. He had been alone for so long that he was having trouble adjusting to having other people around him. Retaining his devotion to his daily prayers, he now recited them in his mind rather than saying them out loud: "I could not abandon what had constituted my only consolation for so many weeks and months."

On the hospital ship, he was kept in bed for the first day. A tall man, he weighed only 116 pounds. During a physical exam, the doctor noted that when he pressed Rodriguez's abdomen, he could feel his backbone. Twice daily, he was given a cocktail of chocolate, glucose, and eggs to fatten him up, a concoction he loved so much that he kept drinking it long after he left the ship.

Despite his emaciation, Rodriguez was judged healthy enough to be allowed out of bed for the rest of the voyage. He spent most of his time outdoors, walking on the ship's bridge and savoring the chill wind in his face. "It was the antithesis of life in a prison cell, and it made me drunk with happiness," he observed. "For me, paradise was the present."

He was always by himself. He spoke to no one, not even at meals, and when someone approached him, he fled, avoiding any presence that might distract him from his constant thoughts of Faye and Vernon in Sonnenburg. He wondered if the bureaucratic machinery was already in motion and if they would be saved in time.

After five days at sea, the ship reached the English coast on February 2. A final physical exam revealed that Rodriguez had gained more than ten pounds during the voyage. When he arrived at Victoria Station in London, Kenneth Cohen's female assistant, whom he knew well, was waiting for him. They fell into each other's arms. He was welcomed equally enthusiastically by MI6 officials, who extensively debriefed him. During his time in the British capital, he was promoted to captain in the army's intelligence corps.

In mid-March, Rodriguez finally returned to Paris. He was reunited with his mother and sisters, whom he hadn't seen for more than two years. And in the Alliance office on Champs-Élysées, he had a joyous homecoming with Marie-Madeleine, Monique Bontinck, and other survivors of the network.

For her part, Marie-Madeleine tried to hide her shock when she saw him: haggard, gaunt, with a glassy look in his pale blue eyes, and looking like a ghost. His wrists still bore the marks of the manacles he had worn for weeks prior to his release. He refused to talk about his own experience, she said, and "his only thought was for the others." He told her about his reunion with Faye at Schwabisch Hall and a bit about their incarceration at Sonnenburg, declaring, "We must act with all speed if we're to save him."

She, in turn, informed him that the news on that front was not good. On January 27, almost two weeks after Rodriguez's release, Berlin radio had announced that Faye was still alive and that the Germans were prepared to let him go in exchange for a German collaborator under a death sentence in Paris. Declining to do so, de Gaulle's government ordered the collaborator executed, despite efforts by at least one French official to commute the sentence. No one yet knew what had happened to Faye.

In the days to come, Rodriguez endlessly walked the streets of Paris, seeking to keep faith with the memory of his friends who'd been executed or were still in captivity. "I cannot abandon my poor dead," he remarked. As he had promised, he went to see the families of the agents who had died at Schwabisch Hall and passed on their final messages. He continued to have, as he put it, "an intense need for loneliness" and would cross the street when he saw someone he knew coming toward him.

At the same time, however, the people to whom he was closest—his family, Marie-Madeleine, and his other Alliance friends—enveloped him in warmth and tenderness, doing everything they could to pull him out of his shell and back to life. Particularly important was his deepening relationship with Monique Bontinck, Marie-Madeleine's young assistant, with whom he had closely worked in the first six months of 1943.

As the weeks passed, Rodriguez, while never forgetting the past, slowly began returning to the present—and the hope and opportunity it offered. His life as Edward Rodney was over; he was done with the secrets and pain that the code name conveyed.

"I look at myself now," he wrote, "and I see only Ferdinand Rodriguez."

CHAPTER 32

THE ROAD TO
GETHSEMANE

T TOOK FOURCADE A LONG TIME TO COAX FROM RODRIGUEZ the full story of what had happened to him and the others in Germany. Bit by bit, he began telling her about it, starting with his and Faye's arrests, his transfers to various prisons, and the trials and death sentences handed down at Freiburg. With great emotional difficulty, he described the night of August 20, 1944, when, paralyzed by fear, he heard the footsteps of his comrades descend the iron stairs at Schwabisch Hall. He also told her how Faye had left his last will and testament, along with other papers, for her behind the radiator in his cell at Bruchsal.

Of Fourcade's three thousand agents, about six hundred had been imprisoned by the Germans during the war. So far, she knew of only about 150 who had survived that ghastly experience. Of the remaining 450, dozens were already known to be dead, among them some of her top lieutenants and agents: Henri Schaerrer, Maurice Coustenoble, Lucien Vallet, Robert Douin, Antoine Hugon, Georges Lamarque, Gabriel Rivière, Pierre Dallas, Ernest Siegrist, and Lucien Poulard. But she had no idea of the fates of the vast majority who were still missing, including Léon Faye.

When the war in Europe finally ended in May 1945, she and Rodriguez set off on a pilgrimage to eastern France and Germany in search of the hundreds who had not returned. It was a heartbreaking journey. Almost immediately, she learned that her anxiety in the late summer and fall of 1944 about the slowness of the Allied advance and the fate of her imprisoned agents had been justified: The eight months of war that followed would claim the lives of many if not most of them.

For Fourcade and Rodriguez, the first horrifying discovery would come even before they crossed the Rhine into Germany.

IN THE SPRING AND SUMMER of 1944, 108 captured Alliance members, sixteen of them women, arrived in three separate convoys at the Schirmeck prison camp in the eastern French province of Alsace. Most of the operatives, ranging in age from twenty to eighty, had been arrested in the massive Gestapo roundup after the arrests of Rodriguez and Faye in September 1943.

Their new place of confinement, located in the Vosges Mountains, had originally been a small training camp established by the French army early in the war. When the Nazis occupied Alsace, they turned it into a prison for resistance members living in the province, who, after being sent there, were forced to help build a new SS concentration camp, Natzweiler-Struthof, a few miles away.

More than half the Alliance operatives at Schirmeck had been involved in collecting intelligence from German submarine bases and shipyards in Brittany, Bordeaux, and Normandy. Several were among the network's most valued agents: Jacques Stosskopf from Lorient; Philippe Koenigswerther, head of the Bordeaux sector; Pierre Le Tullier, one of the French policemen who had helped Marie-Madeleine escape from Marseille and who then had joined Alliance as head of the Rennes subnetwork; and Maurice Gillet (Unicorn), who had been so successful at Brest and who was joined at Schirmeck by six members of his family. (His wife was imprisoned at Pforzheim.)

There were also agents from other regions, including the Paris area and eastern France. One of the Paris-based operatives was Marguerite Brouillet, Marie-Madeleine's dear friend, whose home at Le Lavandou on the Mediterranean coast had sheltered the Alliance chief in the summer of 1942 and had served as the base for General Giraud's escape later that year.

None of the Alliance operatives at Schirmeck had officially been charged or put on trial. Their presence at the camp was top secret, and they were kept strictly segregated from other prisoners. Housed in men's and women's barracks, they occupied their time by staging plays and organizing impromptu classes in English, literature, physics, and mathematics. In August, they learned of the Allied liberation of Paris and talked longingly about their own liberation, which they expected any day. They speculated what France and their lives would be like after the war.

Just a few days after Paris was freed, Julius Gehrum, the Gestapo head in Strasbourg, received an urgent order from his headquarters in Berlin. With Patton's army approaching the Moselle River, it was time, his superiors declared, to take drastic action against the Alliance agents at Schirmeck. No members of other French resistance networks held at the camp were included in the order.

On the evening of September 1, the agents, in groups of twelve, were ordered from their barracks and forced to board trucks that headed off toward an unknown destination. Their exodus was observed by another network operative, a doctor from Le Lavandou who had been recruited by Fourcade and who had been made camp doctor by the Germans; thanks to his job, he was not quartered with his Alliance comrades. That night, he noted with concern that his fellow agents had left without luggage and that empty trucks returned every two hours to pick up more.

He did not learn until later that they had been taken to the Natzweiler-Struthof camp, where they were hustled into a cement block building and told to strip. One by one, they were led down a staircase to an underground vault, where they were shot in the back of the head by SS executioners. Their bodies then were placed on a hoist and hauled up to the camp's crematorium, one floor above, where they were burned.

Inmates at Natzweiler-Struthof reported they had heard repeated gunshots, along with screams and muffled singing. When Fourcade arrived at Struthof, she was told that the crematorium's chimney did not stop smoking for two days after the massacre. Escorted to the vault where the executions took place, she saw dried blood and a flattened bullet in a drainage grid in the ground.

The SS clearly had burned the bodies to cover traces of their crime. There were no records of the agents at the camp; their names were listed on none of its registers. Yet the identities of those killed did not remain a secret for long, thanks to the doctor's testimony, as well as the discovery of bottles filled with sheets of paper that had been buried beneath the floor of one of the barracks. Inscribed on them were the names of the agents kept there—Stosskopf, Koenigswerther, and Brouillet among them—and an account of how they all had spent their last months.*

Although Julius Gehrum had overseen the carnage at Schirmeck, he was not present when it occurred. Of the next spasm of killing ordered by Berlin, he took personal charge. On November 23, 1944, the day the Allies liberated Strasbourg, Gehrum and two henchmen launched a murderous, weeklong tour of a string of prisons in western Germany—several in the Black Forest and all of them close to the French border.

Their first stop was the prison at Kehl, directly across the Rhine from Strasbourg, where Rodriguez had been briefly jailed. A few hours after Strasbourg's liberation, Gehrum and his SS assistants took nine Alliance agents from their cells and herded them to the shore of the Rhine. There they were shot in the back of the head and their bodies thrown in the river. Most of the victims were members of the Nantes sector, including André Coindeau (Urus), the sector's chief.

The following day, the executioners traveled to the prison at Rastatt, thirty miles north of Kehl, where they escorted twelve Alliance agents, all belonging to sectors in central France, to a clearing in the

---

* In 1946, de Gaulle traveled to Lorient to rename the submarine base there in Stosskopf's honor.

woods near the Rhine. Again, they were shot and their bodies dumped into the river.

On November 27, four young female agents from the network were taken from the prison at Offenburg and shot in a nearby forest, where they were buried. On November 28, Gehrum and his assistants returned to the Rhine. After collecting eight network operatives from the prison at Buhl, they loaded them onto a boat and took them to the middle of the river, where they were shot and their bodies dropped over the side.

For the three SS assassins, November 30 was the most murderous day of all. At the prison in Pforzheim, twenty-six agents, including eight women, were transported by trucks from their cells to a clearing in the middle of a forest. There they were killed and their bodies pitched into a water-filled gravel pit. Among the victims were Maurice Gillet's wife, Marie, and Pierre Dayné, the Paris policeman who early in the conflict had acted as Fourcade's personal bodyguard.★

Once they were done at Pforzheim, Gehrum and his men drove thirty miles to the prison at Gaggenau, where they transported nine members of the Toulouse and Bordeaux sectors to a forest clearing and dispatched their victims with a bullet to the head. The bodies were buried in a mass grave near the place of execution. Among the dead were Mouchou Damm, head of the Toulouse sector, and his son.

In what would later be called "the blood week in the Black Forest," Gehrum, aided by his underlings, had murdered sixty-eight Alliance agents for the sole purpose of preventing their rescue by Allied troops. The killings were one more sign of the Reich's remorseless vendetta against a spy network that had played such a major role in its looming defeat and, perhaps just as important, had not stopped actively working until the war's end to achieve that goal.

★ Shortly after the war was over, French troops discovered the mass grave at Pforzheim and forced the citizens of the town to remove the bodies, place them in coffins, and give them a proper burial.

———

IT REMAINS UNCLEAR WHY none of the Alliance members killed at Struthof and in the Black Forest had been tried by the Reich's top military court. Many of them had not actively collected or transmitted intelligence—they had served as couriers or in other ways assisted the network—so the Germans could not legally charge them with espionage. But a number of them, like Koenigswerther and Stosskopf, clearly had been spies. Perhaps the reason for the lack of a trial in their cases lay in the fact that the SS was still gathering evidence, and with Allied troops drawing nearer, there was no more time for legal judgments.

After viewing Struthof and most of the massacre sites in the Black Forest, Fourcade and Rodriguez moved on to Freiburg, where he and many others had been tried by the military court. On every floor of the prison there, Fourcade saw messages and drawings scrawled on the walls and carved in tables by her agents. In the prison's office, Rodriguez examined a long list of names on the inmate register, pointing out to Marie-Madeleine that after their trials, Alliance operatives had been sent to several prisons, among them Ludwigsburg, Bruchsal, and Schwabisch Hall.

The first set of trials involving the network had been held in December 1943; the operatives who were condemned to death then, most of them from the Dordogne and Corrèze sectors, were sent to Ludwigsburg, about 120 miles northeast of Freiberg. When Fourcade and Rodriguez arrived there, they learned that fifteen Alliance agents had been executed on May 25, 1944, outside the prison walls. A Protestant minister who had been with them at the end said that as they were bound to the execution posts, they shouted *"À bientôt au ciel"* (Until we meet again in heaven).

The Ludwigsburg inmates were the only ones to have received proper burials immediately after their deaths. Their graves, which bore their names, had been well kept, with several covered with flowers. One of them belonged to Abbé Charles-Jean Lair, the vicar of Tulle Cathedral who had kept watch in the spring of 1943 while Rodriguez transmitted from the cathedral's belfry. When he found Lair's resting place, Rodriguez, with tears in his eyes, knelt and prayed.

The next stop was Bruchsal, which Fourcade called "the most terrible of all the fortresses" she visited, perhaps because it was the place where Faye had been imprisoned. She was taken to his underground cell, where she saw the chains that had lashed his ankles to the foot of the narrow iron bed. At her request, a Free French general whom she knew had already retrieved the messages that Faye had left for her behind the cell's radiator.

When Faye left in the fall of 1944 for Schwabisch Hall, he had no idea that fourteen other Alliance agents, most of them from the Toulouse and Marseille sectors, had been imprisoned at Bruchsal, too. They were shot on April 1, 1944. At Fourcade's behest, the bodies were disinterred from the pit that had been their mass grave. All of them remained recognizable. They included Jean Philippe, the police superintendent who oversaw the network's intelligence operations in Toulouse, and Robert Lynen, the young actor who had claimed to Fourcade that his work with Alliance would be the greatest role of his career.

And then there was the visit to Schwabisch Hall itself, which, for Rodriguez, was a particularly traumatic experience. As they entered the prison, Fourcade watched with concern as he seemed to metamorphose back into the prisoner he'd been, complete with waxen face and stooped, halting walk. Accompanied by a guard, they climbed the iron stairs to the cell in which he'd been incarcerated on the night of August 20, 1944. The guard had paid no attention to the officer in British uniform until they entered the cell and Rodriguez snarled, "Where are the manacles? What about the chains for the feet?"

The guard recognized his former prisoner, and his face whitened. When Rodriguez demanded to know what had happened to his Alliance comrades, the man produced their luggage for his and Marie-Madeleine's inspection. The suitcases were scuffed and filled with bloodstained underclothes, tattered wallets, and dog-eared photos and notes. When the agents were taken from the cells that August night, they were told that they were being transferred to a new prison but that their personal belongings would remain at Schwabisch Hall.

The twenty-four men had been transferred by truck to a military camp at Heilbronn, about twenty-five miles to the west. There they were informed of their imminent execution. According to a Catholic chaplain who heard their confessions, the Alliance agents embraced one another and, on the way to the firing range, shouted as one, *"Vive la France!"*

After they were shot, they were buried in a nearby apple orchard. Fourcade presided over the bodies' disinterment. For her, it was an agonizing scene, especially the sight of Lucien Poulard wrapped in the dressing gown she had given him.

At the end of her grueling mission, she concluded that the Germans had executed 438 Alliance members, some of whose bodies were never found. Because Sonnenburg prison was in the zone of postwar Germany occupied by the Soviets and declared off limits to their former allies, she and Rodriguez were not allowed to go there to investigate the fate of Léon Faye. But they soon learned what had happened to him.

On January 30, 1945, fifteen days after Rodriguez had been freed, Soviet troops approached Sonnenburg from the east. Berlin sent orders that all inmates in the prison were to be killed before the Red Army arrived, and a special SS unit of twenty men was sent to conduct the executions.

Although several dozen prisoners, aided by guards, managed to escape in the confusion, more than eight hundred did not. That night, the SS executioners escorted them in groups of ten to the back of the prison, where they were shot in the head. After the slaughter, which lasted two hours, the bodies were torched with flamethrowers.

When Red Army troops arrived hours later, they found just four survivors among the heaped, partially burned corpses. Neither Léon Faye nor Robert Vernon was among them. Like the hundreds of other victims, whose charred remains were buried by the Russians in two mass graves, the bodies of Faye and Vernon were never identified.

While the bodies of other Alliance agents were later brought back to France at Fourcade's behest and given ceremonial burials, her beloved Eagle remained, as she put it, an isolated sentinel keeping watch over the wartime front.

EPILOGUE

On a beautiful late-summer afternoon in 1977, Marie-Madeleine Fourcade took her place at the end of a wide grassy field near the town of Ussel, nestled in the verdant foothills of south central France. Standing to one side was a large crowd of onlookers, who had traveled from all over the country to celebrate the thirty-fifth anniversary of Alliance's first Lysander flight to Britain in August 1942.

Plagued by arthritis, the sixty-eight-year-old Fourcade leaned heavily on a cane. Although her hair was now silvery blond and her face bore the lines of age, she still retained distinct vestiges of her once renowned beauty. For those who were there, most of whom had known her since the war, there was no question that her decisiveness, single-mindedness, and legendary organizational skills remained very much intact.

It was she who had made all the arrangements for the festivities that day, including inviting as her escort the slim, elegant, middle-aged man in RAF blue whose arm she clutched tightly. He was Peter Vaughan-Fowler, who, as a twenty-year-old Lysander pilot, had flown her in 1943 from a field near Paris to Britain. Fourcade, whose appreciation of good-looking men had not declined with age, had earlier introduced him to the crowd, to his embarrassed amusement, as "our handsome hero, Peter Vaughan-Fowler."

It was she, too, who had arranged for the plane that would soon appear at the Ussel field to reconstruct the moonlit drama of the network's first aerial pickup. The aircraft, unfortunately, was not a Lysander: Only one wartime Lizzie was still in flying condition, and getting the official clearances needed to fly it from Britain to France proved impossible, even for Fourcade. But she discovered that a French plane, the Broussard, looked very much like a Lysander, and she wangled from French officials the use of one for the day.

As the scheduled time for the plane's appearance drew near, she, Vaughan-Fowler, and the others squinted up at the cloudless sky. And there the Broussard was, suddenly swooping down out of the sun. Its lights flashed a Morse code signal—the letter *M*—to a man standing on the field. A former Alliance agent who had been part of its wartime aviation service, he used a flashlight to beam back his own signal—the letter *C*. Waggling its wings in confirmation, the Broussard descended low over the pine trees surrounding the field and made a perfect landing on the grass.

Climbing down from the little plane's cockpit was another tall, slim, middle-aged man in an RAF uniform—Colonel Hugh Verity, who had led the squadron of intrepid young Lysander pilots during the war. After embracing Verity, Fourcade told the crowd that it was he who had assigned the missions and run the entire Lysander operation, while flying two dozen flights himself in and out of occupied France. "And somehow," she added, "we were all spared to live to see this day."

Fourcade then turned and gave her hand to Jean Vinzant, the wood and coal merchant who had been chief of the Ussel sector and who had repeatedly risked his life by housing Alliance agents before they left for Britain by Lysander and when they returned. He also had allowed Ferdinand Rodriguez and other network radio operators to transmit from his attic, which almost resulted in disaster during a surprise Gestapo raid in 1943. Thanks to his quick-witted maid, Marie, who retrieved the transmitter before the Gestapo could find it, Vinzant managed to get through that incident—and the rest of the war—unscathed.

While Fourcade planned this event as a commemoration of the Lysander operation and its importance to both Alliance and the British, it was also meant as a solemn tribute to Alliance's dead. After all, the operative who had made that first flight twenty-five years ago was Léon Faye, the network's most celebrated martyred hero, who had traveled three times by Lysander to Britain before his arrest and execution.

Remembering Faye and the network's other victims had been a top priority for Fourcade since the end of the war. On November 23, 1945, a solemn requiem mass in their honor had been said at Sacré Coeur Basilica in Paris, attended by hundreds of French and British mourners. In the months that followed, Fourcade made it her mission to bring back to France the bodies of Alliance members found in Germany and to give them proper burials with full military honors.

On that lovely September day in 1977, she and the others honored the dead once more during a ceremony at the Monument des Morts in Ussel's town square, which, like other war monuments throughout France, commemorated local residents killed in the two world wars. After a color guard presented arms, Jacques Chirac, the former French prime minister, made a short speech eulogizing Alliance and its lost members. Fourcade led the crowd in singing *"Chant des Partisans,"* the unofficial anthem of the French resistance, which begins:

> *Ami, entends-tu*
> *Le vol noir des corbeaux*
> *Sur nos plaines?*
> *Ami, entends-tu*
> *Les cris sourds du pays*
> *Qu'on enchaîne?*★

★   Friend, do you hear the dark flight of crows over our plains? Friend, do you hear the muffled cries of a country in chains?

Then it was time to toast the living, also per Fourcade's plan. According to the American journalist and historian David Schoenbrun, who attended the gathering, its organizer saw it as "a weekend of celebration and nostalgia, of tears for those who had fallen and cheers for those who had survived."

After the ceremony at the monument, the hundred or so who were there adjourned to a local inn for a lavish lunch of sausages, ham, boiled potatoes, salads, and a salty local dish called *potée Limousine,* all washed down with multiple bottles of local red wine. It was exactly the kind of thing that Léon Faye had in mind when, in his last will and testament written at Bruchsal, he urged his Alliance comrades to "serve our unhappy country so that it may enjoy peace again and happiness, songs, flowers, and flower-covered inns."

Those at the lunch had traveled to Ussel from Paris and Marseille, Brittany and Nice, Lyon and Bordeaux, Normandy and Toulouse. Car mechanics and plumbers were there, alongside teachers, aristocrats, businessmen, and bureaucrats. Outside the inn, a Rolls-Royce Silver Cloud from Paris was parked next to a small Renault 2CV from Lyon. Men in Guy Laroche sweaters and women in Chanel suits exchanged effusive greetings with wartime colleagues in denim and cotton dresses. Many had not seen one another since the war. Some were meeting for the first time. But none of that mattered: As members of Alliance, they were—and always would be—part of the same tight-knit clan. As Fourcade noted in her memoirs, "The connection formed by a threat to one's country is the strongest connection of all. People adopt one another, march together. Only capture or death can tear them apart."

Throughout the weekend, the participants caught up on what their comrades had been doing since the end of the war. A sizable number of former military officers had returned to the French armed forces. Helen des Isnards, for one, rejoined the air force, serving as a military attaché at the French embassy in Turkey in the late 1940s. After leaving active service, he became president of the Paris subsidiary of an American oil company. But flying remained his great love, and he spent many years in the air force reserve, often delighting his six children by flying low over the family's ancestral château in Provence in a P47 Thunderbolt, a "very loud and powerful American fighter-bomber," his eldest son, Charles-Helen, remembered.

Ferdinand Rodriguez also returned to active military service, but not before taking part in the arrest of Jean-Paul Lien, the network operative and Gestapo informer who had betrayed him, Faye, and more than one hundred other Alliance agents. On a spring night in 1945, Rodriguez was leaving Alliance's Paris headquarters when another network operative ran up to him on the street. He grabbed Rodriguez's arm and hurried him along to a popular bar nearby. Inside, sitting on a stool in the corner and nursing a drink, was Lien. After whispering to his colleague to alert the police, Rodriguez stationed himself at the door of the bar, ready to tackle the turncoat agent if he tried to leave. Within minutes, two plainclothes policemen arrived. They seized Lien, handcuffed him, and led him out. "I mastered the urge to slap him and contented myself with giving him the stare of a ghost," Rodriguez wrote. "Neither Lien nor I exchanged a word. To facilitate the operation, I held the door open for the police." Taken to police headquarters on the rue des Saussaies, the same building to which Rodriguez had been transported in 1943 by the Gestapo, Lien was later tried, convicted, and executed by a firing squad.

Several months later, the former head of Alliance radio operations took part in another momentous occasion—this one filled with joy. On July 28, 1945, the twenty-nine-year-old Rodriguez married Monique Bontinck, twenty-five, at the Basilica of Saint Clotilde in Paris. Among the many guests was Marie-Madeleine Fourcade, who wrote that the couple had "mapped out for us the way of hope."

Shortly after his wedding, Rodriguez was sent by the British army to Indochina, to serve as an intelligence liaison officer with French forces in the current-day countries of Vietnam and Cambodia. When he arrived in southeast Asia, he found another former Alliance colleague, the swashbuckling Jean Sainteny.

Immediately after World War II, Sainteny, who had done business in Indochina in the 1930s, was sent there by de Gaulle's provisional government to try to reestablish France's control over its prewar col-

**WEDDING OF FERDINAND RODRIGUEZ
AND MONIQUE BONTINCK**

ony. In 1946, he reached an agreement with Ho Chi Minh, leader of the wartime Indochinese independence forces, to keep the region in a loose union with France. But the tenuous relationship soon unraveled, and Ho Chi Minh and his band of revolutionaries launched a guerrilla war against French troops. When Indochina was divided in two by the 1954 Geneva accords, Sainteny was named France's envoy to North Vietnam.

Throughout the years of tumult and violence in Vietnam, including America's involvement in the conflict, Sainteny maintained a good relationship with Ho Chi Minh—so much so that in the late 1960s and early 1970s, he served as an intermediary between the Nixon administration and the North Vietnamese leader in talks that eventually led to the secret negotiations ending the Vietnam War.

Ferdinand Rodriguez, meanwhile, returned in 1946 to France and civilian life. Before he left active duty in the British army, however, he was summoned to London and, in honor of his work with the Alliance network, was awarded the Distinguished Conduct Medal, the oldest British decoration for gallantry and one reserved for exceptional acts of bravery. King George VI personally presented the medal to Rodriguez at Buckingham Palace.

Not long afterward, he became involved in the affairs of another Alliance leader—Paul Bernard, Marie-Madeleine Fourcade's successor—who, like Rodriguez, had miraculously survived the horrors of German prisons after his arrest in March 1944. In the fall of that year, Rodriguez had caught a brief glimpse of Bernard at the prison in Kehl. But the former network chief was not among the Alliance operatives taken from there to the Rhine on November 23, 1944, and shot by Julius Gehrum and his henchmen. Two days before the executions, he had been transferred to Moabit prison in Berlin for questioning, and in April 1945, he was liberated by Red Army troops advancing on the German capital.

During his long nights in prison, Bernard was buoyed by recurrent dreams about flying, and he decided that if he survived, he would create an airline. In 1946, he did just that, founding Intercontinental Air Transport (TAI), which became one of France's leading airlines, specializing in routes to Africa, Asia, Tahiti, and other French islands in the Pacific.

An accountant by training, Rodriguez became TAI's chief financial officer. Later he would also assume the same role at Air Afrique, a regional airline operating within Africa. Four years after the Ussel reunion, he would retire as an executive at Air France.

In 1990, at the age of seventy-four, Ferdinand Edward Rodriguez became a French citizen. He died nine years later.

SOON AFTER THE WAR ENDED, the three surviving leaders of Alliance—Paul Bernard, Marie-Madeleine Fourcade, and Georges Loustaunau-Lacau—met in Paris. When Marie-Madeleine asked the other two about their plans for the future, Navarre said he'd like to go into electoral politics, and Bernard mentioned his dream of starting an airline. When they posed the same question to her, she responded that her mission as head of Alliance was still uppermost in her mind. The two of them, she said, had done their full share for the resistance. It was time for them and the network's other survivors to move on with their lives. She, on the other hand, felt that her work for Alliance was not yet done.

Like Bernard, Loustaunau-Lacau fulfilled his dream. Although he never fully recovered from the wounds he had suffered in 1940 and

MARIE-MADELEINE FOURCADE,
FERDINAND RODRIGUEZ, AND
PAUL BERNARD AFTER THE WAR

the savage treatment he had endured at Mauthausen, the indomitable Navarre, who'd always been drawn to political controversy, threw himself into the bear pit of French politics. In June 1951, he was elected to France's Chamber of Deputies as an independent. In February 1955, he was promoted to the rank of brigadier general in the French army and died in Paris eight days later, at the age of sixty.

Marie-Madeleine, for her part, managed to keep Alliance's flame alive while carving out a new life for herself. In 1946, she was divorced from Édouard-Jean Méric, her long-estranged husband, and the following year married Hubert Fourcade, a well-connected young Paris businessman whom she had first met during the war and had tried to recruit for Alliance. Instead he escaped to London, where he joined de Gaulle's Free French forces. According to Michèle Cointet, Marie-Madeleine's biographer, Hubert Fourcade made no effort to curb her freedom as her first husband had done. "Devoid of selfishness and personal ambition, he thought only of her," Cointet wrote. "[H]e would never be a master or a rival."

In 1949, Marie-Madeleine gave birth to her last child, Pénélope. "My mother deeply loved her children, but she was not very demonstrative or affectionate," Pénélope Fourcade-Fraissinet recalled. "She was not what you would call maternal. . . . She was very busy, and we didn't see her much." Her father, Fourcade-Fraissinet added, was the main source of parental affection.

In the late 1950s, Marie-Madeleine became heavily involved in French politics, which she had resolutely avoided during the war. Her husband had been a staunch supporter of General de Gaulle from the early days of the war and remained so even after de Gaulle abruptly resigned as leader of the French provisional government in early 1946 because of his intense frustration with those who opposed his policies. Marie-Madeleine backed the general, too, and in 1958, the Fourcades were two of the leaders of a successful campaign to bring de Gaulle back to power. In later years, Marie-Madeleine would become a member of the European Parliament, dividing her time between Brussels, Strasbourg, her family's elegant apartment on the Quai d'Orsay in Paris, and their country house in the Camargue, a starkly beautiful region of salt marshes and beaches in Provence.

At the same time, her wartime activities remained central to her life. As she saw it, those with whom she had worked during the conflict were as much a part of her family as her husband and children. In May 1945, she became the Alliance network's liquidating officer, a quasiofficial position in which she was required to prove that her three thousand agents had been bona fide members of the resistance, which allowed them access to a government pension, medical care, and other benefits, as well as official honors. She also worked to obtain aid for families of operatives who had been executed by the Germans. Having no jobs of their own, many of the women who had lost their husbands were in dire financial straits, with no money to feed, clothe, or educate their children. Getting sufficient help for them became an increasingly arduous task in a country that was anxious to forget the war, with all its misery and internal strife, and move on. Nonetheless, Fourcade relentlessly pressured the government to do so. "Once the bête noire of the Nazis, Marie-Madeleine has been for more than thirty years the terror of French bureaucrats," David Schoenbrun wrote in the late 1970s. "She storms the corridors and offices of the ministries of Paris seeking every advantage that she can get" for the people of her network. She also raised money from private individuals, among them the parents of Philippe Koenigswerther, who gave a substantial donation to help the widows and orphans of Alliance agents who, like their son, had been killed by the Nazis. In addition, she provided considerable money from her own funds for various projects—setting up a summer camp for her lost agents' children; providing winter clothes for one family; finding a room and paying the rent for the son of a dead operative who had come to Paris to study.

At the same time, Fourcade kept in close touch with her network's survivors. Virtually every month, as Pénélope Fourcade-Fraissinet remembered, her mother would host a gathering of former Alliance agents. "Even if they didn't live in Paris, they came back for those meetings," Fourcade-Fraissinet said. "Everybody stayed in touch. They remained friends for the rest of their lives."

Of this group, Fourcade's closest friends were Ferdinand Rodriguez and his wife, Monique, and Helen and Marie-Solange des Isnards. She became the godmother of Patrick Rodriguez-Redington, the first of Ferdinand and Monique's three children, and Charles-Helen des Isnards, who was the baby Marie-Solange was carrying at the time of Fourcade's escape from the jail in Aix-en-Provence. Fourcade also served as godmother to Colin Cohen, the son of Kenneth and Mary Cohen, born in the summer of 1945.

Fourcade's children remained exceptionally close to Colin Cohen and to the Rodriguez and des Isnards offspring. In their younger years, they spent weekends and vacations together and to this day, as

Charles-Helen des Isnards put it, they have maintained "an extraordinary *esprit de corps*."

Yet, while Fourcade clearly cherished these friendships—and the satisfying life she made for herself after the war—part of her heart remained in the past. Although she rarely talked about her wartime experiences, she occasionally mentioned Léon Faye to Pénélope, who later observed, "He was clearly very important to her." When Fourcade was writing her wartime memoirs, her daughter would sometimes find her in tears.

When Marie-Madeleine Fourcade died on July 20, 1989, at the age of seventy-nine, she became the first woman to be given a funeral at Les Invalides, a splendid complex of buildings in Paris that celebrates

LES INVALIDES

the military glory of France. Napoleon Bonaparte is buried at Les Invalides, as are dozens of other celebrated French military heroes.

On the morning of the funeral, Fourcade's body was greeted by the Republican Guard, the ceremonial regiment that acts as guard of honor at significant state occasions, before being carried by soldiers into the Cathedral of Saint-Louis-des-Invalides. Among the hundreds of mourners were former prime minister Jacques Chirac and Roland Dumas, the French foreign minister and a former *résistant* himself, who persuaded president François Mitterrand to bestow on Marie-Madeleine this signal honor.

It was a fitting farewell to the *grande dame* of the French resistance. Yet in the years that followed, Fourcade and her achievements began to fade into the past. For all the panoply of her funeral, she was never given her full due as one of the most significant leaders in the wartime resistance, nor was Alliance given the credit it deserved as the largest and most important Allied intelligence network in France. The vagaries of French politics played a large role in those omissions, as did Fourcade's gender.

The way in which an individual *résistant* or group was—and is— remembered in France depended to a significant degree on their relationships with other resisters before and during the war. A good relationship with de Gaulle and his supporters was particularly important since, at least in the first few postwar decades, they were the ones who created the dominant narrative of the war and the French response to it. Also playing a key role in shaping the narrative was the French Communist Party, which was a major force of the resistance and emerged from the war as the country's dominant political party.

The Gaullists and Communists didn't agree on much, but on one thing they were in consensus: No one with ties to Pétain or the Vichy government could ever be given credit for defying the Nazis. "For many years it was inconceivable, both to scholars and the public, that a person on the right . . . of the political spectrum could have legitimately been a resister," the historian Valerie Deacon has written. As a result, a large number of early resisters with connections to Vichy were simply airbrushed out of the picture.

Georges Loustaunau-Lacau—and, to a lesser extent, Marie-Madeleine Fourcade—were among them. Navarre, of course, was on the political right, was a former associate of Pétain's, and had launched his fledgling intelligence network in Vichy. He also had made a number of bitter enemies, the most notable of whom was de Gaulle. The two men's ill-natured rivalry went back several decades, to their days at Saint-Cyr. From the first days of their acquaintance, they couldn't abide each other.

The Communist Party, which had not forgotten Navarre's anti-communist crusade in the 1930s, was another old foe. When elections were held in October 1945 to elect a new national assembly, the Communists emerged with the largest share of the vote—26 percent. They used their new political power to wreak vengeance on enemies like Navarre.

Even before the war ended, the Communists and de Gaulle's supporters cast doubt on the war record of Alliance and its founder. A 1945 police report insisted that in forming Alliance, Navarre had only "solicited the cooperation of personalities on the right, members or fellow travelers of extreme parties or organizations." It went on to charge that the network "could only be considered to have been a secret propaganda and intelligence service in favor of Pétain's government." Obviously, neither accusation was true. Alliance agents, as Fourcade pointed out, represented all sectors of society and the entire political spectrum, including Communists.

At the instigation of French Communists, Navarre was indicted in 1947 for prewar rightist political activities and spent six months in jail before he was released. When he was elected to the National Assembly in 1951, he was frequently harassed by Communist deputies, who accused him of having worked with the Nazis. In his book, *A French Paradox,* the Israeli historian Simon Epstein noted that many of Navarre's Communist harassers had in fact refused to stand up against the Nazis in France until Germany invaded the Soviet Union in June 1941, long after Navarre had begun his resistance work.

Although Fourcade did not suffer the retaliation visited on Navarre, her refusal to get involved in the internecine rivalries of de Gaulle and his critics during the war was unquestionably held against her and Alliance. The general's comment to Navarre in 1940 that "everyone who is not with me is against me" indicated his feelings for Navarre's deputy as well. De Gaulle and his men particularly resented the fact that Fourcade and her network insisted on maintaining their ties with the British and would not consent to work directly for the Free French until near the end of the war. Another black mark against Alliance was the role it had played in helping de Gaulle's foremost rival, General Henri Giraud, escape from France, despite the fact that Fourcade was initially unaware of the reason behind the escape.

Thanks in part to her support of de Gaulle's return to power in 1958, Fourcade's political capital had improved enough by the time of her death that she was given the noteworthy funeral at Les Invalides. But she still had one major strike against her: her identity as a woman.

IN NOVEMBER 1940, DE GAULLE had created the Compagnons de la Libération, an elite group of those deemed heroes in the struggle for French liberation during World War II. By the end of the war, only 1,038 persons were considered worthy of the honor. Of that number, 1,032 were men.

Included in the exclusive fraternity were three members of Alliance: Henri Schaerrer, Jean Sainteny, and Georges Lamarque. Also chosen was Édouard-Jean Méric, Marie-Madeleine's former husband, a Free French officer who had commanded a regiment during the Allied landing in southern France in August 1944 that had ended up capturing more than twelve hundred German prisoners near Marseille.

Among others named to the group were leaders of various resistance movements and networks. Henri Frenay, the founder of the Combat movement, was one. Another was Gilbert Renault, the chief of the Confrérie de Notre Dame, the Free French intelligence network that was second only to Alliance in size, breadth, and importance to the Allies.

Renault's counterpart at Alliance, however, was not one of the six women awarded the honor, most of whom had been associates of male movement leaders allied with de Gaulle. Only one—Bertie Albrecht—had played a leadership role in the war, serving as deputy and adviser to Henri Frenay at Combat. The lone woman who had actually been a *chef de résistance* and whose network's intelligence achievements were unparalleled was not judged worthy of the honor.

The omission of Fourcade and the pitifully small number of women named as Compagnons reflected the sexism that had prevailed during the war among the Free French and most resistance leaders; in their view, men fought, and women stayed home. "Discrimination, based . . . on a notion of inequality between the sexes was as solidly rooted in the Resistance as everywhere else in France," noted the historian Henri Noguères, a *résistant* himself.

Notwithstanding men's hesitation to include them in resistance work, tens of thousands of French women had risked and, in many cases, lost their lives by defying the Germans, although virtually none were given leadership positions in resistance organizations. "Just as businesses recruited female personnel only for positions like switchboard operator or receptionist, women and girls were brought into the resistance primarily to be couriers and liaison agents," Noguères recalled. Yet, while these posts may have been regarded as subordinate, they were in fact highly important and extremely dangerous jobs.

Keenly aware of society's norms of acceptable behavior for women, many female resisters during and after the war minimized the importance of their wartime achievements. Unlike a number of their male counterparts, they neither demanded credit for their contributions nor asked for recompense. As the historian Robert Gildea has noted, "After the war, those who had done least in the resistance often spoke the most, while those who had done the most spoke the least." Women, Gildea added, "were particularly modest."

Even Fourcade felt constrained to downplay what she had done, describing herself to an interviewer after the war as "the wife of an officer, the mother of a family, a member of no political party, and a Catholic." As her biographer, Michèle Cointet, aptly noted, it was a "rather humble (and misleading) self-description by the only woman to have led a large and important Resistance network in France. Her words fail to capture her uniqueness before, during, and after the war as a woman who . . . transgressed contemporary gender norms on a regular basis. But they . . . capture the tension between her actions and societal expectations."

Displaying a similar reticence was Jeannie Rousseau, whose reports on the development of the V-1 bombs and V-2 rockets represented one of the greatest intelligence coups of the war. She, too, was excluded from the Compagnons de la Libération, although like Fourcade, she received the Médaille de la Résistance, a lesser honor, along with the Croix de Guerre and Legion of Honor.

After the war, Rousseau remained quiet about her exploits and slipped into the shadows of history. In 1993, almost fifty years after the end of the conflict, the CIA honored her for her "heroic and momentous contribution to Allied efforts during World War II." At a ceremony at CIA headquarters, the agency's director, James Woolsey, noted that her reports about the terror weapons had disrupted their manufacture and testing and as a result had "saved thousands of lives in the West." Soon afterward, a long profile about Rousseau and what she had done appeared in *The Washington Post*. It was the first time she had received public attention.

For several decades following the war, histories of the French resistance, which were written almost exclusively by men, largely ignored the contributions of women. Although that is no longer true, most current overviews of the subject, while certainly mentioning women, have continued to underplay the extent and importance of their participation, treating the subject, in the words of one historian, as "an anonymous background element in an essentially male story."

And although there has been a flurry of books in recent decades that have examined various aspects of French women's experiences during the war, even they tend to shy away from highlighting "atypical" women like Fourcade, whose work as the leader of a military intelligence network was so different from the norm of most female *résistants*.

IF THE LACK OF attention bothered Marie-Madeleine Fourcade, she never showed it. In her view, the thousands of agents in her network were the ones who should be remembered, and she worked hard to keep their memory fresh. "The years have passed, my friends have died, but their spirit is still alive," she wrote in her memoirs. "I should like to know that they will not be forgotten, that the divine flame that burned in their hearts will be understood."

These ordinary men and women never planned to be heroes, but they were—every bit as much (and some perhaps even more) than the 1,038 enshrined in the Compagnons de la Libération. Although they were from varied walks of life and political backgrounds, a moral common denominator overrode all their differences: a refusal to be silenced and an iron determination to fight against the destruction of freedom and human dignity. In doing so, they, along with other members of the resistance, saved the soul and honor of France.

Equally important, they served as an example from the past of what ordinary people can do in the present and future when faced with existential threats to basic human rights. As Jeannie Rousseau noted many years after the war, "Resistance is a state of mind. We can exercise it at any moment."

ACKNOWLEDGMENTS

A COMMON THREAD UNITES THE EIGHT BOOKS I'VE WRITTEN.
They all focus in some way on unsung heroes—individuals of courage and conscience who helped change their country and the world but who, for various reasons, have slipped into the shadows of history. Since seven of those books deal with war, specifically World War II, it's perhaps not surprising that most of the heroes I've spotlighted have been men. *Madame Fourcade's Secret War* is the exception.

I first became aware of Marie-Madeleine Fourcade while doing research on the French resistance for my most recent book, *Last Hope Island*. There were only scattered mentions of her in the books and journals I consulted at the time, but the little I learned about this elegant young mother of two—the only woman to lead a major French resistance network—made me want to know more. As I dug deeper into her story and that of Alliance, I discovered that both were far richer than I could have imagined. I found it hard to believe that she was so little known in the United States, and I decided to correct that deficiency.

My most important source was Fourcade's own wartime memoir. Intensely human, it describes in minute detail the satisfaction and joy, as well as the fear and terror, of fighting back against France's Nazi occupiers. An English translation, entitled *Noah's Ark,* was published in the United States in 1974. The original French version, *L'Arche de Noé,* was published in 1968.

Also helpful were memoirs written by two of Fourcade's top lieutenants—Jean Boutron (*De Mers-el-Kébir à Londres 1940–1944*) and Ferdinand Rodriguez (*L'Escalier Sans Retour*). Rodriguez's memoir, which focuses on his hellish sojourn in Gestapo prisons, is one of the most chilling, moving, and heartbreaking books I have ever read about World War II.

I also learned much from a French biography of Fourcade by the historian Michèle Cointet and from the writings of the American historian Valerie Deacon about the wartime activities of Fourcade, Georges Loustaunau-Lacau, and others belonging to the French right.

My heartfelt gratitude goes to Fourcade's daughter, Pénélope Fourcade-Fraissinet; Rodriguez's son and daughter, Patrick Rodriguez-Redington and Elizabeth Pernet; and Charles-Helen des Isnards, the son of Helen des Isnards, another key figure in Alliance. Their generosity in sharing with me their memories and insights into their parents and other Alliance members, along with providing me with several previously unpublished accounts of the network's activities, was of crucial importance in bringing these amazing individuals to life on the page.

Of the many noteworthy experiences I had while researching this book, the one that immediately comes to mind is a cocktail party hosted by Charles-Helen des Isnards and his wife, Sylvie, in their elegant Paris apartment. The other guests included Pénélope Fourcade-Fraissinet and her husband and des Isnards's five siblings and their spouses, who had traveled from all over France to be there. The warmth of their welcome to me and my friend and colleague, Dorie Denbigh-Laurent, reflected their pride in their parents and their extraordinary achievements during the war.

And speaking of the wise and beautiful Dorie Denbigh-Laurent, I owe her a particular debt of gratitude—not only for helping me with translations but also for her expert guidance and counsel on all things French. I could not have done this book without her.

I'd also like to thank Tom Chapin, the son of Sylvia Bridou Chapin Smith (Marie-Madeleine's onetime sister-in-law), who gave me access to his mother's unpublished *roman à clef* novel about her experiences and those of Marie-Madeleine's family during the war.

Thanks, too, to the historians whose work on the French resistance, Vichy France, and MI6 I learned from and drew on in writing *Madame Fourcade's Secret War* and my other books about World War II. I'd like to single out M.R.D. Foot, Robert O. Paxton, Julian Jackson, Keith Jeffery, Simon Kitson, H. R. Kedward, Douglas Porch, Robert and Isabelle Tombs, and David Schoenbrun.

Also helpful were the French national archives (Archives Nationales de France) in Paris and the archives of the French ministry of defense (Service Historique de la Défense) in Vincennes, both of which have considerable material on Alliance and its members (much of it available online). Their records include an account of Léon Faye's life and his written notes of his capture by the Gestapo, failed escape from 84 avenue Foch, and nightmarish imprisonment in Germany.

The Association of Friends of Alliance (Association Amicale Alliance), an organization of the network's members and families founded by Fourcade after the war, also produced documents relating to Alliance's history, including a lengthy—and poignant—report memorializing its agents who were killed by the Germans.

I want to thank Julie Summers, the author of several wonderful histories set in England during World War II, including *Jambusters* and *Our Uninvited Guests,* for her help on a number of matters, including putting me in touch with Florence Smith, a talented young British researcher and historian. Florence was kind enough to track down for me the unpublished memoirs of the British diplomat Patrick Reilly at the Bodleian Library in Oxford.

The outstanding collection of oral histories at the Imperial War Museum in London also proved to be extremely useful, particularly those of Hugh Verity and Barbara Bertram, who played major roles in the RAF's wartime ferry service of Fourcade and other French intelligence agents between France and England.

Working on this book has been one of the most satisfying and enjoyable experiences of my writing life, in no small part because of the encouragement and guidance of my splendid editor, Susanna Porter, and the rest of the Random House team. I've also had the great good fortune to have the incomparable Gail Ross as my agent and friend—a relationship that has flourished for more than twenty years.

Above all, I must thank the loves of my life—my husband, Stan Cloud, and our daughter, Carly. You are my everything.

NOTES

PROLOGUE

xix **"minute elite"**: Marie-Madeleine Fourcade, *Noah's Ark: A Memoir of Struggle and Resistance* (New York: Dutton, 1974), 10.

xxi **"a tough little animal"**: David Schoenbrun, *Soldiers of the Night: The Story of the French Resistance* (New York: Dutton, 1980), Loc. 3483 (Kindle edition).

xxii **"resisters shared one characteristic"**: M.R.D. Foot, *Six Faces of Courage* (Barnsley, UK: Pen and Sword, 2003), 17.

"She was very independent": Interview with Pénélope Fourcade-Fraissinet.

"not inclined to feminism": Jean Novosseloff, book review of *Marie-Madeleine Fourcade: A Leader of the Resistance,* Fondation de la Résistance, fondationresistance.org/pages/rech_doc/marie-madeleine-fourcade-chef -resistance_cr_lecture55.html.

"She had enormous charisma": Interview with Charles-Helen des Isnards.

xxiv **"To this day"**: J. E. Smyth, *Fred Zinnemann and the Cinema of Resistance* (Jackson: University Press of Mississippi), 206.

"I don't understand": Jeannie Rousseau video interview with David Ignatius, International Spy Museum Archive, Washington, D.C.

CHAPTER 1: LEAPING INTO THE UNKNOWN

5   **"The minds of the French"**: William Shirer, *The Collapse of the Third Republic: An Inquiry into the Fall of France in 1940* (New York: Simon & Schuster, 1969), Loc. 3625 (Kindle edition).

7   **"the stylish":** Harriet Sergeant, *Shanghai: Collision Point of Cultures 1918–1939* (New York: Crown, 1990), 2.
     "You could be": "In the Mood for Cheong Sam: New Women in Old Shanghai Glamour," that-obsession.tumblr.com/post/132366778412/in-the-mood-for-cheongsam-new-women-in-o.

8   **"My mother loved":** Marie-Madeleine Fourcade radio interview, July 2, 1989.
     "They wanted to speak": Ibid.

9   **"tagines of every kind":** Ibid.

10   **"allow a husband":** Michèle Cointet, *Marie-Madeleine Fourcade: Un Chef de la Résistance* (Paris: Perrin, 2006), 17–18.

11   **"people's ineradicable love":** Stacy Schiff, *Saint-Exupéry: A Biography* (New York: Knopf, 1995), Loc. 4875 (Kindle edition).

13   **"You seemed interested":** Cointet, 24.

14   **"One of my Belgian":** Ibid., 24–25.

CHAPTER 2: THE CHAOS OF DEFEAT

16   **"were the reckless agents":** Valerie Deacon, *The Extreme Right in the French Resistance: Members of the Cagoules and Corvignolles in the Second World War* (Baton Rouge: LSU Press, 2016), 84.

17   **"A man of the utmost":** M.R.D. Foot, *Six Faces of Courage* (London: Eyre Methuen, 1978), 46.

18   **"It is neither":** Deacon, 83.

19   **"an anthill":** Julian Jackson, *France: The Dark Years 1940–1944* (Oxford: Oxford University Press, 2001), 100.
     "all the ugliness": Charles Glass, *Americans in Paris: Life and Death Under Nazi Occupation* (New York: Penguin, 2009), 79.
     "We had lost": Jackson, 120.

20   **"a stream of lava":** Eric Sevareid, *Not So Wild a Dream* (New York: Atheneum, 1976), 148.

21   **"too few arms":** Robert Tombs and Émile Chabal, eds., *Britain and France in Two World Wars: Truth, Myth and Memory* (London: Bloomsbury, 2013), 10.
     "the apocalypse": Tom Keene, *Cloak of Enemies: Churchill's SOE, Enemies at Home and the Cockleshell Heroes* (Staplehurst, UK: Spellmount, 2012), Loc. 3878 (Kindle edition).

22   **"How dare you say":** Cointet, 48.

23   **"Whatever happens":** Jean Lacouture, *De Gaulle: The Rebel, 1890–1944* (New York: W. W. Norton, 1990), 225.

CHAPTER 3: FIGHTING BACK

24   **"Never was Vichy":** Schoenbrun, Loc. 3405.

25   **"the physical":** Shirer, Loc. 18120.

26 **"says, 'the Marshal' "**: Jean Guéhenno, *Diary of the Dark Years 1940–1944* (Oxford: Oxford University Press, 2014), 93.

"the Marshal's authority": Lynne Olson, *Last Hope Island: Britain, Occupied Europe, and the Brotherhood That Helped Turn the Tide of War* (New York: Random House, 2017), 129.

27 **"She never operated"**: Interview with Charles-Helen des Isnards.

"aristocracy of defeat": Fourcade, *Noah's Ark,* 25.

"The Marshal received": Jean Boutron, *De Mers el-Kébir à Londres 1940–1944* (Paris: Plon, 1980), 160.

"You know very well": Cointet, 61.

28 **"the first stronghold"**: Deacon, 87.

29 **"The hackneyed phrase"**: Jackson, 406.

"The French have": M.R.D. Foot, *SOE in France: An Account of the British Special Operations Executive in France 1940–1944* (London: HMSO, 1966).

30 **"We must learn"**: Schoenbrun, Loc. 1338.

"watch, resist, and unite": H. R. Kedward, *Resistance in Vichy France* (Oxford: Oxford University Press, 1978), 43.

31 **"the fight must go on"**: Schoenbrun, Loc. 2298.

CHAPTER 4: SPYING IN MARSEILLE

37 **"An immense"**: Boutron, 107.

38 **"But we are not"**: Ibid., 15.

"This bloody armistice": Ibid., 43.

39 **"with the same principles"**: Ibid., 154.

"the pivot around": Ibid, 169.

"the memory": Ibid.

41 **"Marseille residents"**: Simon Kitson, *Police and Politics in Marseille, 1936–1945* (Leiden, Netherlands: Brill, 2014), 5.

"I swear to fight": Antony Beevor and Artemis Cooper, *Paris After the Liberation 1944–1949* (New York: Penguin, 2004), 13.

"discreetly anti-Nazi": Kitson, *Police and Politics in Marseille, 1936–1945,* 96.

"Who wouldn't wish": Ibid.

"Good God!": Fourcade, *Noah's Ark,* 33.

44 **"Collaboration was not"**: Simon Kitson, *The Hunt for Nazi Spies: Fighting Espionage in Vichy France* (Chicago: University of Chicago Press, 2007), 6.

45 **"there was no inherent"**: Frenay, 167.

"all the hopes": Ibid., 97.

CHAPTER 5: THE BIRTH OF ALLIANCE

52 **"a remarkably quick"**: Sylvia Bridou Smith, unpublished manuscript.

53 **"seemed to be everywhere"**: Schoenbrun, Loc. 3624.

55   **"It is, of course, urgent"**: Keene, Loc. 1342.
      "there was no contact": Keene, Loc. 1356.
57   **"very distressing"**: Lynne Olson, *Those Angry Days: Roosevelt, Lindbergh, and America's Fight over World War II, 1939–1941* (New York: Random House, 2013), 291.
      "even now England": Ibid.

CHAPTER 6: DANGER IN PARIS

65   **"it turned out to be"**: Schoenbrun, Loc. 6590.
66   **"enthusiastic volunteers"**: Keith Jeffery, *The Secret History of MI6* (New York: Penguin Press, 2010), Loc. 6990 (Kindle edition).
      "The buffet was groaning": David Pryce-Jones, *Paris in the Third Reich: A History of the German Occupation, 1940–1944* (New York: Holt, Rinehart and Winston, 1981), 71.
68   **"Fashion was, for the French"**: Anne Sebba, *Les Parisiennes: How the Women of Paris Lived, Loved, and Died Under Nazi Occupation* (New York: St. Martin's Press, 2016), Loc. 4104 (Kindle edition).

CHAPTER 7: TAKING COMMAND

72   **"left me gasping"**: Fourcade, *Noah's Ark*, 37.
      "Algeria had felt": Boutron, 184.
73   **"The next time"**: Schoenbrun, Loc. 6409.
75   **"She is the most"**: Fourcade, *Noah's Ark*, 47.
      "She had a natural": Interview with Pénélope Fourcade-Fraissinet.
77   **"For months"**: Boutron, 182.
78   **"Everyone worships"**: Ibid., 194.
      "pronounce the name": Ibid.
80   **"Enough, little one"**: Fourcade, *Noah's Ark*, 66.
81   **N1 ARRESTED THIS MORNING**: Cointet, 109–110.

CHAPTER 8: A NETWORK IN PERIL

87   **"at bars, restaurants"**: Schoenbrun, Loc. 7011.
      "It's open war": Paul Paillole, *Fighting the Nazis: French Intelligence and Counterintelligence, 1933–1945* (Enigma Books, 2003), 253.
      "At the grass roots": Ibid., 254.
      "Vichy is betting": Boutron, 221.

CHAPTER 9: THE MAILBAG

92   **"From the bag"**: Boutron, 232.
93   **"I'm back"**: Ibid., 236.

94 "These are diplomatic": Ibid.

100 "only people with foreign names": Anthony Cave Brown, *"C": The Secret Life of Sir Stewart Graham Menzies* (New York: Macmillan, 1987), 131.

"letting women run": M.R.D. Foot and J. L. Langley, *MI9: Escape and Evasion 1939–1945* (London: Biteback Publishing, 2011), 80.

"Your network *must* last": Fourcade, *Noah's Ark,* 86.

CHAPTER 10: THE RETURN OF LÉON FAYE

106 "At last!": Fourcade, *Noah's Ark,* 166.

109 "I'm prepared to": Ibid., 173.

CHAPTER 11: A GAME OF WITS

115 "Who is ASO 43?": Fourcade, *Noah's Ark,* 107.

116 "a sharp-eyed": Schoenbrun, Loc. 3655.

117 "We're going to arrest": Fourcade, *Noah's Ark,* 111.

118 "By the way": Ibid.

CHAPTER 12: "AN UNDISPUTED LEADER"

127 "They're after you again!": Fourcade, *Noah's Ark,* 131.

131 "She performed": Ferdinand Rodriguez, *L'Escalier Sans Retour* (Paris: Éditions France-Empire, 1984), 138.

"I carried messages": Monique Bontinck Rodriguez, unpublished manuscript.

133 "Faye is obsessed": Cointet, 130.

"fact had outpaced": Fourcade, *Noah's Ark,* 9.

"he, like so many": Adam Bartos and Colin MacCabe, *Remembering Chris Marker* (New York: OR Books, 2017), 28.

"A woman": Léon Faye, biography, Reseau Alliance website, reseaualliance.e-monsite.com/pages/biographie-des-membres/leon-faye-bis.html.

"She was young": "Le Réseau Alliance," French television interview, Sept. 27, 1968.

CHAPTER 13: SITTING ON A BARREL OF GUNPOWDER

137 "We were all": Hugh Verity, *We Landed by Moonlight: The Secret RAF Landings in France 1940–1944* (Manchester, UK: Crécy Publishing, 2000), 197.

"I was rather pleased": Ibid., 84.

138 "were only vulnerable": Ibid., 9.

142 "Well, I've got": Fourcade, *Noah's Ark,* 142.

CHAPTER 14: THE TRAITOR

146 **"We've got you"**: Fourcade, *Noah's Ark,* 147.
148 **"You can't imagine"**: Ibid., 150.
149 **"You're exhausted"**: Ibid., 152.

CHAPTER 15: A GENERAL ESCAPES

152 **"must be given no role"**: Lynne Olson, *Citizens of London: The Americans Who Stood with Britain in Its Finest, Darkest Hour* (New York: Random House, 2010), 220.
153 **"nothing must stand in the way"**: Ibid.
154 **"idiotically self important"**: Schoenbrun, Loc. 7302.

CHAPTER 16: CAPTURED

162 **"Dirty Boche!"**: Fourcade, *Noah's Ark,* 166.
165 **"I only hoped"**: Ibid., 301.
     "I resume my place": Colin Smith, *England's Last War Against France: Fighting Vichy 1940–1942* (London: Phoenix, 2010), 367.
166 **"As I understand it"**: Ibid.
     "Ike had never been": Ibid.
     "Then I shall return": Ibid., 373.
167 **"In a second"**: Boutron, 295.
     "You were to come": Ibid., 296.
168 **"a low, elongated mass"**: Ibid., 302.
     "a bunch of ordinary": Ibid.
169 **"I was going"**: Ibid., 303.
     "Be careful": Fourcade, *Noah's Ark,* 172.
172 **"The whole police"**: Ibid., 175.
173 **"No! Don't move!"**: Ibid., 312.

CHAPTER 17: OPERATION ATTILA

176 **"For my part"**: Lacouture, 349.
     "hit me like a bomb": Boutron, 306.
177 **"Between Giraud and de Gaulle"**: Harold Nicolson, *The War Years: Diaries and Letters, 1939–1945* (New York: Atheneum, 1967), 294.
178 **"looked terribly British"**: Monique Bontinck Rodriguez, unpublished manuscript.
     "I was looking": Rodriguez, 14.
179 **"constant good humor"**: Anthony and Barbara Bertram, eds., Jerome Bertram, *The Secret of Bignor Manor* (Lulu Press, 2014), 134.

CHAPTER 18: "DOWN GO THE U-BOATS"

185 **"A word from us to London"**: Fourcade, *Noah's Ark,* 194.

187 **"moving them"**: Philip Kaplan, *Grey Wolves: U-Boat War 1939–1945* (New York: Skyhorse Publishing, 2014), 18.

"It was a great mistake": Jonathan Dimbleby, *The Battle of the Atlantic: How the Allies Won the War* (Oxford: Oxford University Press, 2016), 116.

188 **"From an operational"**: Daniel V. Gallery, *U-505* (San Francisco: Lucknow Books, 2016), Loc. 2901 (Kindle edition).

189 **"In Breton eyes"**: Jean-Luc Bannalec, *Death in Brittany* (New York: Minotaur Books, 2014), 30.

CHAPTER 19: ON THE RUN

195 **"the terrible year"**: Fourcade, *Noah's Ark,* 189.

196 **"If there had been any bridle"**: Philippe de Vomécourt, *An Army of Amateurs* (New York: Doubleday, 1961), 126.

"almost to a man, thugs on the make": Ibid., 108.

197 **"as if it had been preserved"**: Martin Walker, *The Resistance Man: A Mystery of the French Countryside* (New York: Vintage, 2015), 173.

200 **"I refuse to persecute"**: Jean Philippe, Association l'Alliance, reseaualliance .e-monsite.com/pages/biographie-des-membres/philippe-jean.html.

201 **"we marched off"**: Fourcade, *Noah's Ark,* 206.

202 **"have a hard time"**: Ted Morgan, *An Uncertain Hour: The French, the Germans, the Jews, and the City of Lyon, 1940–1945* (New York: Arbor House, 1990), 124.

"For a clandestine": Jean Overton Fuller, *The German Penetration of SOE: France 1941–1944* (Maidstone, UK: George Mann Books, 1996), 31.

204 **"You forget"**: Cointet, 203.

CHAPTER 20: THE TINDERBOX OF LYON

206 **"a citadel of old money"**: Morgan, *An Uncertain Hour,* 19.

207 **"You couldn't go"**: Douglas Porch, *The French Secret Services: From the Dreyfus Affair to the Gulf War* (New York: Farrar, Straus and Giroux, 1995), 236.

"at me with his": "Klaus Barbie: Women Testify of Torture," *Philadelphia Inquirer,* March 23, 1987.

208 **"In my network"**: Cointet, 209–10.

210 **"Have they gone?"**: Schoenbrun, Loc. 425.

211 **"I had always thought"**: Ibid.

213 **"Marie-Madeleine, there's"**: Fourcade, *Noah's Ark,* 226.

215 **"My son came through"**: Ibid., 232.

216 **"Last Sunday"**: Jeffery, Loc. 8415.

"had been more": Ibid., Loc. 8432.

217 **"Act as if"**: Rodriguez, 103.
    "Of course": Ibid., 104.
219 **"the blood flowed"**: Fourcade, *Noah's Ark,* 233.
    "My guards burst into": Monique Bontinck Rodriguez, unpublished manuscript.

CHAPTER 21: HIGH ANXIETY

221 **"forbidding as fortified"**: Fourcade, *Noah's Ark,* 238.
222 **"They were on the front"**: Marie-Madeleine Fourcade radio interview, French Culture, July 29, 1989.
223 **"Who would ever think"**: Fourcade, *Noah's Ark,* 239.
229 **"Be brave"**: Ibid., 250.
231 **"flood of beacons"**: Ibid., 253.

CHAPTER 22: "HERE YOU ARE AT LAST!"

232 **"Here you are"**: Fourcade, *Noah's Ark,* 252.
233 **"A delightful hostess"**: Anthony and Barbara Bertram, *The Secret of Bignor Manor* (Lulu Press, 2014), 216.
234 **"intimacy and love"**: Barbara Bertram, *French Resistance in Sussex* (Pulborough, UK: Barnworks Publishing, 1996), xv.
    "When they arrived": Ibid., 22.
    "the beautiful Marie-Madeleine": Ibid., 47–48.
236 **"So this is the terrible"**: Fourcade, *Noah's Ark,* 255.
    "You mean you're": Ibid.
    "a most unpleasant": Ben Macintyre, *Double Cross: The True Story of the D-Day Spies* (New York: Crown, 2012), 44.
237 **"eyes of a hyperactive"**: Ibid.
    "Everyone was scared": Anthony Read and David Fisher, *Colonel Z: The Secret Life of a Master of Spies* (New York: Viking, 1985), 12.
    "an utter shit": Ibid.
    "consumed by hate": Patrick Reilly, unpublished memoirs, Bodleian Library, Oxford.
    "one of Dansey's": Read and Fisher, 297.
242 **"I see it's made"**: Fourcade, *Noah's Ark,* 259.
244 **"This material looks"**: Schoenbrun, Loc. 11551.

CHAPTER 23: "THE MOST REMARKABLE GIRL OF HER GENERATION"

246 **"The Germans still wanted"**: David Ignatius, "After Five Decades, a Spy Tells Her Tale," *Washington Post,* Dec. 28, 1998.

"all the things": Ibid.

247 "that would take": Ibid.

"I knew all the details": Ibid.

248 "I had become": Ibid.

"I would absorb it": Ibid.

249 "This afternoon": Michael J. Neufeld, *Von Braun: Dreamer of Space, Engineer of War* (New York: Knopf, 2007), 137.

"the new weapons": Ibid.

250 "stratospheric bomb": R. V. Jones, *Most Secret War* (Ware, UK: Wordsworth Editions, 1998), 351.

"the chilling fear": Ibid., xiv.

"this extraordinary report": Ibid., 354.

the most remarkable: Ibid.

251 "a masterpiece in the history": William Grimes, "Jeannie Rousseau de Clarens, Valiant World War II Spy, Dies at 98," *New York Times,* August 29, 2017.

"would affect the whole course": Martin Middlebrook, *The Peenemünde Raid: The Night of 17–18 August 1943* (Barnsley, UK: Pen and Sword, 2006), 79.

252 "It was like hell": Ibid., 141.

"A substantial proportion": Jones, 346.

"had a far-reaching": Winston S. Churchill, *Closing the Ring* (Boston: Houghton Mifflin, 1951), 207.

"Were the Germans": Tessa Stirling, Daria Nałęcz, and Tadeusz Dubicki, eds., *Intelligence Cooperation Between Poland and Great Britain During World War II* (London: Valentine Mitchell, 2005), 476.

253 "Although we could": Winston S. Churchill, *Triumph and Tragedy* (Boston: Houghton Mifflin, 1953), 53.

CHAPTER 24: PINK HEATHER

257 "If you order him": Fourcade, *Noah's Ark,* 261.

"Damn their law": Ibid.

258 "It's up to you": Ibid., 262.

263 "Good work": Rodriguez, 11.

"We will have": Ibid., 12.

CHAPTER 25: CALAMITY

265 "I'm going mad": Fourcade, *Noah's Ark,* 267.

"with a hand as heavy": Ibid.

267 "Since September 16": Ibid., 272.

268 "the indifference": Paul Bernard, unpublished manuscript.

269 **"I experienced"**: Fourcade, *Noah's Ark, 272.*

270 **"represented a wealth"**: Ibid., 278.

271 **"their uncontested leader"**: Jackson, 428.

272 **"The Resistance, for him"**: Frenay, 206.

"Despite our proven": Ibid., 287.

"full-scale and dangerous": Brown, 333.

"viciously petty": Keene, Loc. 4247.

"Though SOE and MI6": Malcolm Muggeridge, *Chronicles of Wasted Time:* Vol. 2, *The Infernal Grove* (London: Collins, 1973), 174.

273 **"almost incoherent with indignation"**: Keene, Loc. 1812.

"Great news!": Patrick Reilly, unpublished memoirs, Bodleian Library, Oxford.

"an evil man": Ibid.

"was said to be": Ibid.

274 **"Cohen's bitch"**: Ibid.

"all these cumbersome": Fourcade, *Noah's Ark, 290.*

CHAPTER 26: CAPTIVES

275 **"A snake sliding"**: Rodriguez, 40.

276 **"I do not believe"**: Ibid., 44.

277 **"had done absolutely nothing"**: Frenay, 53.

278 **"I walk constantly"**: Rodriguez, 47.

279 **"these separations"**: Ibid., 52.

282 **"a splendid, vague, dreamy"**: Shrabani Basu, *Spy Princess: The Life of Noor Inayat Khan* (Amherst, MA: Omega Publications, 2007), Loc. 1687 (Kindle edition).

283 **"tends to give far"**: Sarah Helm, *A Life in Secrets: Vera Atkins and the Missing Agents of WWII* (New York: Anchor, 2007), 12–13.

"if this girl's an agent": Leo Marks, *Between Silk and Cyanide: A Codemaker's War, 1941–45* (Stroud, UK: History Press, 2013), 311.

"was necessary": Basu, Loc. 1795.

284 **"She told us nothing"**: Helm, 486.

"Kieffer's artist in residence": Ibid., 176.

285 **"The Gestapo boys"**: Ibid., 176.

"His presence was unfortunate": Ibid., 177.

286 **"drunk with happiness"**: Unpublished journal, Léon Faye, French state archives.

287 **"This girl is crazy"**: Ibid.

"magnificent courage": Ibid.

290 **"Water remains permanently"**: Ibid.

"she would have made it": Helm, 487.

CHAPTER 27: THE MAP

294 **"We have the impression"**: Paul Bernard, unpublished manuscript.

295 **"won the lasting respect"**: Patrick Reilly, unpublished memoirs, Bodleian Library, Oxford.

297 **"We Dampierres are not spies"**: Dampierre family history.

299 **"disaster," as one**: Sir Frederick Morgan, *Overture to Overlord* (Garden City, NY: Doubleday, 1950), 279.

   "In this particular": David Irving, *The War Between the Generals: Inside the Allied High Command* (New York: Congdon and Lattes, 1981), 94.

303 **"the most complete"**: Schoenbrun, Loc. 12279.

CHAPTER 28: GOING HOME

305 **"I can't stop now"**: Résistances-Morbihan, resistances-morbihan.fr/alliance-bretagne-2/.

CHAPTER 29: CAUGHT IN THE NET

313 **"Where's the lady?"**: Fourcade, *Noah's Ark,* 321.
   "Hello, Marie-Madeleine": Ibid.

314 **"Do you mean"**: Ibid.

316 **"She would accompany"**: Interview with Charles-Helen des Isnards.

318 **"Where's the man?"**: Fourcade, *Noah's Ark,* 328.

323 **"I've just escaped"**: Ibid., 338.

CHAPTER 30: LIBERATION AND BEYOND

335 **"the animals of the Ark"**: Fourcade, *Noah's Ark,* 357.

336 **"returned, miraculously unaffected"**: Ibid., 361.

338 **"By their work and sacrifice"**: David Schoenbrun, "Animals at War," *New York Times*, Feb. 17, 1974.

339 **"Colonel Bernis"**: Fourcade, *Noah's Ark,* 361.

CHAPTER 31: "HAIL MARY, FULL OF GRACE"

342 **"There is no personality"**: Rodriguez, 169.
   "Where are we going?": Ibid., 162.
   "Commandant!": Ibid.

344 **"And our friends?"**: Ibid.
   "like something out of": Ibid., 82.

345 **"They've landed"**: Ibid., 84.

346 **"God save the king!"**: Ibid., 108.

347 "Hail Mary": Ibid., 133.
348 "Your friends . . . all gone": Ibid., 136.
     "Why are we still alive?": Ibid., 169.
349 "a choirmaster in a crypt": Ibid., 184.
     "Tomorrow!": Ibid., 185.
     "Am I mistaken?": Ibid.
     "Our three lives": Ibid., 186.
350 "You are being exchanged": Ibid., 194.
352 "So, you're all": Ibid., 209.
     "we thought you would prefer": Ibid., 210.
     "Life was worth": Ibid., 215.
353 "I could not abandon": Ibid., 218.
     "It was the antithesis": Ibid., 220.
355 "I cannot abandon": Ibid., 226.
     "an intense need": Ibid.
     "I look at myself now": Ibid.

CHAPTER 32: THE ROAD TO GETHSEMANE

362 "the most terrible of all": Fourcade, Noah's Ark, 365.
     "Where are the manacles?": Ibid., 366.

EPILOGUE

366 "our handsome hero": Schoenbrun, Loc. 336.
     "And somehow": Ibid., Loc. 357.
368 "a weekend of celebration": Ibid., Loc. 363.
     "serve our unhappy country": Ibid.
     "The connection formed": Fourcade, Noah's Ark, 55.
369 "very loud and powerful": Interview with Charles-Helen des Isnards.
     "I mastered the urge": Rodriguez, 230.
     "mapped out": Fourcade, Noah's Ark, 371.
373 "Devoid of selfishness": Cointet, 300–301.
     "My mother deeply loved": Interview with Pénélope Fourcade-Fraissinet.
374 "Once the bête noire of the Nazis": Schoenbrun, Loc. 16308.
     "Even if they didn't live": Interview with Pénélope Fourcade-Fraissinet.
375 "an extraordinary esprit de corps": Interview with Charles-Helen des Isnards.
376 "For many years": Deacon, 30.
377 "solicited the cooperation": Ibid., 95.
     "could only be considered": Ibid.
378 "Discrimination, based . . . on a notion of inequality": Oliver Wievorka,
     The French Resistance (Cambridge, MA: Harvard University Press, 2016), 404–405.

379 **"Just as businesses recruited female personnel"**: Ibid.

"After the war": Robert Gilden, "Jeannie Rousseau Obituary," *Guardian,* Sept. 6, 2017.

"the wife of an officer": Valerie Deacon, "From '*femme d'officier, mère de famille*' to '*grande dame de la Résistance*'*:* Marie-Madeleine Fourcade During World War II," *Contemporary French Civilization,* vol. 42, no. 2.

"rather humble (and misleading)": Ibid.

380 **"saved thousands of lives"**: David Ignatius, "The Remarkable Life of Jeannie Rousseau de Clarens," *Washington Post,* Sept. 4, 2017.

"an anonymous": K. G. Robertson, ed. *War, Resistance and Intelligence: Collected Essays in Honour of M.R.D. Foot* (Barnsley, UK: Pen and Sword, 2000).

"The years have passed": Fourcade, *Noah's Ark,* 15.

381 **"Resistance is a state of mind"**: Olivier Holmey, "Jeannie Rousseau, Spy for the French Resistance," *The Independent,* Aug. 29, 2017.

BIBLIOGRAPHY

ARCHIVAL MATERIAL

Archives of the French Ministry of Defense (*Service Historique de la Défense*), Vincennes. *Gestapo Files on Alliance Network (subseries GR 28P 3)*

Bodleian Library, Oxford. *Patrick Reilly, unpublished memoirs*

Imperial War Museum, London. *Oral histories of Hugh Verity and Barbara Bertram*

International Spy Museum Archive, Washington, D.C. *Jeannie Rousseau video interview with David Ignatius*

National Archives of France (*Archives Nationales de France*), Paris. *Reseau Alliance, 72AJ/35, Dossier No. 8*

PUBLISHED MATERIAL

Aid, Matthew M., and Cees Wiebes, eds. *Secrets of Signals Intelligence During the Cold War and Beyond*. Abingdon, U.K.: Routledge, 2001.

Ambrose, Stephen E. *D-Day: June 6, 1944: The Climactic Battle of World War II*. New York: Simon & Schuster, 1995.

Atkin, Nicholas, and Frank Tallet, eds. *The Right in France: From Revolution to Le Pen*. London: I. B. Tauris, 2003.

Bannalec, Jean-Luc. *Death in Brittany*. New York: Minotaur Books, 2014.

Bartos, Adam, and Colin MacCabe. *Remembering Chris Marker*. New York: OR Books, 2017.

Basu, Shrabani. *Spy Princess: The Life of Noor Inayat Khan.* Amherst, MA: Omega Publications, 2007.

Beevor, Antony, and Artemis Cooper. *Paris After the Liberation 1944–1949.* New York: Penguin, 2004.

Bertram, Anthony, and Barbara Bertram (ed. Jerome Bertram). *The Secret of Bignor Manor.* Lulu Press, 2014.

Bertram, Barbara. *French Resistance in Sussex.* Pulborough, UK: Barnworks Publishing, 1996.

Bodson, Hermann. *Downed Allied Airmen and Evasion of Capture: The Role of Local Resistance Networks in World War II.* Jefferson, NC: McFarland, 2005.

Boutron, Jean. *De Mers-el-Kébir à Londres 1940–1944.* Paris: Plon, 1980.

Brown, Anthony Cave. *"C": The Secret Life of Sir Stewart Graham Menzies.* New York: Macmillan, 1987.

Churchill, Winston S. *Closing the Ring.* Boston: Houghton Mifflin, 1951.

———. *Triumph and Tragedy.* Boston: Houghton Mifflin, 1953.

Clifford, Nicholas R. *Spoilt Children of Empire: Westerners in Shanghai and the Chinese Revolution of the 1920s.* Middlebury, VT: Middlebury College Press, 1991.

Cloud, Stanley, and Lynne Olson. *The Murrow Boys: Pioneers on the Front Lines of Broadcast Journalism.* Boston: Mariner Books, 1996.

Cobb, Matthew. *Eleven Days in August: The Liberation of Paris in 1944.* London: Simon & Schuster UK, 2014.

———. *The Resistance: The French Fight Against the Nazis.* London: Pocket Books, 2010.

Cointet, Michèle. *Marie-Madeleine Fourcade: Un Chef de la Résistance.* Paris: Perrin, 2006.

Deacon, Valerie. *The Extreme Right in the French Resistance: Members of the Cagoules and Corvignolles in the Second World War.* Baton Rouge: LSU Press, 2016.

D'Este, Carlo. *Patton: A Genius for War.* New York: Harper Perennial, 1996.

Dimbleby, Jonathan. *The Battle of the Atlantic: How the Allies Won the War.* Oxford: Oxford University Press, 2016.

Fabius, Odette. *Un Lever de Soleil sur le Mecklenbourg: Mémoires.* Paris: Albin Michel, 1986.

Foot, M.R.D. *Six Faces of Courage.* London: Eyre Methuen, 1978.

———. *SOE in France: An Account of the British Special Operations Executive in France 1940–1944.* London: HMSO, 1966.

——— and J. L. Langley. *MI9: Escape and Evasion 1939–1945.* London: Biteback Publishing, 2011.

Fourcade, Marie-Madeleine. *L'Arche de Noé.* Paris: Fayard, 1968.

———. *Noah's Ark: A Memoir of Struggle and Resistance.* New York: Dutton, 1974.

Frenay, Henri. *The Night Will End.* New York: McGraw-Hill, 1976.

Fuller, Jean Overton. *The German Penetration of SOE: France 1941-1944.* Maidstone, UK: George Mann Books, 1996.

Gallery, Daniel V. *U-505.* San Francisco: Lucknow Books, 2016.

Gildea, Robert. *Fighters in the Shadows: A New History of the French Resistance*. Cambridge, MA: Belknap Press of Harvard University Press, 2015.

Glass, Charles. *Americans in Paris: Life and Death Under Nazi Occupation*. New York: Penguin, 2009.

Grescoe, Taras. *Shanghai Grand: Forbidden Love, Intrigue, and Decadence in Old China*. New York: Picador, 2017.

Guéhenno, Jean. *Diary of the Dark Years 1940–1944*. Oxford: Oxford University Press, 2014.

Harrison, Edward. *The Young Kim Philby: Soviet Spy and British Intelligence Officer*. Liverpool: Liverpool University Press, 2012.

Hastings, Max. *The Secret War: Spies, Codes and Guerrillas 1939–1945*. London: William Collins, 2015.

Helm, Sarah. *A Life in Secrets: Vera Atkins and the Missing Agents of World War II*. New York: Anchor, 2007.

Irving, David. *The Mare's Nest*. London: William Kimber, 1964.

————. *The War Between the Generals: Inside the Allied High Command*. New York: Congdon and Lattes, 1981.

Jackson, Julian. *France: The Dark Years 1940–1944*. Oxford: Oxford University Press, 2001.

Jeffery, Keith. *The Secret History of MI6*. New York: Penguin Press, 2010.

Jones, R. V. *Most Secret War*. Ware, UK: Wordsworth Editions, 1998.

Kaplan, Philip. *Grey Wolves: U-Boat War 1939–1945*. New York: Skyhorse Publishing, 2014.

Kedward, H. R. *Resistance in Vichy France*. Oxford: Oxford University Press, 1978.

Keene, Tom. *Cloak of Enemies: Churchill's SOE, Enemies at Home and the Cockleshell Heroes*. Staplehurst, UK: Spellmount, 2012.

Kershaw, Alex. *Avenue of Spies: A True Story of Terror, Espionage, and One American Family's Heroic Resistance in Nazi-Occupied Paris*. New York: Broadway Books, 2015.

Kitson, Simon. *The Hunt for Nazi Spies: Fighting Espionage in Vichy France*. Chicago: University of Chicago Press, 2007.

————. *Police and Politics in Marseille, 1936–1945*. Leiden, Netherlands: Brill, 2014.

Lacouture, Jean. *De Gaulle: The Rebel, 1890–1944*. New York: W. W. Norton, 1990.

Langley, J. M. *Fight Another Day*. Barnsley, UK: Pen and Sword, 2013.

Loustaunau-Lacau, Georges. *Mémoires d'un Français Rebelle*. Paris: Robert Laffont, 1948.

Lyman, Robert. *The Jail Busters: The Secret Story of MI6, the French Resistance and Operation Jericho*. London: Quercus, 2014.

Macintyre, Ben. *Double Cross: The True Story of the D-Day Spies*. New York: Crown, 2012.

Marks, Leo. *Between Silk and Cyanide: A Codemaker's War, 1941–45*. Stroud, UK: History Press, 2013.

Middlebrook, Martin. *The Peenemünde Raid: The Night of 17–18 August 1943*. Barnsley, UK: Pen and Sword, 2006.

Morgan, Sir Frederick. *Overture to Overlord*. Garden City, NY: Doubleday, 1950.

Morgan, Ted. *An Uncertain Hour: The French, the Germans, the Jews, and the City of Lyon, 1940–1945*. New York: Arbor House, 1990.

Muggeridge, Malcolm. *Chronicles of Wasted Time: Vol. 2, The Infernal Grove*. London: Collins, 1973.

Neufeld, Michael. *Von Braun: Dreamer of Space, Engineer of War*. New York: Knopf, 2007.

Nicolson, Harold. *The War Years: Diaries and Letters 1939–1945*. New York: Atheneum, 1967.

Olson, Lynne. *Citizens of London: The Americans Who Stood with Britain in Its Darkest, Finest Hour*. New York: Random House, 2010.

———. *Last Hope Island: Britain, Occupied Europe, and the Brotherhood That Helped Turn the Tide of War*. New York: Random House, 2017.

———. *Those Angry Days: Roosevelt, Lindbergh, and America's Fight over World War II, 1939–1941*. New York: Random House, 2013.

O'Sullivan, Adrian. *Nazi Secret Warfare in Occupied Persia (Iran): The Failure of the German Intelligence Services 1939–1945*. Basingstoke, UK: Palgrave Macmillan, 2014.

Padfield, Peter. *Dönitz: The Last Fuhrer*. London: HarperCollins, 1987.

Paillole, Paul. *Fighting the Nazis: French Intelligence and Counterintelligence, 1933–1945*. Enigma Books, 2003.

Parry, Dan. *D-Day 6.6.44: The Dramatic Story of the World's Greatest Invasion*. London: BBC Books, 2004.

Paxton, Robert O. *Vichy France: Old Guard and New Order, 1940–1944*. New York: Columbia University Press, 2001.

Porch, Douglas. *The French Secret Services: From the Dreyfus Affair to the Gulf War*. New York: Farrar, Straus and Giroux, 1995.

Pryce-Jones, David. *Paris in the Third Reich: A History of the German Occupation, 1940–1944*. New York: Holt, Rinehart and Winston, 1981.

Read, Anthony, and David Fisher. *Colonel Z: The Secret Life of a Master of Spies*. New York: Viking, 1985.

Read, Piers Paul. *Alec Guinness: The Authorized Biography*. New York: Simon & Schuster, 2005.

Riding, Alan. *And the Show Went On: Cultural Life in Nazi-Occupied Paris*. New York: Knopf, 2010.

Robertson, K. G., ed. *War, Resistance and Intelligence: Collected Essays in Honour of M.R.D. Foot*. Barnsley, UK: Pen and Sword, 2000.

Rodriguez, Capt. *L'Escalier Sans Retour*. Paris: Éditions France-Empire, 1984.

Romanones, Aline, Countess of. *The Spy Wore Red: My Adventures as an Undercover Agent in World War II*. New York: Random House, 1987.

Rosenberg, Tina. *The Haunted Land: Facing Europe's Ghost After Communism.* New York: Random House, 1995.

Rossiter, Margaret L. *Women in the Resistance.* New York: Praeger, 1985.

Sansom, C. J. *Winter in Madrid.* New York: Penguin, 2009.

Schiff, Stacy. *Saint-Exupéry: A Biography.* New York: Knopf, 1995.

Schoenbrun, David. *Soldiers of the Night: The Story of the French Resistance.* New York: Dutton, 1980.

Sebba, Anne. *Les Parisiennes: How the Women of Paris Lived, Loved and Died Under Nazi Occupation.* New York: St. Martin's Press, 2016.

Sergeant, Harriet. *Shanghai: Collision Point of Cultures 1918–1939.* New York: Crown, 1990.

Sevareid, Eric. *Not So Wild a Dream.* New York: Atheneum, 1976.

Shirer, William L. *The Collapse of the Third Republic: An Inquiry into the Fall of France in 1940.* New York: Simon & Schuster, 1969.

Smith, Colin. *England's Last War Against France: Fighting Vichy 1940–1942.* London: Phoenix, 2010.

Smyth, J. E. *Fred Zinnemann and the Cinema of Resistance.* Jackson: University Press of Mississippi, 2014.

Sullivan, Rosemary. *Villa Air-Bel: World War II, Escape, and a House in Marseille.* New York: Harper Perennial, 2007.

Summers, Julie. *Our Uninvited Guests: The Secret Lives of Britain's Country Houses 1939–1945.* London: Simon & Schuster, 2018.

Tombs, Robert, and Émile Chabal, eds. *Britain and France in Two World Wars: Truth, Myth and Memory.* London: Bloomsbury, 2013.

Verity, Hugh. *We Landed by Moonlight: The Secret RAF Landings in France 1940–1944.* Manchester, UK: Crécy Publishing, 2000.

Vomécourt, Philippe de. *An Army of Amateurs.* New York: Doubleday, 1961.

Vosjoli, P. L. Thyraud De. *Lamia.* Boston: Little, Brown, 1970.

Wake-Walker, Edward. *A House for Spies: SIS Operations into Occupied France from a Sussex Farmhouse.* London: Robert Hale, 2011.

Weitz, Margaret Collins. *Sisters in the Resistance: How Women Fought to Free France, 1940–1945.* New York: John Wiley and Sons, 1996.

West, Nigel. *MI6: British Secret Intelligence Service Operations 1909–1945.* New York: Random House, 1983.

Wieviorka, Oliver. *The French Resistance.* Cambridge, MA: Harvard University Press, 2016.

INDEX

PHOTO: © TAMZIN B. SMITH

LYNNE OLSON is the *New York Times* bestselling author of *Last Hope Island: Britain, Occupied Europe, and the Brotherhood That Helped Turn the Tide of War; Those Angry Days: Roosevelt, Lindbergh, and America's Fight Over World War II, 1939–1941;* and *Citizens of London: The Americans Who Stood with Britain in Its Darkest, Finest Hour.* Among her five other books is *Troublesome Young Men: The Rebels Who Brought Churchill to Power and Helped Save England.* She lives with her husband in Washington, D.C.

lynneolson.com

Facebook.com/lynneolsonbooks

ABOUT THE TYPE

This book was set in Bembo, a typeface based on an old-style
Roman face that was used for Cardinal Pietro Bembo's tract *De
Aetna* in 1495. Bembo was cut by Francesco Griffo (1450–1518) in
the early sixteenth century for Italian Renaissance printer and
publisher Aldus Manutius (1449–1515). The Lanston Monotype
Company of Philadelphia brought the well-proportioned letter-
forms of Bembo to the United States in the 1930s.